The Ecocentrists

The Ecocentrists

A History of Radical Environmentalism

Keith Makoto Woodhouse

Columbia University Press   New York

Columbia University Press
Publishers Since 1893
New York   Chichester, West Sussex
cup.columbia.edu
Copyright © 2018 Columbia University Press
All rights reserved

Cataloging-in-Publication Data available from the Library of Congress

ISBN 978-0-231-16588-4 (cloth)
ISBN 978-0-231-54715-4 (e-book)

♾

Columbia University Press books are printed on permanent
and durable acid-free paper.
Printed in the United States of America

Cover design: Julia Kushnirsky
Cover photograph: © Richard Schultz

Contents

Preface

The year before I began graduate school, I spent a summer as a Forest Service ranger in the Weminuche Wilderness, a half-million acres straddling the Continental Divide in southwestern Colorado. I hiked dozens of miles each week, checking backcountry conditions and making visitor contacts. Other rangers enforced Forest Service regulations by issuing citations. Still others sat at desks in Creede, Durango, or Pagosa Springs, overseeing the administrative work of wilderness management according to guidelines set by foresters in Golden, Colorado or Washington, D.C. Even my brief and limited view of the Weminuche made clear how much human effort went into keeping this piece of the country wild.

The trail crews best demonstrated this incongruity. Winter in the mountains of Colorado brought blowdown: wind-felled trees that often obstructed hiking trails. In the spring and throughout the summer, trail crews cut through the dead trees to clear a path. In the forest at large the crews used all-terrain vehicles and chainsaws. As soon as they reached a wilderness boundary, they abandoned their motorized equipment, saddled horses and mules, and continued up the trail with handsaws and axes. Cutting through a downed tree with a handsaw is strenuous work; what might take minutes with a chainsaw can take over an hour without one.

The Forest Service's commitment to using livestock and hand tools inside wilderness was both noble and odd. Thanks largely to a very human political process, the forest on one side of an administrative boundary was subject to roaring chainsaws and motor exhaust and on the other side free from both.

That summer I read William Cronon's "The Trouble With Wilderness," an essay that had sparked an ongoing debate among academics and environmentalists. "The Trouble With Wilderness" describes the paradox that I encountered high in the Rockies: wilderness is both defined by human absence and also "quite profoundly a human creation," a creation shaped by administrative policies that are themselves the product of deeply rooted assumptions.[1] Even when wilderness is thousands of miles away and almost never visited—in fact, especially then—it remains culturally and socially situated. The lone hiker escaping into a nature devoid of human influence is beguiled, stirred by a set of preconceptions packed in along with water and sunscreen.

Like many readers, I found the essay as disconcerting as it was compelling. Even more nettlesome than the idea of wilderness as artifice was the claim that just as human influence streams into wilderness, so artifice trickles out. Wilderness, Cronon writes, "serves as the unexamined foundation on which so many of the quasi-religious values of modern environmentalism rest." The idea of wilderness sits within and informs a larger idea called "nature," which in turn frames the political movement called environmentalism. That movement's critiques often assume that people have wandered away from nature-as-it-should-be. As "the ultimate landscape of authenticity," wilderness offers a baseline against which to measure how far the human world has strayed. If wilderness is a false beacon, then the environmental movement as a whole may be misled.[2]

In graduate school I learned that Cronon's wilderness essay was an incisive and provocative statement of a larger trend within the field of environmental history. That trend involved questioning basic categories and was part of what the environmental historian Richard White in 2004 called "the cultural turn." One of the most significant consequences of this turn, according to White, was an emphasis on "hybrid landscapes rather than the wild, rural, and urban landscapes that were once treated as pure types." Environmental historians smudged whatever clear lines they once thought existed between city and country, and between human landscapes and natural ones. They recognized that urban places never lacked in nature, and that apparently wild spaces were in fact profoundly shaped by human activity. Natural and human worlds did not stand apart on either side of city limits.[3]

This smudging erased more than an imagined boundary between boulevards and fields. Cronon's own *Nature's Metropolis*, in demonstrating the inextricable connections between a city and its hinterland, commingled geography with philosophy as easily as it did Chicago with the plains beyond. Cronon described his "deepest intellectual agenda" as not simply to remove lines on a mental map but "to suggest that the boundary between human and nonhuman, natural and unnatural, is profoundly problematic." Part of the cultural turn in environmental history was a willingness to question the category of "nature" itself.[4]

The cultural turn had deep implications for environmental history as well as for environmentalism. The implications for environmental history were overwhelmingly salutary. First and foremost, the cultural turn led to a welcome reconsideration of timeworn narratives. An untethering of the field from its most familiar renderings of "nature" produced innovative scholarship that corrected myopic views. Long-cherished subjects, like the conservation movement, received a newly critical treatment. Historians began to describe how conservationists' fixation on an unpeopled nature allowed them to disregard the established practices—and sometimes even the existence—of already marginalized groups, privileging recreation and sightseeing over subsistence hunting or Native American treaty rights. The decentering of wilderness as an idea, meanwhile, reflected the decentering of wilderness as a place. Historians found in cities and suburbs stories about how people related to the natural world, and even about the origins of the environmental movement. Since the cultural turn, environmental historians have better resisted narrow assumptions about how people understood and used natural resources, and have avoided too-easy morality tales about the innocence of nature and the danger of human influence.[5]

In the era of climate change and accelerating human impacts on the planet, it is worth revisiting the cultural turn and its place in environmental history. Paul Sutter began to do so several years ago. "Hybridity has challenged declensionist narratives and pushed American environmental historians into new terrain," Sutter wrote, "but those scholars have found this world, without Eden or sin—without a pure nature or universal human transgression against it—a disorienting place." Acknowledging the many insights that arose from the cultural turn, Sutter nevertheless suggested that as much as hybridity fueled environmental history's conversations and debates, its limits grew more apparent in a time of intensifying human influence over nonhuman nature. "Environmental historians," Sutter wrote, "have not done a great job of reengaging metanarratives of environmental decline after the hybrid turn."[6]

It is easy to understand why not. Metanarratives of decline are less compelling when the idea of "nature" is less stable. Scholars have argued forcefully that a too-fixed definition of nature—and maybe even more importantly of the word "natural"—leads to exclusionary systems and practices, and to essentialisms that can be used to marginalize people as much as to explain the nonhuman. The concept "nature" has served to calcify and delimit as much as to enlighten, and so its meaning has to remain fluid and subject to reinterpretation.[7]

What does this mean for environmentalism, a movement that is in many ways predicated on a nature that exists, at least in part, beyond human conceptions of it? As a graduate student I tried to think about that question by examining a group of environmentalists who proclaimed, more than any others, that nature held meaning and value regardless of what people thought, and who insisted that a felled tree made a sound and subtly altered a forest whether or not people heard the crash or understood its ecological implications. These radical environmentalists wanted above all to challenge human preeminence. They argued that people were no more important than any other living things on the planet or than the ecosystems those things inhabited. They claimed, ultimately, that human beings and human society held no greater moral value than did nonhuman species and ecological systems, a philosophy called "ecocentrism."

Ecocentrism was a leveling philosophy in that it claimed a moral equality for all of the planet's inhabitants, but it grew out of a sharp distinction between people and nonhuman nature. Radical environmentalists were not beatific egalitarians. They were angry. They believed, fundamentally, that as modern human society gradually destroyed wild nature it veered toward catastrophe, and that its self-destruction would take much of the planet with it. That belief assumed an oppositional relationship between the human and the natural. To reject ecocentrism, radical environmentalists argued, was to embrace anthropocentrism—human-centeredness. Beyond those two positions lay only equivocation.[8]

It is easy to dismiss such extreme ideas. They lead in many troubling directions. Chief among them is the way in which the idea of an autonomous nature reinforces one of environmentalism's most problematic impulses: the tendency to group all people into a single, homogenous category called "human," a tendency Cronon has criticized as "an oversimplified holism."[9] Environmental holism risks ignoring social and cultural difference and suggesting that all people are equally culpable in modern civilization's effects on the natural world despite unequal distribution of resources and vast inequities of economic and political power. Environmentalists have often criticized "humanity" in the singular without recognizing the unending diversity to which that term refers.

But as easy as it is to dismiss radicals' ideas, it is less easy to define an environmentalism without them, or at least without some semblance of them. A world without Eden or sin, Sutter worried, could produce "a haze of moral relativism" in which the basic claim that humans might harm nonhuman nature becomes more and more tenuous.[10] In the recent past environmentalism's critics have produced such a haze, one that has grown more opaque in the era of climate change. As a presidential candidate in 1980, Ronald Reagan downplayed concerns about air quality by claiming that nearly all nitrogen oxide pollution came from plants, and he discounted fears about oil drilling off of the West Coast by comparing spills to naturally occurring oil seepage.[11] Years later similar arguments proved just as useful. After the 1989 Exxon Valdez oil spill, the libertarian writer Llewellyn Rockwell said, "Oil is natural, it's organic, and it's biodegradable." Ozone holes, Rockwell claimed, "open and close naturally." A Mobil Oil ad from 1995 described the nonhuman world as "resilient and capable of rejuvenation," insisting that "nature itself has produced far more devastating changes than any caused by man . . . and the environment has survived."[12] The literary scholar Rob Nixon notes a similarly cavalier attitude among politicians and managers who tried to minimize fallout over the BP Deepwater Horizon spill in 2010. The blowout was "a natural phenomenon," BP's defenders argued, comparable to regularly occurring oil seeps in the Gulf and just as easily cleaned up by ocean filtration. The endpoint of this logic is the claim that climate change should cause little concern, because changing climates are natural and the planet has survived countless instances. As early as 1990, Rockwell suggested that global warming could "lengthen growing seasons, make the earth more liveable, and forestall a future ice age"—by now familiar talking points for climate change apologists. "The recent turn within environmental studies toward celebrating the creative resilience of ecosystems," Nixon writes, "can be readily hijacked by politicians, lobbyists, and corporations who oppose regulatory controls and strive to minimize pollution liability."[13]

The challenge for environmental historians, and for environmentalists, is to insist that humans should carefully consider their impact on nature even as terms like "humans," "impact," and "nature" lose much of their ballast. "Hybridity may be a source of hope," Sutter wrote, "but at this moment of unprecedented human influence over the global environment—what many call the Anthropocene—environmental historians must better contend with and communicate the cultural, material, and moral complexity implicated in the term."[14] The notion of a geological age of humans, "the Anthropocene," captures a tension between urgency and complexity. "Anthropocene" is primarily descriptive but can easily tip in one of several prescriptive directions. In one of those directions is acute anxiety over the ways that people are more and more rapidly refashioning the planet. In another direction is the celebration of an earth made over by human design, or a complacent insistence that there remain no meaningful differences between people and nonhuman nature and so less reason to worry about one's effects on the other.

Radical environmentalists believed very strongly that a planet dominated by humans should be a source of anxiety rather than complacency or celebration, and that environmentalism without anxiety and even anger is less meaningful. Their ideas deserve more of a hearing today. In the Anthropocene, when the human and the natural are more and more of a piece, environmentalism can become a narrower and more technical matter of simply measuring risk and reward. That narrow version of environmentalism loses what Jedediah Purdy calls "the prophetic strain of environmental politics, which has always been a part of its power, and is more important than ever today."[15] In the Anthropocene, environmentalism must be a view from somewhere.

An environmental point of view is not necessarily an ecocentric one that draws distinctions between people and nature. There are many reasons why it shouldn't be. But an environmental point of view must wrestle with the vital questions that ecocentrism raises. The more I learned about radical environmentalists the more I understood them as serious thinkers, engaged in conversations that held great relevance for the broad environmental movement and for the way that anyone might think about climate change and the Anthropocene. Their ideas were sometimes deeply wrongheaded, but their conversations were often thoughtful and even urgent. And their false turns came from confronting issues that were and are complicated, distressing, and maybe even irreconcilable.

Critics of radical environmentalism confronted the same issues, and the same irreconcilability. It is easy to forget, after the influence of "The Trouble With Wilderness," just how carefully that essay made its points. Although many writers who have used Cronon's arguments have done so single-mindedly, Cronon himself remained painfully aware of what might be lost along with romantic views of wilderness. He admitted a "deep ambivalence" about what wilderness meant for environmentalism, and was uneasy not only about the binaries that wilderness advocacy could encourage but also about diminishing the power of an autonomous nature to act as "an indispensable corrective to human arrogance." However much people shaped wilderness, they did not finally control it. Always beyond complete human understanding, wilderness provided an unmistakable encounter with "something irreducibly nonhuman, something profoundly Other than yourself." And that encounter could unsettle as many assumptions as it might reinforce. Whether a false beacon or not, the idea of wilderness continued to point toward what Cronon called a "critique of modernity that is one of environmentalism's most important contributions to the moral and political discourse of our time."[16]

The Weminuche Wilderness and "The Trouble With Wilderness" unsettled and reinforced many of my own assumptions. Since hiking the one and reading the other, I have kept asking questions about what wilderness means for environmentalism and what environmentalism might mean in the twenty-first century. This book is an attempt to answer them.

The subject of this book has made me think about human beings as a species; the writing of it has made me deeply appreciative of people as individuals. No one has inspired this project more than Bill Cronon. As much as Bill's scholarship shaped my thought and my writing, his mentorship has been even more meaningful. Through countless conversations and through his own example, he helped me understand what sort of thinker I wanted to be.

Many other faculty members at the University of Wisconsin taught me what historians do. Particularly important were the members of my dissertation committee: Jennifer Ratner-Rosenhagen, Lou Roberts, Bill Reese, and Gregg Mitman. At Amherst College, Kevin Sweeney and David Blight made being a historian look exciting long before I actually decided to do it.

At Wisconsin, I joined what I am sure is one of the best and certainly one of the most fun communities of graduate students in the country. I suspected this before I even arrived because I had already met Jim Feldman. I knew it beyond doubt after I met Marc Hertzman, and spent the better part of the next decade becoming his close friend. I met many more people in Madison who became intellectual companions and good friends, including Cydney Alexis, Lauren Bresnahan, Emily Brown, Scott Burkhardt, Liese Dart, Elizabeth Feldman, Laura Haertel, Marian Halls, Jenn Holland, Tim Lenoch, Marilen Loyola, Dan Magaziner, Adam Malka, Adam Mandelman, Jen Martin, Brittany McCormick, Nic Mink, Alissa Moore, Ryan Quintana, Tom Robertson, Kendra Smith-Howard, Courtney Stein, Zoe Van Orsdol, Tara Waldron, Erica Wojcik, Tom Yoshikami, and Anna Zeide. At Northwestern I have gotten to know a warm and supportive group of colleagues with whom it is a pleasure to work. During my first few years, Ken Alder served as department chair and Mike Sherry acted as a mentor. Both were and are full of generous wisdom. Paul Ramirez in particular has become a great friend.

A Charlotte Newcombe Fellowship proved crucial in completing my dissertation, and I am grateful to the Woodrow Wilson National Fellowship Foundation for its generous support. I spent several semesters as an adjunct instructor during and after graduate school, and I worked with smart and friendly colleagues at both the University of Wisconsin-Stevens Point and the University of Wisconsin-Oshkosh. In a very difficult job market that leaves far too many stellar applicants adrift, I was lucky enough to find harbor in a postdoctoral fellowship with the Huntington Library-University of Southern California Institute on California and the West (ICW). Before arriving in Southern California I was likely one of the last people in the world not to have met ICW director Bill Deverell. Now I consider myself fortunate to count him as a friend. I had the chance to return to Southern California, and to put the finishing touches on this book, during a fellowship year at the Huntington Library. The Huntington runs a remarkable fellowship program that attracts an extraordinary group of scholars, and I was extremely lucky to have been a part of both.

While researching radical environmentalism, I had the chance to work with several excellent library staffs. The State Historical Society of Wisconsin served as a second home in graduate school, and the librarians in special collections, in the periodicals department, and in the microform room shared their expertise time and time again. The Denver Public Library is one of the great public libraries in the United States, and its special collections staff patiently helped me navigate its excellent conservation collection. I also relied on the friendly professionalism of librarians at Northwestern University, the University of California-Davis, the University of California-Santa Barbara, and the University of Southern California. Most of all, however, I worked with the staff of the Bancroft Library at the University of California-Berkeley. I spent hundreds of hours at the Bancroft and find it hard to imagine a nicer library or a more competent, knowledgeable, and welcoming group of librarians.

I owe a particular debt of gratitude to four Earth First! founders. I spent several hours on the phone with Howie Wolke and Bart Koehler, both of whom talked to me at length despite the fact that Bart was busy with family matters and Howie hates long phone calls. I visited Mike Roselle in West Virginia and talked to him for the better part of an afternoon. Mike was generous with his time and with his opinions, and I learned a great deal from our conversation. Most of all I owe thanks to Dave Foreman. I spoke with Dave on several occasions at his home in Albuquerque, and he let me look through many boxes of documents stacked in his garage. A historian at heart, Dave told me stories about Earth First!'s early years and encouraged me to look through the papers he'd kept, never once questioning what I intended to do with any of it. I have tried to approach Earth First! critically, but I hope that the group's founders recognize the admiration I hold for their spirit and dedication.

Andie Tucher and the Society for American Historians guided my dissertation to Columbia University Press, and Philip Leventhal received it there. Working with Columbia has been a pleasure, thanks largely to Bridget Flannery-McCoy and her team. I did not really understand what editors do—and how essential their work is—before working with Bridget. Receiving her extensive comments on drafts was at first daunting and at last revelatory. She did far more work than I could reasonably expect, and the final product is much, much better for all of her suggestions and insights as well as her uncanny sense of argumentative structure. Several other people did me the great favor of reviewing drafts. The editors and readers of the *Journal for the Study of Radicalism* helped me work through some initial ideas. (Some material originally appeared as "The Politics of Ecology: Environmentalism and Liberalism in the 1960s" *JSR* 2 (Fall 2008) and is reprinted here with permission of Michigan State University Press). Mark Stoll read an early version. Derek Hoff and Michelle Chihara offered trenchant feedback on individual chapters. Steve Hahn graciously took time out of a leave year to read several chapters. Tom Robertson provided thoughtful comments on the manuscript as a whole that guided crucial revisions. Alex Moisa spent a summer helping me with research. And anonymous readers for Columbia University Press provided important feedback. Whatever you might like about this book is thanks in part to these careful readers; anything you don't like is my responsibility alone.

I lived with an assortment of people during the many years I spent researching and writing. In Madison I lived for two years with Scott Burkhardt and for two years with Tom Yoshikami (including a brief overlap with Ryan Quintana), years that deepened already dear friendships. I spent my last year in Madison on East Johnson with Jonny Hunter, Sarah Christopherson, Matt Robertson, Jamie Duffin, and Mia Cava, all of whom I was happy to run into in the kitchen. In Berkeley I spent a year with two old friends: Nick Collins and Micah Porter. In Los Angeles I lived with Tim Lenoch and then with Ray Chao, and spent hours on the phone talking politics with Adam Malka. Daniel Immerwahr generously provided room and board for three crucial days of apartment hunting. There were others who hosted me for days or weeks, including Max Nanao, Ben Bloch, and Zana Ikels. I spent my last year of writing in Pasadena with Jessica Biddlestone, who more than anyone else endured the hardships of living alongside an all-consuming project. I hope that, much more, she lived with all of my love and affection and continues to do so.

Finally, I lived on and off with my family. I spent time with my sister Miya, who looks out for me even from far away; with my brother Leighton and sister-in-law Carolina, who made living in Los Angeles a real joy; and with July, the sweetest if not the most energetic dog in the world. And I spent many weeks with my parents, who have given me much more than I can ever repay and to whom this is dedicated.

The Ecocentrists

Introduction

"It is environmentalism gone mad," John Benneth of the American Forest Institute told a reporter in 1986. Benneth was talking about "tree spiking," an act of sabotage by radical environmentalists who inserted metal spikes into trees designated for logging. To cut down spiked trees was to risk damaging chainsaws and mill saws, as radical environmentalists made clear, and to risk the safety of the loggers themselves, as the forest industry pointed out. Tree spiking explicitly threatened expensive equipment and implicitly risked the safety of forest workers in order to protect ancient trees, an equation that struck Benneth, and many others, as morally despicable.[1]

Benneth's comment suggested that tree spiking took the logic of environmentalism and twisted it into something different, something wicked. But radical environmentalism was not an inversion of mainstream environmentalism. Although radicals made claims and took actions that most environmentalists disavowed, they were not operating from entirely different principles. Radicals took basic beliefs that many environmentalists subscribed to—that the natural world was in a state of crisis, that modern society was often to blame, and that people should change their behavior accordingly—and extended those beliefs beyond what others found acceptable. Radicals were an example of extremism, not madness.

Because tree spiking targeted industrial equipment but also threatened human life, the tactic forced a reckoning with radical environmentalists' core belief, a philosophy called "ecocentrism." That philosophy—also called "biocentrism" or "deep ecology"—ascribed an equivalent value to human beings and nonhuman nature, and rejected the premise that people should occupy a privileged place in any moral reckoning.[2] Ecocentrism was the defining feature of the radicals under consideration here. These radicals considered industrial society's accelerating transformation of the natural world a crisis, not just because of the threats such a transformation posed to people and resources but because of the damage it inflicted on nature regardless of human well-being or even survival. Seeing catastrophe on the horizon, radicals held a dark view of the world, and that pessimism spurred their activism.

Because radicals cared first about the integrity of the nonhuman world, they worried about wilderness especially. They considered the existence of natural places defined by human absence to be the best measure of planetary health. Potential wilderness disappeared every day as logging companies felled trees, governments built roads, and cities sprawled into suburbs, exurbs, and beyond. Industrial manipulation of natural places was so immediate and so constant, radicals believed, that conventional reform did little to slow it, and so mainstream environmental groups that bided their time and relied on political compromise abetted the forces they claimed to oppose. Radical environmentalists refused to wait for the outcome of negotiations or the possibility of new legislation. Instead, they sat in roads as bulldozers approached and ascended trees before loggers arrived. Over time laws and lawsuits might save a forest, they understood, but in the moment only direct action backed by fierce commitment could.

By pushing environmental principles as far as they might go, radicals emphasized the differences between environmentalism and humanism. Radical environmentalists questioned beliefs that most late twentieth-century Americans considered beyond question—the necessity of economic growth, the soundness of human reason, and the inviolability of individual freedom—and ignored debates about inequity and social justice that marked the same period. Their controversial views revealed the powerful critique as well as the selective shortsightedness of environmental thought at its most obdurate.

Despite a diversity of beliefs and goals in the broad sweep of environmentalism, radicals maintained that their own ecocentric doubts about human virtue pointed to something essential in the environmental movement. For radicals, the central concern of environmentalism was always with limits: to natural resources, to industrial expansion, and to human population. Most contentious and in some ways most basic of all was what radicals understood as environmentalism's interest in limiting individual human freedom. Radicals believed that mainstream environmentalists, whether or not they admitted it, were similarly at odds with individual freedom and with the basic liberal commitments such freedom anchored.

"Liberal" is a slippery term. Relative to environmentalism it has several valences, three of which are crucial here. The first is liberal individualism, what Alan Wolfe calls liberalism's "core commitment to individual autonomy."[3] For liberals, the individual is the fundamental unit of politics and governance. Liberal political thought is rooted in individual liberty and committed to the belief that people should reach their own definitions of the good life, as long as those definitions do not violate another's freedom. The authority of the state should be used for procedural purposes, to facilitate individual opportunity rather than to dictate particular values or perspectives. Environmentalism, however, tends to focus on collective ends and shared conditions, often to the point that individual freedom is subordinated to a perceived common good. Environmentalists worry that, left to their own devices, most people would choose to act in ways detrimental to the natural world. Even fully aware of the consequences, people might act in their own short-term interests, whether those interests involved something as innocuous as using a disposable bottle or as consequential as bulldozing a forest. Because of their concern for the nonhuman world and for the systems that sustain it, environmentalists have a particularly strong preference for sacrificing some degree of individual freedom in order to safeguard a greater good.

The second valence is liberal humanism: a prioritizing of human inter-ests and a faith in human reason. Environmentalists' conviction that people should restrict their actions in order to minimize their impact on the natu-ral world, and by implication that unrestricted human freedom is a threat to nature, is constructed from different building blocks than those that compose liberal political thought. Liberalism is fundamentally human-istic in that it advocates human reason as the best means of achieving a desirable world. Environmentalism is generally skeptical of humanism in that it suspects limitations to human reason and so proposes limitations to human behavior.[4] Liberal humanists tend to place a great deal of faith in the capacity of rational thought to solve most problems, while environ-mentalists tend to believe that the natural world is far more complicated than people can reasonably understand. Environmentalists insist that the planet in all its complexity is beyond the scope of human comprehension, and they stress the importance of humility, a virtue rarely associated with liberal humanism.[5]

Liberal individualism and liberal humanism are ideas that have been a part of liberal political thought for several centuries. The third form of lib-eralism relevant here, what some scholars have called "growth liberalism," is more particular and more contextualized. Especially after World War II, Americans thought of economic expansion as the surest path to democracy and social equality. Material production and consumption fed political ide-als, tying lofty principles to everyday wants and needs. For modern Ameri-cans economic growth became the great leveler. Production, consumption, economic expansion, and social reform all made up a virtuous cycle that offered more things and more freedoms to more and more people. Growth liberalism braided economic expansion with social progress and national identity.[6] Environmentalists worried about the implications of this associa-tion, questioning not only the centrality of economic growth in American life but even whether the social benefits of growth liberalism were worth the environmental costs.

The points of tension between environmental and liberal commit-ments are easy to miss. Mainstream environmental organizations have operated through conventional liberal democratic procedures, appealed to broadly shared values, and often framed their cause as little more than common sense. The widespread (although fragile) support that environmental policies have enjoyed since the 1970s is a testament to the success of this political strategy.[7] But the notion that environmentalism is a simple matter of prudence belies the degree to which strong environmental protections can require abstention and even abnegation. Radical environmentalists had no illusions about what robust environmental commitments might demand, and radicals' ideas and campaigns made clear just how difficult such commitments could be—and perhaps should be. Long before climate change activists insisted that confronting global warming meant confronting an entire way of life, radical environmentalists protested industrial civilization itself.

Radical environmentalists have more often been objects of derision than subjects of serious study. Rob Nixon calls radical environmentalism "shallow" and "hokey," its average follower easily caricatured as "a whiter-than-white, hippy-dippy-tree-hugging-dopehead deep ecologist from an overprivileged background."[8] That caricature is not wholly inaccurate. Environmentally minded scholars and activists have exposed the many ways an ecocentric environmentalism, originating in and privileging the United States, can gloss over social difference, cultural complexity, and economic inequality, and how it can draw a too-stark line between the human and the natural. By pushing green ideas to their extremes, radical environmentalists risked stripping those ideas of the sort of nuance and malleability that might help them fit into a diverse and complicated world.

Why study a movement with such a narrow and unyielding point of view? Environmental historians have often chosen not to. The few broad histories of the modern environmental movement tend to mention radical environmentalism only in passing and to treat it as an isolated phenomenon. Whether because they considered radicals' views to be marginal or overly simplistic, historians have dispensed with them quickly, offering little more than a brief explanation of radical doctrine and its limitations. Historians have for the most part placed environmentalism within conventional American political thought rather than outside of it or even straddling its edges. That tendency is diminishing, as a growing literature on the modern environmental movement complicates an older view of environ-mentalism as an ideological extension of modern liberalism or a pragmatic consequence of postwar affluence. As some scholars have pointed out, even at the far edges of belief and principle are substantive debate and conflict. Sometimes that is the best place to find them.[9]

A history of modern environmentalism that includes radical ideas starts with the rise of mainstream environmental politics in the 1960s, as well as the sense of planetary crisis that gripped the movement in the 1970s. It especially involves telling the story of Earth First!, the premier ecocen-tric, radical environmental organization of the 1980s and 1990s. A small group of renegade conservationists founded Earth First! in 1980, frustrated by the increasing professionalization and, they believed, the decreasing effectiveness of mainstream groups. The acquiescence of mainstream envi-ronmentalists to moderate reform was, for Earth First!, an abandonment of the ecocentrism that had constituted at least a tacit part of American environmentalism since John Muir and Aldo Leopold. Earth First! claimed that mainstream organizations, by emphasizing the interests of people and accepting the limitations of conventional politics, shirked environmental-ism's basic commitment to the nonhuman.

Freed from the strictures of lobbying strategy, the imperatives of nego-tiation, and a frustrating cycle of compromise, the original Earth First!ers began to engage in a radical form of environmentalism that rejected con-ventional democratic methods in favor of direct action and even sabotage. Earth First!ers fought to protect wilderness not only as an end in itself but also as the best means of preserving biodiversity and opposing a crisis fed by rampant industrialism. Championing ecocentric principles, Earth First! tried to model what an uncompromising environmental group looked like: it insisted that disaster was imminent and even unfolding, refused to negotiate politically or philosophically, and challenged the humanism that radicals found arrogant and destructive. This uncompromising view, Earth First!ers claimed, remained true to the principles that made environmental-ism significant and urgent in the late-twentieth century.

Ecocentric thought was the heart of Earth First!'s political vitality and the inspiration for its dedicated activists. It gave radicals a piercing voice. Ecocentrism also encouraged the sort of holism in radical thought that could quickly slide into a sweeping antihumanism. The simplicity of radical environmentalism's claims made them elegant and inspiring if taken as rallying cries, but dangerous and malevolent if taken as unqualified truth. The great shortcoming of the radical environmental movement was a neglect of social issues, a denial that social difference had anything to do with the human relationship to the natural. Increasingly misanthropic statements by some Earth First!ers drove several wedges into the radical environmental community. Earth First!'s most important internal and external critics tried to reconcile radical environmentalism with social justice—among them the social ecologist Murray Bookchin, the Northern California Earth First! leader Judi Bari, and a disparate community of Pacific Northwest anarchists who took Earth First!'s tactics in new directions. Different stripes of anarchism coursed through these debates, giving radical environmentalists a language with which to critique liberal democratic reform and even human society without abandoning any sense of political order and direction. The late 1980s and the 1990s tested some of Earth First!'s most uncompromising views of nature and of people, and pointed to fundamental and persistent philosophical debates within the broad environmental movement. Those debates concerned the limits of democracy and of individual freedom, the effects of the state and of the market on environmental policy, the role of inequality and difference in environmental politics, and the relationship between humans and the nonhuman world—questions that are ever more vital in an era of people's expanding influence over the planet.

Radical environmentalists focused on what mainstream groups too easily lost sight of: that doubt is at the center of environmentalism. They cast a wary eye on much that humans thought and did, and that wariness guided their politics. Environmentalists at their most useful have been skeptics, and groups like Earth First! highlighted one of the environmental movement's most enduring critiques: a questioning of material progress for its own sake and a mistrust of the presumed wisdom behind it.

Not all environmentalists embrace skepticism. Since at least the early 2000s, a growing number of optimistic environmentalists have argued that what was once understood to be a cause of environmental decline may in fact be a solution.[10] New technology and market-based fixes, from this perspective, can not only heal the planet but also save environmentalism from itself, since the environmental movement's problem is that it has always lacked a hopeful and enthusiastic view of the future and has fought against the forms of innovation best suited to confronting environmental crises. Solving these crises will not require great sacrifice or radical change, optimists claim, but only a purposeful application of the very forces that environmentalists have long tried to restrain. The most enthusiastic environmental optimists point to the conceptual malleability of "nature" in order to justify more intentional efforts to remake the natural world.

There is certainly a great deal to learn from this point of view. Adapting to climate change will demand significant manipulation of habitats and ecosystems, and technology and markets have a crucial role to play. But an environmentalism that enthusiastically embraces this new dispensation is an environmentalism that has lost much of what makes it most significant. This is partly because there is a lack of proportion in the arguments of environmentalists who, as Naomi Klein puts it, "paint a picture of global warming Armageddon, then assure us that we can avert catastrophe by buying 'green' products and creating clever markets in pollution."[11] Mostly it is because one of the environmental movement's most valuable contributions to political thought is a check on deep-seated assumptions about human ingenuity and economic growth. Caution, and even pessimism, is what makes environmentalism vital.

Radicals insisted that doubt and pessimism remained key tools in all environmental thought. At the same time, they advocated a more pure version of environmentalism. "More pure" is an important oxymoron. As much as radicals reached for pure qualities and categories, they never fully subscribed to them. In reaching, though, they pushed the boundaries of the conversation. It is easy to depict radical environmentalists as little more than bitter misanthropes or naïve idealists. They were hardly that simple. They doubted human wisdom and fulminated against human arrogance, but they also insisted on a basic connection between people and the natural world and they believed that within every modern person lay a dormant piece of the wild. They revered and glorified wilderness and nonhuman nature, but they also understood them pragmatically. Many radicals worked at one point in the political trenches of the conservation movement and were used to negotiating for parcels of land in practical and technical terms rather than with sweeping declarations. And even sweeping declarations functioned as a useful sort of idealism. "Ideals are real: they direct our striving, our plans, our legal processes," writes Martha Nussbaum.[12] Radical environmentalists could lament the last ten thousand years of human history and then talk about how to preserve space for wilderness and wildlife alongside modern civilization. One cleared a path for the other. Only by stating their views in the most extreme terms, radicals believed, could they nudge human interests from the very center of political decision making. Some radical environmentalists did step off of this path and wallow in nihilistic antihumanism, reactionary authoritarianism, or simple bigotry. Most, however, wrestled with the environmental movement's place in a democratic society, confronting some of the difficult questions about individualism and material progress that environmentalism, at its worst and its best, seeks to ask.

I

Ecology and Revolutionary Thought

Because radical and mainstream environmentalism have the same intellectual roots, they have a common history. Both grew in part out of twentieth-century conservation and its commitment to moderating industrial society's effects on natural resources and amenities. At the center of the conservation movement was the Sierra Club, at various points the most recognized and most politically influential conservation organization. The Club was also in many ways the most democratically structured conservation group, so its point of view shifted with its membership rolls.[1] The Club's evolution over the course of the twentieth century tracked the development of key ideas about conservation and environmentalism that would structure the environmental movement and its relationship to the social politics of the 1960s and 1970s. Spurred by its executive director, David Brower, the Club focused increasingly on ecological ideas that described an interconnected world without human beings at its center and in which nonhuman nature might be worth protecting for its own sake. Those changes and ideas set the terms under which some environmentalists in the 1970s walked away from the movement's mainstream and toward more radical thought and action.

EARLY YEARS OF THE SIERRA CLUB

The oldest and most storied of all conservation organizations, the Sierra Club was founded in 1892 as a regional outdoors association with modest political ambitions. John Muir served as its first president and like every other officer of the Club he drew no salary. In its early decades, the Sierra Club represented what Stephen Fox has called the "amateur tradition," in which those interested in natural places carried out conservation work in their spare time. Because they had little to risk economically or professionally, Fox explains, amateur conservationists benefited from "time and taste to consider intangibles," championing aesthetic and even spiritual enjoyment of forests and mountains against the more utilitarian views of professional conservationists such as the chief forester of the United States, Gifford Pinchot.[2] Sierra Clubbers had no direct material interest in the places they worked to protect, a fact that would define the organization politically and legally for decades and which meant they fought more out of passionate enthusiasm than practical expedience.

The same amateur standing that would become synonymous with grassroots activism by the late twentieth century meant nearly the opposite during the Progressive Era. To be an amateur was to have money. At a time when leisure was a privilege of the wealthy, the same was true of politics as avocation. Even among career conservationists like Pinchot, concentrated wealth was important; among amateurs, it was essential. "Conservation and business are natural enemies," Fox writes.[3] But despite the larger truth of that claim, early Club leaders were overwhelmingly professionals and businessmen—"the prime movers," according to Michael Cohen, "in what one might call the philanthropic tradition of conservation, where business provided the individuals, progressivism provided the ideology, and American industrial growth provided the economic power."[4] There were other conservation organizations that represented even higher social strata, like the Save The Redwoods League, but few that reached lower. By mid-century this began to change as conservation groups relied more heavily on lobbying backed by popular support. As late as the 1960s, though, the Club's work still took place in private rooms at San Francisco steak houses, the banquet hall at the Sir Francis Drake Hotel, and meetings at the Bohemian or Pacific Union clubs.[5]

In the early days of the Sierra Club, private wealth shaped not only public lands but also particular views of democracy. The Club may have had somewhat democratic goals—in its first few decades it was dedicated to opening the Sierras to the public in a way it was not later—but early twentieth-century conservationists generally had mixed views of popular support. On the one hand, they rallied the public to their causes; on the other, conservationists like Rosalie Edge in the 1930s and Paul Sears in the 1960s insisted that independent wealth with fewer strings attached was the most effective means of protecting natural resources.[6] Early conservationists often worked behind the scenes rather than in the public eye. This could produce a heroic sense of the exceptional point of view. In the 1950s, Harold Anderson of the Wilderness Society predicted that conservationists would always make up "a very small minority" but also thought "there is no good reason why our influence should not be out of all proportion to our numbers."[7] Initially, the wilderness movement championed this argument from the margins. "One of the dominant strains of early wilderness thought," writes historian James Morton Turner, "was the role of wilderness in forging American independence and respecting the rights of the minority."[8] The intellectual commitment to a perspective shared by a relative few could lead to an affinity for business conducted by a select group rather than for a broad base, done with a handshake instead of through a mass appeal. "The amateur pioneers of the movement hated politics and doubted the people could appreciate what they were doing," Fox writes of Muir's battles with "consummate politician" Pinchot.[9] When the Sierra Club expanded purposefully beyond California's borders in the mid-century, director Marjory Farquhar resigned from the board. Fellow director Richard Leonard believed it was because the Club had sacrificed intimacy and close-knit control for breadth and a larger membership. "Her Club is lost," Leonard said. "It is now a powerful, impersonal political force."[10]

The shift from one Club to the other—from a group of relative intimates and fellow enthusiasts to an organization national in scope—followed nearly a half century during which the Club engaged in only one major political slugfest on the national stage, over the damming of the Tuolumne River in the Hetch Hetchy Valley. That fight spanned the first dozen years of the century and involved several mayors, the national press, Congress, and three presidential administrations. By 1913, the Club was defeated: the O'Shaugnessy Dam held back the Tuolumne River, and the Hetch Hetchy Valley disappeared under a reservoir that provided municipal water to San Francisco. A year later the Club lost Muir himself to pneumonia. For several decades after, the Sierra Club limited itself to little-publicized political efforts and much-publicized trips into the Sierra Nevada Range. Limited in both its goals and its constituency, it defined itself as a regional organization dedicated to the protection and appreciation of the Sierras.

THE CLUB AT A CROSSROADS

The Club found a newly combative and expansive spirit in the 1940s and 1950s when a new generation of conservationists advanced different ideas about the relationship between people and nature and took a more confrontational stance toward those agencies and industries that would exploit the nation's scenic places. The Club grew combative in fights with federal agencies and grew expansive in its geographical reach and philosophical discussions. In particular, its shifting views on the purposes and the politics of national parks led to the organization's reappearance on the national stage. Its views were simultaneously more democratic in methods and less democratic in goals, appealing to a wider base in order to further restrict park use. It became more populist at the same time as it grew more critical of people. In Yosemite and Grand Canyon national parks and in Dinosaur National Monument, Club leaders found cause to fight with the federal government and with each other, and to reconsider what the Club stood for and against, as well as how it went about its business.

There was no place more closely associated with the Sierra Club than the Yosemite Valley region on the western slope of the Sierra Nevada Range. Born of fire and ice, its walls originating as magma deep underground and sculpted by glaciers over several million years, it was John Muir's favorite. He called it "the incomparable Yosemite." Protecting Yosemite National Park may have been the main impetus behind the Sierra Club's founding in 1892; much of the Club's energies in its first two decades went toward park management, up to and including the battle over Hetch Hetchy. That initial sense of purpose informed the Club for much of the twentieth century. Its mission was shaped by the twin beliefs that scenic places should be protected as parks and that people rallied around the parks they most enjoyed. Muir spent many years popularizing the Yosemite area, extolling its beauty under the assumption that greater public appreciation would provide a defense against industrial development.

Muir's assumption was reasonable during the Progressive Era but became less and less so in the decades after. During the interwar years, outdoor recreation spread at the speed of a Model T as more and more Americans owned automobiles and used them to find pretty locales. Private businesses aided this trend by creating a commercial infrastructure of shops, motels, and advertising, all part of a celebration of consumption and middle-class American life. The federal government promoted car camping too, primarily as the nation's largest road-builder. Quickly, the most immediate threat to the quiet and contemplative parks of Muir's heart was no longer loggers or ranchers but the very Americans that Muir had been calling to the parks for decades. Popular outdoor recreation, and the roads that facilitated it, compromised the sanctity of the remote outdoors more than did private industry.[11]

The mass consumption of the outdoors by the 1940s did not alarm most Sierra Club leaders, many of whom viewed recreational infrastructure and conservation as aligned. Their membership agreed. Most Sierra Clubbers "were not refugees from civilization," Susan Schrepfer writes, and "rarely challenged the nation's economic interests."[12] Others, including the younger generation of Club directors led by David Brower, Richard Leonard, and Ansel Adams, felt differently, and this difference of opinion emerged during two fights in the 1940s: one over the possibility of building a ski resort on the San Bernardino National Forest's Mount San Gorgonio, just east of Southern California's Inland Empire, and the second over plans to develop the road that crested Yosemite's Tioga Pass.

The Club's board divided over San Gorgonio both in its meetings and in the *Sierra Club Bulletin*, which published articles for and against. Brower laid out the opposition to a ski resort, and Bestor Robinson, at the time the Club's new president (and later remembered by Brower as "the developer") wrote anonymously in favor of it. Robinson considered skiing every bit as legitimate an outdoor activity as hiking and camping and stressed the sport's growing popularity.[13] He made a democratic appeal: parks had roads, after all, to allow more people to enjoy them. "Our club purposes," he noted, "include 'rendering accessible.' Any other policy would confine the use of the wilderness to the aristocracy of the physically super-fit."[14] Brower argued for the "absolute" value of wilderness even against the adventuring of tourists, vacationers, and thrill-seekers. He ducked accusations of elitism by referring to a "relatively small number" of skiers, and claiming in a sidebar that "wilderness for all should take precedence over its development for any special group."[15]

Two years earlier Brower had even more directly challenged Robinson's populist sentiments. Still stationed in Italy, where he fought with the Tenth Mountain Division in the last months of World War II, he wrote an article for the *Sierra Club Bulletin* called "How to Kill a Wilderness," with Europeans' misuse of their remote mountain valleys and peaks in mind. There were two basic steps to killing a wilderness, Brower explained: "Improve and exploit it," and "Rely always on the apparently democratic argument that you must produce the greatest good for the greatest number." Here Brower took issue with straightforward utilitarianism and also with democracy being understood as whatever most people wanted. He asked whether anyone could reasonably think of dividing Michelangelo's Sistine Chapel frescoes into bits so that more people could see them. Satisfying the immediate whims of many, he suggested, risked destroying the world's irreplaceable treasures, and attending to contemporaries risked ignoring posterity. Brower may have been arguing that majoritarian democracy was not the only kind, or that democracy should take into account future generations, or that democracy of whatever variety might lead to regrettable choices.[16] He was certainly wrestling with what historian Paul Sutter has called "an increasing confusion and conflation of democratic politics and consumer choice" in the mid-twentieth century, as a culture of mass consumption traveled out of cities on newly paved roads and arrived at the forest's edge.[17]

Paving the roads was the first step in bringing people to the mountains. For many decades, getting city people outdoors had been part of the Sierra Club's mission. Brower later complained that the long-held view of the Club's older generation was "that roads were just peachy, that we must get more roads into the Sierra to get more people there." The road over Tioga Pass tested this view.[18] The Tioga Road in 1915 was a steep, rugged, privately owned route that ran from the eastern to the western slope of the Sierras and bisected Yosemite. Stephen Mather, the energetic new assistant secretary of the interior and a Sierra Club member, bought the road with donations from wealthy friends, some of his own fortune, and funds from the Club itself. He donated the road to the federal government and for several decades the new National Park Service maintained and gradually improved it.

Until the late 1940s, the Sierra Club supported the Park Service's plans to upgrade the road from a narrow and windy drive to a wider and more direct thoroughfare. Then some of the newer directors and one veteran of the old guard, Harold Bradley, began to question the need for high-speed travel through the park. Particularly at issue were plans to blast through slabs of Sierra granite and skirt the edges of Tuolumne Meadows and Tenaya Lake. Brower, Bradley, Adams, and Leonard opposed the improvements from different ethical standpoints but shared an opposition to road development for the sake of faster travel times. If the circuitous Tioga Road forced visitors to slow down and take their time crossing the park, so much the better. If it limited the number of visitors to higher elevation lakes and valleys, it served its purpose. Improving and exploiting the park's wilderness and swelling its motorized crowds threatened to kill it, as Brower had warned several years earlier. In order to grant more people a view, the Park Service was dividing the chapel's ceiling into bits.[19]

Much of the Sierra Club's leadership remained either unmoved by Tioga Road development or else more concerned with preserving the Club's working relationship with the Park Service. In the early and mid-twentieth century, such relationships constituted the Club's main currency. Years later, when the Club had garnered a mass membership that it could rally to its causes, it began loudly opposing the Park Service and Forest Service. Before it gained the leverage of nationwide public support, though, it relied on collegiality between its own leaders and federal land managers. Forest and Park Service administrators regularly consulted the Club when making major decisions about scenic places.

In the case of the Tioga Road, maintaining friendly relations won out. The Park Service expanded the road with convenience and speed in mind. Brower and the other directors who stood against the development plan lost both the fight and, it seemed to them, a place they had been charged with protecting. "I haven't gotten over that yet," Brower remarked a half century later.[20] Ansel Adams grew so disheartened in the immediate aftermath of the Park Service's improvements to the road that he resigned from the Club's board of directors and sent furious telegrams to the Park Service, the Department of the Interior, the Bureau of Public Roads, and the Army Corps of Engineers. Despite Adams's breach of protocol, the Club did not want to lose one of its best-known directors to an internecine battle and refused the resignation. After venting his anger, Adams stayed on.[21]

Having lost the fight over Tioga Road, however, Brower, Adams, and the others gained a sense of conviction that would gradually reshape the Club. As the Park Service moved philosophically and administratively toward Mission 66, its decade-long effort in the late 1950s and early 1960s to expand visitor services and road access to national parks, the Sierra Club moved haltingly in the opposite direction.[22] It began to see-saw between protecting parks for people and protecting parks from people, a balance the Club struggled with for many years—as did the environmental movement more broadly. The new Tioga Road changed Yosemite's high valleys forever, and it changed the Club as well. In 1951, the board proposed and the membership approved amending the Club's statement of purpose from "explore, enjoy, and render accessible the mountain regions of the Pacific Coast" to "explore, enjoy, and preserve the Sierra Nevada and other scenic resources of the United States."[23] The Club had grown wary of the overcrowded mountains encouraged by its founding documents, as it was becoming even warier of the actual multitudes inhabiting the planet.

THE BATTLES OVER THE PARKS

The Sierra Club's revised statement of purpose suggested not just chariness about teeming crowds of people but also a much more sweeping purview, far beyond the Sierra Nevada. Extending its reach nationally complicated the Club's work both politically and philosophically. While the new statement's wording took in the whole nation, and while the Club had founded its Atlantic Chapter a year earlier, few directors spent much time outdoors east of the Sierras. The Club, and conservationists in general, at times argued for preserving places because of their popularity and at other times argued for preservation on principle. If the threatened place sat a few hours away in the Sierra Nevada Range, organizing pack trips could rally support; if the site was in Alaska, it was the idea of that vast place alone worth protecting. Sometimes bringing more people to the mountains saved the wilderness, and sometimes the wilderness was worth saving because so few people made it there. Conservationists continued to balance the democratic impulse of appealing to a broad public against the fear of that public's potential impact on a delicate landscape. They were in the business of manipulating space—at times expanding it by keeping roads narrow and slow and at other times shrinking it by bringing images of distant lands into people's living rooms.

Dinosaur National Monument in northwestern Colorado was one of those distant lands that even most Sierra Club leaders had never visited. Richard Leonard was an exception. In 1950, Leonard served as secretary of the Sierra Club and as a councilmember of the Wilderness Society when he attended the Society's annual meeting at Twin Springs, Colorado, and took a tour of nearby Dinosaur. The monument was then under the shadow of a giant: a Bureau of Reclamation proposal for ten dams on the Colorado River and its tributaries that would capture nearly fifty million acre-feet of water for irrigation and hydropower throughout the Southwest. Despite its anodyne name, the Colorado River Storage Project (CRSP) was, as the writer Marc Reisner later wrote, "as big as the universe itself."[24] The plan included a reservoir at the confluence of the Green and Yampa rivers just above Echo Park, where the Bureau hoped to build one of two dams within Dinosaur. The CRSP pitted two wings of the Department of the Interior—the National Park Service and the Bureau of Reclamation—against each other, one opposed to any dams within national monuments and the other eager to build several of them. Secretary of the Interior Oscar Chapman sided with the Bureau and in 1950 forced the resignation of Park Service director Newton Drury.[25]

Dinosaur left the Wilderness Society council awed at the monument's surprising beauty and shocked by the possibility of the first dam since Hetch Hetchy to be built on Park Service land. Leonard took that shock and awe with him to the Sierra Club, which elected him president in 1952. As he discussed Dinosaur with his board of directors, he also decided that the Club's growing commitments required a more businesslike approach. Leonard proposed that the Club hire an executive director, and he recommended Brower.[26] This would be the first paid staff position in what had been an all-volunteer organization, a pivot away from the amateur tradition and toward professionalization. Although the Club took on paid staff later than most conservation groups, it made up for lost time with its first hire. The two independent decisions that Leonard encouraged—to defend Dinosaur and to make Brower executive director—remade the Club in ways that he could never have predicted. Director Edgar Wayburn later called the combination of Dinosaur and Brower "the turn of the hinge."[27] Brower accepted the position of executive director in 1953, and soon began to hire more paid staff members. "The Sierra Club," Stephen Fox writes, "moved irrevocably into the big time."[28]

The proposed dam at Echo Park amounted to just one small piece of the CRSP, but fighting even one piece of such a monumental project was far beyond what the Club had taken on before. Nevertheless, Leonard and Brower made Dinosaur the Club's top priority, leading an effort that allied the Club with the Wilderness Society, National Audubon Society, National Parks Association, and several other groups. This quickly assembled coalition caught its government adversaries by surprise. Brower famously embarrassed the Department of the Interior during a Congressional hearing in 1954 when he used a chalkboard to demonstrate that the Bureau had miscalculated evaporation rates and that raising the height of the proposed Glen Canyon Dam—outside of Dinosaur—would save more water than constructing an entire dam at Echo Park.

But it was publicity and constituent pressure, much more than closed-door hearings, that won the battle. Brower worked obsessively to raise the ire of voters and their representatives with every means he could think of. He made a short film, *Two Yosemites*, that compared the proposed dam at Echo Park to the actual dam at Hetch Hetchy; he published a book of essays and photographs called *This Is Dinosaur: Echo Park Country and its Magic Rivers* with an introduction by Wallace Stegner and a conclusion by Alfred Knopf; and he took out a full-page advertisement in the *Denver Post*. Brower waged a public-relations battle with the United States Congress and with Congressman Wayne Aspinall of Colorado in particular, and the longer the battle went on, the more public opinion began to swing in favor of the conservationists. Brower, the Club, and their allies mobilized broad public support in a way that conservationists had not tried to do since Hetch Hetchy, and with far greater success. Aspinall and the Bureau of Reclamation finally relented, and in 1956 they scratched plans for a dam at Echo Park.

It was, from Brower's point of view months later, a Pyrrhic victory. Several of the organizations that opposed dams in Dinosaur, in particular the Wilderness Society and National Parks Association, did so to keep major projects out of Park Service lands. The Sierra Club went along with this basic reasoning and agreed to allow a series of dams that would not violate national parks or monuments. Brower's own testimony suggested that saving Echo Park meant building a bigger dam at Glen Canyon. And so, a few months after the defeat of the dam at Echo Park, the Bureau of Reclamation began construction on Glen Canyon Dam. Even as Brower and his friends celebrated their victory, the photographer Eliot Porter sent Brower photos from a float trip through Glen Canyon. The beauty of Porter's photos shocked Brower and he decided to visit Glen Canyon himself. After taking three separate trips down the Colorado through a canyon now consigned to flooding, he sunk into depression. At a time when conservation decisions could come down to purely aesthetic questions, Glen Canyon's beauty alone led Brower to reevaluate what many considered the Club's greatest success (see figure 1.1).

Richard Leonard and other Club leaders praised their new executive director's restrained tone and reasoned approach to the Dinosaur fight.

Figure 1.1 David Brower in Labyrinth Canyon, near Glen Canyon (1961). Sierra Club pictorial miscellany [graphic], BANC PIC 1971.026.006:10—AX. Courtesy of the Bancroft Library, University of California, Berkeley.

Brower would never again be accused of either. After losing Glen Canyon, he resolved never to surrender anything worth saving, especially for the sake of compromise. Even his allies came to refer to the feistier, post-Dinosaur Brower as "a shin kicker." Brower got his chance to make up for Glen Canyon ten years later when the Bureau of Reclamation proposed another set of dams that threatened another national park, in order to complete another massive irrigation and power scheme for the Southwest. The plan was called the Central Arizona Project, and the dams would not be in the park itself but at Marble Gorge and Bridge Canyon on either end of Grand Canyon National Park. The upper dam would calm the rapids of the Colorado through the park, and the lower dam would back the river up several dozen miles, flooding parts of the canyon.

Brower went to work with two San Francisco advertisers, Jerry Mander and Howard Gossage, and together they created what became known as the Club's "Grand Canyon battle ads." Much of the work to defeat the Grand Canyon dams took place in Washington, D.C., where the Sierra Club had grown more influential than it had been during the Dinosaur fight. Public opposition again played a crucial role, and Brower, Mander, and Gossage rallied it with some of the most effective pieces of persuasion in conservation history. Most famous was the ad that responded to the Bureau's claim that a partially flooded Colorado would give tourists a better view of the Grand Canyon's walls from motorboats. Echoing Brower's wilderness and development analogy from twenty years earlier, the ad asked, "Should we also flood the Sistine Chapel so tourists can get nearer the ceiling?" Congressional mail turned overwhelmingly against the dams. *Reader's Digest* and *Life* published anti-dam articles. Representative Morris Udall condemned the ads from the floor of Congress while his brother, Secretary of the Interior Stewart Udall, fought Brower behind the scenes. But the opinions of voters swung against any threat to the Grand Canyon, and the Department of the Interior retooled the Central Arizona Project to work without the Marble Gorge and Bridge Canyon dams. Brower and the Club had again cultivated and then appealed to broad sentiment, portraying the Department of the Interior's plans as not just misguided but a betrayal of the public trust.[29]

In one sense, the middle decades of the century were a time of renewed leadership and resolve for the Club. "A quiet regional group of mountaineers in 1945," Fox writes, "two decades later the Sierra Club had become the focal point of modern American conservation under the leadership of a man who seemed to be Muir reincarnate."[30] In another sense, it was a period when the Club, and Brower in particular, confronted the limits of conservation work and the inevitable losses that accompanied every victory. Glen Canyon was the most obvious example and would remain a symbol for conservationists decades later. But there were others. Defeating the Grand Canyon dams prevented development in one of the nation's iconic parks but may have contributed to air pollution in the Four Corners region and to the strip-mining of Black Mesa on northern Arizona's Navajo Reservation. In order to complete the Central Arizona Project, the Department of the Interior substituted the power that would have come from the Grand Canyon dams with electricity generated by the coal-fired Navajo Generating Station.[31] Sierra Club policy at the time was to never sacrifice scenic places for the sake of energy production because one was rare and the other plentiful. Club leaders had not yet come to understand that the two issues could not be separated.

During the various park battles of the 1940s, 1950s, and 1960s, the Sierra Club acted selectively, not systemically. Conservationists had long recognized the broad forces behind specific threats such as consumer culture or the spread of roads and automobiles. Aldo Leopold's *A Sand County Almanac* and its call for a "land ethic" was a sacred text for conservationists, if not yet for a wider public.[32] But more often than not the Club and its allies focused their efforts on easily bounded places, patrolling borders instead of confronting root problems. That began to change. In 1963, Brower, who ran the Club's publication program, used Eliot Porter's photographs of Glen Canyon in a book called *The Place No One Knew: Glen Canyon on the Colorado*. It was both a lament for a lost place and a regret for a too narrow definition of conservation. Brower's foreword began, "Glen Canyon died in 1963 and I was partly responsible for its needless death. So were you." He had appealed to public sentiment in the defense of Dinosaur, but several years later he blamed that same public's own myopia in the drowning of Glen Canyon. He warned of other treasured places threatened by other development plans, and he pointed his finger not at the Bureau of Reclamation or the agricultural lobby but at an entire way of thinking. "The rest will go the way of Glen Canyon," he predicted, "unless enough people begin to feel uneasy about the current interpretation of what progress consists of—unless they are willing to ask if progress has really served good purpose if it wipes out so many things that make life worthwhile."[33]

Soon even that sweeping condemnation was overly timid. "The alternatives that could have saved Glen Canyon are still unused. Fossil fuels, for one," Brower argued in *The Place No One Knew*. Nuclear and solar power, he continued, would "make the destruction of Glen Canyon appear to have been the most naïve of choices in the search for electricity."[34] By the mid-1970s Brower had reconsidered this position. "The alternative I talk about now," he told an interviewer, "as I'm always looking for alternatives, is to have a new look at growth. We don't want atomic power, we don't want more hydroelectric power, we don't want a lot of strip mining, we don't want to use up the fossil fuels which are, as someone has described it, the earth's life savings of energy."[35] In a few years the idea of "alternatives" evolved from different sources of power to different ways of thinking. In the 1960s, Brower questioned whether economic growth demanded invading the nation's most scenic resources. In the 1970s, he questioned economic growth itself. As would be the case for many thinkers in the emerging environmental movement, the tradeoffs involved in any source of energy or economic expansion forced Brower to consider increasingly fundamental premises.

Among those premises was the assumption that people knew what was best for themselves and for others. Brower described the "moral" of the Glen Canyon story as "Progress need not deny to the people their inalienable right to be informed and to choose. In Glen Canyon the people never knew what the choices were."[36] Confident that "the people" would have chosen his own position, Brower put his faith in democratic procedures. Instead of arguing that conservationists articulated a crucial minority view, Brower liked to assume that they spoke for the masses. In 1957, he talked about Echo Park on a conservation panel for the Democratic National Conference. "The conservationist force, I submit, is not a pressure group," he said. "It merely demonstrates the pressure of man's conscience, of his innate knowledge that there are certain things he may not ethically do to the only world he will ever have. . . ."[37] In 1959, he spoke to the North

American Wildlife Conference, declaring, "Support for the Wilderness Bill comes from no hastily organized battalion of rugged hikers, no 'wilderness lobby'; it reflects broad public concern about direction."[38] In 1960, he addressed the Sixty-Sixth National Conference on Government in Phoenix and defined "conservation" as "humanity fighting for the future." He argued against undue restrictions on political advocacy by conservation groups because such work was done by "citizens" representing "a corporation which is duly, naturally, and quite effectively taking care of its own self-interest. I don't say 'selfish interest' because that is merely to use a label as a substitute for thought."[39] Conservation, in this view, was simply the commonsense work of people protecting common interests. Brower would always hold on to this idea, but like other conservationists he would also begin to ask whether people acting on their own behalf might sometimes cause more harm than good. A decade and some years after Glen Canyon, he said, "My own thinking has evolved a long way away from finding the handy *geographical* alternative to something; the alternative is inside our own heads: Stop demanding so much for ourselves now, at the cost of all the other people who are ever going to show up and all the other living things."[40] Self-interest and selfish interest had become synonymous.

THE NEW LEFT AND ECOLOGY

The year 1969 was transformative for the Sierra Club and for the conservation movement it often led. The change most likely on the minds of the Club's directors was the resignation of David Brower. A majority of the board had come to believe that Brower, despite his preternatural skills as a publicist and political strategist, held little respect for the board's own views and too often acted on his own without consulting any of his staff or his superiors. When Brower spent over $10,000 on a page-and-a-half advertisement in the *New York Times* calling for an "Earth National Park," many had had enough, including Brower's onetime fellow upstarts Richard Leonard and Ansel Adams. Club president Ed Wayburn suspended Brower's financial authority. The next board election pitted a Brower slate against an anti-Brower slate, and when the latter won, the board pressured Brower to resign.

Brower's resignation was only a change in personnel, even if it involved the most influential person in the Club. More significant was a change in the direction of the Club, and even of the conservation movement as a whole, in response to what would soon be called "the environmental movement." Although the two movements overlapped considerably, environmentalism distinguished itself from traditional conservation in its concern with nature close at hand in suburbs and cities rather than in faraway parks and forests, and with the pollution of living spaces more than with the extraction of natural resources.[41] Those ideas emerged gradually in the early and mid-twentieth century and then grabbed the nation's attention with the publication of Rachel Carson's *Silent Spring* in 1962. Carson's warnings about the invisible threat of pesticides like DDT, as they wandered from bugs to birds and from produce to people, took conservationists' dim view of unthinking "progress" and rendered it in human terms. Instead of worrying about what industrial development and technological change might mean for wildlife and wild places, Carson asked what they might mean for families and neighborhoods.

In September 1969, the Club's new executive director, Michael McCloskey, spoke to his board amid what the Conservation Foundation's Rice Odell called "the Big Bang of the Environmental Revolution," a year that began with a major oil spill off of the Santa Barbara coast and ended with the enactment of the National Environmental Policy Act.[42] McCloskey asked the assembled directors whether the Club should consider taking on new priorities, including "environmental survival," a catch-all category centered on overpopulation and pollution. New priorities would mean a broadening of Sierra Club interests beyond traditional conservation and into the realm of environmentalism, a not uncontroversial decision for the Club's directors. Eliot Porter argued for the new priorities, as "shotgun attacks" to protect particular places would be meaningless in the long run if population and pollution ran rampant, whereas Martin Litton and Edgar Wayburn opposed stretching the Club too thin and taking on too many issues. No group more effectively protected remaining wilderness, Litton said, and "saws can destroy redwoods faster than environmental pollution." The board finally decided that the Club should reach beyond its traditional responsibilities and take on new concerns.[43] In truth the Club had sporadically and unofficially involved itself in such issues for years, often against the judgment of most directors. But what had once been haphazard was now policy. The Sierra Club would no longer limit itself to conservation in the most conservative sense.

Eight months later, just weeks after the first Earth Day brought tens of millions of Americans into parks, onto streets, and alongside rivers and lakes to celebrate the planet and protest industrial pollution and waste, McCloskey reported to his board again. "Congress has never been more receptive," he said. "And public understanding has never been greater." The sudden surge of attention that buoyed Earth Day also lifted the profile of traditional groups like the Sierra Club that were quickly becoming environmental as much as conservation organizations. Along with the unprecedented attention and leverage, however, came criticism. McCloskey reported "skepticism . . . from a variety of sources." Most of those sources supported the Club's philosophy while objecting to its strategy. But there was also doubt "from those who believe established institutions are beyond reform and must be made to tumble entirely, whether through paralysis or revolution; and these people are often allied with those who believe the environmental movement is merely a diversion of public attention from other more pressing social issues."[44] That position—that environmentalism amounted to little more than a distraction from real problems—was not an isolated one. It characterized much of the New Left for most of the 1960s and persisted well into the 1970s and after. In its most sophisticated forms, it offered a substantive and vital critique of environmentalism from a humanistic perspective. For several decades, environmental thought would be shaped in part as a response to that critique. New Left groups and ideas were both distinct from and a vital influence for the environmental movement.

It was easy enough to assume by 1970 that environmentalism and the New Left went together, and that years of popular protest would combine with growing awareness of environmental harm to produce a more socially just and ecologically sound society, or at least produce a dedicated effort in that direction. Yale law professor Charles Reich predicted "a renewed relationship of man to himself, to other men, to society, to nature, and to the land," in his best-selling *The Greening of America*.[45] Reich believed this relationship would come about through a shift from a collective "consciousness" tied to materialism and technology to one based in equality and community. The green and the just were intertwined. "If he thinks wilderness areas should be 'developed' he is quite likely to favor punitive treatment for campus disruptions," Reich wrote of a hypothetical American stuck in the old consciousness. Opinions about society and opinions about the environment reflected each other.[46]

The opposite was more often the case. In the 1960s, the politics of social justice and the politics of conservation and environmentalism had little resemblance. The New Left—that amorphous movement that often emanated from university campuses and was most concerned with civil rights, economic inequality, opposition to the Vietnam War, and eventually feminism—came to environmentalism late, and only with misgivings. Because the New Left comprised several movements and many organizations, it was ideologically indeterminate; historians have argued about what the New Left was and what exactly it represented.[47] Motley as it appeared, though, it prioritized some issues and principles over others, and for most of the 1960s environmentalism and conservation were not among them. A fundamentally humanistic movement, the New Left tended to regard an emerging interest in the nonhuman environment with skepticism or even hostility.

Students for a Democratic Society (SDS), the most voluble and politically plastic New Left organization, was never synonymous with the New Left as a whole but its views and actions carried weight far out of proportion to its numbers, and whether SDS followed the larger movement or the larger movement followed SDS, its pronouncements, manifestoes, and strategic decisions tended to approximate the views of a broad swath of protesters, especially those based on campuses. SDS was a weathervane of sorts; because the group organized itself not around a particular cause but around questioning the social and economic conditions that many Americans took for granted, it remained open to new issues and concerns. "Thus," onetime SDS president Todd Gitlin wrote in 1967, "we offer alternatives to a wide variety of people and foment movements of different sorts, each of which . . . attunes us to new outlooks."[48]

The group rose to national prominence in 1965 when it took the lead in staging an April demonstration in Washington, D.C. against the Vietnam

War. Although Vietnam was only one issue among many for SDS, the demonstration turned into the largest antiwar protest in U.S. history, prompting many months of organizational hand-wringing, soul-searching, and position paper after position paper as SDS debated what to do with its newfound prominence. Paul Booth, who helped create the vibrant Swarthmore chapter of SDS and was twice elected vice-president of the national office, wrote in 1966 of SDS's organizing efforts, "there is little clarity as to the content of the radical program in behalf of which the organization is carried out."[49]

Even amid that uncertainty, the group held strong political commitments. SDS first articulated its key issues and core values in 1962 at a national conference in Port Huron, Michigan. SDS was only two years old and the conference attracted just a few dozen attendees, but the document the conference produced, the *Port Huron Statement*, became a key expression of New Left thought in the early 1960s, and a point of reference for years after. The *Statement* highlighted a raft of problems needing attention, including labor relations, colonialism, higher education, the military-industrial complex, and especially the American South's racial segregation and the Cold War's potential for nuclear annihilation. There is the sense, in the several dozen pages of the *Statement*, that its authors could have gone on listing more and more causes for concern. Still, tying them all together were the organization's—and, the document implies, the generation's—basic values: "human beings, human relationships, and social systems." Tom Hayden, the principle author of the *Statement*, and his co-writers explained SDS's guiding principle as a faith in people. "Men," they wrote, several years before women in the New Left would point out the movement's inherent sexism, "have unrealized potential for self-cultivation, self-direction, self-understanding, and creativity."[50]

To a large degree SDS owed its faith in the innate dignity and promise of individuals to the influence of the Civil Rights Movement, the greatest and most immediate source of inspiration for the New Left. The taproot of the Civil Rights Movement was a humanistic defense of fundamental freedoms, a principle voiced by Martin Luther King, Jr. and demonstrated by black Southerners standing up to violent repression. In the 1950s and early 1960s, the movement fought for the very same liberal values—equal rights, civil liberties—that were at the heart of American political discourse, and that many white Americans believed had already been achieved. Early New Left leaders learned the importance and the tenuousness of those values not only by witnessing the Civil Rights Movement but also by participating in it; many activists in groups like SDS and campaigns like the Free Speech Movement began their political lives by spending several weeks or months in the South working with the Student Non-Violent Coordinating Committee (SNCC). The South's aggressive defense of segregation shocked the conscience of white student volunteers from the North and the West. They assumed the wrongs of segregation were obvious. In supporting the Civil Rights Movement, the future New Left relied less on a new set of ideals than on a reaffirmation of the liberalism that theoretically grounded modern American democracy. Tom Hayden, reporting on attempts to suppress SNCC's 1961 voter registration efforts in McComb, Mississippi, felt no need to explain what was at stake; in an account that relied almost exclusively on straight description and that assumed the common values of its readers, Hayden wrote, "This report is intended to make facts real and evoke not reader interest but productive commitments. The method need not be demagoguery however. Just read the facts. And read them again. And again."[51]

Less than a decade later, SDS and the New Left embraced a radicalism that rejected the middle-class order of mainstream liberalism. But that rejection came gradually, and never completely. A few months after he reported from the South, Hayden used the *Port Huron Statement* to articulate SDS's particular interpretation of the common values he had taken for granted in Mississippi. As a group that fundamentally believed in democratic participation, SDS had to also believe in human wisdom, and so the *Port Huron Statement* emphasized "human independence," "love of man," and the search for the "personally authentic." These vague descriptions differed little from the basic commitments of mainstream liberal thinkers in the 1960s, the thinkers behind many of the policies SDS came to oppose. The primacy of the individual, and the importance of individual freedoms in a democratic society, bound together student protesters and establishment political figures. "Every liberal, of course," Arthur Schlesinger, Jr. wrote in 1967, after the New Left had begun to attack the liberalism he represented, "will define liberalism in his own way. But liberalism has always seemed to me in essence a recognition that the world is forever changing and a belief that the application of reason to human and social problems can enlarge the dignity and freedom of man."[52] On this, even if on little else, Schlesinger and SDS agreed. The New Left were humanists just like the mainstream liberals they came to criticize. Schlesinger's definition unwittingly echoed the *Port Huron Statement*, which stated, five years earlier and with emphasis on the object of its admiration, "We regard *men* as infinitely precious and possessed of unfulfilled capacities for reason, freedom, and love." Schlesinger put his faith in the Democratic Party, and SDS invested itself in grassroots activism; Schlesinger held that politics was the art of compromise, and SDS gave no quarter; but liberals like Schlesinger and New Leftists like SDS believed, fundamentally, that maximizing individual freedom would produce social good, and that given enough freedom people had the competence to create conditions favorable to all.

Ecological conditions did not figure prominently in this perspective. SDS paid almost no attention to the state of the natural world and natural resources or even to pollution in cities and suburbs. In the *Port Huron Statement*, the absence is notable. In dozens of pages of criticism and analysis is a single sentence registering concern with environmental decline, noting the threat of overpopulation and the "sapping of the earth's physical resources." A year later SDS refined its critique of American society in *America and the New Era*.[53] Again the group focused its attention on the Cold War, civil rights, and economic inequality, and ignored environmental concerns. In the year between the *Port Huron Statement* and *America and the New Era*, Rachel Carson's *Silent Spring* became a bestseller. But Carson's warnings about the unintended consequences of modern technology did not resonate with early New Left activists. Although SDS leaders expressed grave concern about nuclear technology and "the Bomb" in 1962 and 1963, they drew no connections between nuclear fallout and the subtler sorts of technological threats to which Carson alerted the nation.

SDS held this non-stance toward ecology for the rest of the decade. The SDS newsletter, *New Left Notes*, one of the most widely read journals of the student movement, published practically no articles about environmental issues before 1970. Throughout the 1960s, *New Left Notes* reported on race relations, urban poverty, and the war in Vietnam; late in the decade, it addressed the Black Power movement, the counterculture, U.S. imperialism, and radical feminism. But *New Left Notes* paid scant attention to environmental issues or to the emerging environmental movement until the first Earth Day in April 1970. SDS conventions demonstrated the same set of concerns. At the 1967 national convention in Ann Arbor, Michigan, attendees discussed draft resistance, whether to march on Washington to protest the war, and supporting SNCC.[54] The convention agenda included workshops on first-time topics such as "cultural revolution" (in recognition of the growing importance of the hippie counterculture) and "liberation of women" (an issue several women in SDS had been pushing for years), but delegates to Ann Arbor did not discuss environmental matters, and nor did delegates to Clearlake, Iowa, in 1966 or to East Lansing, Michigan, in 1968.

The New Left assigned itself the daunting tasks of reducing poverty, helping to end segregation, and ending the Vietnam War. Next to these formidable responsibilities, cleaning up lakes and rivers and protecting forests seemed beside the point. More important, the New Left valued the liberatory potential of social movements and the idea that regular people held the knowledge necessary to address social ills and achieve social harmony. "Man is the end and man is the measure," declared an anonymous 1966 essay in *New Left Notes* as SDS debated the direction it should take in the second half of the decade. "The rock bottom foundation of radical ideology is a view of man—human nature and human possibility."[55] Social justice, for the New Left, meant delivering power from an entrenched elite to a democratic mass, and believing that doing so would quickly lead to a better world. Putting restrictions on people and suggesting that individual freedom could lead to social harm—as environmentalism seemed to imply—remained anathema to the New Left's general faith in liberation.

THE CLUB AND THE NEW LEFT

By the time the "ecology movement"—soon to be renamed "environmentalism"—arrived in 1969, the New Left had climbed aboard what Todd Gitlin later called the "express train of antiauthority."[56] Escalation of the Vietnam War played a large role, as growing frustration with American foreign policy fueled a split between liberal antiwar groups and New Left activists, the former anticommunist and the latter often sympathetic to North Vietnam. Street fighting between police and protesters outside the 1968 Democratic National Convention in Chicago, which led to hundreds of hospitalizations and one death, radicalized both participants and observers[57] Looking back, Carl Oglesby marked the shift as early as 1965, the year he was elected president of SDS and "the black and white sectors of the movement explicitly abandoned reformism and took up that long march whose destination . . . is a theory and practice of revolution for the United States."[58] In the space of just a few years, SDS and much of the New Left gave up on not just institutional liberalism but on modern American society, as the group accepted the need for fundamental, sweeping change.

A more radical and more antiestablishment New Left found even more fault with the ecology movement. Where once SDS simply disregarded environmental issues, now the New Left actively disparaged them. Still fundamentally committed to social justice and a humanistic philosophy, many activists worried that pointing to environmental harm did little to cut to the core of what was wrong with the nation. The politics of ecology, some activists felt, blunted the movement's radicalism. Claiming that industrial production harmed everyone smudged the differences in race, class, and gender that had become central to the New Left's criticisms of the modern state. The New Left's humanism was rooted in inequities of power between different social groups, and the notion that American society unwittingly poisoned itself ignored an unequal distribution of political influence and material resources as it promoted a "we're-all-in-this-together" attitude. The ecology movement's holism diverted attention from exactly the sorts of differences that most concerned the New Left.

Radicals skeptical of ecology made their doubts clear in the pages of the vast and raucous underground press. *The Fifth Estate*, Detroit's best-known alternative newspaper, declared, "Ecology sucks! It sucks the life out of social reform. It sucks the energy out of campus movements. It sucks the irritants out of capitalism. It sucks change out of politics. It sucks reason out of thought." According to *The Fifth Estate* the ecology movement siphoned money away from crucial social programs, shifted blame from industrial polluters to society as a whole, and distracted from more urgent issues. "Limpid water in our lakes and rivers will not help the worker who doesn't have a job. . . ."[59] The week before Earth Day, the *Berkeley Tribe* reminded its readers that "there will be no peace between man and nature until there is peace amongst men and women." Radicals questioned any framing of environmental concern that did not indict American society as a whole. "Pollution control," the *Tribe* argued, "at this point is merely another means of social control: to prevent America's children from realizing that the crisis in the environment represents nothing less than a crisis in America itself."[60] In a more sanguine piece about ecology in New York's *Rat*, "Pocahontas" nevertheless warned that supposedly radical ecology groups were in fact firmly in the mainstream: "They don't make the connection between violence on the environment and the society that perpetrates that violence."[61]

The conventional media unwittingly confirmed the underground press's suspicions about ecology's antiradicalism, covering the story of ecology on campus as the issue to overshadow Vietnam and using words like "responsible," "conservative," and "unpolitical."[62] Earth Day, created by a United States senator, was for many on the Left the clearest sign yet of ecology's potential for co-opting the radical movement. According to the editors of *Ramparts*, Earth Day organizers were attempting to "banish everything but environment to the back pages of our minds."[63] That same month, *New Left Notes* called overpopulation worries "racist hysteria," and argued, "The problem of non-white people . . . is super-exploitation and racist oppression, not 'overpopulation.' "[64] Criticism spilled over into friendly publications, too. An "angry reader" of Bellingham, Washington's *Northwest Passage*, an alternative newspaper that dedicated itself to environmental issues, called ecology "the white liberal's cop-out," and complained, "People figure that if they stick with a subject which is controversial as Apple Pie . . . then they won't get hasseled [sic] by those in power."[65]

The Sierra Club's attempts to reach out to a younger generation furthered the New Left's disdain. Hoping to take advantage of student activism, the Club made an early appeal to younger Americans through a campus outreach program. In September 1969, the Club hired Connie Flateboe as its first campus coordinator. Flateboe started organizing activities immediately, contacting and collaborating with local environmental groups in the Bay Area, publishing handbooks for students about environmental activism, and organizing a conference in Santa Cruz, California, with the new Environmental Protection Agency's Youth Advisory Board. The outreach program also acted as the Club's primary campus presence on Earth Day, and ambassador to a younger generation. "Conservation is an old word," Flateboe explained to the board. "Environment, or Ecology is with it today."[66] And the program talked tough. "The fad is over and it's time for the hand wringing and bitching to stop," staffer Ron Eber wrote to his campus contacts late in 1971. "To save the California coast will take action and not rhetoric."[67] Eber did not ask students to take to the streets, though, but rather to support AB 1471 in the state assembly, which would set up a statewide coastal commission. While the Sierra Club campus program encouraged student groups to chart their own courses, often the Club used the network as little more than an extension of its own political activities. These students were not firebrands. Flateboe described them as "pragmatic," "concerned," and "working within the system and making it work."[68]

The Club's praise for a new generation of activists usually betrayed its own skepticism as much as its excitement. While the *Sierra Club Bulletin* noted the importance of "ecological revolutionaries," it described the revolutionaries' groups as "ill equipped to pursue conservation goals through the courts or to conduct a protracted battle to stop pollution." And while the younger groups enjoyed "enthusiasm and dedication," they were short "the political muscle of a national organization with thousands of members."[69] Even the Club's attempts at outright pandering rang hollow. Paul Brooks, a member of the Club's board in 1969, wrote knowingly that the conservation movement, "though it operates within the law, is in principle revolutionary." Many Americans mistook the movement's revolutionary potential for traditional values. "The younger generation understands this," Brooks explained, before going on to discuss the need to marshal facts in debates with experts, to gain recognition in courts, and to otherwise pursue decidedly non-revolutionary tactics.[70]

In 1972, two campus coordinators warned the Club's board of directors, writing, "At this point in time you must realize that students are very doubtful that the system is capable of bringing about meaningful change." It was the job of the Sierra Club, they went on, to show that "the system" could work, as "we cannot abandon our effort to inform and involve this country's students."[71] Soon after, the board dissolved the campus program due to budget constraints. The mixed messages of the Club's student outreach, which used the language of environmental revolution but advocated more conventional reform, underscored the environmental movement's conflicted relationship with radical politics and student activism in the late 1960s and early 1970s. Even an established organization like the Sierra Club experimented with the idea of environmentalism as an inherently radical movement, but soon the Club and other leading groups pushed forward their programs of reform along the well-worn paths of the established political process.

THE 1969 WILDERNESS CONFERENCE

Whatever success the Club had in reaching the New Left and a broader youth culture was mostly unintentional, and much of it began with the 1969 wilderness conference in San Francisco. The conference showcased some of the ideas that had been percolating at the Club for years and even decades. A growing sense of ecological relationships and an embrace of Darwinism gave shape to a more ecocentric perspective, which in turn nudged human beings from the moral center of some Club leaders' cosmologies. The 1969 conference was one vector through which these ideas traveled outward, onto the pages of newspapers and into conversations between activists across the Bay.

The concept of the wilderness conferences started with Norman Livermore, a livestock wrangler, economist, timber executive, Sierra Club director, and California's secretary for resources under Governor Ronald Reagan.[72] After an extended debate, the Club went ahead with Livermore's idea and held the first biennial wilderness conference in 1949, across the Bay from San Francisco in Berkeley. Livermore initially proposed gathering land managers, recreationists, and conservationists to consider a management plan for the Sierras, but soon the conferences became a much more wide-ranging discussion of wilderness. The Wilderness Society enthusiastically participated in the conferences but its director, Howard Zahniser, let the Sierra Club take the lead.[73]

"I attended two and they were the dullest things I've ever been to in my life," Ansel Adams remembered.[74] This was an uncommon view. Michael Cohen makes clear the importance of the wilderness conferences, where issues and positions would emerge for discussion years before the Club rendered final judgment. The conferences served as a sort of incubator for ideas that grew into organizational and sometimes national policy, including the Wilderness Act itself.[75] Brower, an early enthusiast of the conferences, began publishing their proceedings in the late 1950s, effectively putting the Club's seal on informal talks not yet vetted by the board. At the 1959 conference, speakers raised the issue of overpopulation years before the Club took a formal stance on human numbers.[76]

Even more consequentially, the 1959 conference was, according to Cohen, "filled with speakers who presented an ecological view of nature."[77] Soon an ecological perspective on wilderness became less notable at the conferences, only because it was by then a given. The more traditional aesthetic and romantic justifications for wilderness never disappeared, but they made room for scientific explanations of why wilderness mattered as a baseline for measuring change, as habitat for particular species, and as preserves of biodiversity. "By the 1960s environmental militants in the club had come to have a dynamic perception of a wilderness park," Susan Schrepfer writes, using the word "militant" somewhat loosely. "Rather than a preserve frozen in time, to them a wilderness park was a living organism within which disease, fire, and all natural processes must play a continuous and creative role."[78] Earlier conservationists assumed they knew exactly how to manage and protect wild places. A more ecological approach was one that presumed human ignorance and protected natural systems, which were likely doing more work and offering greater benefits than managers could fully comprehend. Even John Muir could get it wrong. Although he thought in ecological terms decades before most conservationists, Muir opposed any and all forest fires, while many Native Americans—including Yosemite's Miwok Indians—and a handful of forest commissioners recognized the role of fires in forest health. Brower later dismissed Muir's "unecological attitude toward fire in the forests," noting that it was the view of the Forest Service's mascot, Smokey Bear. "He didn't know a damn thing about forest ecology," Brower said of Smokey, "and all he tried to do was make people practice conservation through feeling guilt."[79]

Brower wanted conservation to spring from "higher motives" than guilt, but in fact conservationists like Brower were moving away from any sense of hierarchy at all, whether of motives or of species. Schrepfer stresses the shift in thought among Club leaders in the 1960s from the ordered world of Muir, filled with intimations of divine intention, to the random sense of evolutionary history captured in the popular writing of anthropologist Loren Eiseley.[80] Brower, an Eiseley enthusiast, convinced him to contribute to several Sierra Club books. The lean toward Eiseley was also a nod at the modern evolutionary synthesis, which reasserted Darwin's theory of natural selection after several decades during which scientists considered more directed theories of evolution. The renewed influence of Darwin in the mid-twentieth century, popularized through writers like Eiseley, pointed to a world without divine order and in which *Homo sapiens* was a chance occurrence rather than an inevitable end product. If modern, industrial society was happenstance rather than inexorable, it deserved greater scrutiny and doubt.

An emphasis on ecology and a darker view of the human place in evolution contributed to what Schrepfer calls "an ontological equality—that is, men are not better than trees."[81] That idea would become an increasingly important and vexing one in environmental thought and activism. Few held it in the extreme before the 1970s. Most Club members and leaders thought that men were, in fact, better than trees, or at least more valuable. But many conservationists began to edge slowly toward the trees. James Morton Turner describes how wilderness activists by the late 1960s and early 1970s used more technical and scientific arguments for protection of wild places. As those arguments gained favor, "what began to dwindle were sweeping claims on behalf of the public interest, appeals to patriotism, and an emphasis on the historic value of wilderness . . ."[82] In conservation work, people were less and less central to conceptions of the natural world and to arguments for its protection, and that de-centering had inevitable moral implications.

An ecological emphasis and a pessimistic view of modern human societies were fully in evidence at the Club's eleventh wilderness conference at the San Francisco Hilton in March 1969. The conference foregrounded wilderness and wildlife in Alaska, but looming in the background was the threat that people posed to the planet. The media covered both. The Associated Press reported on the howling timber wolf that played over speakers during a talk on Canadian wildlife; the *Los Angeles Times* and *St. Paul Dispatch* told readers about the important role of Alaska in wilderness politics, as did, predictably, the *Nome Nugget*, *Alaska Empire*, and *Kodiak Mirror*. Other papers focused on the more controversial topics addressed by the conference's opening and closing speakers, Paul Ehrlich and Garrett Hardin. The *San Diego Union* and *Los Angeles Times* relayed Ehrlich's gloomy prediction that more and more people would inevitably degrade not just wilderness but food, air, and water. The *Philadelphia Inquirer* and the *San Francisco Examiner* described Hardin's recommendation that wilderness be restricted to only those physically capable of strenuous hikes.[83] Hardin had recently published "The Tragedy of the Commons," the essay that would make him both famous and infamous. In that piece, Hardin considered how to conserve a resource when unrestrained individual gain could lead to collective loss. Now he asked the same question of wilderness, a resource that could easily be enjoyed to oblivion. Hardin concluded that while other systems of selection might be more fair and democratic, one based on "merit" would best match those most appreciative of wilderness with places worth appreciating.[84] Hardin argued unapologetically for exactly the position that Bestor Robinson had called unconscionable during the San Gorgonio debate more than twenty years earlier: a policy that would, in Robinson's words, "confine the use of the wilderness to the aristocracy of the physically super-fit."[85] Not everyone in the Club approved of Hardin's view and his talk received a mixed response. But conference chairman Dan Luten, fishing for bold statements, had invited Hardin in order to leave the audience with "a persisting uneasiness."[86] In 1947, that unease had been acute for many Club leaders. By 1969, it was part of the program.

Saving wilderness, Hardin told his audience, was "a problem of human choice" as population increased and wilderness acreage did not.[87] The idea of human choice and its profound consequences echoed through the conference. John Milton of the Conservation Foundation lamented a culture "dominated by an assumption that our economy must always continue to expand," and advised, "There may still be time to choose a better vision, but with each new dawn our options narrow." Geographer George Macinko warned, "In man's headlong flight to conquer nature, he tends to behave as though he were not subject to any ecological laws." Brower suggested that only by combining human self-interest with the interests of wildlife would humanity survive.[88] Beginning with Ehrlich's pessimistic view of population growth and ending with Hardin's cold calculations for limiting human freedom, the Club's eleventh wilderness conference left little doubt that people and their modern comforts lay at the root of environmental problems.

What was there to do? Conference attendees knew that few Americans shared their particular interests and concerns, or at least their sense of urgency. As the *Providence Journal* joked of the roughly one thousand people participating in San Francisco, "The hedonistic delights of that most wonderful of all convention cities in North America will mean little to them."[89] Some speakers walked gingerly up to the line separating conventional reform from radical acts, disapproval of modern society from outright resistance, but none crossed it. Chairing the first day's afternoon session, Richard Cooley asked the Club's Northwest representative, Brock Evans, whether environmentalists should be revolutionaries. "I have a split feeling whether we should or not," Evans answered. "Some decisions we cannot accept," he said, tempering that declaration by expressing hope for judicial action to protect Oregon's Cascade Range.[90] When Ray Sherwin told George Macinko that he had voiced "profoundly radical and subversive" ideas and asked whether conservationists should use "civil rights tactics," Macinko demurred. To plan for the long-term future, he said, was "prudent, not subversive."[91] The Club's leaders and friends had started to question economic growth, democratic principles, and human primacy in the world, but they held firm to traditional methods of reform and suggested that their arguments were little more than common sense.

THE BATTLE OVER THE PARK

Not everyone at the Hilton in 1969 found the program commonsensical. The poet Gary Snyder told attendees between sessions that he would be willing to sit in front of a bulldozer to prevent the destruction of the Earth. He passed out copies of his "Smokey the Bear Sutra," a poem that depicted Smokey Bear as a Buddha appearing in "the American era" while the human race "practically wreck[s] everything in spite of its own strong intelligent Buddha-nature."[92] To Snyder, the dire warnings of the conference signaled something profound, a threshold in human history. "Mankind has reached the point of his greatest knowledge and power," he said months later, "and has come to a dialectical turning point when, if he is to become greater, he has to become smaller."[93]

Snyder had convinced his friend Keith Lampe, a fixture in the Bay Area's hip community, to join him at the conference. Lampe had been a Beat poet in the early 1960s and a Yippie later in the decade, one of the organizers of the 1967 effort to exorcize the Pentagon of evil spirits. He had never been especially interested in conservation or ecology until the Sierra Club's conference changed his political and moral point of view. "People in the Movement and subculture will have to take to the streets with disruptive Save-Our-Species-Week demonstrations in order to give the liberals of the Sierra Club any lobbying leverage with the U.S. regime," he wrote the following week in the *Berkeley Barb*, at once measuring the ideological distance between radicals and liberals and recognizing the possibility of aligned interests. Where the New Left had generally disparaged the ecology movement as narrow and reformist, Lampe acknowledged both its limits and its possibilities. The conference was "middle-classy," with few young people in attendance and even fewer nonwhite audience members. Ecology had the potential, though, to bring together old and new leftists. "All of us now hung up with the industrial revolution," Lampe told his readers, "have got to move from the disastrous notion of man-versus-nature into a peaceful coexistence with nature."[94] After the Sierra Club conference, Lampe dedicated himself to proselytizing for that cause. He started a newsletter called *Earth Read-Out* that turned into a syndicated column in the underground press, and he appointed himself the voice of the environment among hippies and New Left radicals.

Lampe tapped into what was already a swirl of issues and activists in the Bay Area. Several years before Earth Day, the New Left, the traditional conservation movement, and an emerging environmentalism intersected in and around San Francisco.[95] Before 1969 this confluence was difficult to see, visible only to those in the back reaches of the Bay Area political scene where the various streams of thought met. They ran together most often in Berkeley, where in 1967 a University of California student named Cliff Humphrey met Chuck Herrick, who was just back from serving in

Vietnam. Cliff Humphrey and his wife, Mary Humphrey, took an interest in ecology not only as a way of understanding the natural world but also as a way of framing political decisions. Herrick, who had studied zoology, shared their point of view. The Humphreys and Herrick chose the new Peace and Freedom Party as a vehicle for their ideas. In late 1967 and early 1968 they distributed essays and articles about ecology and politics to Peace and Freedom Party members. Humphrey wrote one piece, "A Unifying Theme," with help from forestry doctoral student Fred Bunnell and professor of geography Dan Luten, a member of the Sierra Club's board of directors and later chair of the 1969 wilderness conference. "A Unifying Theme" tried to connect war, overpopulation, racial hierarchy, and economic inequality through the overarching theme of ecology. "Radical movements in the United States are responses to inequities that constitute ecological blasphemy," the authors declared.[96]

The Humphreys and Herrick formed a group called Ecology Action, recognized as an official caucus of the Peace and Freedom Party even as Ecology Action shifted away from formal politics and toward education. Ecology Action tried to convince the New Left of ecology's critical role in radical politics. "The relationship between current campus unrest and a blindly expanding human population is not yet recognized," Humphrey wrote in 1968 after transferring to San Francisco State University. "Ecology offers the beginnings of an alternative to the present value structure that many have rejected," he said in a radio broadcast on KPFA in June. Humphrey lamented students' lack of an ecological perspective, a shortcoming compounded by a missing sense of urgency about environmental decline.[97] Eugene Anderson, founder of the Southern California chapter of Ecology Action, described conservation (the term "environmentalism" was not yet coined) as "universally approved and universally unsupported," an issue that inspired none of the attention it deserved. Conservatives subordinated environmental concerns to those of business, Anderson felt, and liberals were generally pro-growth and pro-development. New Left radicals, the group Anderson expected the most support from, felt that "somehow other issues are 'more important.' " A "narrow interpretation of Marx' attack on Malthus," Anderson complained, "has led some radical friends of mine to opposition of all conservation on principle."[98]

But many New Left radicals opposed conservation on much more than principle. Even as Ecology Action tried to combine the urgent concerns of the New Left with the emerging issues of environmentalism, it often unwittingly set them against each other by privileging one over the other. "The magnitude of these problems reduces the Vietnam War to an absurdity," Humphrey and Bunnell wrote of environmental concerns in 1967.[99] "Ethnic studies and campus autonomy are backlog issues, needed certainly, but a settlement of these issues alone will not automatically move us toward the search for behavior that is not self-destructive," Humphrey insisted in 1968.[100] Campus activists had little sympathy for Ecology Action's holism, its tendency to look only at the big picture and to insist on the primacy of an environmental perspective.

Ecology Action thought of its holism as synthetic rather than hierarchical, an overarching politics rooted in ecological principles and a step beyond the traditional conservation movement of Aldo Leopold's *A Sand County Almanac*, which Anderson derided as "The prototypic statement of the pretty-pretty, Wilderness-values, nice-weekend-farm school attitude."[101] Uninterested in pastoral nature, Ecology Action carried money sacks weighed down with Bay fill to financial institutions supporting the Bay's development and issued a statement of ecological relationships called "The Declaration of Interdependence" at a press conference in front of the Berkeley dump. The group insisted that environmental issues touched on all others, implying that environmental issues were therefore always central.

The most influential project Ecology Action created was not initially a political act. In May 1968, Chuck Herrick died in a car accident driving to a Peace and Freedom Party conference in Ann Arbor. In response Ecology Action took an abandoned lot on the corner of Dwight and Telegraph, several blocks from the University of California campus, and designated it Herrick Peace and Freedom Park. Ecology Action and its sympathizers planted a garden in the lot and put up petitions on the fence which read, in part, "CITOYENS: IF YOU WISH TO KEEP THIS AS A PARK, YOU MUST ACT. THIS WILL BE A PEOPLE'S PARK. RATHER THAN ANOTHER STRETCH OF ASPHALT TO SERVE THE AUTOMOBILE . . . THE SIMPLEST WAY TO EXERT PRESSURE ON THE CITY OF BERKELEY, WHICH OWNS THIS LAND, IS TO CALL A CITY

OFFICIAL."[102] The city removed the flowers and trees soon after, but Cliff Humphrey began to work with Berkeley's parks commission and city council to find a site for a permanent park honoring Herrick.

The saga of Herrick Peace and Freedom Park remained in the collective memory of the Telegraph Avenue community a year later when an avenue merchant named Mike Delacour tried to find a performance space for a local band. He picked an open area just off of Telegraph Avenue and bordered by Haste Street, Bowditch Street, and Dwight Way, less than half a block from the original site of Herrick Peace and Freedom Park. Lot 1875–2 belonged to the University of California, which had torn down several buildings and let the three acres collect mud and garbage. Through the *Berkeley Barb*, Delacour invited community members to help transform the lot. Dozens showed up on April 20 to lay sod and plant shrubs in the lot's northeast corner. Landscaping continued for the next three weeks, sometimes with a handful of workers and sometimes with several hundred, all cleaning and planting by day and celebrating at night. By the middle of May much of the lot sprouted grass, flowers, and vegetables, and locals began calling it the People's Park (see figure 1.2).[103]

Figure 1.2 "Volunteers at People's Park, Berkeley, California, 1969." Photo by John Jekabson, Sunday, May 11, 1969.

State and University officials, unwilling to cede the land but wary of confrontation, spent several weeks debating the best course of action. Chancellor Roger Heyns met with a group of park supporters in early May to search for a compromise. Professor of architecture Sim Van der Ryn suggested a park maintained by the Telegraph Avenue community under the university's sponsorship. Heyns considered and then abandoned the idea, citing pressure from the Board of Regents. Finally, he declared that the university would erect a fence in order to prevent further unauthorized use of university land.

On May 15, a combined force of 250 officers from the Berkeley Police Department, Alameda County Sheriff's Department, and California Highway Patrol arrived in the early morning to evict overnight campers and protect a work crew ordered to put up a fence. Several thousand locals gathered in response just a few blocks away and, after hearing a string of speakers, surged toward the park. Halfway there the crowd collided with the police and highway patrol. The confrontation quickly escalated into rock- and bottle-throwing on one side, and tear gas and birdshot on the other. Later, the police switched to more lethal buckshot. At the end of the day over a hundred people were shot and wounded, some seriously and one fatally. Governor Ronald Reagan mobilized the National Guard, which occupied downtown Berkeley for seventeen days. Those two-and-a-half weeks saw scattered skirmishes and clouds of tear gas floating through the city, and finally the withdrawal of the Guard and outside police forces. Still the Reagan administration, and through it the University, refused to lease the park to the city, and the lot remained contested space for years after.

People's Park has long been understood as a violent clash between radical activists and established institutions at a time when those two sides were most determinedly opposed. Robert Scheer, a reporter for *Ramparts*, described it in these terms just months after the fighting: "The park confrontation was a battle in a war between the mainstream of society, as represented by the University of California's administration, and the counter-community of revolt which thrives in the South Campus-Telegraph Avenue area, with the People's Park site at its heart."[104] Winthrop Griffith of the *New York Times* explained the clash over the park as "part of the accelerating conflict between the tightly structured and self-proclaimed 'rational' institutions of society and the unordered and yearning youth of the nation."[105] *The Black Panther* described the Park as "socialism in practice" and the fight over it as an extension of "The Fascist State."[106] Ronald Reagan said the conflict centered on a group of local activists "challenging the right of private ownership of land in this country."[107] *New Left Notes* agreed with Reagan's analysis, if not with his position; both sides, the newspaper explained, "understand that the question of OWNERSHIP AND CONTROL OF PROPERTY is the basis of the current struggle."[108]

For much of the New Left, Berkeley was the likely epicenter of a nationwide uprising, and People's Park was simply a potential catalyst to growing militancy, little different from the Democratic National Convention in Chicago the previous year. Dazzled by direct action, they remembered People's Park for the street fighting that followed it rather than for the planting and growing that preceded it. Months after the confrontation over the park, New Left leaders Tom Hayden and Frank Bardacke called Berkeley "an example of rebellion to others" and "a kind of 'front' in the worldwide battle against American capitalism." In the *Berkeley Tribe* Hayden and Bardacke took stock of what the movement had learned about revolution and about itself in the East Bay "stronghold." They discussed police tactics, divisions within the radical community, proletarianization, and internationalization, but not ecology or the environment. Hayden and Bardacke's wide-ranging evaluation of what Berkeley had taught American radicals showed no interest in the ecology movement nor in growing concern with land use and resource destruction. People's Park was a moment when "we ripped off the Man's land" rather than a sign of new goals and concerns.[109] Its significance was quantitative, signaling escalating confrontation, rather than qualitative, signaling a new set of ideas.

Local activists had a different take. Keith Lampe published an open letter to Hayden and Bardacke explaining how "astounded" he was that "you guys could type out so many pages of words without once relating to what we've learned in recent months about the fragility of the earth's life-support system." That absence, he went on, "renders your material naïve and dated."[110] People's Park, for Lampe and other Berkeley activists, infused the movement with a green ethos and with a new concern for the natural world. Here, finally, was the convergence of ecological concerns with New Left radicalism. "We will never forget that if they win this simple struggle, the planet will soon become a slag-heap of radioactive rubble," one activist wrote of the state and university, "but if we, in our own way, overcome the official agents of uniform death, the earth will become a park." Another predicted, "We will fight with strange new weapons. With dirt and water. With flowers and trees. . . . Can you legislate against the earth? We will be the earth."[111]

A year later, and a month before Earth Day thrust environmentalism into the national spotlight, the *Berkeley Tribe* reported, "People's Park was the beginning of the Revolutionary Ecology Movement. It is the model of the struggle we are going to have to wage in the future if life is going to survive at all on this planet." The new struggle, according to the editors of the *Tribe*, combined the social politics of the New Left with a growing ecological sensibility, a fusion first seen at People's Park. "What we did with one city block last spring is going to have to be done more and more on a larger and larger scale," the editors of the *Tribe* explained.[112] While another People's Park never materialized, in the year or so following the original event the radical community in Berkeley grabbed hold of ecology as a paramount concern. Just days after the National Guard pulled out of Berkeley, over two thousand people gathered on campus for an "Ecology and Politics in America" teach-in sponsored by two American Federation of Teachers locals. "The questions raised by this issue," the event's flyers read, "reach into two worlds at once: the world of power, politics and the institutional shape of American society on the one hand, and world of ecology, conservation and the biological shape of our environment on the other." Ecology and politics, the flyer explained, "are no longer separate or separable issues." Ecology Action held an ecology workshop and an "extinction fair" over the summer; the Eco-Liberation Front temporarily hijacked a meeting of the Bay Area Pollution Control District in early 1970; and a coalition of eco-minded groups launched a months-long campaign to grow trees on unused Bay Area Rapid Transit land.[113]

By late 1969, the seed of radical interest in the environment planted at People's Park took root as Left thinkers and writers began to think and write about the natural world more than they ever had. In response to an interviewer's question about the place of poetry within the movement, Allen Ginsberg began talking about how contemporary activism was "a little wavelet on a larger awareness that's growing in people, which is a biological awareness rather than a political awareness."[114] Unprompted by any question at all, another interviewer recorded, the Hog Farm commune's Hugh Romney said, "What I'm really into is the Whole Earth trip, because that's something that everyone can agree on. Everyone can see that the planet is in bad trouble and we've all gotta get together and melt our flags and hang a rainbow on a pole and share all the food."[115] And Todd Gitlin, by 1969 a veteran of the New Left and increasingly skeptical of ever-newer movements, offered grudging admiration for Gary Snyder's *Earth House Hold*. "Snyder can help us do one thing we've scanted," Gitlin wrote, translating Snyder into his own terms, "which is to understand how American capitalism rips up everything of value."[116]

While People's Park helped trigger a blossoming of radical interest in ecology, that interest was sustained by an emerging view that ecology played a role in an overall, radical analysis. The environment, New Left activists came to argue, was not an isolated issue but rather an essential element in a larger critique of American society. Lampe had been making this point for months. By late 1969, he decided it was time to "begin to define a more specifically radical ('root') approach to the emergency." The coming mistakes in addressing ecological issues, he predicted, would be programs based on competition, faith in technology, the profit motive, and centralized authority. Lampe associated such approaches with "the OLD TIME, i.e., the industrial-revolution phase of history." Nations themselves, he argued, must be phased out and replaced with "tribal and regional cooperative post-monetary steady-state post-technocratic heliocentric economic models, eco-models." Lampe recognized earlier than many others that, spun out to its extreme, the logic of ecological activism could call into question the foundations of modern industrial society, including property, economic growth, and centralized government.[117]

Few committed themselves to a radical ecotopia as Lampe did, but many other activists began to consider what Ecology Action had long argued: that the environment was an issue tailor-made for opposing the establishment. Because concern for human survival was so basic, environmentalism—as it was beginning to be called—could point to fundamental and even sui-cidal flaws in modern American society. Holism, the tendency to group all people together and reduce complicated issues to single causes like over-population, was rhetorically both environmentalism's worst characteris-tic and its greatest strength. "The environment" could connect disparate issues like racism and sexism and war, and offer an overarching symptom (or cause—it worked both ways). "The notion of man's ability/need to completely control his environment is ancient," the Austin *Rag* suggested. "This idea should be critically analyzed by radicals. This analysis should be prompt, for the consequences of a new understanding of man *in* nature are far-reaching."[118] New York's *Rat* agreed. "An exploration of ecological trends demonstrates that the present ecological crises cannot be separated from the social crisis," a writer called "Pantagruel" explained. "An attack against environmental destruction is an attack on the structures of control and the mechanisms of power within a society."[119]

For Ecology Action, the news was old but the sudden interest welcome. "well, we finally hit the big time, sort of," Eugene Anderson wrote from Riverside with his typical disdain for capital letters. "i think it is a good idea on the whole that Ecology Action's part in people's parks hasn't been publicized. still, it gives me a feeling of great satisfaction that we, in our quiet peaceable way, have been responsible for a genuine revolution!!"[120] Ecology Action tried to capitalize on People's Park by helping to write and distribute a special issue of Philip MacDougal's magazine *Despite Every-thing*, explaining how a green flag had flown at People's Park "beside social-ist red and anarchist black," a flag that signaled "new indelible connections in the mind which will re-color popular protest in every country in the world, from this time on." The environment, MacDougal claimed, held the potential to unite the Left and even garner mainstream support because it touched everybody.[121]

It was one thing to enthuse about environmentalism's all-encompassing meaning, but another to establish it. On the one hand, Eldridge Cleaver, writing from exile in late 1968 after his parole was revoked but still the Black Panther's minister of information, seemed to have a sense of what MacDougal meant. Cleaver compared the Black Panther's Breakfast for Children program with People's Park as, respectively, a black and a white response to the failures of "the system." One addressed vital needs and the other addressed what might be perceived as leisure, but "they both pose precisely the same question" about the distribution of goods and amenities. "I find myself very enthusiastic about these developments," Cleaver said.[122] On the other hand, MacDougal imagined Panther Bobby Seale, shovel in hand, telling reporters that the park was a crucial issue for black Americans, and then lamented that this scenario was "a mere dream."[123]

People's Park triggered a growing interest in integrating New Left radicalism with ecology—working at the roots, both figuratively and literally—but the analytical framework for such a combination remained unclear at best. "The underground culture is beginning to groove on conservation and ecology, but a comprehensive radical viewpoint needs to be developed," Pantagruel noted. "Lewis Herber, in his breakthrough essay 'Ecology and Revolutionary Thought,' provides a starting point."[124] In fact, Lewis Herber provided much more than a starting point. "Lewis Herber" was a pseudonym for Murray Bookchin, an Old Left anarchist who became a New Left guru by creating a school of political thought called "social ecology." In 1969, abridged versions of Bookchin's essay "Ecology and Revolutionary Thought" appeared regularly in the alternative press. Bookchin followed the New Left closely, occasionally writing to their publications and offering advice based on his many years of radicalism. After a long and underappreciated career as a radical thinker, Bookchin enjoyed belated recognition within the New Left exactly because he offered an analysis that tied together social and environmental politics.[125]

Bookchin, in other words, provided a pre-assembled philosophy for integrating the "new" issue of environmentalism into the Left's overall radical analysis. Social ecology argued, essentially, that people's abuse of the natural world resulted directly from social inequality, that control and exploitation among human beings of each other led to control and exploitation by human beings of nature. "The truth of the matter," Bookchin wrote, "is that man has created these imbalances in nature as a direct outgrowth of the imbalances he has created in his own society." As an anarchist, Bookchin placed the blame for the modern world's predicament squarely on the shoulders of social hierarchy and the suppression of the individual. "The mass society, with its statistical beehive approach," he wrote, "tends to triumph over free expression, personal uniqueness and cultural complexity. This creates a crisis not only in natural ecology but in social ecology."[126]

Such an analysis resonated with the New Left, opposed as it was to the impersonal, bureaucratic "establishment," and supportive as it was of free expression and cultural pluralism.And so, many radical thinkers adopted environmental concerns into a Bookchin-like framework. "Environment destruction is merely another manifestation of the fundamentally fucked-up system," a contributor called "Panurge" wrote in the *Rat*. Such destruction "is the more subtle effect of a social system no longer in the hands of the people."[127] *The Old Mole* of Cambridge, Massachusetts agreed: "The problem we face cannot be solved if we think about it in terms of pollution, which is a result of the crisis and not a cause," wrote Roxanne O'Connell. "It has to do with the way we operate and the way people and nature are viewed—as something to be used and exploited."[128] After People's Park, the environment became a canary in a coalmine for some on the Left, a chief indicator of just how oppressive and self-destructive modern establishment society had become.

CONCLUSION

"The Environmental Movement is coming to be more than a re-labeled Conservation Movement," Michael McCloskey told the Sierra Club's membership several months after Earth Day. The boundaries of the environmental movement stretched to embrace the consumer movement, population stabilization, pacifism and participatory democracy, an action-oriented youth movement, and "a diffuse movement in search of a new focus for politics," McCloskey said. "The varied groups are still learning to understand each other." McCloskey found this fragmentation and diversification jarring. It remained unclear whether the coalition could hold. It might be possible, he speculated, "to try, eclectically, to combine many of these perspectives." It was equally possible, though, that the Club was "entering into a period of competing strategies."[129]

What seemed like a sudden efflorescence to McCloskey had been emerging for years and even decades. Going back to early battles over recreation, roads, parks, and the balance between economic imperatives and the protection of scenic places, the Sierra Club had wrestled with questions of democracy and legacy. New understandings of ecological relationships and the place of humans in the natural world complicated those questions, and conservationists increasingly made judgments based not just on what best served the public but on how people affected the nonhuman. More and more, the view that human action must be restrained—a view epitomized by David Brower—informed the environmental movement. That view would shape the topography of environmental politics in the late twentieth century. In 1969, New Left activists and environmentalists struck a brief and tenuous balance in and around People's Park, connecting ecological concerns with a much broader critique of capitalism and inequality. "At some point," McCloskey wrote presciently, "either a better synthesis of philosophy must develop or hard choices will have to be made."[130] Those choices would be made again and again, and would delineate the relationship between the environmental movement and democratic procedures, social justice, and individual freedoms.

2

Crisis Environmentalism

Environmental issues played a starring role in the Congressional campaigns of 1970, a first in American politics according to *New York Times* reporter Gladwin Hill. "While the 'environmental crisis' has not become the major national issue that some militants predicted last spring it would be," Hill wrote, "it has clearly emerged as a new and possibly portentous fixture of the political landscape." Just a few months after Earth Day demonstrated Americans' strong interest in environmental issues, major environmental organizations planted their flags in Washington, D.C. The nascent environmental lobby helped put conservation and pollution on the agendas and on the lips of every candidate fighting to retain a seat. However, while many politicians talked about environmental issues, few debated them; the topic, Hill reported, remained "in the category of 'motherhood and apple pie.' " Frank Denholm, a Democratic candidate for Congress from South Dakota, said, "Pollution is not an issue with me until I find someone who is for it." Alabama state senator Pierre Pelham told Hill, "Nobody's going to take a stupid side of the issue in the campaign."[1]

Environmentalism was in fact riven with controversy, but on the national political stage much of that controversy took time to emerge. In the first flush of Earth Day, those who felt regulation did not go nearly far enough stayed hidden from view, limited mainly to local organizations and the alternative press. A strong anti-regulatory push by pollution-generating industries also remained out of the spotlight, negotiated in private or else papered over with green slogans. Critics of regulation's ecological ineffectiveness (as opposed to its economic harms) wanted to be heard, and so emerged more quickly. "We are strapped in, crisis dead ahead, we can see it, are evaluating it, but not acting on it yet, even though we are already suffering from pains of inaction," Environmental Action's Cliff Humphrey wrote in 1969.[2] For Environmental Action, and for a new organization called Zero Population Growth, "inaction" included anything less than systemic change that restructured the national economy and reoriented the mind of the modern consumer. The environmental crisis was not metaphorical but real, and it demanded a proportional response.

People had created the crisis, Humphrey believed, in their pursuit of material comfort. "We have taught ourselves to believe in a man created image," he wrote, "but we are beginning to detect natural limits. The American dream images of the fifties are beginning to fade."[3] To find fault with the high-consumption "American dream" of the 1950s was to condemn more than nostalgia; 1970s environmentalism was in many ways a referendum on 1950s affluence. Critics like Humphrey questioned some of the most basic premises of postwar American society, including economic growth, individual freedom, and even democratic government. These bedrock premises, they believed, might have to be limited or abandoned for crisis to be averted. In the late 1960s and early 1970s when the mainstream environmental movement steadily advanced its agenda through litigation and legislation, crisis-minded environmentalists doubted the efficacy of conventional reform and instead treated environmental issues as a national emergency. In a state of emergency, they argued, fundamental assumptions should be questioned and unprecedented political sacrifices made.

Edmund Muskie of Maine, running for a third term in the Senate, seriously considered the question of limiting economic growth at a press conference just before Earth Day. He rejected the idea but worried that attending to environmental concerns in an expanding economy might require Americans to "give up the luxury of absolute and unlimited freedom of choice."[4] Muskie's dilemma was the environmental movement's too.

Most environmentalists advocated a moderate approach even as they wondered whether settling for moderate reform might necessitate radical change. Environmental organizations began to master the tools of incremental improvement at the same time as environmental ideas pointed toward desperation, crisis, and even questioning industrial society itself. While major environmental organizations secured a part in the familiar machinations of government, others asked whether human survival might require giving up some of what Americans held most dear.

ENVIRONMENTALISM GOES TO WASHINGTON

By the end of the 1970s, Michael McCloskey, executive director of the Sierra Club, could look back and identify unequivocally the Club's primary strategy for protecting the environment: "I think the Sierra Club has mastered the theory of lobbying, particularly with respect to Congress, better than any other organization in the environmental field," he said. By then the Club took pride in its reputation as a leader in conventional methods of reform. "The club has become known preeminently as *the* environmental lobby," McCloskey said. "We tackle more issues; we are there on more occasions and before more committees than any other organization is."[5] Chief lobbyist Brock Evans told a reporter, "Whenever there is a big issue of any kind on the hill, and we meet in coalition with other environmental groups, we are always the ones who are turned to to deliver the mail."[6] The Sierra Club had, over the course of the decade, become an influential organization in Washington, D.C., scoring victories over bigger and better-funded industrial groups. And it was part of a much larger trend. "The environmental movement, nurtured by Earth Day's youthful enthusiasm, has matured into a political lobby of formidable sophistication," the *Washington Post* reported in 1979. "More than a dozen environmental groups now have Washington offices that rival the best corporate lobbies."[7]

Major environmental groups had committed to a strategy of lobbying and working through the federal government years before the *Washington Post* acknowledged that strategy's effectiveness. Beginning in the early 1970s the environmental movement focused on Congress and the courts, organizing its advocacy around lobbying and lawsuits. Out of the varied ideas and approaches that characterized the movement soon after Earth Day, the major groups emerged with a clear plan of action: to use the federal government to institute legal protections for the natural world. Three developments in particular furthered this goal, creating the foundation for environmentalism's legislative approach to protecting natural resources and hitching the movement to the liberal democratic state.

The first major change occurred when the Sierra Club lost its tax-deductible status. Between 1954 and 1976, the deductibility of donations to conservation organizations remained a murky question. In 1954 the Supreme Court upheld the Federal Lobbying Act of 1946, making it a criminal offense to engage in lobbying without registering to do so. Being an official lobbyist, however, risked an organization's tax-deductible status, and lobbying was defined only as directing a "substantial" portion of funds or activities toward influencing legislation. What that meant was never clear; organizing letter campaigns certainly counted as a form of lobbying, but did testifying before Congress? Although David Brower would later warn environmentalists against the centrifugal pull of Washington, D.C., in 1954 he argued that the Club should simply forego its tax status and commit itself to lobbying. Other directors worried how members would react to this aggressive stance and voted to set up a separate, non-deductible organization called Trustees for Conservation so that the Club could stand apart from the rough and tumble of politics.[8]

Once the home of the amateur tradition, by the 1970s the Club had moved purposefully if haltingly toward a more professionalized environmentalism. In the early 1960s more traditionally minded directors like Edgar Wayburn continued to insist that the Club was not a lobbying organization.[9] The battles over dams in Dinosaur and Grand Canyon, however, forced the issue. Soon after Brower's "battle ads," the IRS suspended the Club's tax-deductible status. Having lost its high perch, the Club took the path Brower initially advised and switched from a 501c3 tax-deductible organization to a 501c4 non-deductible group free to lobby for or against legislation (although not yet for or against specific candidates). The Club lost many large contributions between 1966 and 1968, but its newfound pugnaciousness and notoriety attracted many more small donations and its membership grew from 39,000 to 60,000. "We should almost be grateful," Brower told the *San Francisco Chronicle*.[10]

The Club's experience led, eventually, to greater clarity for other environmental organizations. Several groups gave up their tax-deductible status and established charitable foundations for non-political work, while others limited their lobbying to 5 percent of their overall program expenses. Finally the National Audubon Society pushed the IRS to specify what qualified as an acceptable amount of lobbying for a 501c3 organization, and in the Tax Reform Act of 1976 the IRS designated that amount at 20 percent of a group's overall budget. Audubon opened a Washington office soon after. The Club, having lost its tax-deductible status and gained a much wider constituency, found nothing to hold it back from direct involvement in legislative debates, and it led the way toward more active lobbying by many other groups. Almost accidentally, the Club remade itself and the movement as a political force.[11]

The second development pushing environmental organizations toward the nation's capital, and toward a close relationship with the federal government, was the legislative infrastructure for protecting natural resources and natural areas constructed by the Nixon administration. During Nixon's presidency, Congress passed some of the most far-reaching environmental protection laws in U.S. history. Revised and strengthened Clean Air and Clean Water acts, the Endangered Species Act, the Resource Recovery Act, and the Environmental Protection Agency (EPA) all came to fruition between 1968 and 1973. Most significant of all was the 1969 passage of the National Environmental Policy Act (NEPA), a law with implications far beyond the estimations of the senator who championed it—Henry Jackson of Washington—and the president who signed it into law.[12] NEPA established the Council on Environmental Quality (CEQ), a three-person board that advised the president on environmental matters and oversaw the implementation of NEPA's regulatory aspects, and NEPA required that any government agency planning a significant project first file an environmental impact statement (EIS) that described all reasonable alternatives to the planned approach. Within a few short years, environmental groups used NEPA to temporarily halt construction of the trans-Alaska pipeline and the Tennessee-Tombigbee Waterway, and to force further review of their potential effects; to postpone the operation of several nuclear power plants; and to delay the sale of oil and gas leases off of the Gulf Coast. By April, 1972 federal courts had ruled on more than 160 decisions related to NEPA, and continued to do so almost weekly.

Historians have disagreed on the motivations behind Nixon's environmental credentials but generally attribute them to opportunism. Believing that environmentalism excited many and offended few, Nixon seized on it as an issue that might gain him respect among younger and more liberal voters without losing support among conservatives. In private, the president complained about environmentalists and criticized his own appointees as unreasonable in their support of environmental regulation. But, despite himself, Nixon declared the 1970s the "environmental decade," and he appointed Russell Train chairman of the CEQ, William Ruckelshaus administrator of the EPA, and Walter Hickel Secretary of the Interior, all of whom proved friendlier to environmentalists than either Nixon or environmental groups could have guessed. Nixon also implemented a legal regime that would come to define the environmental movement for the rest of the twentieth century. Under Nixon-era laws, environmental organizations developed close working relationships with federal agencies, found new bases for lawsuits, and gained clout on Capitol Hill. Intentionally or not, the Nixon administration invited the environmental movement to Washington, D.C.[13]

The third development furthering a strategy of lobbying and litigation was the expansion of environmental law. At the same time as more established groups honed their lobbying operations, many new organizations extended the boundaries of the environmental movement's legal activities. Major legislation like NEPA depended on enforcement, and enforcement required watchdogs that would poke and prod federal agencies with lawsuits. These watchdogs could employ staff attorneys and pursue expensive litigation thanks to the Ford Foundation, which committed funds to public interest law in the 1970s. Over several years, the Ford Foundation awarded tens of millions of dollars to public interest law groups in fields like consumer advocacy, civil rights, and especially environmental law. Ford Foundation grants allowed the establishment or expansion of the Environmental Defense Fund (EDF), the Natural Resources Defense Council (NRDC), and the Sierra Club Legal Defense Fund. Continuing legal success further bound the Club and the broader environmental movement to an approach based on legislative gains in Congress and on enforcement of those gains in the courts.[14]

The Sierra Club's shift in tax status and newfound freedom to lobby, the Nixon administration's environmental protection laws, and the establishment of environmental law organizations all molded the environmental movement in the early 1970s. These shifts worked together like interconnected cogs: lobbying produced—and litigation fortified—key environmental laws; those laws provided opportunities for successful lawsuits; and legislative victories bolstered the reputation of environmental organizations, expanding membership and providing greater support for renewed lobbying.[15]

A strategy centered on legislators and litigators furthered the professionalization of the environmental movement. Older groups like the Sierra Club, the National Audubon Society, and later the Wilderness Society, along with new groups like NRDC, EDF, and the League of Conservation Voters (LCV), shifted the movement's focus from grassroots organizing and major publicity campaigns to technical expertise in environmental policy and direct involvement in the legislative process. The major organizations began to fashion common goals and a shared strategy and to focus on the daily business of politics. Collectively, the primary environmental groups employed only two or three full-time lobbyists in 1969; by 1975 they had forty lobbyists in the halls of Congress, and ten years later more than eighty.[16] Environmental organizations grew rapidly, taking advantage of the sudden popularity of environmental issues and using improved direct mail techniques. By 1971 the Sierra Club had added over three thousand new members a month, the Wilderness Society signed up over twenty thousand each year, and the relatively unknown Friends of the Earth surpassed twenty thousand members before its second anniversary.[17]

Professionalization also meant expanding funding by broadening environmental organizations' appeal, and that often meant toning down their rhetoric. "Many of the 'eco-freaks' who had marched on Washington on Earth Day did not leave the capital when the event concluded," Arthur Magida wrote in the *National Journal* in early 1976. "Gradually, their long hair was shorn, their pockets were filled with grants from foundations or donations from members of their environmental groups, and their naivete was replaced by the sophistication of experienced Washington lobbyists." Creating a wider base of support meant not just looking the part but sounding dispassionate, often relying on technical arguments rather than ethical principles. The new lobby's success, Magida suggested, rested on a less zealous approach to its work. "Environmentalists have been able to phrase their arguments on non-environmental grounds," Magida wrote, "and to pick up a greater variety of allies because of their growing confidence, decreasing doctrinairism and increasing tolerance."[18]

"Tolerance" meant accepting the give-and-take of politics. "As one Congress ends and another begins, it is well to ask whether we and other groups like us are solely the victims of compromise," Michael McCloskey wrote in 1977.[19] "Might we not more properly be viewed as beneficiaries as well, and really, as time goes by, more beneficiaries than victims?" Brock Evans explained the benefits of compromise in his regular column for the *Sierra Club Bulletin*: "We win some and lose some—that's the nature of the business," he reassured readers in 1975. "Being realists, we cannot hope to succeed at every point."[20]

The environmental movement's tone of detachment, its acceptance of compromise, and its calculated political gamesmanship did not signal a lack of ideology. It signaled exactly the opposite. The shift to Washington, D.C. meant an embrace of institutions and processes as well as a particular set of values. Environmental groups mastered the methods of liberal democratic politics and accepted the premises behind those methods. Despite the early-1970s rhetoric of "environmental revolution" and a "new ecological ethic" heard among grassroots activists and established groups alike, for the most part the major organizations appealed to trusted and familiar political principles. Sierra Club director William Futrell called NEPA an "environmental magna carta" and described environmentalism as part of the "grand struggle for justice, which is the haunting theme of our history."[21] Environmentalists frequently called for an "environmental bill of rights" to delineate government's various ecological responsibilities, and Michael McCloskey justified political compromise as "the means by which legitimate interests in a democracy come to understand that they are being given fair consideration."[22]

Mainstream environmental groups took the public favor generated by Earth Day and turned it into political influence in the nation's capital. The blossoming of small-scale activity in 1970 was encouraging, McCloskey thought, but finally ineffective: "The powerful who were polluting," he later wrote of Earth Day's aftermath, "needed to be confronted with the power of government, not just with hit-or-miss voluntary action."[23] With Nixon-era laws firmly in place, the environmental movement gravitated toward Washington, D.C. and the authority of the regulatory state.

ZERO POPULATION GROWTH

Even in Washington, D.C., amid the environmental movement's emergence as a savvy public interest lobby, a more dissident sort of environmentalism surfaced. Zero Population Growth (ZPG) was not much more than a year old when it opened its Washington, D.C. office just before Earth Day in 1970. In late 1968, an entomologist named Charles Remington and an attorney named Richard Bowers incorporated the group in Connecticut in order to fight overpopulation by advocating "zero population growth."[24] The group's goal was an end to population growth; the means, troublingly, were not yet specified. Within three years, ZPG had thirty-two thousand members.

Anxiety about population politics stretched back to at least the mid-eighteenth century, decades before Thomas Malthus's 1798 *Essay on the Principle of Population*, when Europeans and American colonists weighed the benefits and harms of a growing population for a polity's resources and governance. The idea of global overpopulation, however, and the concern that there might be too many human beings in existence, was largely a twentieth-century phenomenon. The fear of planetary overpopulation stitched together a complicated tangle of issues including agriculture and the distribution of resources, migration and national borders, reproduction and human rights, economic theory and policy, and ecology and conservation.[25] That fear could also be reduced to a narrow relationship between a particular species and its resource base. In the United States, Aldo Leopold spelled out the ecological bases of overpopulation concern in his work on animal populations and carrying capacity in the 1930s (work that environmentalists would explicitly compare to global human population in the 1960s). In 1948 conservationists William Vogt and Fairfield Osborn, in *Road to Survival* and *Our Plundered Planet*, respectively, considered a global carrying capacity for the human population and how overstepping it could trigger resource shortages and environmental degradation.[26] An American optimism born of material abundance and technological advancements kept population worries muted but never silent in the 1950s and early 1960s. In the late 1960s, the emerging environmental movement stoked fears of excessive human numbers again.

The environmental movement's emerging view that people were the problem led almost inevitably to concern with overpopulation. Only a few mainstream environmentalists, such as Brower, articulated this holism in no uncertain terms. But conservation groups' increasing discomfort with the crowds at national parks, the roads through forests, and the loss of countryside to suburbs made it a short step to the view that there were simply too many people in the world. The sharp criticisms of people's impact on the planet at the Club's 1960s wilderness conferences made ZPG's message all the more urgent.

Within months of incorporating, ZPG relocated its headquarters to Los Altos in the San Francisco Bay Area. In the late 1960s the Bay Area was one of the centers of population activism. The move allowed Stanford biologist Paul Ehrlich, author of *The Population Bomb*, to serve as the group's first president. Ehrlich was the most famous overpopulation alarm-raiser in the country—the first edition of *The Population Bomb* was reprinted twenty-two times between 1968 and1971—but he was just one of many in the Bay Area. In 1969 Stephanie Mills proclaimed her refusal to have children as she delivered the valedictory speech at Oakland's Mills College. As much an activist for women's rights as for environmentalism, Mills connected the two causes whenever she wrote or spoke. Ehrlich in particular hovered behind Mills's valediction; she had read *The Population Bomb* a few months earlier and decided that a rosy graduation speech amid the population crisis would be little more than "a hoax." Mills was instantly a divisive figure, celebrated for her environmental credentials and her refusal to accept a predetermined place in society, and criticized for questioning the choices of others and for dismissing centuries of tradition. After her graduation address she spoke widely, joined several boards of directors, headed the campus program for Alameda County Planned Parenthood, and edited a new magazine called *Earth Times* for *Rolling Stone* publisher Jann Wenner. Mills continued to believe in rousing the public to attention, even if "some people won't get bothered about the smog in Los Angeles until it blocks the view of their TV screen."[27]

In October of that same year, in a parking lot in Hayward several miles south of Oakland, *Whole Earth Catalog* publisher and founder Stewart Brand invited anyone interested to surround themselves with a plastic wall and subsist on only water for a week.[28] Brand hoped his "Liferaft Earth" would illustrate the dangers of overpopulation and limited resources. More than one hundred people—including Stephanie Mills—participated. Just north of Oakland, Berkeley folksinger Malvina Reynolds wrote songs about sprawl and the harm wrought by too many people. Long before Mills, Brand, and even Ehrlich concerned themselves with overpopulation, Reynolds had satirized the endless conformity of "ticky tacky" suburban houses south of San Francisco in "Little Boxes," a song made famous by her friend Pete Seeger. In "Song of the San Francisco Bay," Reynolds wrote about highways that paved over countryside so that cars could travel miles and miles "To find a place where they can see a plant, a bush and a blade of grass, and a lady bug and a bee."[29]

ZPG pushed further what was already a key issue for mainstream environmental organizations. The Sierra Club's interest in overpopulation predated ZPG by many years. Population discussion emerged at the Club's wilderness conferences by the early 1960s, encouraged by Club director Daniel Luten, and continued in its board of directors meetings soon after. In 1968 the Club's directors assembled an advisory committee on population policy, and in 1969—the year ZPG was founded—the Club released a series of statements calling for the liberalization of abortion law and an end to pronatalist policies. David Brower persistently called attention to the issue of overpopulation and continued to do so after he left the Club. ZPG's first lobbyists worked out of the Washington, D.C. offices of Brower's Friends of the Earth. In 1970 Club president Phil Berry listed population first among "central subjects of concern for conservationists in the '70s," ahead of both wilderness and pollution.[30] Berry suggested that the Club work with Planned Parenthood and the still little-known ZPG, a suggestion the Club's National Population Committee passed on to Sierra Club chapters. Even though Club staffers like Louise Nichols questioned the wisdom of taking strong stances on population politics and especially immigration policy as early as 1973, overpopulation remained among the Club's main priorities for the rest of the decade thanks largely to the efforts of John Tanton and Judy Kunofsky, two population activists who worked with both the Club and ZPG. When the U.S. House of Representatives considered a bill to establish an "Office of Population Policy" in 1982, Kunofsky testified in favor of the bill on behalf of the Club.[31]

The Wilderness Society came to population politics largely at the behest of its own supporters, though it did so more slowly and cautiously than did the Sierra Club. "All attempts to preserve wilderness areas will come to naught if mankind does not soon limit his numbers," one member wrote to Society director Stewart Brandborg and several Wilderness Society councilmembers in 1969. Councilmember James Marshall responded sympathetically, acknowledging the importance of overpopulation but noting that the Society "has the responsibility, believing as it does, to concentrate on conservation problems."[32] Later that year Congressman Morris Udall wrote to Brandborg, stating, "It is my conviction that, increasingly, the conservation movement is going to have to get involved in the population problem."[33] By 1971 the Society felt impelled to take a stand. "As the one species ever to undergo long-term, large-scale population growth," the Society's "Statement Concerning the Need for a National Population Policy" explained, "we must take seriously our responsibility to make our demands upon the earth finite by limiting the growth of our numbers."[34]

Unlike more established environmental organizations, ZPG did not consider overpopulation an issue connected to its core interests; overpopulation *was* its core interest. ZPG emerged near the end of a period that historian Thomas Robertson has called "the Malthusian moment," from the end of World War II to the mid-1970s, when phrases like "spaceship earth" gained wide currency and overpopulation grabbed the attention not just of environmentalists but of policymakers.[35] ZPG leveraged this attention in its Washington, D.C. office and in its relationships with better-known groups, but whereas many environmental organizations treated overpopulation as a gradual problem to be dealt with over time, ZPG tapped into a vein of acute distress that ran through the environmental movement. Beneath the earnest concern of mainstream environmentalism lay a deeper dread about immediate threats and irreversible trends.

Stressing the worst-case scenario did not always endear ZPG to potential supporters. While the Sierra Club bragged of "delivering the mail" and environmental lobbyists pointed to Earth Day as evidence of their broad mandate, ZPG took pride in its relative unpopularity. "All new ideas seem extremist to those who uncritically support the established way of doing things," one of the group's early pamphlets read. "Thus it is right and proper that ZPG should seem like an extreme group to the general public."[36]

ZPG did strike many as extreme, even with environmentalism ascendant. "The degree of antagonism and hostility I encounter at the very mention of ZPG seems to ensure that the members of our chapter will go on having true communication only with the other members of our chapter," one ZPG member from Rhode Island complained less than a year after Earth Day.[37] ZPG did itself no favors by taking on cherished ideas, the most cherished among them "pronatalism"—policies and beliefs that encouraged reproduction and presumed that "parenthood is the natural, expected and proper status to achieve," in the words of board member Judy Senderowitz. The inevitability of parenthood was "in most cases so ingrained as to be unnoticed and thus unquestioned."[38] ZPG wanted to debate a subject that most Americans did not even consider debatable.

To heighten the public's concern about overpopulation, ZPG focused on education as much as on legislation. In this regard it was not unlike Cliff Humphrey's Ecology Action in Berkeley. Humphrey believed that "almost all governmental programs are irrelevant to the crisis we face, as our officials can only propose solutions to problems that they publicly acknowledge."[39] ZPG, which pushed for a national population policy, had more regard for federal action than did Humphrey, but like Ecology Action it found the national political conversation profoundly attenuated, and its view of social and environmental problems in the United States sprang directly from a sense of crisis. In the late 1960s and the 1970s this acute sense of crisis defined a vital strain of environmentalism, distinguishing it from the mainstream movement and marking one of the key elements of environmental radicalism.

CRISIS ENVIRONMENTALISM

Some environmentalists viewed democratic politics as inadequate to the task of preventing social and ecological collapse. At the same time as most mainstream organizations worked to better lobby Congress and shepherd legislation, other environmentalists put little faith in conventional reform. These environmentalists shared the belief that human impact on the natural world was approaching a breaking point beyond which lay certain catastrophe. They disavowed gradual reform and urged immediate action, insisting that anything less would bring about disaster. "Environmental crisis" was a common and almost casual phrase in newspapers and magazines after Earth Day, but these dissenting environmentalists took the idea literally, insisting that the nation and the world had reached a crucial moment in which humanity would save itself and the planet or assure the destruction of both. Crisis was the precondition for casting doubt on traditional methods of reform and for advocating extreme measures. Just as an acceptance of compromise and faith in either the electorate or its representatives i nformed mainstream environmentalism, a belief in crisis galvanized the radically minded environmentalists of the 1970s and later the ecocentric radicals of the 1980s.[40]

A small but influential group of thinkers assembled the intellectual scaffolding of crisis environmentalism.[41] Best known was Paul Ehrlich, who warned about the peril of overpopulation in articles and public lectures until David Brower convinced him to put his warnings into a book. *The Population Bomb* was one of the first in a series of dire predictions at the turn of the decade about human society and natural limits that together formed a sort of doomsday canon for environmentalists. These foreboding works shared the basic premise that any society based on continued growth, whether of people or products, was bound to run up against the simple fact of finite natural resources. In 1968 Paul Ehrlich and his wife Anne Ehrlich were among the first environmentalists to successfully draw attention to the idea of limits at a time when Americans still lived comfortably within the nation's longest economic boom—a boom that just a few years earlier had prompted Lyndon Johnson to declare "unconditional war on poverty" and to champion a "Great Society" that set its goals higher than mere affluence. In *The Population Bomb* the Ehrlichs warned that the world's exponentially increasing population could lead to widespread famine and political instability in just a few years. They argued that the number of people in the world, combined with environmental degradation and ever-higher consumption, was already outstripping available resources and would soon trigger wars and social turmoil. The Ehrlichs took the central points of Malthus's 1798 *An Essay on the Principle of Population* and placed them squarely in the American present. But instead of claiming that society approached the edge of a demographic cliff, the Ehrlichs claimed it had already overshot and was now hanging in midair, ready to plummet.[42]

Few took crisis environmentalists entirely seriously, but few ignored them outright. As historian Derek Hoff has shown, federal concern with population growth declined steadily during the Nixon administration. But that concern received "a very temporary shot in the arm" from the publication of *The Limits to Growth*, a report authored by a group of scientists known as "the Club of Rome" and funded by an Italian businessman named Aurelio Peccei. Headed by another husband-and-wife team, Donella and Dennis Meadows, the group based its findings on computer models that estimated population growth, food supply, availability of natural resources, pollution, and industrial production to predict worldwide conditions many decades into the future. From that seemingly objective point of view, the group discerned a dark horizon: unless the rates of industrial growth, population increase, and natural resource depletion slowed dramatically, "the limits to growth on this planet will be reached sometime within the next one hundred years. The most probable result will be a rather sudden and uncontrollable decline in both population and industrial capacity."[43] A more concise statement of this grim view appeared in *Blueprint for Survival*, a book based on a special issue of the British magazine *Ecologist*: "The principal defect of the industrial way of life with its ethos of expansion is that it is not sustainable," the editors stated in the book's opening pages.[44] The belief that human wealth and comfort could be achieved and expanded by greater and greater industrial production was an illusion, and people could ignore this difficult truth "only at the cost of disrupting ecosystems and exhausting resources, which must lead to the failure of food supplies and the collapse of society."

The literature of crisis environmentalism offered more than just simple apocalypticism. These ominous books provided a critique, implicit or explicit, of the modern assumption of endless consumption. That critique came into greatest focus among a group of heterodox economists who were both convinced that crisis was at hand and interested in different ways of thinking about the economy. Most proposed some version of a steady-state system as a means of preventing destructive growth. A steady-state economy was one in which the total population and the total amount of natural resources remained constant, at a particular level and with a minimum of "throughput" (that is, the fewest births and deaths and the lowest levels of production and consumption). The ecological economist Herman Daly argued that a steady-state system was inevitable, given finite resources.[45] The only question was whether nations would ignore this fact until the point of human extinction (which, given its balance of no people maintained by no throughput, would simply be another sort of steady state) or else try to shape their economies around the inescapable limits set by the planet itself.

The British economist E. F. Schumacher held views similar to Daly's but used a different language to express them: Schumacher called his approach "Buddhist economics"—a view of the economy that focused less on material wealth and more on human happiness. Its hallmarks were simplicity, moderation, and an orientation toward the local. Economic sense, for Schumacher, was a matter of achieving "the maximum of well being with the minimum of consumption." The unsustainable use of resources constituted a form of violence, and following Buddhism's pacific teachings there was "an ineluctable duty on man to aim at the ideal of non-violence in all he does."[46]

With discrete vocabularies, Daly and Schumacher articulated the same view of modern economic thought and modern patterns of consumption. Daly called the problem "growthmania," the "mind-set that always puts growth in first place—the attitude that there is no such thing as enough, that cannot conceive of too much of a good thing."[47] Schumacher echoed this thought: "An attitude to life which seeks fulfillment in the single-minded pursuit of wealth—in short, materialism—does not fit into this world," he wrote, "because it contains within itself no limiting principle, while the environment in which it is placed is strictly limited."[48] A society oriented toward economic growth, both Daly and Schumacher believed, was a society hammering away at its own foundation.

The problem resided not just in the habits and practices of the modern world but in the very goals that world set for itself. Industrialization in the late twentieth century, Schumacher explained, "produced an entirely new situation—a situation resulting not from our failures but from what we thought were our greatest successes."[49] Daly articulated this position in even more specific terms: modern accounting considered "defensive expenditures" incurred to counteract the effects of production (building deeper wells and bigger pumps to pursue a dropping water table, building new refineries to process lower-grade ores from depleted mines, and making fertilizers to encourage depleted soil) as part of the gross national product, and so a part of beneficial growth. "This" Daly said, "creates the illusion of becoming better off, when in actuality we are becoming worse off."[50] Economic activity demanded by diminished resources counted as positive expansion, and so liabilities were measured as assets.

Environmentalists concerned with limits to growth challenged some of the most fundamental assumptions of the mid-twentieth-century United States. More goods, more jobs, and greater production might signal an imperiled economy rather than a healthy one, and more products for more people might be a disastrous rather than a noble goal. "We now have a vested interest in our own destruction," Cliff Humphrey said. "What generates capital or credit today? A field lying fallow, seeded in legumes, building up its nitrogen, or a housing tract on the same parcel?"[51] What had been thought to be the promise of the modern age was in fact its greatest threat; material wealth did not mean boundless progress but instead meant impending crisis. Simple reform in that case held little promise. The vaunted environmental lobby fought a forest fire with a garden hose.

The line between incremental reform and sweeping change grew all the more apparent in the 1970s. All environmentalists considered the harms of economic and population growth but not all sided against them. Few if any major environmental organizations would go as far as Cliff Humphrey, who called the stock market "merely a device for signalling [sic] an imminent or successful act of destruction or contamination of some part of our surroundings."[52] Humphrey readily disavowed established institutions and abided extreme solutions because he remained convinced that anything less would flirt with calamity. The more an environmentalist like Humphrey accepted the existence of environmental crisis, the more he rejected the world as it was.

CRISIS AND SURVIVAL

At the edge of crisis simple endurance was the first order of business. If the planetary environment was in a state of crisis, environmentalists concerned themselves with survival as much as with quality of life. "The mounting evidence of environmental degradation in the 1960s," historian Adam Rome writes, "provoked . . . anxieties about 'survival,' a word that appeared again and again in environmentalist discourse."[53] Even though radical environmentalists of the 1980s read and took to heart the major works of crisis environmentalism, those works' focus on human survival suggested how non-ecocentric crisis environmentalism was by comparison.

For a few years, Cliff Humphrey did not just shout from offstage when he warned of crisis and survival. At the beginning of the 1970s his existential concerns surfaced even at the Sierra Club, where he sat on the "survival committee." Officially known as the "environmental research committee" but never referred to that way, the survival committee described itself to the Club's board as a "think tank" charged with providing advice on issues "outside the 'traditional' areas of concern of the Club." Responding to the amorphous state of environmentalism early in the decade and the growing array of ideas associated with it, the survival committee went far outside the areas of concern the Club had favored for nearly a century. Although it couldn't bring itself to disavow economic growth in 1971, it willingly questioned many other premises of modern American society. Richard Cellarius, one of the Club's directors and the committee chair, assigned committee members futurist tracts like Jean-Francois Revel's *Without Marx or Jesus: The New American Revolution Has Begun*, and Warren Wagar's *Building the City of Man*. Cellarius told the committee he believed "reformation/ revolution is our only hope. I accept Revel's thesis that it is beginning. . . . The environmental years of 1969-70-(71?) made up one early 'campaign' of the revolution." The end goal of the Sierra Club, he suggested, should be a global, steady-state civilization without nations and centered on the sustainable use of all resources.[54]

The Sierra Club never adopted Cellarius's idea as a stated goal, and the handful of directors who retreated to a cabin on the California coast or to a lodge in the Sierra Nevada to discuss the possibility of a drastically changed world finally had little impact on the Club's program. But in the early 1970s the Club took the committee's ideas seriously. Phil Berry, president of the Club when it formed the survival committee, attended several of the committee's meetings and remembered it as an attempt to consider the many dire predictions for the future that circulated in those years. "We were talking about the elements of a program essential to global survival," he explained. The environmental movement was broadening itself to consider issues far afield from national parks and forests, Berry said, and "We were talking about how to put this into a Sierra Club agenda for action. That's really what the survival committee was."[55]

The rhetoric of survival revealed two key characteristics of early 1970s crisis environmentalism. The first was that despite its frequent references to the decimation of natural resources and the destruction of natural places, crisis environmentalism was overwhelmingly oriented toward people. The ecocentrism of later radicals remained either rare or inchoate in the early 1970s. Whereas radical environmentalists of the 1980s would prioritize nonhuman nature, crisis environmentalists worried most of all about the fate of humanity. John Fischer, a contributing editor and columnist at *Harper's*, suggested as much when he proposed an experimental university—"Survival U."—structured entirely around "the study of the relationship between man and his environment, both natural and technological." The crucial question for students at Fischer's imagined campus would be how long people could last on a degraded planet. The loss of forests and animals was frightening, but the potential loss of people was the greater tragedy. "For the first time in history," Fischer declared, "the future of the human race is now in serious question."[56]

What was a thought experiment for Fischer was a serious undertaking for Paul Ehrlich. In 1971, Ehrlich and political science professor Robert North first proposed a program in "social ecology" at Stanford University to study the intersection of biological systems, social institutions, and cultural values. "It is apparent that mankind is moving toward a crisis of unprecedented magnitude," the program's official proposal began.[57] The crisis of human existence that Ehrlich and North feared arose from a combination of industrialization, overpopulation, environmental degradation, and above all a culture of endless expansion. Ehrlich and North wanted to approach social and biological systems as interconnected and ultimately unsustainable, in courses like "Environment, Ecology, and Survival" and "Social Institutions and the Survival Problem." People faced the greatest risks on a dirty and crowded planet, and so the social ecology curriculum focused on "stimulating social action for reducing mankind's peril."

The second characteristic of crisis environmentalism was an orientation toward the future and a certainty about its dire condition. Crisis environmentalism rested on the conviction that the house of cards would inevitably topple. Crisis environmentalists demanded a dramatic and purposeful response, not to a clear and present danger but to a disaster that was, ostensibly, moments away. They called attention both to what was easily demonstrated, such as oil spills, pollution, or plans for a dam or power plant, and to more serious but less apparent events lurking in the near future. And so, because the public reflexively dismissed overly pessimistic outlooks, they battled optimism. They dealt with the public's rosy disposition in several ways: by making the pragmatic argument that preparing for the worst entailed the least risk, by claiming that the die had been cast and that it was no longer a matter of if but of when, or by making predictions as rigorously as possible. Ehrlich tried all three. He claimed that planning for disaster would yield benefits even if disaster never arrived, he opened *The Population Bomb* with the words "the battle to feed all of humanity is over," and most of all he tried to buttress his prophecies with data.[58]

Jay Forrester—a member of the Club of Rome, a mentor to the Meadowses, and a founder of the field called system dynamics—specialized in anticipating what the near future would hold. Forrester claimed that complex social systems, from corporate management to urban poverty to the interaction of population, industrialization, and pollution, could be modeled and predicted with the help of a computer. In an article first published in *Technology Review* and later reprinted in the *ZPG National Reporter*, Forrester argued that social policy was often ineffective and even counterproductive because it relied on linear thought and failed to understand the complicated relationships between different social and natural systems.[59] Ehrlich read the article with interest and proposed using, at Stanford, something similar to Forrester's DYNAMO (Dynamic Modeling) computer program. Intrigued by the Club of Rome and its computer simulations, Ehrlich arranged for the Meadowses to visit Stanford. The predictive dimension of system dynamics made it compelling for Ehrlich and vital to crisis environmentalists. Only some claim to scientific rigor would allow policymakers to take crisis environmentalism seriously. Explaining to readers why they had published Forrester's article, the editors of *ZPG National Reporter* wrote, "ZPG is a fortune-telling organ. . . . The roads to doom seem many and broad. The path to a desirable, or even tolerable, life seems intricate and narrow. Professor Forrester tells the future. And he tells it the way we want to hear it told."[60] The first step to survival was knowing what was to come. And the presumption of knowing quickly led to a second step: political reaction.

CRISIS AND DEMOCRACY

So urgent was the crisis environmentalist sense of imminent catastrophe that some willingly questioned not just demographic and economic growth but also democratic governance. The political implications of crisis environmentalism often simmered beneath the surface of calls for more drastic measures, and on occasion they rose into plain sight. Crisis environmentalists found it difficult to reconcile the state of emergency they described with democracy's meandering procedures and its tendency to favor compromise over decisive and dramatic action. Radical environmentalists of the 1980s would become similarly frustrated with the gradualism of democracy, but while those later radicals used direct action to either accelerate or circumvent conventional reform, crisis environmentalists pondered a wholesale abandonment of democratic procedures.

Democracy's great strength and weakness, political scientist David Runciman argues, has always been indecisiveness. Lacking centralized authority and a consistent vision, modern democracies have relied on trial and error. Democratic governments, according to Runciman, think in the short term and succeed in the long term. They take on problems as they arise, and while this ad hoc approach can appear aimless in the moment it tends to bear fruit over time. What democracies have lost through equivocation they have gained through flexibility. At various points of crisis in the twentieth century, this was not a reassuring method of decision-making; experimentation became a less palatable mode of governing as the point of no return approached. And democratic nations, Runciman explains, held tight to the belief in a bright future in order to remain confident of their haphazard mode of politics, even when optimism seemed foolhardy. "Could any democratic politician be expected to point out the limits of growth," he asks, "and to dampen expectations of continued expansion in living standards?"[61]

Crisis environmentalists argued that the more urgent the issue at hand, the less effective were democratic governments at taking necessary action. Ecologist Garrett Hardin explicitly linked environmental problems to broad political and social values in his 1968 essay, "The Tragedy of the Commons," arguing that the use of any shared resource in a manner that maximized individual gain would inevitably harm the general good. If individual actors behaved in a rational manner, seeking to advance their own interests, the net result would be to degrade any commons. Hardin's example was a grazing pasture, on which the advantage for any single herdsman of adding an animal to his herd (the value of that animal on the market) was significant, while the disadvantage (the effects of overgrazing borne by all the herdsmen) was marginal. Logically, each herdsman would keep adding to his herd to increase its value, and in doing so help destroy the pasture. "Freedom in a commons," Hardin wrote, "brings ruin to all."[62]

Hardin suggested that the tragedy of the commons could be applied to many resources, including the oceans, national parks, and unpolluted air. But his chief interest was in the planet as a whole—the greatest commons of all—and the growing human population that threatened to bring ruin to it. Hardin's basic argument was that overpopulation created a problem with no technical solution. Technology and ingenuity, he insisted, would not be sufficient in addressing growing human impact on the planet. The sacrifice of some freedoms, including the freedom to breed, would be necessary. Appealing to individual consciences, and thus relying on the responsible behavior of some to outweigh the self-interested behavior of others, would likely produce more resentment than results. Only "mutual coercion, mutually agreed upon," in Hardin's much-repeated phrase, would work. Individual freedom created the tragedy of the commons, and collective restraint would solve it.

Hardin never explained in his original essay exactly what he meant by "mutual coercion, mutually agreed upon," although he implied that it would involve a combination of public education and enforcement. On its own, mutual coercion was not an argument against democracy—all democracies, in fact, depended upon the proscription of some freedoms through mutual agreement—but the political scientist William Ophuls, who wholeheartedly agreed with Hardin, pushed the logic of Hardin's essay to its ultimate, antidemocratic conclusion. Ophuls pointed to "striking similarities" between "The Tragedy of the Commons" and *Leviathan*, Thomas Hobbes's seventeenth-century justification for a strong, centralized state. Like Hobbes, Hardin advocated giving up certain individual liberties in order to gain social order, and argued that the loss of particular political rights actually led to greater freedom by handing the state the power to improve the general social good and, through it, individual opportunities. The path to social stability, for Hobbes and, Ophuls claimed, for Hardin, ran not through freedom and democracy but through something approaching authoritarian control. The tragedy of the commons illustrated the need for quick and selfless action, and the leisurely pace and self-interested nature of democratic reform could only lead to disaster. "Real altruism and genuine concern for posterity may not be entirely absent," Ophuls admitted, "but they are not present in sufficient quantities to avoid tragedy. Only a Hobbesian sovereign can deal with this situation effectively, and we are left then with the problem of determining the concrete shape of Leviathan."[63]

Crisis environmentalists' willingness to abandon personal freedoms did not arise from philosophical considerations alone. A larger sense of decline hung over the 1970s, fed by energy crises, runaway inflation, and political scandals. The Trilateral Commission, founded in 1973 to foster close relations between North America, Western Europe, and Japan, called the halting political response to the decade's adverse conditions "The Crisis of Democracy" in a 1975 report. The oil shock of 1973, in particular, raised alarms about overpopulation and the conservation of natural resources despite that event's largely political origins. In 1974 the economist Robert Heilbroner suggested basic social and political change might be the only safeguard against overpopulation, environmental destruction, and nuclear war. Caught between the individualistic and growth-oriented consumer culture of the mid-century and the era of limits that the 1970s seemed to inaugurate, fundamental and difficult changes might be realistic "only under governments capable of rallying obedience far more effectively than would be possible in a democratic setting. If the issue for mankind is survival, such governments may be unavoidable, even necessary."[64]

A year later, Heilbroner felt even more convinced that the tension between individual freedom and commonweal that characterized liberal society could not be eased through democratic means. "The *malaise*, I have come more and more to believe, lies in the industrial basis on which our civilization rests," he wrote. Democratic reform could not address such a fundamental problem; so entrenched was the culture of individualism and material gain that only force, backed by authority, could undo it. At certain historical points, Heilbroner said, "It is not possible to reconcile the hopes of the moment and the needs of the future, when a congruence between one's personal life and the collective direction of all mankind cannot be established without doing violence either to one's existence or to one's understanding." Balanced against each other, personal lives could not match the weight of the species and planet. Eventually human society as a whole would have to make a grim choice that Ophuls described as either "the coercion of nature" or "an iron regime."[65]

ZPG AND THE THREAT OF COERCION

Crisis environmentalism in theory was often a far cry from crisis environmentalism in practice. As an established environmental organization with an office in Washington, D.C. and a relationship with federal legislators, ZPG held a stake in public opinion. As a group trying to save civilization from itself, however, ZPG confronted possibilities and considered methods that many others would not. The antidemocratic theories entertained by crisis environmentalists got the sort of consideration in the offices of

ZPG that they would never get in the halls of the Environmental Defense Fund or the National Audubon Society.

Throughout the 1970s, ZPG wrestled with the question of coercion. The ease with which overpopulation could theoretically be ended by fiat made obligatory measures seductive. Kingsley Davis, the demographer often credited with coining the term "zero population growth," liked to make this point in the most clinical terms: "If ZPG were the supreme aim," he wrote, "*any* means would be justified. By common consent, however, raising the death rate is excluded; also, reducing immigration is played down. This leaves fertility reduction as the main avenue." The problem, Davis contended, was simply a matter of what people were or were not willing to give up to achieve demographic stability. "If having too many children were considered as great a crime against humanity as murder, rape, and thievery," Davis pointed out, starting with a premise few people would support, "we would have no qualms about 'taking freedom away.'" In fact, he continued, having children would be understood as a violation of others' rights.[66]

This sort of turning of the moral tables was a common and often effective gambit for ZPG. The organization liked to refer to laws restricting abortion as "compulsory pregnancy," and to describe those laws as arising from "a particular segment of the population . . . imposing its religious and moral doctrine upon others who do not share their views."[67] But pointing out the wrongness of one form of coercion did not establish the rightness of another, as ZPG was well aware. Executive Director Shirley Radl wrote to Ehrlich in early 1970 to assure him that the young organization was learning how to present itself publicly. "We have good readings from the membership, the general public, and our legislators, and an understanding of what is acceptable to all such factions," she explained. "We know, for example, that to discuss hard-line compulsory birth control is totally taboo."[68] The question persisted, though, among those most concerned with overpopulation. ZPG supporters like Edgar Chasteen strongly advocated compulsory birth control, and Radl had to explain the impracticality if not the undesirability of such a position. "We have so many really serious problems with which to cope," she wrote to Chasteen, "I'm not sure any of us are ready to take on the controversy which will result if we adopt a resolution endorsing compulsory birth control."[69]

Having the discussion and taking the position were different matters, as ZPG came to understand. The group started off swimming against the current. "We aren't afraid to discuss the possibility that population pressure may force compulsory family limitation," ZPG stated in 1969.[70] That fearlessness would quickly fade, however, in ways illustrated by one of the odder episodes in ZPG's history. In November 1971, director Michael Campus contacted ZPG about his new film based on the novel *The Edict*, to be called *Z.P.G.* Like the novel, the film would tell the story of an overpopulated future in which a "World Federation Council" makes reproduction a capital offense. Campus claimed to be inspired by *The Population Bomb* and wanted ZPG's endorsement of a film he hoped would alert Americans to the perils of too many people.[71]

Privately, ZPG's leadership discussed the financial implications of the film, which might produce significant royalties as well as a relationship with billionaire Edgar Bronfman, who partially funded *Z.P.G.* After seeing an early version of the movie, executive director Hal Seielstad recommended endorsing it as long as Paramount Pictures agreed to a prologue and epilogue scripted by ZPG.[72] Publicly though, ZPG began to put strategic distance between itself and the film, uncomfortably aware of how even fictional suggestions of coercion might tar the group. A week after Seielstad recommended endorsement to ZPG's executive committee, he sent a "crisis alert" to chapters: "Since ZPG advocates personal responsibility for voluntarily restricting child birth rather than government decrees enforced by pain of death," he said, "this association is very damaging to our image with the movie viewing public."[73]

Paramount rejected the idea of a prologue and epilogue despite an appeal by Campus himself. ZPG had not trademarked its name and so had no guarantee of financial gain either. Weeks before the film's release, ZPG filed suit to block the use of its name and began organizing leafleting by its members to make sure that audiences knew the difference between *Z.P.G.* and ZPG. No injunction was granted, and *Z.P.G.* hit theaters in March. Increasingly concerned about its brand, ZPG polled moviegoers in the Bay Area, asking them whether they were aware of an organization called Zero Population Growth, whether they thought such an organization called for government restrictions on childbirth, and whether they thought the organization endorsed the film. A plurality—before and after viewing—believed that population activists advocated government regulation of reproduction. On the other hand a majority had never heard of ZPG, so it was unclear whether there was much of a brand to damage. By May, ZPG felt comfortable declaring victory as it became clear the film was a flop.[74]

ZPG never in fact endorsed any form of coercion, although it confronted the possibility more seriously than did any other environmental group. At the organization's founding, several board members, including Garrett Hardin, pushed the idea and were soon outvoted. Richard Bowers, a negligible presence for most of ZPG's history despite helping to found the group, later regretted that initial shift toward voluntarism. By the 1990s, Bowers believed Hardin had been proven right and that "human coercion is needed and the sooner the better for humankind and more so for wildlife."[75] For the most part, though, controversies about coercion remained more talk than action. ZPG staffers never actively sought legal strictures to limit human numbers. They just believed in the urgency of the environmental crisis enough to hazard the conversation. Walking up to the line without ever overstepping it, ZPG's discussions of coercion suggested how environmentalists could question, however hesitantly, the unalloyed good of individual freedom, material comfort, the nuclear family, and mid-century liberalism.

ZPG AND LIBERALISM

After the movie's brief run, ZPG's staff kept busy "carefully logging the hate mail we receive in response to the film." But the public's discomfort with ZPG could arise as much from the group's holism as from its depiction on screen. Arguing that people were inherently problematic was never a popular position. When ZPG made the point in the most sweeping terms, it tended to produce equal parts support and strenuous condemnation. Many of those who condemned ZPG assumed, not without some justification, that ZPG was saying what the broader environmental movement believed. Environmental holism, though, was rarely as sweeping as the movement's rhetoric sometimes suggested. Some environmentalists lumped people, or

certain classes of people, into a homogenous mass. Most environmentalists, including ZPG, wrestled with the implications of gender, race, and
nationality even as they talked about a collective humanity. Holism offered
a stark framework for pressing concerns. It also fed a more pointed critique
of modern, growth-oriented liberalism.[76]

New Left activists pointed to overpopulationists as an example of
environmental antihumanism. "ZPG says that there are too many people,
especially non-white people, in the world," *New Left Notes* reported in 1970,
"that these people are terrifying and violent, and that their population
growth must be stopped—by 'coercion' if necessary." *New Left Notes* made
two specific critiques of population politics: first, it was coercive; second, it
blamed all people for environmental destruction instead of recognizing the
much greater guilt of the wealthy and the privileged. Population activists
abetted the most powerful in society by failing to expose the powerful's
outsized responsibility. "This is not the first time that racist hysteria and
fascist practices . . . have been advocated by capitalist agents," the newspaper
observed.[77]

Students for a Democratic Society (SDS) accused ZPG of reckless simplification, reasoning that by treating all people as a single flat category, population activists ignored not only human difference but also human value.
Ehrlich heard this complaint from both sides of the political spectrum. His
two chief antagonists were the Left-leaning biologist and environmentalist
Barry Commoner and the Right-leaning economist Julian Simon. Commoner said that Ehrlich never took account of social inequality, capitalism's
drive for profits, or how some people were polluters and other people were
victims; Simon argued that Ehrlich failed to appreciate human ingenuity,
capitalism's knack for innovation, and how more people could mean more
solutions to the problems of scarcity and pollution. Both critics accused
Ehrlich of failing to treat people as complicated and autonomous individuals rather than as simply part of the human horde.[78]

This was a key grievance against not only population activists but also
against environmentalists more generally. Too often, critics said, environmentalists treated all people as the same in the good and the harm that they
did, ignoring the ways people could help as much as hinder and suffer as

much as perpetrate. SDS, Commoner, and Simon, despite their differences, could all make this critique of population politics because they shared a commitment to liberal individualism. The environmental movement, less committed to individualism, could subordinate individual autonomy to the interests and faults of a collective "people." ZPG and its sympathizers took this further, questioning the obligation to individual freedom that had informed liberal political thought for centuries, and in particular questioning a twentieth-century liberalism that embraced consumption and economic growth and emphasized social distinctions. By criticizing material prosperity and minimizing social difference, ZPG cut against the grain of a particularly modern liberal ethos. These points of tension were basic and informed much of the debate between ZPG and its antagonists. But ZPG was also a bridge between crisis environmentalism's harsh rhetoric and mainstream environmentalism's more pragmatic reformism. As a crisis-oriented group that operated in a broad political context, ZPG challenged modern liberal commitments while still trying to pay heed to pluralism and to how categories like gender and race structured society.

Any objections to material consumption challenged the essence of mid-twentieth-century American liberalism. "Growthmania" was not simply a matter of acquisitiveness. The shift in emphasis among policymakers from economic stability to economic growth in the mid-twentieth century was good for business, for organized labor, and for the middle class, as well as for social reform. Government-sponsored economic growth provided steady profits for the corporate sector, a rising standard of living for workers and suburbanites, and increased military funding for the Cold War, and it allowed politicians to talk less of redistributing wealth and resources and more of expanding them. In this calculus, social reform was not a matter of taking away from some to give to others but instead a means of letting everyone have more. "The interpenetration of growth economics and liberal politics," Robert Collins writes, "produced a defining feature of public life in the 1960s—the ascendancy of what might be labeled 'growth liberalism.' " Economic growth was not an end in itself, Collins makes clear, but rather the means to many ends: the formula that solved for all problems social, political, and material.[79] Consumption was not only an economic activity but also a civic responsibility and a political process. According to Lizabeth Cohen, never-ending growth constituted the engine of "an elaborate, integrated ideal of economic abundance and democratic political freedom, both equitably distributed, that became almost a national civil religion from the late 1940s into the 1970s."[80]

For much of the American public in the postwar decades, social reform, an expanded state, and material affluence were not just coincidental but connected. Consumption aligned closely with liberal political ideals. Economic growth stood at the center of a broad social and political vision that celebrated population growth in economic as well as cultural terms. More people producing and consuming would lead to ever-greater benefits for all. Nonetheless, as historian Derek Hoff has shown, many policymakers found reasons to reconcile a lower birth rate with assumptions of continued increases in production and consumption. Departing from some of John Maynard Keynes's demographic views, these legislators and pundits subscribed to what Hoff calls "stable population Keynesianism" (SPK), essentially the view that state-induced consumption could offset lower numbers of consumers. In fact, fewer consumers might even raise wages and encourage gains in per capita consumption. According to SPK adherents, the incomes and purchasing power of buyers mattered far more to the overall economy than the mere number of buyers. "By contending that the size of the population means little to the economy compared to spending and saving habits," Hoff writes of SPK, "it contributed to the rise of consumerist liberalism in the United States."[81]

Population politics contributed, and eventually population politics took away. By the 1960s and 1970s, Hoff explains, environmentalists had to decide whether to argue that limiting the population would foster economic growth and benefit everyone materially or that economic growth itself was inherently harmful to the planet and so must be limited too. They had to decide, in other words, whether or not to challenge what had become part of the scaffolding of twentieth-century American liberalism: economic expansion and material affluence. Different environmentalists made different arguments about the benefits and drawbacks of an expanding economy and its relationship to environmental degradation. Most, however, at least agreed that economic growth, population growth, environmental harm, and political beliefs were all intricately related.

The Sierra Club waffled on these questions, at times critical of consumption for consumption's sake but more often uneasy with dismissing the engine of national prosperity. Even the survival committee, which discussed dystopian and utopian possibilities as a matter of course, found itself conflicted. Members of the committee discussed the problem of "credit, which has led people to have a vested interest in their own destruction," and lamented "the lack of a rational measure of quality other than profit," but generally agreed that "the Sierra Club should not oppose growth as such."[82] To oppose an ever-expanding economy, the Club knew, was to oppose many Americans' dreams for the future.

Crisis environmentalists had fewer qualms. ZPG argued that economics and ideology combined in a system it called "structural pronatalism." This system was part and parcel with mid-century suburbanization and the consumer lifestyles that went along with it. The public and private institutions that facilitated middle-class consumption, ZPG believed, also encouraged people to have children in both obvious and subtle ways. The most obvious was the tax code, which offered deductions for children and which treated married couples as a unit rather than as individuals, discouraging two-income households. Somewhat less obvious was the suburb itself, which presented a host of problems. A report by ZPG's population policy committee noted how suburban homes wasted energy; suburban neighborhoods "increased the racial, social, and age segregation of American society"; and suburban living patterns were "associated with a high-fertility life-style" as well as "the increasing isolation of women from the job market." Large automobiles further contributed to suburban expansion, to large families, and to air pollution. One member of the committee advocated the elimination of federally insured loans for houses larger than 1,500 square feet. Another recommended a ban on all but subcompact vehicles.[83]

For crisis-minded environmentalists the birthrate alone was far from the whole story. The problem was people, but even more so people's consumption. This sort of systemic view did not always endear environmental groups to their supporters. George Mumford of Grayling, Michigan, wrote to Paul Ehrlich in 1970 to complain about *The Environmental Handbook*, which was published by the organizers of Earth Day and edited by Garrett DeBell, one of ZPG's lobbyists. The book included "some shockingly-dangerous notions," Mumford said. "For example, on pages 6 and 7, a kook named Keith Lampe advocates phasing out nations and capitalism."[84] This was true. Lampe had long advocated a dismantling of capitalism and industrialism. In his own newsletter he told his readers, "enormously overcrowded planetary conditions make necessary a rapid evolution from competition to cooperation, that in the U.S. specifically . . . means shucking capitalism and evolving a community for which there is yet no label, a community within which the notions of ownership and money no longer have meaning or appeal."[85] Ecology Action pushed beyond simple math too. "Simply stated," one of its editorials read, "a few people with what most of the world considers a high standard of living have an infinitely greater negative impact than few or even many people with a low standard of living."[86] ZPG sought to put this theory into action, proposing in 1973 a Center for Growth Alternatives that would advocate "selective limitation of growth in population, consumption and development," and that would seek to "reverse the general thought that affluence carries with it the right to disproportionate use and degradation of the public environment."[87]

By opposing an economy based on ever-greater consumption, environmentalists picked a fight with a key element of twentieth-century American liberalism. By opposing more products and more purchases, they set themselves against what many people viewed as an essential quality of American citizenship. While the nation yelled, "More," environmentalists cried, "Less." Sometimes population activists glossed over the ways that different social and economic contexts shaped different levels of consumption and environmental impact. At other times they paid close attention to such distinctions. At their most discerning, population activists considered the ways that environmentalism and twentieth-century liberalism overlapped but never aligned.

Unlike many environmental groups, ZPG frequently discussed gender equality. This was a matter of both conviction and convenience. It was a point of conviction for ZPG that normative gender roles both subordinated women and encouraged childbirth. ZPG called this "psychological pronatalism," a cause and a consequence of structural pronatalism. While structural pronatalism was easy enough to identify once described, psychological pronatalism was so ubiquitous as to be invisible. "The enormous power exerted by this set of social attitudes results from its pervasiveness in all aspects of our lives," one member of the population policy committee reported.[88] This ever-present point of view was buttressed by a lack of professional options for women and the assumption that most women should raise children at home; restrictions on advertising contraception alongside television's regular celebrations of sex and parenthood; and hostility to sex education in schools. In the mid-1970s ZPG argued that addressing the unquestioned association of women with domesticity started with passage of the Equal Rights Amendment, aggressive affirmative action programs, and state-level commissions on the status of women. But laws were not enough. Women would not dutifully take responsibility for birth control, Rhonda Levitt and Madeline Nelson wrote in a special issue of the *ZPG National Reporter* by and about women, "unless we are able to assert our humanity outside of motherhood and servitude to our husbands."[89]

It was a matter of convenience for ZPG and for reproductive rights groups like Planned Parenthood that they could set aside some of their key differences and unite in defense of abortion rights, which they both supported wholeheartedly. In the 1970s ZPG and Planned Parenthood adopted each other's ideas and language to further their common goal. "Never before had we been so aware of the crucial interdependence of peoples and economies on our fragile, finite planet," the Planned Parenthood Federation of America said of the previous year in its 1974 annual report. "We have learned to speak of food production, population growth, economic development, environmental protection and human rights not as 'separate problems,' but as interrelated dimensions of a single world crisis of survival."[90] ZPG, for its part, dedicated several issues of the *ZPG National Reporter* to reproductive rights. "Legalizing abortion will be the final step in giving women control over their own reproduction," the editors of one of those issues wrote.[91] Planned Parenthood of Alameda and San Francisco participated in the Bay Area's "World Population Day" in 1974 along with ZPG and the Sierra Club, while ZPG signed on to a letter Planned Parenthood sent to every member of Congress on the second anniversary of the key abortion decisions *Roe v. Wade* and *Doe v. Bolton*.[92]

For several years, ZPG and Planned Parenthood, and the communities they represented, stood on political and philosophical common ground.

But eventually feminists grew increasingly concerned about population groups' focus on a vague "greater good," and how that focus might restrict women's right to have children rather than their right to terminate pregnancies. Between 1968 and 1971, *The Birth Control Handbook*, a popular Canadian feminist text published by McGill University students, reversed its view of overpopulation and the groups associated with it. The original edition had linked birth control to both women's liberation and the welcome reduction of human numbers. After 1971 the pamphlet described population control—and in particular, Ehrlich and ZPG—as a racist project that relied on coercive methods. ZPG recommended its members avoid subsequent editions.[93]

Even more volatile for population activists than the issue of gender was that of race. *The Population Bomb* famously opened with Ehrlich's description of his family's taxi ride through New Delhi, a white family inside of the car and an endless mass of nonwhite people outside of it, the defining moment when Ehrlich understood the population problem "emotionally." He immediately drew a line from the United States to the crowded streets of urban India, writing, "The problems of Delhi and Calcutta are our problems too. Americans have helped to create them; we help to prevent their solution."[94] But the visceral sense of the insideness and outsideness of that taxi characterized population politics for decades.

African American leaders from Julian Bond and Jesse Jackson to Roy Innis criticized population activists for using a white, middle-class point of view to frame the population issue while claiming population as a universal problem.[95] As Samuel Hays suggested in the late 1970s, environmentalists presented limits to growth as a problem for all people although the issue often arose from concern for open space rather than for the state of cities.[96] Conservation groups like the Sierra Club and the Wilderness Society took up the issue more readily than did antipollution activists. Terms like "survival," applied frequently by population activists to the entire human race, held different meanings when applied to particular social groups. In March 1972 the Black Panthers organized a Black Community Survival Conference in Oakland, where they registered over 11,000 voters, tested more than 13,000 people for sickle-cell anemia, and gave away 10,000 chickens to local families. Environmentalists' rhetoric of survival inspired little sense of urgency among the Black Panthers, who understood survival as the economic and political vitality of communities of color. "Primarily," Panther chairman Bobby Seale said, "we want to unify the people and let them know that the party can institutionalize concrete survival programs that serve their basic political desires and needs."[97]

By 1969, stung by African American leaders' criticisms and increasingly cognizant of the shortcomings that those leaders so easily identified, Ehrlich and other ZPG activists had begun to stress the disproportionate impact of white, middle-class families. "Our goal is to change the hearts and minds of middle-class America," ZPG claimed in 1970.[98] Racism and paternalism continued to inform many population activists, however. That same year a ZPG chapter coordinator from Albuquerque wrote to the *ZPG National Reporter* about the possibility of compulsory birth control classes. "There is a great deal of resentment about the welfare mothers being able to have as large a family as they want, at the taxpayer's expense," the coordinator said, "while the taxpayer is being asked to limit himself to only one or two natural children." Explaining that she served on the board of the local Planned Parenthood Association and knew firsthand that compulsory classes were something that "welfare mothers" wanted, she noted, "A lot of the women actually do not know how a conception takes place, let alone that anything can be done about preventing it."[99]

The most severe critics of Ehrlich and ZPG accused them of opening the door to racial genocide. Such accusations sprang from the close connection between family planning and eugenics in the early twentieth century. Well into the 1940s and 1950s, writers considering the relationship between population and environmental limits—most notably William Vogt—continued to organize their ideas according to a strict sense of racial hierarchy.

The assumption, however, that eugenics persisted as practice and theory throughout twentieth-century population politics is misleading, as Hoff has argued, and it ignores the many differences among efforts to limit population from decade to decade. While individual population activists continued to harbor racist views, by the 1960s and 1970s population organizations were trying to break with the movement's disturbing past. In 1971 the Council on Population & Environment, concerned about rifts between business, labor, social justice, and environmental groups, organized a meeting with representatives from each to discuss how to address population and environmental issues while paying heed to matters of employment, housing, and poverty.

Where Ehrlich once used India as an example of overpopulation, ZPG increasingly used India as a point of comparison to illustrate American overconsumption. "This is why ZPG has directed its educational campaign toward the affluent consumptive middle classes," executive director Hal Seielstad wrote.[100] ZPG member Lewis Perelman insisted that to achieve a global steady state would require "a vastly more equitable distribution of wealth and power among all the people of the world than exists today."[101] Increasingly, ZPG called into question suburbs, cars, and middle-class lifestyles as much as it did the birth rate. In 1972 it adopted a "local growth resolution" that recognized municipalities' right to limit population through local ordinances but noted that such regulations "must at all times be administered so as to protect and enhance the opportunities of the disadvantaged, including the poor, the aged, and racial and religious minorities."[102]

Nevertheless, the taint of eugenics stayed with population activists for many decades. Black leaders tended to point out how proportional balance between different social groups was every bit as important as overall numbers. Jesse Jackson argued that numbers were a source of strength for minority communities, and that limiting childbirth meant limiting political power. Keith Lampe, always trying to reconcile his environmentalism with the broader Left, wrote, "Most black people in North America fear that all the talk about population control might really be a cover story for genocide. For this reason it is urgently important that groups like Zero Population Growth (ZPG) make abundantly clear their opposition to genocide in any form."[103] Although not at Lampe's bidding, ZPG-California did take on the question. Its 1972 convention included a panel discussion called "Population Control, Racism, and Genocide," which put Paul Ehrlich on stage with several African American community leaders from the Bay Area. "I think the discussion was very valuable in bringing out some of the basic misunderstandings and legitimate concerns that black people have toward the population-stabilization movement," secretary-treasurer Jean Weber wrote to Ehrlich afterward. As though speaking for the movement as a whole, she continued, "I know I learned a great deal from the discussion, but I still have a long way to go."[104]

Race was an obvious if at times surreptitious dimension of population policy in discussions of immigration. A focus on immigration was to some degree inevitable for population activists during the 1970s, a decade during which the fertility rate declined in the United States and blame for population growth shifted from childbirth to new residents. Environmental organizations had wrestled with immigration since at least the early 1960s, when the Sierra Club began to debate the "population explosion," but it was in the 1970s that immigration grabbed the attention of the environmental movement as a whole. The shift was in part the work of John Tanton, appointed chairman of the Club's population committee in 1971 and several years later president of ZPG's board.[105]

"Any population policy that fails to deal with illegal immigration can be of little worth," Tanton reported to ZPG.[106] He was in favor of restricting legal immigration and fighting illegal immigration as determinedly as possible. ZPG largely agreed, proposing in 1975 a reduction of immigration to roughly the level of emigration, and recommending a restriction of illegal immigration through better funding for the Border Patrol; a crackdown on employers hiring undocumented immigrants; and an increase in foreign aid to improve potential immigrants' economic opportunities at home.[107] Because immigration of any kind did not actually increase the number of people in the world, environmentalists often had to explain why they paid any attention to it. They made two broad arguments that came close to contradicting each other. The first was that Americans had a responsibility to safeguard American resources, and that any increase in the population of the United States jeopardized the American parks, forests, waterways, cities, and ecosystems that environmentalists fought to protect. The second was that more people in the United States meant more people living a profligate and costly American lifestyle. Sometimes both arguments appeared at once. Gerda Bikales warned members of the National Parks & Conservation Association that "immigrants come, essentially, because they want to eat, dress, live, and consume like Americans—a luxury our planet can no longer afford," and at the same time spoke of avoiding "the ultimate sacrifice from us—the social and ecological ruin of our land."[108]

Americans were at once the scourge of the planet and the stewards of a fragile landscape.

Tanton represented both the balance of interests that could coalesce around the population question and the troubling directions in which it could all lead. An ophthalmologist with a practice in Petoskey, Michigan, Tanton worked not just with the Sierra Club and ZPG but also with the Michigan Audubon Society and the Michigan Natural Areas Council. He was president of the Northern Michigan Planned Parenthood Association, chairman of Planned Parenthood's Great Lakes public affairs committee, and a member of the Sierra Club's survival committee. Many in the Club—and even in ZPG—began to ignore or oppose the increasingly severe proposals that Tanton fired off.[109] The Sierra Club's Louise Nichols wrote to Chuck Clusen about Tanton and immigration in 1973, stressing the potential for embarrassment and offense. "I always suspected Petoskey Michigan might not be the best place to live and understand what's really going on in the world," she wrote.[110] Ehrlich, responding ambivalently to Tanton's occasional requests that Ehrlich call for immigration restriction, acknowledged the role of immigration in population politics but stressed the many problems with immigration restriction.[111] But both the Club and ZPG took immigration seriously as an environmental issue, ceding Tanton's basic point and hoping that he would stick to ecological arguments. That hope was misplaced. By the end of the decade, frustrated with inaction by both organizations, Tanton began to set up anti-immigration organizations, including Numbers USA, the Center for Immigration Studies, and the Federation for American Immigration Reform. During the 1980s and 1990s he increasingly talked about immigration in terms of race, language, and culture, and was less concerned with natural resources than he was with "a European-American majority, and a clear one at that."[112]

Tanton was an extreme example of the ways that environmental arguments could be used to support bigoted, jingoistic ideas. Well into the twenty-first century, a vocal minority of mainstream environmentalists pushed for closed borders. There were also more subtle and complicated ways that environmental activists questioned basic claims underlying twentieth-century liberalism, many of them rooted in a fundamentally ecological perspective as opposed to a fundamentally social one. The anarchist

Murray Bookchin pointed this out when he criticized Gary Snyder's widely published essay "Four Changes," which claimed, "there are now too many human beings." Bookchin called this statement "a social problem . . . being given biological dimensions in a wrong way, a biological primacy that it still does not have." The issue was almost purely a political one, according to Bookchin. "The solution to this kind of 'overpopulation' lies not in birth control within the existing system, but in a social revolution that will harmonize man's social relations with man and man's relationship with the natural world."[113]

Bookchin gestured toward a set of concerns that would become central to radical environmental debates in the 1980s: whether environmental problems were essentially social or ecological, whether justice preceded sustainability or vice-versa, and eventually whether human welfare mattered more than did the integrity of the natural world. Bookchin continued to argue the points that he made in the 1960s when a new school of radical environmentalists appeared in the 1980s. Those radicals would be both more dedicated to the uncompromising protection of the natural world and more dubious of modern liberalism's commitments to individual freedom and economic growth.

CONCLUSION

In 1976, the environmental scholar Timothy O'Riordan wrote of Garrett Hardin's essay, "The commons parable is powerful because it drives right at the heart of environmentalism—the moral relationship between short-term selfishness and enlightened longer-term community interest."[114] Environmentalists often understood the tragedies of various commons in these terms: the unrestrained advance of individual interests jeopardized a collective reliance on a resource, an ecosystem, or a planet. When too many people tended to their own sheep, they failed to notice the entire meadow disappearing in front of them.

Democratic governance could not attend to the common good, some environmentalists believed, because it focused on short-term action (or inaction) to fix problems in the present rather than on long-term planning to prevent greater problems in the near future. It improvised and muddled through. Even the centralized state created by the New Deal—evidence of democracy's shortcomings when immediate action was required—could not confront acute environmental problems. It was procedural rather than goal-oriented, relatively efficient in form but relatively agnostic in purpose. And most Americans found no conflict between individualism and the common good, believing instead that the one produced the other. What Robert Collins calls "growth liberalism" tied consumerism to social benefits, so that individual material achievement amounted to a form of civic participation.

Environmentalists like Ehrlich, Hardin, and Ophuls insisted that the planet was in a state of crisis, and that both conventional politics and economic growth fed that crisis. Mainstream organizations, from this perspective, tended to abet the worst qualities of democratic inefficiency. After 1970 environmental organizations eagerly embraced the political power of key pieces of legislation like the National Environmental Policy Act. In doing so, they accepted the necessity of compromise that democratic reform entailed, and they rarely challenged the primacy of economic growth. The rhetoric of crisis made clear the scale and the immediacy of environmental threats and allowed crisis environmentalists to discuss alternatives to conventional reform and to a growth-oriented economy, but it also tended toward holism: broad characterizations of people and human civilization that ignored the complexities of inequality, social difference, and relative culpability.

ZPG had a foot in each camp, working within the confines of Washington, D.C. but using the rhetorical urgency of crisis environmentalism. ZPG was willing to entertain extreme measures, to insist on the imminence of potential catastrophe, and to paint a picture of the human relationship to the natural world with the broadest of brushstrokes, but it was also attendant to the basic requirements of democratic politics, and it tried to take heed of social distinctions and human complexity, even if it never fully succeeded.

Crisis was a powerful idea that tried to clear a path to action by flattening the unevenness of the world. It was a basic ingredient of radical, ecocentric environmentalism in the 1980s, and its adherents would borrow liberally from the environmentalists of the 1970s. Like their predecessors, ecocentric radicals claimed the planet had been pushed out of balance by industrial and agricultural processes. They also blamed a flawed scale of values that used human welfare to measure ultimate good. Only crisis could justify the circumventing of conventional democratic procedures and the questioning of modern society's moral structure. But crisis-driven politics always provoked the same difficult questions about what interests were in jeopardy, from which perspective, and saved at greatest cost to whom. They were questions that soon no environmentalist could afford not to ask.

3

A Radical Break

"I heard that you are a bunch of radical, crazed environmental lunatics!" a reader wrote to the *Earth First! Journal* in the summer of 1983. "That your methods are unorthodox, destructive, and extreme! That you take matters into your own hands with pragmatic—even vengeful—action! I've heard also that all the proper environmental organizations look down on you with disdain and often anger! That you are setting back years of proper environmental progress!! So how the hell can I join?! Where do I sign up!"[1]

The zeal of Earth First!'s supporters was a function of not only the group's uncompromising politics and daring actions but also its unforgiving critique of mainstream environmentalism's sober gradualism. In the 1960s and early 1970s, environmental advocacy had been a matter of influencing legislators with reasoned arguments and the measured application of public pressure—what the Sierra Club's Michael McCloskey called "the theory of lobbying." Professionals who understood legislative procedure and accepted the necessity of negotiation performed this work in offices and conference rooms in Washington, D.C. By the mid-1980s, environmental advocacy might involve barricades, heated confrontations, and occasional acts of sabotage. Grassroots activists who possessed a fervor that bred near-total dedication carried out this work in the forests of the Pacific Coast and intermountain West.

This shift involved a tiny fraction of those Americans who called themselves "environmentalists" and, for most of the mainstream groups, remained an isolated phenomenon that had little to do with their larger campaigns. But radical environmental groups like Earth First! exerted an influence over popular perception, political climate, and philosophical debate that far outweighed their numbers. What radicals perceived as the failures of mainstream environmentalism by the late 1970s, stemming from the major groups' overreliance on conventional methods of reform, led to a breakaway faction of conservationists who sought to reenergize the movement with new ideas and new strategies.

Three elements in particular structured this radical break, all of them intertwined and justifying one another. First, frustrated activists subscribed to an ecocentric philosophy that placed nonhuman nature on an equal moral footing with people, a philosophy they believed distinguished their work from that of mainstream groups and explained mainstream environmentalists' shortcomings. Second, radical environmentalists focused on wilderness preservation, the clearest and most vital example of ecocentric environmentalism because wilderness—as radicals conceived it—meant the absence of people. And third, radicals bypassed the incrementalism of liberal democratic processes through direct action, both because they prioritized natural over political processes and because they believed that where lawsuits and injunctions failed to stop bulldozers, human bodies could succeed. The clarity of Earth First!'s principles and the militancy with which it advanced them was, for environmentalists who were discouraged by the half-steps of conventional reform, irresistible. "Please send your newsletter" wrote one supporter from California. "I wait with baited breath [sic] . . . has the eco-revolution begun?"[2]

ECOCENTRISM

The philosophical foundation for 1980s and 1990s radical environmentalism had many labels. Generically it was "ecocentrism" or "biocentrism," but its brand name, by the 1970s, was "deep ecology." Whatever its name, its most basic idea remained straightforward: the moral equivalence of humans and nonhuman nature. Ecocentric thought assumed that trees, bears, fish, and grasshoppers should receive as much consideration as humans in decisions large and small about the shape of modern society. An ecocentric outlook granted no more value to people—at least in terms of a basic hierarchy of existence—than it did to plants, animals, and ecosystems.

No major environmental organization ever embraced ecocentrism, but many environmental groups with a background in conservation worked with the basic tools of ecocentric thought, even if they never built a lasting structure.[3] At the Sierra Club's mid-century wilderness conferences, interest in the ecological significance of wilderness began to replace discussions of aesthetics and recreation. According to Michael Cohen, Club director Bestor Robinson uncomfortably recognized "two contradictory philosophies underlying wilderness preservation—philosophies that came to be called anthropocentric and biocentric," the one centered on people's enjoyment of wilderness and the other unconcerned with what people wanted or felt.[4]

Few issues better tracked the emergence of this bifurcation in the Sierra Club than the organization's shifting positions on the Mineral King Valley in the southern Sierras. The Mineral King debate grew out of the Mount San Gorgonio controversy of the late 1940s in which David Brower had fought against a ski resort that would mar the mountain's wilderness characteristics. Not yet an enemy of reflexive compromise, Brower fought against the location rather than the construction of a ski resort and undertook an aerial survey of Southern California mountains to find an alternative site for skiers. He recommended Mineral King, a scenic valley nestled against Sequoia National Park. In 1949 the Club's directors, while not advocating a resort, declared their willingness to tolerate one at Mineral King, should one be proposed.[5]

A proposal materialized in the early 1960s in the form of a plan by Walt Disney, Inc. for a massive ski resort. In the decade-and-a-half since San Gorgonio, the Sierra Club had put itself on battle footing in Dinosaur National Monument and the Grand Canyon, and even before Disney submitted its plan the Club's Kern-Kaweah chapter formally recommended protection of Mineral King from all development. The collision of the Kern-Kaweah recommendation with the Disney proposal triggered a four-hour debate during one of the Club's board meetings, at which some directors argued for consistency and for accepting the inevitability of skiing while others claimed that "in view of a new appraisal of the conflicting values involved," Club policy should be reversed. Change won the day, and the board passed a resolution overturning the 1949 decision and opposing any development that might threaten "the fragile ecological values" of Mineral King.[6]

Having switched its position, the Club filed suit against the Disney development in 1969 and won a temporary restraining order. The Forest Service appealed, and both an appellate court and the U.S. Supreme Court ruled that the Club lacked standing to sue because its members did not hold any "direct interest" in Mineral King. By then the National Environmental Policy Act offered another means of blocking development: Disney and the Forest Service would have to file an environmental impact statement (EIS). Completing a satisfactory EIS under the scrutiny of conservationists proved too arduous for Disney, which eventually shelved its plan (see figure 3.1)

Figure 3.1 Mineral King Valley in 1974. [Sierra Club Photograph albums], BANC PIC 1971.031.1974.01:14a—LAN. Courtesy of the Bancroft Library, University of California, Berkeley.

The Mineral King fight stretched over several decades, during which environmentalists considered and reconsidered their justifications for protecting undeveloped places. In the 1940s, conservationists focused on the scenic qualities of San Gorgonio and Mineral King. By the 1960s, the Club grew increasingly concerned with Mineral King's ecological integrity. In the 1970s, new arguments emerged. Among the many flaws Michael McCloskey found in the Sequoia National Forest's draft EIS was an almost exclusive focus on economic and recreational concerns. "A statement is made that Mineral King in a natural state provides little or no benefits, has no value in and of itself," McCloskey wrote. "Does the USFS believe that the natural environment has no ecological benefit or is of no scientific value?"[7] Several years earlier, the Club's own Proclamation on Wilderness had called for a new land ethic to make clear how "it is essential that wilderness be preserved for its own inherent value." The Forest Service EIS and the Supreme Court's decision assumed that public lands policy should prioritize use by people. The Sierra Club increasingly disagreed with this view. So did a law professor named Christopher Stone, who followed the Mineral King case and in 1972 published an article called "Should Trees Have Standing?: Toward Legal Rights for Natural Objects," in which he considered how the interests of the nonhuman world might gain an independent voice within the legal system.[8]

Why grant the nonhuman world legal status? Stone listed several advantages for people, including a more pleasant environment, a greater sense of empathy and interconnectedness, and a more developed moral sense. But the question of what purpose his idea served was an "odd" one, he said, because "it asks for me to justify my position in the very anthropocentric hedonist terms that I am proposing we modify." Stone implied that there were nonutilitarian, non-anthropocentric reasons for granting legal protection to the natural world—reasons beyond any benefits gained or interests held by people.[9]

Stone wrote with Mineral King in mind, knowing that the question of the Club's standing would soon come before the Supreme Court. He published his article in a special issue of the *Southern California Law Review* on law and technology for which Supreme Court Justice William Douglas had agreed to write a preface. The ploy worked: Douglas read Stone's essay, and the most influential part of *Sierra Club v. Morton* was not the decision itself but Douglas's dissent, in which he cited Stone and suggested the case would be more properly titled *Mineral King v. Morton*. Those parts of the natural world subject to "the destructive pressures of modern technology and modern life," Douglas argued, had their own interests. "The river as plaintiff speaks for the ecological unit of life that is part of it."[10]

Stone's article, and Douglas's dissent, spoke to a broader discussion about the prerogatives of humans and the integrity of the nonhuman world, about ecocentric thought and liberal humanism. It was a fragmented discussion whose participants did not always know of each other but nonetheless addressed some of the same concerns. Soon after *Sierra Club v. Morton*, the San Francisco Ecology Center held a "news ceremonial" at which several people—dressed as a ponderosa pine, an Arctic loon, and a tan bark oak—gathered to dance, make bird calls, and praise the "genius" of Douglas's dissent. The tan bark oak told assembled reporters that "non-human species have not been afforded dignity. . . . The only way to preserve your democracy is to extend it to us."[11]

Behind the news ceremonial was Living Creatures Associates, a media group operated through the Ecology Center and founded by Keith Lampe, who by the 1970s called himself Ro-Non-So-Te. In the summer of 1970, just two months after Earth Day, Lampe wrote to a friend, "Seems to me that by autumn or winter there needs to be a second generation of radical eco-rhetoric & eco-actions in order to keep things moving. But I have little idea what it should be except probably it should stress a post-humanist perspective, ie, protection of *all* beings, habitat thought, human logic gone."[12] A year later, Lampe started Living Creatures Associates in order to shift public perceptions "from thinking in human-centered terms (anthropocentrically) to thinking in life-centered terms (biocentrically)."[13] In the late 1970s he organized an All-Species Rights Day parade down San Francisco's Market Street, "a sort of *spectacular* of the biocentric focus."[14] By the 1980s he had started a new group, "All-Species Projects," whose slogan was, "Let us join together to end human-centered behavior."[15]

Lampe combined ecocentric thought with crisis environmentalism. Crisis environmentalists rarely subscribed to ecocentric values, but nearly all ecocentric activists thought in terms of crisis. To avoid anthropocentrism was, potentially, to avoid catastrophe. After the publication of *The Limits to Growth* in 1971, "The public . . . simply drove its ostrich head deeper into the sands," Lampe wrote to Tom Hayden in 1975 as Hayden prepared to run for a U.S. Senate seat. Lampe recommended that Hayden make "biocide" central to his campaign and that he encourage students to think in terms of the planet rather than themselves: "Hey, that trip you're about to major in can't possibly be out there in 1987 because it has such a gross negative environmental impact we'll all have blowing sands by then."[16]

Hayden did not take Lampe's advice, but while Lampe occupied the radical edge of Bay Area environmentalism he was not the only one advocating nature-centered thought. Biocentricity, Debra Weiners reported for the Pacific News Service in 1975, was not only "the latest trend" but also an underlying ethic of environmentalism. Weiner noted the views of Ponderosa Pine (Lampe's third name), and described recent direct actions to prevent whaling.[17] But she also interviewed movement stalwart Jerry Mander, who had worked with David Brower and the Sierra Club on the Grand Canyon battle ads and several other campaigns in the 1960s. "Biocentricity is really a very simple idea," Mander said. "There is no reason to believe there is something better in humans that makes up [sic] superior to other species."[18] The idea of biocentricity, or ecocentrism, came not just from people on the outer fringes of the movement but from those near its established center.

Environmental philosophers of the 1970s and 1980s traced the principles of ecocentric thought back to Aldo Leopold, John Muir, Henry David Thoreau, and an amalgam of Native American cultures. But it was a Norwegian philosopher named Arne Naess who most successfully placed the concept into a modern political context and articulated a philosophy based on that context, a philosophy he called "deep ecology." Most of the environmentalists who later called themselves deep ecologists did not closely follow the seven-point outline that Naess proposed in 1973, which he described as "rather vague generalizations, only tenable if made more precise in certain directions."[19] The ideas that did stick, and which became characteristic of deep ecology, were "biospherical egalitarianism," the "equal right to live and blossom" of forms of life other than human beings; "local autonomy and decentralization," an acknowledgment that governing or managing from afar tended to jeopardize local stability; and the claim that the modern environmental movement consisted of two strains, one of which was "shallow," professionalized, and anthropocentric; and the other "deep," grassroots, and ecocentric.[20]

Few Americans outside of academic philosophical circles had heard of Naess, and he owed his sudden rise to prominence among environmental thinkers late in the decade to the efforts of his greatest American proponents, two northern California professors named Bill Devall and George Sessions. Devall and Sessions began discussing Naess's ideas in the 1970s. By the early 1980s, through a series of conference papers, journal articles, and newsletters, they had established deep ecology as an essential subject in any discussion of environmental ethics. In 1983 a Canadian philosopher named Alan Drengson started *The Trumpeter*, a journal of environmental philosophy with a strong interest in deep ecology; and in 1985 Devall and Sessions published *Deep Ecology: Living as if Nature Mattered*, a summary of the philosophy and a description of its intellectual context.[21]

Ecocentric thought came in milder and harsher forms. The Sierra Club tended to adopt the language and ideas of ecocentrism even as it never accepted its furthest implications. When John Tanton testified on the Club's behalf before the Commission on Population Growth and the American Future, he complained that the Commission's interim report was "an anthropocentric document" that "regards man and his institutions, recent though they may be, as the most central and important feature of the natural scene." The Club preferred to ask what was best "for the welfare of the bio-physical world." Tanton's testimony made clear, however, that the Club understood human and nonhuman interests as aligned rather than opposed: "If the farmer will take care of his land," Tanton quipped, "the land will take care of the farmer."[22]

An ecocentrism rooted in tension rather than cooperation was a harder sell. Few environmentalists were comfortable with deep ecology as a legitimate ethical stance when it posed people and nature as set against each other. Many activists already struggled with the antidemocratic and illiberal sentiments that sprang from crisis environmentalism's talk of "coercion." Disavowing those sentiments, they tried to frame environmentalism as a fundamentally humanistic movement. Well-known environmental thinkers like Barry Commoner and Frances Moore Lappé already accused Paul Ehrlich and other neo-Malthusians of ignoring social inequality.[23] Lesser-known environmentalists made the same point. "By and large," wrote two contributors to the Canadian journal *Alternatives*, "it is man who is the concern of the ecologist."[24] The project of environmentalism, wrote another, was to protect human habitat. "This is not a rejection of the concept of human rights," he wrote, "but its extension."[25]

Founded in 1970 by activists, students, and faculty at Trent University, *Alternatives* would by the end of the decade become the official journal of Friends of the Earth-Canada. Its contributors called crisis environmentalists like Garrett Hardin "counter-productive" and "dangerously wrong."[26] Like the mainstream movement, Friends of the Earth-Canada hoped to bridge the ethics of environmentalism with the principles of liberal humanism and social justice. *Alternatives* advocated a "conserver society" that would minimize waste and pollution while remaining committed to "social justice and political democracy."[27] In the 1970s, the environmental movement's growing clout in matters of public policy gave it all the more reason to situate its ideas in the broadest and most inclusive frame. For many activists, environmentalism was an idea that went with the grain of liberal humanism.

Deep ecology could cut against that grain, and from the beginning it made many environmentalists wary. In 1983 the philosopher Richard Watson claimed deep ecology's internal contradictions were "so serious that the position must be abandoned." Watson made what would become a common and important criticism of deep ecology: that its adherents complained about the notion that humans deserved separate moral consideration, and then treated humans as morally distinct by demanding they restrain their behavior, their population, and their impact on the planet. Deep ecologists could not decide whether people were a part of nature or nature's antithesis.[28] In a response to Watson, Arne Naess explained that deep ecology was less a matter of strict rules and prescriptions than of broad principles and attitudes. Certainly, Naess granted, humans must be treated differently than the rest of the natural world; that, in many ways, was the point of environmentalism. But people were nonetheless capable of considering the degree to which they privileged their own interests over others' or set aside their interests for the good of the natural world and the planet as a whole.[29] Deep ecologists tended toward the latter more than did other people and even other environmentalists.

For most people it went without saying that human interests and human life were paramount political and philosophical concerns. And most people, the biologist David Ehrenfeld claimed in *The Arrogance of Humanism*, put a near-absolute faith in reason, technological innovation, political planning, and the long-term viability of human civilization. Where others saw the steady advance of material comfort and social stability, Ehrenfeld saw a series of haphazard attempts to address narrow problems, attempts that nearly always produced unintended consequences that injured people and the nonhuman world. The greater the ambition to plan for the future and to control the conditions of human life, the greater the distance would grow between expectations and results. "There are no navigators on this humanist ship," Ehrenfeld wrote, "and the few steersmen we have are caught in the same system of lies and pretense that enfolds us all."[30]

Ehrenfeld's critique was notable less for its complaints about reason and technology than for its fundamental distrust of the most basic human motivations, and for the fact that Ehrenfeld found environmentalism as much to blame as anything else. Conservationists, he said, operated within a humanist framework that rendered their work almost meaningless. The standard justifications for the protection of nature—recreation, beauty, scientific interest, stabilization of ecosystems, etc.—were all "anthropocentric values." The dilemma for conservationists, Ehrenfeld explained, was that in order to make a case in humanist terms they labeled everything a "resource" of one kind or another, diluting the meaning of the term and rendering their arguments less and less convincing. All of the anthropocentric claims for the value of nature were subjective, speculative, or so long-term as to be easily ignored. "There is no true protection for Nature," Ehrenfeld wrote, "within the humanist system—the very idea is a contradiction in terms." The only way around this dilemma was through honoring "the Noah Principle." Noah's Ark, which Ehrenfeld called the greatest conservation effort ever described in Western culture, made an implicit argument for the equal importance of all animal species. Ehrenfeld believed that such a nondiscriminating approach should ground the ethics of environmentalism. "Long-standing existence in Nature," he wrote, "is deemed to carry with it the unimpeachable right to continued existence." Countering the humanist tendency to judge nature in purely utilitarian terms required countering the standards of judgment themselves and insisting that the natural world had value independent of human reckoning. "For those who reject the humanistic basis of modern life," he said, "there is simply no way to tell whether one arbitrarily chosen part of nature has more 'value' than another part, so like Noah we do not bother to make the effort."[31]

To reject the humanistic basis of modern life was to reject liberal individualism, a stance made clear, ironically, by radical environmentalism's general distaste for animal rights. "The Noah Principle" and ecocentrism more broadly focused on species and ecosystems rather than individual beings. Because they had little concern for human interests, ecocentric environmentalists distanced themselves from a mainstream, "anthropocentric" environmentalism. And because they had little concern for individual rights—whether of humans or non-humans—ecocentric environmentalists distanced themselves even from animal liberationists, their likely allies. Animal liberationists insisted that only the capacity to suffer should matter in considering a particular being's interests. Animal liberation, the environmental philosopher J. Baird Callicott explained, offered little more than a "humane moralism" (moral standing to any sentient beings) against the "ethical humanism" that characterized most philosophical thought. Environmental ethicists, meanwhile, did not limit their concern to individuals or bound it by sentience. Aldo Leopold, the prototypical philosopher of a "land ethic" and also a lifelong hunter, showed little interest in the welfare of individual animals. For Leopold, the integrity of the "biotic community" was of paramount importance and the individual lives of all its members of secondary concern. Callicott went further, arguing that the stability of the community and the lives of its inhabitants could easily be at odds; overpopulation of any particular species diminished the value of its individual members and threatened the community as a whole. As Callicott suggested, "humane moralism" was only a small step beyond conventional liberalism; animal liberationists' concern for particular beings and their interests put them in line with modern liberal thought and its focus on individual liberties and protections. The humane moralism of animal liberation, he wrote, "centers its attention on the competing criteria for moral standing and rights holding, while environmental ethics locates

ultimate value in the 'biotic community.'" For environmentalists like Callicott, animal liberation was the same individualistic liberalism with fur and
feathers, and it similarly ignored the sense of interconnectedness that lay at
the heart of environmentalism.[32]

For ecocentric environmentalists, liberal individualism and the "arrogance of humanism" were of a piece and had for too long occupied a privileged position above nonhuman communities. Ecocentrics' willingness to
upset that hierarchy followed a sort of moral gravity. As value and concern flowed toward biotic communities, they flowed away from individual
beings, and especially humans. Deep ecologists' abundance of regard for the
nonhuman world could mean a poverty of consideration for humans. "The
extent of misanthropy in modern environmentalism," Callicott explained,
". . . may be taken as a measure of the degree to which it is biocentric."[33] Few
were as misanthropic as Paul Watson, founder of the Sea Shepherd Conservation Society and a radical environmentalist who held little respect for any
of the supposed achievements of human civilization. Music, architecture,
and art were "vanity," Watson wrote in the 1990s. A Van Gogh painting
was little more than "a bit of coloured hydro-carbon splattered on canvas,"
and human cultural achievements were "worthless to the Earth when compared with any one species of bird, or insect, or plant."[34] Arne Naess never
suggested that valorizing the nonhuman world demanded a proportional
denigration of human civilization, but for those who most passionately
championed deep ecology, defending the one often meant attacking the
other. Ecocentric thought lent environmentalism an intellectual energy
and a political fervor that roused old-timers and newcomers alike, and it pit
radical environmentalists against human civilization in ways that became
increasingly difficult to maintain in both thought and practice.

THE POLITICS OF WILDERNESS BEFORE EARTH FIRST!

Ecocentric environmentalism would have been little more than an interesting line of thought had environmentalists not applied its ideas to a timely
issue. The emerging radical environmental movement of the late 1970s and
1980s cohered around the cause of wilderness, a purpose that gave shape to
the philosophy of deep ecology. Radical environmentalists' commitment

to protecting wilderness sprang from the same principles as did their philosophical values. Their primary ethical claim was that the natural world had
as much moral value as did the human world. Given the imbalance between
the destructive force of industrial society and the delicate processes by which
nature renewed itself, radicals believed the best way to advance their ethics was to protect an autonomous nature from human influence. In the late
1980s, Earth First! described its 'central idea' as "that humans have no divine
right to subdue the Earth, that we are merely one of many millions of forms
of life on this planet," and the 'practical application' of this idea as "that large
sections of Earth should be effectively zoned off-limits to industrial human
civilization."[35] Wilderness was the greatest expression of the radical belief in
the moral standing—and therefore the sovereignty—of the natural world.
Earth First! emerged as a direct result of wilderness politics in the late 1970s
and in particular of the Forest Service's second Roadless Area Review and
Evaluation (RARE II), a wilderness inventory of thousands of roadless areas
in national forests that Earth First!'s founders considered the nadir of mainstream environmentalism's politics of appeasement. In a narrow sense, Earth
First! spent a decade trying to revisit RARE II as a matter of policy in order
to save millions of acres that might still be protected as wilderness; in a broad
sense, Earth First! spent those years challenging RARE II as a set of political
and ethical premises in order to question the principles of an increasingly
professionalized environmental movement and to assert the primacy of wild
nature among environmental causes.

Wilderness protection prefigured the conservation movement itself,
and by Earth Day it was an old idea. In the swirl of new issues that constituted the modern environmental movement, the Sierra Club's Michael
McCloskey worried that "wilderness preservation appears to many as
parochial and old-fashioned."[36] But wilderness advocates reinvented the
meaning of their work every few decades: wilderness was a refuge from
industrialization at one point and from unrestrained recreation at another,
it was solitude and escape for some and a heightened aesthetic sensibility
or a repository of democratic values for still others, and increasingly it was
a storehouse of biological diversity.

The decline of democratic justifications presaged the rise of ecocentric
thought. Early on, the democratic argument could be made in at least two

ways that tended to contradict each other. On the one hand, early Wilderness Society leaders like Aldo Leopold and Robert Marshall appealed to the democratic concern for protecting minority interests from a dominant and flattening popular culture. On the other hand, the Society's longtime executive director Howard Zahniser described wilderness as a national interest and a public good. Wilderness advocacy swerved between pluralism and populism. These tendencies did not always fit neatly into the small offices of a single organization like the Wilderness Society. For early Society leaders, Paul Sutter writes, "there would be a nagging tension between wilderness as a democratic ideal and wilderness as a minority preference."[37] During the campaign for the Wilderness Act in the 1950s and 1960s, James Morton Turner notes, an "emphasis on the interests of the minority . . . was overwhelmed by a focus on the nation's collective interest in protecting wilderness as a national good."[38] In the 1970s democratic arguments for wilderness both crested and splintered. The notion of wilderness as a national good plateaued in the fight over Alaskan public lands, where ecological arguments began to eclipse it. At the same time, a more pluralist approach to wilderness fragmented in the aftermath of RARE II, a process more heavily dependent on grassroots support. In the 1980s radical environmentalists largely abandoned democratic claims as they gave wilderness one of its most powerful and troubling meanings, finding in it an order and a set of values beyond—and often at odds with—those of human society.

There was no more powerful example of wilderness in the United States than the wild lands of Alaska. The Sierra Club's John Muir extolled the state's vast public lands, as did the Wilderness Society's Robert Marshall and Olaus Murie, Adolph Murie, and Margaret Murie. Among those lands were the valleys of the Koyukuk, Alatna, and Hammond Rivers in the Brooks Range, straddling the southern edge of the Arctic Circle; the vast northeast corner of the state between the Yukon River and the Beaufort Sea, home to one of the nation's largest caribou herds and nesting grounds for migratory birds; the sprawling point of convergence for the Wrangell, St. Elias, and Chugach mountain ranges; and, on Alaska's southernmost tip, a collection of islands and coastal strips that together made up the Tongass National Forest. The remoteness and the scale of these places both set them apart from and made them symbolic of all other American public lands. Alaska was, in many ways, the wilderness movement's greatest prize.

Wilderness politics in the late 1970s converged on several approaching legislative deadlines. One of the most important would determine the final disposition of federal lands in Alaska, lands that contained the nation's greatest concentration of de facto wilderness. The slow process of deciding jurisdiction began with the Alaska Statehood Act of 1958 and gained greater urgency after the discovery of oil deposits at Prudhoe Bay in 1968. It accelerated in 1971, when the Alaska Native Claims Settlement Act designated forty-four million acres for Native Alaskans, withdrew tens of millions more as "national interest lands" and "public interest lands" managed by the Department of the Interior, and gave Congress until December 1978 to accept or reject Interior's designations of those lands.[39]

By the middle of the 1970s environmental organizations had committed themselves to Alaska lands as the movement's top conservation priority. Protecting tens of millions of acres of Alaskan lands as wilderness, parks, or refuges would require unprecedented cooperation between a collection of large and small environmental groups. Those groups banded together under the Alaska Coalition, led by the Sierra Club, the Wilderness Society, the National Audubon Society, Friends of the Earth, and the National Parks and Conservation Association, and encompassing many smaller organizations. The Coalition's efforts stretched from grassroots work in Alaska to over a dozen staff members working full-time in Washington, D.C. Edgar Wayburn, the most tireless advocate of Alaskan wilderness on the Sierra Club's board of directors, would later call it "the conservation battle of the century."[40]

The seven years between the Native Claims Act and the deadline for designation of public lands were marked by political trench warfare as conservationists and their opponents fought to a standstill. By December 1978, Congress remained deadlocked. As a stopgap measure President Jimmy Carter, who had been heavily lobbied by both sides, used a patchwork of environmental laws and agencies to temporarily protect 110 million acres—more territory preserved by a president than at any single moment since Theodore Roosevelt's final days in office. A year later Congress passed the Alaska National Interest Lands Conservation Act (ANILCA), permanently protecting 103 million acres of Carter's temporary withdrawals and more than tripling the total acreage of the National Wilderness Preservation System.

The Carter administration celebrated Alaskan lands as a national interest, treasured by all Americans. "Alaska is a reflection of our national spirit," the White House Press Office explained to reporters. "It is the only place left in the United States where the vast open spaces, unmarred scenery and free roaming wildlife that shaped early America can still be found."[41] The administration's supporters echoed the notion that Alaska belonged to the American people. Over 150 members of Congress signed a letter to the president that stressed "the strong desire of the American people who want their natural heritage in Alaska protected."[42] The Alaska Coalition itself, powered by national organizations based in Washington, D.C. and doing battle with Alaska's own congressional delegation, reflected the idea that a New Yorker had as great an investment in Alaska's public lands as did an Anchoragite.

But the campaign for Alaskan lands also advanced a newer language for defending wilderness. In 1978 the Wilderness Society said of the proposed Wrangell-St. Elias National Park, "The issue is clear: whether the boundaries of our largest national park will embrace the full ecological richness of this choice mountain region . . . or little more than ice and rock heights."[43] Just after passage of the final Alaska lands bill in 1980, Wayburn praised it for protecting wild territory "in an ecological manner with boundaries that we hope will sustain the land and its wildlife."[44] Wilderness Society conservation director Chuck Clusen agreed, writing, "Nowhere else in the free world can one find such majesty, vastness and ecological diversity which for the most part has escaped the impact of industrial civilization."[45] More than in any previous wilderness campaign, the arguments in favor of protecting Alaskan lands focused on an undisturbed natural world where people rarely made an appearance. The Alaska campaign championed a form of wilderness advocacy less concerned with preserving grand vistas for visitors to enjoy and more concerned with protecting the natural processes that took place in people's absence rather than in their presence.

While the Alaska campaign brought the environmental movement together in a grand coalition, RARE II revealed its points of fracture.

RARE II involved another approaching deadline, this one triggered by the Wilderness Act of 1964. The Wilderness Act stipulated that only Congress could designate wilderness, and it immediately set aside nine million acres of public land and directed the secretaries of Agriculture and the Interior to determine the suitability of their roadless lands for wilderness and to make recommendations to Congress within ten years. The Forest Service managed the bulk of potential wilderness in the United States, and the agency followed a multiple-use mandate that required it balance the competing interests of industry, recreation, and agriculture. Because of its wide jurisdiction—in terms of both geography and use—the Forest Service sat in the very center of wilderness politics.[46]

In the initial fight over roadless areas in national forests, legislation and litigation proved a winning strategy for environmentalists. In the early 1970s, RARE I (the Forest Service's first attempt at classifying its holdings) examined fifty-six million acres of roadless area and promised either a massive addition to the wilderness system or an enormous loss of potential wilderness.[47] "We face both our greatest opportunity and crisis now," McCloskey told the Club's board.[48] Rather than issuing environmental impact statements for each area under review, the Forest Service designated the review itself as a single, sweeping EIS. In 1972 the agency announced it would recommend 274 areas comprising just over twelve million acres as wilderness study areas (potential wilderness). Environmentalists considered this a paltry recommendation, especially because a third of the acreage recommended was already well on the way to wilderness classification. Further, they charged that the Forest Service used overly narrow definitions of wilderness in order to limit the number of sites under consideration, and that the entire RARE process had been rushed. The Sierra Club sued, accusing the Forest Service of submitting an insufficient EIS and therefore violating the National Environmental Policy Act (NEPA) when it allowed logging on nonrecommended sites. As was the case with Mineral King, the EIS requirement of NEPA offered environmentalists their most expedient tool. The chief of the Forest Service agreed to issue instructions to all foresters directing them to comply with NEPA—generally, drafting an individual EIS—before developing any roadless area. This new policy effectively overturned and ended RARE I.

Five years later, wilderness remained a point of contention both for environmentalists who claimed the Forest Service dragged its feet on wilderness recommendations and for timber companies that complained the Forest Service did not open enough land to logging. Rupert Cutler, the new Assistant Secretary of Agriculture, hoped RARE II would address the concerns of both the environmental movement and industry by making final recommendations for 62 million acres of roadless area by 1979. Over the next two years, even as the Alaska campaign dominated the major environmental organizations' agendas, the Forest Service examined close to three thousand sites, held hundreds of public hearings, and tabulated hundreds of thousands of public comments.[49]

In theory, the Wilderness Society was the group best suited by its mission and its structure to take charge of the RARE II fight. Stewart Brandborg, executive director of the Society in the late 1960s and early 1970s, believed in the protection of wild places through grassroots citizen involvement. A charismatic leader in the mold of David Brower, Brandborg took special interest in grassroots training programs that would shape the next generation of field organizers. "In the early 1970s," James Turner writes, "the Wilderness Society's emphasis on citizen organizing reflected Brandborg's faith in participatory democracy."[50] While the amateur tradition of the early twentieth century Sierra Club had relied on relatively affluent conservationists working in San Francisco, Brandborg's grassroots wilderness activism involved a cadre of conservationists who spent their time in the field and cultivated local support.

But the Society overextended itself under Brandborg, who spent money on current campaigns with little thought as to funding future endeavors. By 1974 the Society's finances dipped into the red. Brandborg began firing employees to reduce costs, tarnishing his once sterling reputation among the Society's staff. This was especially the case in the Denver office headed by Clif Merritt, which absorbed much of the downsizing. In the summer of 1975, with staff morale plummeting and staff resignations climbing, the Society's governing council spent four days hearing from the skeleton crew remaining. On the advice of a management consultant, the council fired Brandborg at the beginning of 1976.[51]

Between early 1976 and late 1978, the Wilderness Society managed to put its finances back in order and to remain involved in the ongoing Alaska campaign. But Brandborg's replacement, George Davis, lasted barely a year, and so the governing council turned to one of its own longtime members, Celia Hunter, while it searched for a permanent director. The council hoped to point the Society in a new direction—one that emphasized the sort of structure and professionalism that council members thought befitted a major environmental organization. The administrative turmoil, Hunter explained to the Society's members, grew out of "our rapid growth from a fairly small, close-knit organization featuring easy camaraderie between staff and management . . . to a large enterprise with two major offices and widely dispersed field representatives."[52]

The Society found itself pulled between its grassroots efforts and its determination to streamline and professionalize. Even Hunter, beloved by field staff and in possession of more backcountry bona fides than almost any other Society director, fought against longtime staff members to consolidate the organization. When Hunter tried to shut down the Denver office and move its field representatives to Washington, D.C., she collided with Clif Merritt. "We want to make use of Regional Reps for lobbying in Washington on issues with which they are familiar . . . ," she explained to Merritt in 1977. "In all of this, the role and function of the Denver office is uncertain."[53] Merritt responded by stressing how important—and, he claimed, underappreciated—Western issues like RARE I and RARE II were for the Society, and how essential the Denver office had been and continued to be in coordinating those campaigns.[54] "It could make a thinking person wonder," Merritt complained the following year, "whether the objective [of] The Wilderness Society was to promote more centralization of authority and bureaucracy or to save wilderness."[55]

Merritt offered a view from the field, where staffers worked close to the roadless areas at risk in the RARE II fight but far from the upheaval at the Society's headquarters. Throughout the mountain West, the conservationists who would later found Earth First! organized local participation in Forest Service hearings and pushed for the maximum inclusion of wilderness in each state and forest district. "The bulk of my time was involved in researching and worrying about RARE II," Bart Koehler wrote in a monthly activity report for late 1977.[56] Koehler, a Wilderness Society regional representative in Wyoming, dedicated even more of his time to RARE II the following year, doing interviews for *Wyoming News* and Rapid City television, writing pieces in *Wyoming Issues* and *Wyoming Wildlife Magazine*, and even speaking before the American Petroleum Institute. Bob Langsenkamp, a Society field consultant in New Mexico, described his RARE II work in mid-1978 as "Hectic." Langsenkamp set aside work on the Bureau of Land Management's already neglected wilderness review because "RARE II & Ak [sic] taking most of my time." October, he reported, "was a month of 'cooling my heels' and regrouping from RARE II," after having responded to the Forest Service's draft EIS. Langsenkamp cleaned his office for the first time in six months.[57]

Future Earth First!ers in other organizations also sought to expand national forest wilderness as much as they could. Late in 1978, Friends of the Earth's (FOE) Washington, D.C. office asked its staff members to file inventories listing which issues gained most of their attention. "Alaska—This goes without saying," wrote Howie Wolke, FOE's Wyoming field representative, before offering an unsolicited opinion: "Perhaps this is a regional bias of mine, but I do feel that FOE has not put enough emphasis on wilderness and public lands issues in general (except for Alaska). With RARE II due to be completed shortly, there will soon be a whole bunch of Administration wilderness proposals . . . which will need action."[58] Wolke was right about his regional bias; the Alaska campaign and the RARE II fight both involved national and grassroots work, but "Alaska" brought to mind clear images of mountains and glaciers for most Americans while "national forest wilderness" remained an abstract idea until rendered in local terms. All conservationists followed the Alaska fight, but east of the Mississippi fewer kept close tabs on RARE II. Most Forest Service roadless lands sat in the American West, where RARE II would be fought and from which Earth First! would soon emerge.

The Wilderness Society found new leadership just as it entered the final stage of the RARE II process. William Turnage, a graduate of the Yale School of Forestry who spent several years as photographer Ansel Adams's business manager, assumed the directorship in November 1978.

Turnage was an aggressive administrator who wasted no time overhauling the organization by cultivating new sources of revenue and centralizing operations in Washington, D.C. During his first few months as executive director the Society lost a quarter of its staff to termination or resignation. Turnage finally closed the Denver office for good, after which Merritt declined Turnage's offer of a position at the Society's headquarters. For years the Society had tried to keep at least one field representative in each Western state in which it worked. Celia Hunter, during her tenure as executive director, centralized that network of field staff by bringing several key field representatives—including Tim Mahoney, Debbie Sease, and Dave Foreman—to Washington, D.C. to live in a bunkhouse in Virginia and help with lobbying. Turnage went a step further, paring down the field staff to a handful of regional representatives. When Turnage closed the Wyoming office, Bart Koehler left, complaining of the new administration's "complete absence of respect for the regional representatives as professionals and as human beings." When Turnage closed the Utah office and fired Dick Carter, upsetting many Western conservation leaders, he explained that despite Carter's good work, "He is not philosophically committed to the idea that the central organization needs to make decisions."[59] Turnage's plan for the coming decade, according to the executive committee's recording secretary, was "an augmented staff capability in economics and in forestry . . . on a highly professional basis. This would not include so-called 'high-spirited' people, as there was of course not an automatic conflict between professionalism and dedication."[60] Foreman, certainly one of the "high-spirited" people Turnage had in mind, later described the new executive director as "the businessman" who "replaced virtually the entire experienced and grassroots staff . . . with 'professionals.'"[61]

In one view, the Wilderness Society's administrative transformation came many years late. "The shift to managerial executives has been an inevitable one," Michael McCloskey wrote three years after the Sierra Club fired David Brower and three years before the Society fired Brandborg, "but it has marked the passing from the scene of charismatic, beloved, and esteemed figures."[62] In another view, the Society held out longer than the Club had managed against an enervating focus on lobbying, efficiency, and political negotiation: "Since the Sierra Club's firing of David Brower,"

Earth First!'s Dave Foreman wrote in 1984, ". . . the environmental movement has been slowly co-opted by the concept of professionalism to the
detriment of the vision, activism, ethics and effectiveness of the cause."[63]
The professionalization of the Society was never a simple matter of MBAs
managing from flow charts. Esteemed figures like Brandborg and Hunter
either refused to acknowledge fiscal and organizational imperatives or else
acquiesced to the changes those imperatives necessitated. But the Society's
turn toward professionalization was a sharp one, too sharp for some of its
most experienced field representatives. For them, the governing council's
answer to the Society's management concerns solved technical problems
by abandoning core principles, putting the interests of the Society ahead of
the wilderness the Society pledged to protect. To already disgruntled field
representatives, the aftermath of RARE II provided the most damning evidence that mainstream environmental groups could no longer stand firm.

At the very moment the Wilderness Society adopted a more professional approach in the mold of the Sierra Club, RARE II demonstrated
the potential limits of that approach to environmental work. Major lobbying campaigns depended on the cultivation of delicate alliances with
senators, representatives, and agency officials. The Alaska Coalition had
already committed the bulk of its staff time and its political capital to the
fight over Alaska lands and had little left for RARE II. By 1979 a handful
of field organizers and national staff had already been working toward a
RARE II endgame for years, but the full weight of the environmental lobby
seemed unlikely to materialize. Brock Evans warned the Sierra Club's board
of directors that it remained unclear what sort of congressional support
existed for a fight with the Forest Service given that most environmentally
friendly legislators had already invested themselves in the Alaska campaign.
With the Alaska fight approaching a climax and battle lines forming around
hundreds of RARE II sites, environmentalists' congressional to-do list had
grown uncomfortably long.[64]

More importantly, while the Alaska campaign was an ideal issue for a
powerful Washington lobby, RARE II was not. As an idea and as a political entity Alaska constituted a single issue that wilderness advocates could
debate with a single set of terms. RARE II was a fight that encompassed
several industries, many landscapes, and dozens of states. An internal memo

from early 1979 for the Environmental Study Conference (a collection of senators and representatives organized in part by the Sierra Club to confront environmental issues) noted that although RARE II tried to determine the fate of sixty-two million acres of public lands at once, "that goal may well be thwarted by the wide sweep of the proposal—ninety-two congressional districts in thirty-eight states. And environmental, timber and energy interests all have problems." The Carter administration hoped to address the RARE II lands with an omnibus bill, the memo explained, but was unlikely to succeed because "the bill is just too unwieldy to deal with in a package." Regardless of pressure from both environmentalists and industry representatives to reach a speedy decision about the RARE II lands, the Interior Committee would likely "handle the entire Alaska lands issue right away, including Alaska's RARE II areas, and then deal with the other controversial RARE II areas one by one." The comprehensive, unified approach that defined the Alaska campaign—and that had shaped the Wilderness Act itself—was one that centralized political organizations tended to favor but that did not fit the RARE II process.[65]

The Sierra Club, which prided itself on both its influential Washington, D.C. office and its nationwide network of chapters, generally tried to coordinate these two assets. In the lead-up to the RARE II recommendations, the Club and the Wilderness Society sent regular bulletins and updates out to their collective membership, stressing the importance of local efforts but also reminding members that national coordination remained crucial. *"It will be most effective to make a single, comprehensive national challenge through the Sierra Club/Wilderness Society network,"* a bulletin from late 1977 emphatically advised. "This comprehensive approach will allow us to organize the challenge most effectively, direct it to the proper officials, and follow it up on a day-to-day basis in Washington, D.C."[66] Because RARE II involved site-specific reports, recommendations, and hearings for hundreds of potential wilderness areas, the Sierra Club and the Wilderness Society benefited greatly from their active base of members. Still, both organizations worked hard to funnel all information and planning through their Washington offices and to choreograph a single, nationwide strategy.

The Carter administration announced the RARE II results in April 1979. The Forest Service recommended 15.4 million acres for wilderness,

10.6 million acres for further study, and 36 million acres for nonwilderness. Environmentalists expressed deep disappointment. The Wilderness Society, Sierra Club, and FOE jointly called the RARE II recommendations "an imbalanced and shortsighted decision," and Turnage described the outcome as "among the most negative decisions in the history of public land management."[67] RARE II, which environmentalists had followed with guarded optimism, quickly became a major environmental defeat.

The tricky question of how to respond to RARE II revealed lines of fracture among wilderness advocates. Well before some of the Society's organizers broke away to start Earth First!, even moderate staffers struggled to balance professionalism with a strident response. The Society approached RARE II with caution, wary of alienating Carter and congressional moderates with Alaska lands still at stake. Soon after Carter's announcement, Tim Mahoney, one of the Society's RARE II experts, wrote to Turnage and conservation director Chuck Clusen to report on how the Society's delicate response to the Forest Service recommendations played out on Capitol Hill. Two of the environmental movement's greatest congressional allies— Ohio's John Seiberling and Oregon's James Weaver—sprinted ahead of environmental leaders. "Weaver is calling Eizenstat [Carter's chief domestic policy advisor] today," Mahoney reported. "Sieberling is calling again and will threaten new oversight hearings on disputed RARE II areas. Weaver himself and Weisner are asking how they can go out on a limb if [the Wilderness Society] and [the Sierra Club] will not." The situation, Mahoney wrote, amounted to "the worst of all possible worlds with forestry, mixed with bad Alaska timing. Our congressional friends are sticking their necks out and [Wilderness Society] lobbyists have their hands tied."[68]

"This is B.S.—*when* have we been unwilling to go out on a limb," Turnage wrote in the margin of his own copy before forwarding it to Clusen. "I really do not agree with the thrust of this memo—a lot of allusions & innuendoes adding up to hysteria," he wrote at the top. "I do not feel—I really emphasize this—that our lobbyists have 'had their hands tied.' "[69] Environmental leaders like Turnage had a hard time understanding those who criticized the environmental movement rather than the industrial interests it fought against. The movement, after all, had just completed a decade of stunning successes and stood on the cusp of passing a monumental Alaska lands bill.

Political negotiations involved give-and-take, and the major environmental organizations had fared well according to their own particular goals.

Those limited goals were, for the most militant wilderness advocates, exactly the problem. Dave Foreman wrote to sympathetic activists about the need for a new, more radical group. "Conservation groups," he said, "have been especially co-opted by the Carter presidency: for the one sweet plum of Alaskan National Monuments, they have failed to sue over the illegal RARE II process—the greatest single act of wilderness destruction in American history."[70]

For years Foreman nursed a grudge over the Society's failure to sue in response to RARE II. After Carter announced the Forest Service recommendations, Sierra Club and Wilderness Society leaders began working with other environmental groups to salvage RARE II. One obvious tactic was a lawsuit. Given the similarities between RARE I and RARE II, and the Sierra Club's successful lawsuit after the original inventory, it stood to reason that the courts would find RARE II wanting as well. But environmental leaders worried that a successful lawsuit might trigger a backlash in Congress and ruin any opportunity to improve on RARE II's minimal protections.

Huey Johnson, the California Secretary of Resources and a strong proponent of wilderness, felt differently. The Forest Service recommended 2.4 million acres of federal lands in California for nonwilderness, slightly more for further study, and less than a million acres for wilderness. Johnson, who had said of RARE II, "A proper approach would start with the objective of producing the greatest possible returns to society in perpetuity, not simply the immediate profits of cutting, digging or drilling," thought that the Forest Service favored industry and slighted posterity. Despite personal visits from Wilderness Society and Natural Resources Defense Council staffers urging restraint, Johnson filed suit. In early 1980 a district court ruled in Johnson's favor, and in 1982 the Ninth Circuit Court of Appeals affirmed the ruling. Echoing the decision that ended RARE I, the courts decided that RARE II did not demonstrate an adequate consideration of public sentiment and the potential impact of development on wilderness areas and so did not satisfy the National Environmental Policy Act.[71]

California v. Block insured that the RARE II fight would stretch into the 1980s and beyond. By the time Johnson sued, the Sierra Club and the Wilderness Society had embarked on a state-by-state strategy, shepherding through Congress state-specific wilderness bills in order to circumvent RARE II and pressure wilderness opponents. The state-by-state strategy quickly became a complicated set of negotiations—made even more complicated by Johnson's lawsuit—that hinged on the fate of the acres left to "further study." Fearful that the Johnson suit opened the door to innumerable legal challenges by environmentalists, the timber industry pushed for statutory release—also called "hard release"—that would definitively designate certain lands *not* wilderness. Environmentalists fought the concept, arguing that Congressional review of wilderness already contained "sufficiency language" that effectively released nonwilderness to logging. They advocated "soft release" language that indicated nonwilderness while leaving open the possibility of future wilderness designation. Occasionally, the need for soft release led the Club and the Society to advocate state bills that recommended even less acreage than did RARE II.[72]

The final disposition of roadless lands in national forests remained a subject of negotiation for decades, and for radical environmentalists those negotiations were evidence of the mainstream groups' culture of compromise. Years later, Foreman described RARE II as a decisive moment that convinced him of the modern environmental movement's ineffectiveness. "We didn't want a lawsuit," he wrote, "because we knew we could win and were afraid of the political consequences of such a victory. We might make some powerful senators and representatives angry. So those of us in Washington were plotting how to keep the grassroots in line. Something about all this seemed wrong to me." Soon after the initial RARE II announcement, Foreman left the Wilderness Society and helped found Earth First![73]

EARTH FIRST! AND WILDERNESS

Earth First! was a question before it was an answer. The question was how to avoid the compromises of RARE II and the political process more generally. The wilderness movement, as James Morton Turner makes clear, was for most of the twentieth century a reform movement that worked comfortably within the bounds of conventional political institutions. Even as social protest movements took a radical turn in the 1960s, for wilderness advocates "a liberal faith in the federal government and the legislative system remained an animating force."[74] Turner considers wilderness a political process as much as a place, a process that involved people who lived near wilderness, national groups that lobbied for it, and congressional representatives with the power to designate it. When Dave Foreman and Bart Koehler left the Wilderness Society in 1979, they questioned that process and that liberal faith, and the Society's increasing commitment to professionalization, centralization, and a political culture marked by the failures and compromises of RARE II. Earth First!ers never abandoned conventional reform, but they never stopped criticizing it and insisting that it succeeded only so far as it was spurred by radical thought and action.

To the degree that the word makes any sense applied to Earth First!, "officially" the group's founding took place at a ranch in Wyoming in the summer of 1980. But the group was born several months earlier, when Dave Foreman, Ron Kezar, Bart Koehler, Mike Roselle, and Howie Wolke spent a week in and around the Pinacate Desert of northern Mexico. Most of the five were either current or former staffers of major environmental organizations: Wolke of FOE, Kezar of the Sierra Club, and Koehler and Foreman of the Wilderness Society. Their long association with mainstream groups insulated them from charges of not giving conventional methods a chance. They had tried convention and found it insufficient to the task. On the way back from northern Mexico to Foreman's home in Albuquerque, the conservationists began to imagine a new group based both geographically and culturally outside of Washington, D.C. and committed to a no-holds-barred form of environmental advocacy. They chose the name Earth First. Later they would add a mandatory exclamation mark as radical ecocentrism increasingly punctuated their actions.[75]

The group drove all the way to northern Mexico in part because the environmental writer Edward Abbey called the Pinacate "the final test of desert rathood."[76] A few years earlier Abbey had finished *The Monkey Wrench Gang*, a novel about a band of eco-saboteurs who traveled throughout the Southwest disrupting or dismantling development projects. Earth First! drew inspiration from the spirit and the form of Abbey's fictional group.

Like the Monkey Wrench Gang, Earth First! would fight against industrial society directly. And like the Monkey Wrench Gang, Earth First!
would avoid professionalism whenever possible. Although it eventually
established a journal, a nonprofit foundation, and a modest publication
business, Earth First! never maintained offices, membership lists, formal
chapters, or salaried employees. Earth First!ers considered themselves part
of a movement rather than an organization. To be part of Earth First!, all
an aspiring radical had to do was show up (see figure 3.2).

If there is a particular reason that so much environmental activism in the
twentieth century sprang from the American desert, it is probably the character of industrial development there. Aridity defines not only the desert's
geographical identity but also its industrial infrastructure. Agriculture and
human habitation in the American desert require water, and water requires
large-scale engineering. The arid West is crisscrossed with aqueducts,
siphons, and tunnels carrying water, with empty riverbeds where water

Figure 3.2 Earth First!ers, Ron Kezar, Ken Sanders, Bart Koehler, Howie Wolke, Dave Foreman, Mike Roselle, Roger Featherstone, Nancy Morton, and Shaaron Netherton in Tucson
in 1985. Earth First! had no formal offices but in the early 1980s, the group was informally
based in Tucson. Photo courtesy Dave Foreman.

used to be and full riverbeds where water never flowed before. Water in the West is impounded in hundreds of reservoirs and contained by thousands of dams. The energy to move all of that water, and to electrify the cities and farms that consume it, comes from generators within dams or from coal mined in desert mountains and fed to power plants throughout the region. The industrial base of human civilization is more apparent and glaring in the desert West, where it is thrown into relief by not only the stark, open space but also the monumental effort required to establish cities and towns in such an unforgiving environment.[77]

But amid that network of pipes and pump stations, strip mines and sluices, one single structure came to represent the ethos of industrialization in the desert more than any other: Glen Canyon Dam. Glen Canyon Dam was not the biggest dam in the West; it was not even the biggest dam on the Colorado River. It was not the most expensive or the most obtrusive, and it did not contain more water than any other dam. But it was the most despised. In the early twentieth century, conservationists in California regretted few projects more than the O'Shaugnessy Dam, over which John Muir and Gifford Pinchot had their greatest battle and which, in the end, held back the Tuolumne River and inundated Hetch Hetchy Valley. Glen Canyon Dam, which checked the Colorado and flooded Glen Canyon with a reservoir called Lake Powell, produced an equal sense of despondency but even greater anger among late-twentieth century conservationists in the West.[78]

In David Brower's own estimation, Glen Canyon was his greatest mistake, the canyon he sacrificed sight unseen for the sake of political expediency, "the place no one knew." The dam remained for the rest of Brower's career a reminder of what compromise could lead to. For Edward Abbey, it was a symbol of industrial civilization's disregard for wilderness and the natural world. In his more measured moments he recommended systematically dismantling the dam and letting nature reclaim the drained reservoir. More often, he fantasized about blowing it up. The cover illustration for his 1977 collection of essays, *The Journey Home*, showed the Colorado breaking through a crumbling Glen Canyon Dam.[79]

Earth First! adopted Abbey's attitude, acknowledging Glen Canyon Dam's place at the top of any list of industrial offenses in the desert.

The group staged its first action, or prank, at the dam in March 1981. "The finest fantasy of eco-warriors in the West," Dave Foreman wrote soon after, "is the destruction of the dam and the liberation of the Colorado." With dozens of sympathizers watching, Foreman and several others unrolled a three-hundred-foot strip of black plastic down the front of the dam, creating the illusion of a crack in the solid concrete barrier and, by implication, in the entire industrial infrastructure of the West. Abbey himself addressed the crowd soon after, telling them to oppose the development of the region by corporations and public agencies. "And if opposition is not enough," he said, summarizing his own philosophy and that of the new group that had embraced it, "we must resist. And if resistance is not enough, then subvert."[80]

Subversion, for Earth First!, followed from the ecocentric ideas that distinguished its own view of wilderness advocacy from that of mainstream organizations. Earth First! considered the wilderness bills of the early 1980s nothing but half measures, and said so in letters to the Sierra Club, Wilderness Society, FOE, and National Audubon Society, as well as in personal visits to the offices of the Oregon Natural Resources Defense Council and the Idaho Conservation League. When Montana's congressional delegation tried to determine the disposition of the state's RARE II lands with the Montana Wilderness Act of 1984, Earth First! slammed the Wilderness Society for supporting a version of the bill that would release millions of acres from wilderness designation, asking whether the Society—and in particular lobbyist Peter Coppelman—"is now supporting the destruction of defacto wilderness."[81] Coppelman defended the Society's position. "In my view the coalition proposal is a strong proposal which will be taken seriously in the legislative process," he explained. "That distinguishes it from the Earth First! proposal to designate as wilderness every single acre of forest roadless area remaining in Montana." Earth First!'s position, Bill Devall responded, might be less realistic but it advanced a set of views that compromise would undermine. "For supporters of a deeper ecology movement," he told Coppelman, "it is important to work within the political process but to always remember that our values are very, very different from the dominant social paradigm." To abandon those values, Devall insisted, was to "provide more legitimacy for the existing political system."[82]

Wilderness preservation could be as much a critique of "the existing political system" as an example of it. Even more: it could be a critique of modern society itself and what David Ehrenfeld called "the arrogance of humanism." This was true in both a philosophical and a material sense. For Earth First!, wilderness and ecocentric thought aligned. "In a true Earth-radical group," Foreman wrote in 1981, "concern for wilderness preservation must be the keystone. . . . Wilderness says: Human beings are not dominant, Earth is not for *Homo sapiens* alone, human life is but one life form on the planet and has no right to take exclusive possession."[83] To respect wilderness was to recognize the ethical limits of human activity. Wilderness constituted a moral boundary as much as a geographical one.

As much as wilderness was morally freestanding, though, it was also materially connected to a much larger collection of environmental harms and potential catastrophes. When radical environmentalists talked about the erosion of wilderness, crisis environmentalism never strayed far from their minds. For most radicals, wilderness degradation acted as both a sign and a cause of much broader environmental disaster. Pollution, extinction, overpopulation, and the disruption of planetary cycles all intersected with the plight of wilderness. This was not a new view; it had been percolating at the Sierra Club's wilderness conferences in the 1950s, and the Club's Proclamation on Wilderness of 1970 stated, "Portions of this planet must be protected from that impact of man which is now producing ecological catastrophe."[84] The following year David Brower—by then head of Friends of the Earth—spoke before a congressional subcommittee about population stabilization. Brower turned immediately to the topic he considered most vital to questions of planetary survival. "It is wilderness, and what it stands for," he told the subcommittee, "that taught conservationists the folly of the idea of numbers without end."[85]

Earth First! took that lesson to heart. Although wilderness remained the political and philosophical focus, a much broader assault on nonhuman nature constituted the crisis at hand. "Clearly, the conservation battle is not one of merely protecting outdoor recreation opportunities, nor a matter of elitist aesthetics, nor 'wise management' of natural resources," read an Earth First! pamphlet explaining the group's purpose. "It is a battle for life itself, for the continued flow of evolution."[86] For Earth First!, wilderness made up the philosophical bedrock of ecocentric thought and the material base of the nonhuman world. It also sat, stated or unstated, at the center of any environmental crisis.

Earth First!'s fixation on wilderness as the antithesis of modern human civilization and as the source of all balance in a roiling world earned it criticism in the 1980s and for long after. According to critic Emma Marris, a "high opinion of pristine wilderness and low opinion of human changes to the landscape" marked the guileless views of wilderness absolutists, views that devolved from the "pristineness approach" of the Wilderness Act to the "purist conservation" of Earth First![87] Skeptics have pointed out the particular, romantic, and often exclusive premises of wilderness valorization; the ways that wilderness parks have catered to a white, middle-class visitorship while both marginalizing and dispossessing longtime users and inhabitants; and how supposedly pure wilderness has always been at least in part the product of human action and intention. There is, William Cronon writes, "nothing natural about the concept of wilderness. It is entirely a creation of the culture that holds it dear, a product of the very history it seeks to deny."[88]

These were and remain essential questions about the idea of wilderness, so essential that Earth First! could never answer them to even its own supporters' complete satisfaction. But wilderness enthusiasts were never as naïve nor as reductive as some of their detractors have suggested. The debate about what can be classified as "wilderness" and whether human changes rule out such classification began within the environmental movement itself. While wilderness advocates spoke to the public in sometimes soaring language, in their own private discussions with each other and with legislators they inevitably dealt in the practical details that rendered wilderness management a series of human choices. At the Sierra Club's third wilderness conference in 1953—more than a decade before passage of the Wilderness Act—a panel on "the wilderness idea" dealt not with absolutes but with degrees of wilderness, including buffer zones, accommodation of livestock, and the use of built structures. Olaus Murie grouped wilderness protection with gardening, both part of a shift toward "appreciation of natural things"; and Howard Zahniser said, "The concept of wilderness is something man has thought of; its values are human values."[89]

As James Morton Turner has explained, by the 1970s the Forest Service, not conservationists, insisted on a strict definition of wilderness that ruled out most human activity. The agency's "purity policies" were a way of limiting wilderness designation by defining it as narrowly as possible.[90] During the Alaska campaign Pamela Rich of Friends of the Earth wrote to Harold Sparck of Bethel, Alaska, to assure him that FOE supported limited use of snowmobiles by Native Alaskans in wilderness areas while the Forest Service might "interpret the Wilderness Act in a very 'puristic' sense" in order to restrict such use.[91] Several years later the Wilderness Society's Bill Cunningham told the Owyhee Cattlemen's Association that the Forest Service "has used impossibly strict grazing management in wilderness areas to turn ranchers against future wilderness designations."[92] In 1983 when Howie Wolke criticized the Wilderness Act as too weak, one of the few qualities he found praiseworthy was the act's flexibility and its strategic ambiguity in defining wilderness as an area "which generally appears to have been affected primarily by the forces of nature, with the imprint of man's work substantially unnoticeable." That loose definition with its many modifiers, Wolke noted, allowed for consideration of even places that had suffered mining or clear cutting. In drawing boundaries around wilderness, the environmental movement was more often agnostic and the Forest Service dogmatic.[93]

Within the Earth First! community wilderness served more as a general orientation than as an absolute. From the beginning, Earth First! advocated "rewilding"—the remaking of wilderness through the removal of development and infrastructure, including even roads—so pristine, "untouched" nature was never a fundamental concern. In 1984, the year after they celebrated some of Earth First!'s early forest actions, the editors of southwest Oregon's bioregional journal *Siskiyou Country* wrote, "Our bioregion no longer exists in a pristine 'natural' state. We find ourselves inhabiting a place which has a history: millenia upon millenia [sic] in which people have lived with, on, or against the land."[94] Some Earth First!ers agreed. "Many recent wilderness management plans exemplify a tendency to view human presence in wild places as unnatural," George Wuerthner wrote years later. "This philosophical assumption is based on a mythical and sentimental view of pristine wilderness."[95]

That mythical and sentimental view had a place in Earth First!, but moral certainty could also demand rather than preclude subtle distinctions. To pine for pure wilderness was to understand that it had disappeared long ago and so to accept whatever remained. "Earth has been so ravaged by the pox of humanity that pristine wilderness . . . no longer exists," said Earth First! stalwart Reed Noss. "A place may feel wild and lonely, but it is injured."[96] Noss echoed what Aldo Leopold once suggested in a more measured tone: "One of the penalties of an ecological education is that one lives alone in a world of wounds."[97] In that wounded world conservationists had to fight for what they could, including rewilding places profoundly transformed by human activity. Sometimes they dreamed big: Howie Wolke insisted that wilderness meant "multi-million acre chunks that represent all major eco-systems complete with all known biological components."[98] At other times their dreams were more modest. "Yes, let's battle for wilderness," Earth First!er Tony Moore replied to Wolke, "but let's fight equally hard to pro-tect this planet in every way we can. Wilderness is not removed from Earth, it's part of Her."[99] Protecting big wilderness remained the ultimate form of respect humans could pay to the nonhuman world, but never the only one.

DIRECT ACTION

"In my view, Earth First! means direct action," Mike Roselle wrote in 1987. "In fact, it is because of direct action that EF! exists."[100] Radical environ-mentalists' use of their own bodies to protest whaling, logging, and road-building signaled a deep suspicion of what James Morton Turner calls the wilderness movement's "liberal faith in the federal government and the legislative system."[101] To engage in physical protest was to circumvent established political processes. By harassing whalers or blockading log-ging trucks, radicals expressed their opposition not only to the plundering of the natural world but also to what they considered the protracted and ineffective methods of the mainstream movement. Direct action consti-tuted a political position as much as a tactical choice. Roselle, who woke up practically every day ready to be arrested, was the kinetic center of civil disobedience for Earth First! and believed in "letting those actions speak for our philosophy." He threw together actions and ideas until they became completely entangled.[102] So did Doc Sarvis of Edward Abbey's *Monkey Wrench Gang*, who advised his fellow eco-saboteurs, "Let our practice form our doctrine, thus assuring precise theoretical coherence."[103]

In one form or another direct action had always been a part of the modern environmental movement. Well before Earth Day, the alternative press regularly reported on environmental sabotage. In 1968 the *Express Times* described how a saboteur called "the Wasp" blew up a Pacific Gas & Electric tower in California's Bay Area, hoping to stop factories from polluting by cutting off their power.[104] In 1971 *Harry* related the exploits of "the Fox," a Midwest "ecoguerilla" who sealed an industrial smokestack, clogged a factory's drainage system, and dumped a jar of effluent in the offices of U.S. Steel. "The eco-guerilla movement is growing," *Harry* observed, "as patience with the 'proper authorities' wears thin."[105] The Ann Arbor *Argus* told of a group of "billboard bandits" who targeted roadside advertising throughout Michigan.[106] And *Northwest Passage* described how Florida's clandestine "Eco-Commando Force '70" dropped seven hundred pre-addressed cards in sealed bottles into sewage outlets that discharged near the ocean, over a hundred of which ended up on the desks of the *Miami News* and the governor's office, mailed from towns and cities all along Florida's east coast.[107]

Direct action on behalf of the environment in the 1970s was usually anonymous and covert, and often limited to isolated incidents. Some of the acts targeted particular projects or companies, and others implicated modern industry more generally. Most were one-time actions designed to promote awareness or to inspire others. When the perpetrators communicated with the public, they tended to describe themselves as catalysts trying to trigger a chain reaction. Their deeds, if they worked, would make sparks that could ignite a popular and sympathetic response.

The first environmental group to successfully adopt direct action not just as a tenuous gambit but as an organizing principle was Greenpeace. As Frank Zelko has made clear, Greenpeace excelled at drawing attention to dangers and injustices by staging audacious encounters. Neither furtive nor shy about its actions, Greenpeace confronted its industrial enemies in broad daylight. Instead of focusing on single escapades the group garnered enough support to organize long campaigns of persistent agitation that generated controversy and produced political pressure. Greenpeace was less a single spark than a steadily burning fuse.[108]

When Greenpeace began it was not really an environmental group, and it was not called Greenpeace. In 1969 a group of peace activists in Vancouver, most of them Quakers, formed a group to oppose U.S. testing of atomic bombs underneath the island of Amchitka, near the western end of Alaska's Aleutian chain. They were too late to stop a one-megaton explosion in October 1969, but they vowed to fight the next blast. The group—initially called the Don't Make a Wave Committee, in reference to fears of a tidal wave from the underground nuclear tests—decided to sail a boat close to Amchitka during the next explosion. This tactic, arrived at largely because so few other options were available, was designed to illustrate the threats posed by nuclear tests and to give the military some pause. It was also an extension of the Quaker philosophy of "bearing witness" to injustice, a silent condemnation that became a hallmark of Greepeace.[109]

The boldness and, for some, foolhardiness of sailing toward an atomic explosion demonstrated not only the sense of urgency within the Don't Make a Wave Committee but also the limitations of more mainstream peace and environmental organizations. Those organizations took Amchitka seriously, not least because of the island's status as a national wildlife refuge. But the authority of the Atomic Energy Commission's claims to "national security" and the rapid pace of events worked against conventional tactics like lobbying and litigation. The Sierra Club had been following the AEC's plans since 1965, publicly opposing the tests alongside several major environmental groups. Quickly, however, environmentalists realized the limitations of their influence as they confronted a powerful and determined Cold War state. An internal Sierra Club memo from 1969 advised, "Alaskan conservation groups should not go out of their way to pick a fight with AEC. We are already against 'progress' and can't afford to be against national defense too."[110] Just a few days later, James Moorman, one of the Club's lawyers, submitted a report on Amchitka strategy that pointed out loopholes allowing the AEC to circumvent the Department of the Interior and the Endangered Species Act. Given the competing claims to national as against environmental interest, he guessed that federal courts were unlikely to grant a temporary restraining order or a preliminary injunction. When the time frame was not years but months, and the stakes were not the siting of a dam or the designation of a park but the conduct of nuclear war, the legal system on which environmental groups relied turned sharply against them. "Unless we have some solid evidence of serious damage," Moorman concluded, "we would be in the position of trying to stop a $200,000,000 defense expenditure for the principle of the thing. Under the circumstances, I would not recommend a suit."[111]

What Moorman did recommend were "legal guerilla actions."[112] Leading up to the initial test, environmental groups flooded federal agencies with requests for complete documentation of the possible effects of a nuclear blast at Amchitka. When the requested information came slowly or not at all, the organizations threatened lawsuits.[113] These tactics failed to stop or even slow the AEC's plans. When the AEC announced it would stage another test in 1971, environmental and peace groups banded together to form the Committee for Nuclear Responsibility and promptly filed suit against the AEC for an insufficient environmental impact statement. Suing over an EIS, a tactic that had worked in environmentalists' favor so many times, in this case achieved only brief delays.[114]

The strongest legal weapons the environmental movement wielded were no match for an atomic bomb. Major environmental organizations knew this, as did the AEC. The Don't Make a Wave Committee suspected this as well, and so it chartered a fishing boat, the *Phyllis Cormack*, which left Vancouver for the treacherous North Pacific seas in the fall of 1971 amid considerable press coverage. After a temporary AEC cancellation, a ship change, and inclement weather, the Don't Make a Wave Committee was still several hundred miles from Amchitka on November 6 when the United States detonated a five-megaton blast several thousand feet underneath the island.

The Amchitka blast did not cause the earthquake or tidal wave that many environmentalists feared and there was little evidence of leaked radiation, but it created a half-mile wide impact crater, killed hundreds of sea otters and an unknown number of fish and birds, and sent a shock wave measuring 7.2 on the Richter scale through the island, the nearby ocean, and a small, spring-mounted concrete bunker on the far side of Amchitka where James Schlesinger, the chairman of the AEC, sat with his family in a risky bid to reassure the public of the test's safety. The blast also propelled the Don't Make a Wave Committee to international recognition and lent it a reputation for brash, confrontational actions.

The Don't Make a Wave Committee soon changed its name to Greenpeace and changed its focus to whaling and ecological concerns. Even as the group's founding members sailed toward Amchitka, they had begun to move toward more specifically environmental issues. Robert Hunter later described a formative moment when the *Phyllis Cormack* docked at Akutan, Alaska, the site of an abandoned whaling station, and the crew discussed how few whales they had seen on their voyage across the Gulf of Alaska. One of Hunter's disgusted companions asked, "Who wants to save the human race anyway?"[115] Greenpeace's founders lived and worked in a coastal city that lay along the migratory routes of gray whales, humpback whales, and orcas. The group drew from the city's countercultural community, and it took little to convince its members that whales were part of a "planetary consciousness" threatened by the modern world. Greenpeace activists began using fast and maneuverable inflatable boats called Zodiacs to position themselves between whales and the harpoon guns of whaling fleets in what would become the organization's signature tactic. "Since 1975," Greenpeace explained to its supporters after a confrontation with Spanish whalers in 1980, "Greenpeace has conducted direct action campaigns against commercial whaling fleets operating in both the Pacific and Atlantic oceans. These peaceful non-violent confrontations are based on the belief that it is useless to wait for governments to act while the last of the great whales die."[116]

Greenpeace's commitment to peace and nonviolence was absolute. Despite its best intentions, though, the group opened the door to a more aggressive style of activism, and Paul Watson walked through it. One of the Don't Make a Wave Committee's earliest members, Watson's penchant for confrontation led to his ouster from Greenpeace in 1977. He would go on to found the Sea Shepherd Conservation Society, a close ally of Earth First! and a group known for mining whaling ships in port and ramming them at sea. "Sometimes the only way you can stop outlaws," Watson said in 1981, "is by becoming an outlaw yourself."[117]

The year Earth First! was born was the year direct action seemed to grip the environmental movement. In January 1979 the Sea Shepherd Conservation

Society set sail on its first ship, the *Sea Shepherd*. By the end of the year the *Sea Shepherd* lay at the bottom of a Portuguese harbor after its crew rammed an illegal whaler, surrendered to the Portuguese Navy, and then scuttled their own ship rather than risk its falling into the hands of whalers. In May a rag-tag conservation group called Friends of the River (FOR) took on the Army Corps of Engineers in Northern California. FOR had spent years battling the construction of New Melones Dam on the Stanislaus River, a dam that would tame a spirited river and flood a canyon treasured by whitewater raf-ters. FOR tried rallies, legal actions, an appeal to the Historic Preservation Act, and a ballot initiative to protect the Stanislaus under California's Wild and Scenic Rivers Act. None of those efforts worked. Finally, as the recently completed New Melones Dam slowly flooded the river canyon, FOR's Mark Dubois walked to the river's edge and chained himself to a rock. A few close friends knew where Dubois was and where he had hidden the key. The Army Corps of Engineers knew only that filling the reservoir would mean killing him. Dubois remained hidden for a week until the Corps agreed to des-ignate a temporary fill-level limit. "I always knew I would have to make a personal statement at some time," Dubois said of his risky act.[118]

By the end of the 1970s the door that Greenpeace had cracked was wide open. "Now, according to some—a growing number—it is time to mutiny," the *Chicago Tribune* reported in 1981. "Nature's bounty, they believe, is on the brink of disaster. Normal channels lead nowhere. Ecological activism, a movement of mutineers, has been born."[119] Greenpeace's Robert Hunter, long an advocate of nonviolence, began to question that inflexible principle in the wake of his old comrade Paul Watson's militance. Sensing a moment of crisis, he wrote about eco-radicalism for *New Age*, saying of nonviolence, "so far history has not shown much evidence that the strategy is inevitably going to triumph. It is nice to think it must, but the trouble is, even if the meek do finally inherit the earth, there may not be much of it left to enjoy."[120]

"It is past time for this discussion," Dave Foreman wrote approvingly to the editor of *New Age*. "I think that the basic problem, however, goes beyond merely the question of whether violence (directed against either machines or people) is justified in protecting the earth. The real question is that of radicalizing the environmental movement." The answer to that question, Foreman made clear, was aggressive action in defense of the wild and a de-centering of human beings politically, geographically, and philosophically. "The only hope for Earth and her millions of residents (besides humans) is to declare vast areas of the globe off limits to industrial civilization," Foreman wrote. The answer, then, was an ecocentric, direct-action wilderness movement. The answer was Earth First! (see figure 3.3)[121]

Born in the southwestern desert, Earth First! grew into maturity in the forests of the Pacific Coast. Those forests stretch from southern Alaska to northern California and, together, constitute the greatest conifer forest on the planet. By the late twentieth century, the trees had been disappearing for a hundred years. Having decimated the hardwood forests of the Northeast and the pine forests of the upper Midwest, Americans began intensively logging the Pacific Coast in the late nineteenth century. Much of what remained in the 1980s stood on public land, and attempts to protect it pitted environmentalists against a Forest Service that, Earth First! believed, reflexively served the logging industry. It was during these campaigns that Earth First! established itself as a direct-action group willing to push far beyond conventional tactics.

The trees that environmentalists hoped to protect could only exist on the Pacific Coast. Over many millennia of competition, conifers lost out to more adaptable broad-leaved trees throughout North America, but on the steep mountains and hillsides of the Pacific Northwest a temperate climate that mixed dry periods with rain and fog allowed the conifers—spruces, cedars, hemlocks, redwoods, and Douglas firs—to thrive. While the rugged conditions supported fewer species of life overall than some other forests, the size of the trees produced a greater mass of life, per acre, than even the tropical rainforests. Within this idiosyncratic forest environment was an even more unusual place: the Siskiyou Mountains in northern California and southern Oregon. Never breaching eight thousand feet and lacking a view of the ocean, the Siskiyous might have been overshadowed by the towering Sierra Nevada and Cascade ranges to the east or the more scenic Coast Range to the west had they not distinguished themselves as one of the greatest storehouses of biological diversity in the United States, a result of having started as a string of volcanic islands before gradually migrating to the mainland to make an east-west bridge linking nearby ranges.[122]

Figure 3.3 Dave Foreman, Bart Koehler, and fellow activists demonstrate Earth First!-style wilderness activism. Photo courtesy Dave Foreman.

Some of that biological diversity already enjoyed protection as the Kalmiopsis Wilderness. But the Kalmiopsis sat amid many thousands of acres of "de facto wilderness," roadless and undeveloped land lacking the Wilderness Act's thick armor. Each logging road was another chink in a de facto wilderness's shield. The Forest Service—the greatest roadbuilding agency in the world, its network of logging roads far longer than the interstate highway system—started to penetrate the area around the Kalmiopsis soon after passage of the Wilderness Act. During the 1970s, as the Forest Service began and completed RARE II only to have it mired in legal challenges, environmentalists in Oregon worked with Senator Mark Hatfield on a statewide wilderness bill. Especially at issue was the area directly to the north of the Kalmiopsis Wilderness, an area that included old-growth trees treasured by both environmentalists and logging companies, although for different reasons. An ally of environmentalists except when it came to forests and the timber industry, Hatfield defeated several legislative attempts to create a northern addition. Then in the early 1980s the Forest Service began to build a road to Bald Mountain that would run just north of the Kalmiopsis, effectively cutting the established wilderness off from any potential additions and opening up a large portion of the remaining de facto wilderness to logging.[123]

Earth First! wed itself to direct action—and specifically to civil disobedience—on Bald Mountain. First drawn to the region in 1982 to fight the Gasquet-Orleans (G-O) Road in Northern California, Earth First! quickly shifted its attention to Bald Mountain when a court halted construction of the G-O Road for violating the religious protections of several Native American peoples. Volunteers from Oregon and Northern California, introduced to Earth First! through the G-O Road fight or during one of the group's "road show" tours through the region months earlier, mounted blockades on the still incomplete Bald Mountain Road in late April 1983. A half dozen or fewer people would stand across the road, arms linked, preventing bulldozers from moving any further. Local sheriffs and deputies took several hours to reach the remote site, so each blockade shut down construction for at least half a day. By early May, activists were locking themselves to roadbuilding equipment with chains and handcuffs, costing the construction crews even more time. The blockades wavered unpredictably between long periods of quiet standoff and brief moments of angry confrontation. On May 10 a bulldozer charged a group of activists with its blade down, burying them in a pile of dirt. On May 12 road workers drove a pickup truck straight into Dave Foreman, knocking him down and then dragging him for dozens of yards. In June Earth First! took the fight to the courts, joining the Oregon Natural Resources Council (ONRC) in a lawsuit against the Forest Service modeled after Huey Johnson's challenge to RARE II years earlier. A U.S. district court judge granted a temporary restraining order that halted the road's progress. Earth First! held its fourth annual gathering in the Siskiyous, bringing together hundreds of support-ers for what was to be the largest direct action yet. The swift decision by the court left Earth First!ers celebrating rather than blockading.[124]

The Bald Mountain fight ended up in front of a judge, but Earth First!ers believed their blockades played a key role. The Sierra Club Legal Defense Fund had failed when it sued to prevent a road over Bald Mountain a year earlier without challenging RARE II. After Earth First! stirred up renewed interest, the ONRC found locals willing to fund a more aggressive suit. Perhaps even more important in shaping long-term efforts to protect and expand wilderness in Oregon, the Earth First! actions radicalized those who participated. "I no longer have doubts about my commitment to action NOW for the wilderness," Molly Campbell wrote of her experience in the blockades. "If we wait and go through the 'proper channels' one more time, there will be no forests left . . . the strength of my beliefs and convic-tions grew after facing the angered bulldozer driver." Ric Bailey explained, "We feel in our hearts that we have contributed to a great cause, and helped with the advent of a new tactic in the protection of wilderness in America: Direct Action."[125] And Karen Pickett told a judge after her arrest that if her dedication to wilderness and species diversity was sincere, "then it is my *responsibility* to act when I see things being destroyed."[126] Earth First! paired particular campaigns for wilderness protection with the greater goal of convincing others that the interests of the natural world were no less important than those of humans, and worth great risk.

Because participants often found their own convictions either confirmed or strengthened, Earth First! actions tended to produce further Earth First! actions. When legal measures failed, activists quickly took matters into their own hands. The year after the Bald Mountain blockades, protesters launched actions around the proposed Middle Santiam Wilderness, drawing bigger crowds and producing more arrests than the year before. The Middle Santiam sat in the Willamette National Forest in Oregon's Cascade Range. At less than nine thousand acres, its size left it especially vulnerable to industrial activities nearby. For years the Forest Service allowed logging in Pyramid Creek, just upriver from the wilderness. To avoid landslides the Forest Service had moved Pyramid Creek Road several times, inadvertently rendering the steep hillside slopes unstable and showering silt into creeks and rivers. Local activists, who organized as the Middle Santiam Wilderness Committee, filed lawsuits and requested restraining orders against timber sales and roads in the Pyramid Creek area, although the Middle Santiam was only de facto wilderness. In June Congress passed an Oregon wilderness bill, protecting hundreds of thousands of acres as wilderness and releasing millions of acres to potential logging. In the Middle Santiam, the bill protected 7,500 acres, a fraction of what environmentalists had hoped for. Even before final passage of the Oregon wilderness bill, activists associated with the Middle Santiam Wilderness Committee and Earth First! formed a new outfit, the Cathedral Forest Action Group (CFAG). CFAG declared that it would fight for a complete moratorium on logging and roadbuilding in old-growth forests; for protection for an eighty-thousand-acre area the group dubbed the "Santiam Cathedral Forest"; for an end to construction of the Pyramid Creek Road; and for a restructuring of Forest Service policy away from logging and toward wilderness protection.[127]

The summer of 1984 saw more traffic than usual on Pyramid Creek Road, much of it protesters heading in to block logging trucks and sheriffs heading out to take protesters to jail. At the end of the summer, about a hundred activists gathered at a park in Portland before marching to the Region 6 Forest Service main office. The regional forester slipped out of the building before the protesters arrived, but a handful of Earth First!ers and Greenpeace members managed to slip in before police surrounded the office. The group emerged on the fourth-floor balcony and unfurled a banner that read, "Stop The U.S. Forest Service/Save Our Old Growth/Earth First!" Eventually a deputy regional forester agreed to a meeting with two activists. When that meeting produced no results, two members of CFAG chained themselves to the office's doors. The Portland Police called in a SWAT team to clear the office and place the two chained to the doors under arrest.[128]

Direct action, because it demonstrated an unusual degree of commitment and conviction, served as an implicit statement of the basic Earth First! philosophy that people could and should care as much about nature's interests as about their own. As such, it was also an implicit statement of the difference between mainstream and radical environmentalism. Direct action made clear the belief—righteous to some, naïve to others—that the urgency of environmental destruction demanded an immediate, uninhibited response, and that the larger environmental movement had failed to provide it.

The riskier the action, the more resonant the statement. In the Middle Santiam, Earth First! pioneered one of the riskiest tactics used to prevent logging: the tree sit. It quickly became one of the archetypal actions employed by radical environmentalists, the land-based version of Greenpeace's placing their Zodiacs between whales and harpoons. Tree sitters on platforms high in old-growth forests not only caught the attention of reporters but also forced loggers to choose between sparing the occupied trees or risking a human life. The original Earth First! tree sitter was Mikal Jakubal, an experienced rock climber who had heard of Australian activists occupying trees and experimented with the idea early in June 1985. Several months later Earth First! perfected the tactic and managed over a month of consecutive tree sits in the Squaw Creek watershed of the Middle Santiam. For decades after, tree sits persisted as a standard feature of environmental battles in the Pacific Northwest, involving on one side more and more elaborate platforms and strategies for resupplying sitters, and on the other side stakeouts, cranes, and eventually professional tree climbers trained in dismantling the platforms.[129]

Earth First!'s use of increasingly audacious direct actions made mainstream environmentalists wary. Even before the Oregon tree sits, radicals had caused enough of a stir that established organizations felt moved to comment or else remain conspicuously silent. "They're sort of a parody: they don't do anything," one Sierra Club staffer told a reporter, contrasting Earth First! with those environmentalists "who are actually out there slugging away, putting on their neckties, going into offices, writing legislation, turning up at the hearings, filing comments on EISs, doing all that grungy work that actually produces results." The Wilderness Society's William Turnage worried that Earth First! reinforced an image of environmentalists as "irresponsible and rather bizarre characters." Cecil Andrus, the former Secretary of the Interior, called Earth First!'s tactics "extremism that is irresponsible, illegal and totally unacceptable to responsible conservationists in America." The Club's deputy conservation director, Doug Scott, agreed: "I don't think you can be a monkeywrencher and still expect to be taken as a serious player in the political process," he said. Michael McCloskey, the Club's executive director, refused to talk about Earth First!.[130]

Critics who considered direct action more flash than substance made an important point: the protection offered by blockades and tree sits lasted only so long as activists did. For that reason, Earth First! had to pair its tactics with a philosophy that bred commitment and devotion. "Thus," Bill Devall and George Sessions wrote in 1984, "the process of ecological resistance is both personal and collective."[131] Despite the blockades of 1983, the 1984 Oregon wilderness bill left the de facto wilderness north of the Kalmiopsis open to logging. In 1987 the Forest Service began planning timber sales there. In the intervening years, Earth First! had maintained not just an interest but a physical presence in the north Kalmiopsis. Earth First!er Lou Gold, a retired law professor from Brooklyn, kept a sporadic vigil from a campsite near the Bald Mountain Road every summer from 1983 to 1987. With the north Kalmiopsis threatened again, Earth First! activists returned to the area to rejoin Gold. By then Mike Roselle had organized Earth First!'s Nomadic Action Group, a rapid response team ready to use direct action to halt imminent threats. In 1987 Earth First! initiated several years of blockades, lockdowns, tree sits, and at one point a group of protesters sitting in the road with their feet encased in concrete. Although the Forest Service took advantage of a fire to allow salvage logging in the north Kalmiopsis, well over a decade of Earth First! actions helped prevent any significant roadbuilding and kept alive the hope of enlarging the Kalmiopsis Wilderness. After his arrest for blocking a bulldozer outside the Kalmiopsis in 1987, at the same time as four other Earth First!ers began a two-week jail term for occupying a log yarder, Roselle insisted that the arrests and imprisonments couldn't shake activists' resolve. "They haven't stopped Earth First! from protesting old growth cutting," he said. "In fact, we're now even stronger."[132]

CONCLUSION

The radical break that cleaved Earth First! from the mainstream environmental movement was a political one that quickly became tactical and philosophical too. Radicals grew frustrated with conventional liberal democratic reform of the sort so many environmental organizations had come to rely on. Conventional reform, they believed, could never be a proportional response to the planetary crisis at hand. The professionalization of the movement and the culture of compromise that radicals believed it bred, represented especially by RARE II, convinced some disgruntled conservationists that environmentalism needed an infusion of energy and ideas. The key idea radicals embraced, believing that it had always animated what was most powerful about environmentalism, was ecocentric thought: a rejection of the humanism that underlay so much of the modern world. The most vital manifestation of that idea was the protection of wilderness. The energy came from direct action, from no longer depending on partial and incremental change and instead demanding, urgently and emphatically, that species and ecosystems should be spared from destruction.

The theory and practice of ecocentric, radical environmentalism raised questions about what was central and what was marginal to the environmental movement. Earth First!ers believed they were returning to the basic premises of early conservation, to the ideas that had always given environmentalism its most piercing cries. Its critics, throughout the 1980s, asked to what degree such ideas bred reaction and misanthropy and ignored social justice.

Even before Earth First! gained wide notoriety, Eugene Hargrove, the editor of *Environmental Ethics*, worried about its ideas. Earth First! had been inspired by Edward Abbey's novel *The Monkey Wrench Gang*, Hargrove wrote, and was at risk of moving from legitimate protests to violent and immoral acts, acts which might "create a terrible backlash undoing all the good that has been done" by the environmental movement.

Environmentalists had often talked about "*extending* moral consideration in some way to include nature," but for Earth First! "nature, rather than being included, is given priority." That combination of an extreme philosophy and a willingness to act on it was, for Hargrove, cause for concern. "In the twentieth century," he reminded readers, "terrorism . . . has been the last resort when normal political action was frustrated," but such measures were uncalled for in protecting the natural world, as environmentalism "has been an immensely successful political movement."[133]

"Let's have some precision in language here: terrorism means deadly violence . . . carried out against people and other living things. . . . Sabotage, on the other hand, means the application of force against inanimate property," Abbey wrote in response. Bulldozers tearing up hillsides and dams flooding canyons and valleys were acts of terrorism, he said, and the characters in his novel—as well as, by implication, the activists those characters inspired—"engage in industrial sabotage in order to defend a land they love against industrial terrorism." Dave Foreman, one of the founders of Earth First!, let Abbey defend direct action and in a separate letter took up the cause of greater limits to industrial civilization. "You say the environmental movement has been immensely successful . . . ," he wrote. "It appears to be successful because it asks for so little and actually threatens the corporate state to such a minor extent." For both Abbey and Foreman, Hargrove's warnings about Earth First! epitomized exactly what was wrong with the modern environmental movement. Too concerned with political niceties, that movement would never risk serious confrontation with those in power in order to defend the natural world. Too satisfied with token victories, it would never present a significant challenge to the basic values of industrial civilization. When Hargrove responded to Abbey and Foreman by asking how anyone could support acts "both criminal and morally reprehensible by normal moral or ethical standards," Hargrove confirmed his opponents' most fundamental complaint: conventional ethics was exactly what they objected to. For them, effective environmentalism rested on countering the anthropocentric values that were at the very center of industrial society.[134]

4

Public Lands and the Public Good

On July 4, 1980 several hundred residents of Grand County, Utah gathered in Moab, the county seat, to cheer on a bulldozer with "Sagebrush Rebel" bumper stickers. As county commissioners denounced federal bureaucracy, the bulldozer scraped a road up to and just over the boundary of a Bureau of Land Management wilderness study area, a violation of federal law and one of the few direct actions in the anti-wilderness movement known as the "sagebrush rebellion." The slapdash road transgressed not just a wilderness boundary but also the broader system of environmental regulations governing public lands and even the authority of the federal government. Grand County officials organized the event in opposition to highhanded federal agencies, environmental extremists, and the misbegotten alliance between them.[1]

It is tempting to think of the environmental movement as a product of midcentury liberalism and as an enemy of the late twentieth-century conservative ascendancy. That story allows historians to saddle Ronald Reagan's administration with major shifts in environmentalism's fortunes: the modern movement emerged in the 1960s and leapt to the top of the nation's political agenda on the strength of overwhelming public concern and strong support in a still relatively liberal Washington, D.C., only to

be hobbled when Reagan's election signaled the end of the modern liberal era. But the Grand County bulldozer plowed into federal wilderness
months before Reagan's election. As historians have looked more closely at
the 1970s and 1980s, they have found years of complicated political negotiation in which the Reagan presidency was the culmination of political,
economic, and ideological trends already well under way rather than the
beginning of an inchoate conservatism.[2]

Any attempt to map environmentalism onto the Left or the Right
means negotiating the unruly terrains of both the state and the market.
Conservatives from Barry Goldwater to Ronald Reagan used government as a rhetorical foil, defining their own principles in opposition to
the state and defining liberalism as synonymous with "big government."
But just as conservatives did not oppose the state as thoroughly as they
sometimes claimed, liberals did not uncritically align themselves with the
federal government. The historian Paul Sabin argues that public interest environmental law brought to bear "an intensifying 1960s critique of
federal agencies and government power" in the name of a public good
that the state did not necessarily represent. "A new kind of liberalism—
skeptical and distrustful of government, yet still committed to collective
action by the state—had emerged in the heart of the liberal establishment," Sabin writes.[3]

Skepticism and distrust of the government emerged far outside of the
liberal establishment as well. Mainstream environmentalists who had relied
on state power for years began to question its effectiveness by the 1980s.
Radical environmentalists went much further, calling natural resource
agencies fundamentally corrupt and little different from extractive industries in their human-centered assault on the wild. Placing little faith in government or the democratic virtues it was supposed to represent, radicals
appealed to a sense of order and structure beyond human design. Generally,
this was a natural order of ecological relationships, but translating that natural order into policy was difficult to achieve through conventional liberal
democratic processes.

Uneasy with established procedures and institutions, radicals turned
to other political architectures. From its earliest days, Earth First! drew
from anarchist thought to explain the pitfalls built into systems of human

devising. Far less often but at times significantly, Earth First! subscribed to an economic order of market relationships, and in doing so made common cause with a New Right that was ostensibly the environmental movement's chief adversary. That partnership remained narrow, fleeting, and difficult, but it made clear that radical environmentalists held few political commitments beyond what they considered the interests of the nonhuman world. And it suggested that environmentalism, like many other postwar political movements, was neither liberal nor conservative in any obvious and consistent way. In the 1970s mainstream environmentalists locked arms with the federal government for pragmatic purposes. In the 1980s radical environmentalists made clear the political and philosophical limits of that partnership.

ENVIRONMENTALISM, CONSERVATISM, AND THE SAGEBRUSH REBELLION

The state framed the relationship between environmentalism and conservatism. During the 1970s the environmental movement drew itself closer to the federal government while the conservative movement set itself apart, and those distinct trajectories made room for growing conservative hostility toward environmental regulation. The distance between the two movements stretched especially wide in the West, where debates over public land management produced strenuous appeals to local autonomy and declamations against a faraway bureaucracy. Those appeals and declamations rang loudest during the "sagebrush rebellion," an attempt by Western legislators to seize federal lands and hand them to state governments. Even as the sagebrush rebellion heightened the differences between environmentalists and anti-environmentalists, it demonstrated how each side had a vacillating relationship to government. Westerners were not entirely at odds with the federal government, and environmentalists were not entirely aligned. Radical environmentalists, in particular, viewed federal agencies with suspicion as much as with favor. The difficulty of reconciling competing views of how public lands should be used, and even of defining a "public good," marked the limits of a plural approach to land management.

The modern environmental and conservative movements were contemporaneous. Environmentalism gained broad support in the United States at the same moment as conservatism reestablished its political relevance. After several decades on the sidelines of American politics, conservatives took the field in the late twentieth century. As scholars have recently emphasized, the 1960s was as much a decade of right-wing organization as of left-wing agitation. Young conservatives grew frustrated with what was, in their view, a centrist Republican Party cowed by the New Deal and decades of liberal control in Washington, D.C. This New Right sought to take over the party both politically and ideologically, its efforts coalescing around Barry Goldwater's 1964 presidential campaign. Although Goldwater lost the election, he inspired a generation of conservative activists who worked to elect Ronald Reagan governor of California in 1966 and president of the United States in 1980. At the same time, conservative thinkers as disparate as Russell Kirk, Milton Friedman, Jerry Falwell, Irving Kristol, and William Buckley, Jr. contributed to a collective critique of liberal ideas and policies. In just two decades conservatism shifted from the margins to the center of American politics and culture.[4]

As the New Right defined itself in reaction to the politics of race and gender in the late twentieth century, so it defined itself against the environmental movement. But that intellectual work had to overcome the ways environmentalism and conservatism were not natural enemies. William Buckley's *National Review*, by the 1960s the voice of a nascent New Right, briefly supported environmentalism. In early 1970 its editors acknowledged that "conservation" would be one of the most important public issues of the coming decade and worried that the Left would claim it. "This must not happen," they wrote. "As the very word itself suggests, 'conservation' is intrinsically a conservative concern." Equating conservation with the mythical American frontier and the "virgin land" that the magazine's editors felt defined the early republic, they warned readers, "Conservation is likely to be a powerful, indeed an overriding *spiritual* issue, which it would be political suicide to concede to the Left."[5] Young Americans for Freedom (YAF), which Buckley had also helped found, was similarly sanguine. YAF emerged as the conservative alternative to Students for a Democratic Society, and like SDS it had paid little attention to environmental issues throughout the 1960s. But in the lead-up to Earth Day, YAF nodded approvingly, if hesitantly, at efforts to clean up the American landscape. "It doesn't take a genius to see that pollution is potentially just as much an enemy of freedom as Communist expansionism, statist legislation, and the violent left," YAF leaders advised. "Environmental control," they insisted, "is not something we can allow to become a monopoly of the liberal and radical left."[6]

Even the ultra-conservative weekly *Human Events* tempered its skepticism of the environmental movement with recognition of pressing environmental issues. "No question exists that the majority of the public is desperately in support of our national goal to bring pollutants under control and restore the planet to the balance of nature commensurate with the existence of mankind," Robert Bailey said.[7] The race between Democrats and Republicans to capitalize on environmentalism's sudden popularity was, John Chamberlain wrote, "the sort of political competition that must help more than it can possibly hurt"; while James Jackson Kilpatrick welcomed "so much apparent evidence that the public, at long last, has awakened to the situation and is prepared to take action."[8]

What sort of "action," however, quickly became a point of contention. Doctrinaire conservatives could be for the environment and against environmentalism. More often than not, the wedge between the cause and the movement was federal authority and the role of the state. A YAF board member said of environmentalism, "I have heard 'conservatives' and YAF leaders, hopefully without too much thought, proclaiming that here really is an area where the Federal Government must play a larger and larger role. This disturbs me not only from a political and philosophical perspective, but from a factual one."[9] Neoconservatives, those ex-Leftists migrating steadily to the Right in the late-twentieth century, grew particularly wary of environmentalism's relationship to state power. *Commentary* editor Norman Podhoretz warned that declarations of an environmental crisis sacrificed the public interest and served those motivated by "the desire to govern the rest of us."[10]

More and more, conservatives associated environmentalism with excessive state power. From its New York offices *Commentary* railed against an imperious environmental movement and its tendency toward "extraordinary measures of political control."[11] In the West, though, the shadow of environmental regulation was coterminous with federal lands in the public imagination. Along the Atlantic Coast, conservatives worried about regulation of industry; deep in the American interior, critics of environmentalism assailed the management of public lands. Resource users—in particular ranchers—grew increasingly frustrated with federal control of Western acreage. At the political and emotional center of that frustration sat the Bureau of Land Management (BLM), an agency whose vast holdings in the eleven westernmost contiguous states included nearly a quarter of surface lands and a majority of the subsurface mineral estate.

Western hostility toward federal land management grew in part out of the BLM's evolving policies in the 1970s and especially the passage of the Federal Land Policy and Management Act (FLPMA) in 1976, a law that offered the BLM the sort of coherent policy guidelines it had long operated without. While the Forest Service and Park Service enjoyed relatively clear identities and broad constituencies, few Americans outside of the rural West knew the BLM. It was primarily ranchers who paid close attention to the public domain (a general term for BLM holdings), having enjoyed decades of grazing rights on public lands at below-market rates. FLPMA pushed the BLM onto a more public stage, mandating a multiple-use approach to management and requiring that the BLM pay heed to scientific, ecological, recreational, and historical values and consider wildlife as well as domesticated animals. FLPMA also directed that the BLM review all roadless areas over five thousand acres that possessed "wilderness characteristics," a directive that the Carter administration took seriously and interpreted generously. The law and its application caused consternation in the rural West, stoking anger toward environmentalists and the federal government. "When Kruschev was dictator of Russia," A. C. Wilkerson of the Uintah Cattlemen's Association said at a hearing on wilderness designation in the Ashley National Forest, "he promised us he would bury us and with the help of the environmentalists, he probably will."[12] Ranchers worried about the loss of grazing lands, a general shift toward more environmentally minded policies, and federal agencies' assertion of control over lands many Westerners relied on. Like rising water, FLPMA extended government's reach into the narrowest spaces of rural Western life.

Western anger flared most during the sagebrush rebellion. In the strictest terms, the sagebrush rebellion took place almost entirely in the legislatures of nearly a dozen Western states with a few brief skirmishes in Washington, D.C. In the summer of 1979 the Nevada legislature passed a law that declared all BLM lands in Nevada the property of the state, created a board to oversee the transfer of public lands from federal to state hands, and reserved funds for the inevitable court battle ahead. Utah Senator Orrin Hatch embraced the issue and the anti-federal sentiment behind it, introducing a bill in Congress designed to transfer all BLM lands to state jurisdiction. For the next year and a half, more and more Western legislators at the state and federal levels declared themselves sagebrush rebels, passing or proposing legislation modeled on Nevada's. The legal basis of the sagebrush rebellion was always tenuous. None of the measures ever took effect, and by 1982 enthusiasm for large-scale land transfers began to fade away. But the rhetoric and spirit of the sagebrush rebellion lasted for another decade and beyond, framing environmental debates in the West.[13]

Antistatism and anti-environmentalism fit together neatly in the sagebrush rebellion, bringing into further alignment the politics of the rural West and the New Right. For movement conservatives and rural Westerners alike, public land controversies were another instance of elite liberals imposing their values on others. The Nevada State Legislature's Select Committee on Public Lands, which helped engineer the original legislation, described the sagebrush rebellion as a reaction to "colonial" treatment by a federal government that made policies "for a so-called national constituency without regard for western problems." Pointing to FLPMA, the Alaska lands campaign, RARE II, and the BLM wilderness review, the committee complained of an assault on Western autonomy at the behest of an environmental establishment. The Alaska lands campaign, U.S. Representative Don Young told his congressional colleagues, was by and for "special interest groups in San Francisco and New York that would like to turn Alaska into a park." At the moment that conservatives and Western politicians made political hay by opposing Washington, D.C., the environmental movement's flurry of activity in the capital left it a perfect target.[14]

Environmentalists tried to fight back by claiming that the "special interest" label better fit their antagonists, and that it was anti-environmentalists who sought their own narrow advantage. The Sierra Club described the sagebrush rebellion as "another attempt by energy, mining, and livestock interests to shuck off reasonable and lawful federal regulations and take advantage of the American public." Debbie Sease, the Wilderness Society's BLM specialist, told her colleagues, "The public lands belong to the nation and cannot continue to be managed for the benefit of an *elite* minority."[15]

Both sides claimed to stand for the public good and the most democratic use of public lands. FLPMA required that the BLM honor what James Skillen has called "the new pluralism in public lands management," in which the BLM and Forest Service had to plan for the varied ways Americans used and valued public lands rather than simply the various economic benefits those lands offered.[16] But as the agencies shifted away from a focus on industry and toward a consideration of wilderness and ecological integrity, they struggled to reconcile different opinions and philosophies. In 1953 Richard McArdle, Chief of the Forest Service, had said of his agency's multiple-use mandate, "I believe that our inability to satisfy completely each and every group of national-forest users is a definite sign of success in doing the job assigned to us."[17] Allotting equal degrees of dissatisfaction might have worked in the 1950s, but by the 1970s that ideal could not accommodate what had become not just competing uses but also competing ethical claims. Sagebrush rebels and wilderness advocates did not follow the rules of interest-group pluralism. They were not seeking a compromise that left everyone equally frustrated. They argued over the very premises of public lands policy.

Mainstream environmentalists had to make a particularly delicate argument. The alliance between environmentalism and federal agencies had always been one of convenience rather than conviction. When William Voigt of the Izaak Walton League wrote an account of grasslands management in the twentieth century, he called it *Public Grazing Lands: Use and Misuse by Industry and Government*, pointing to a shared culpability.[18] For decades environmentalists had offered measured criticisms of federal agencies, including against the Department of the Interior over roads and dams in Yosemite and Dinosaur. David Brower amplified those criticisms in places like Mineral King and Grand Canyon.[19] But during the 1970s the most influential environmental organizations grew increasingly tied to federal agencies and compelled to argue that the government served a common interest.

Radical environmentalists were less hemmed in and so distributed blame more broadly. "Only the most naïve ever believed that the true intent of the so-called Sagebrush Rebellion was to gain title to the federal public lands in the western states," the *Earth First! Journal* cautioned in 1980. The actual purpose of the sagebrush rebels, the *Journal* claimed, was to remake the BLM into the pre-FLPMA "Bureau of Livestock and Mining"—environmentalists' nickname for an agency they felt catered to Western industry— "to cow conservationists, the Forest Service, and Washington politicians, and to encourage local and state politicians to make stronger anti-environmental statements. They have admirably succeeded."[20] From Earth First!'s point of view ranchers and mining companies wore the black hats, but federal agencies were often little better than scared townspeople. Among ranchers, politicians, land managers, and even mainstream conservationists there were few heroes.

The success of the sagebrush rebellion, Earth First! argued, was political rather than legal. While it failed in its stated goals, the sagebrush rebellion reoriented Western land management, pushing back on federal agencies' modest steps toward environmental protections. Earth First! found sagebrush rebels and the broader New Right both exasperating and instructive. "Is the Moral Majority timid? The NRA apologetic? The Sagebrushers hesitant?" Dave Foreman asked rhetorically, urging a more militant environmental movement. "If you believe in wilderness, if you love the Earth, if you are appalled at what humankind is doing to the biosphere," he advised, "then don't be timid. Speak out. Act with vigor and pride in your convictions!"[21] More and more, radicals' convictions were less about what was popular or democratic than about what was environmentally sound. The point was to defend nonhuman nature, not any particular agency or even political process. The state did not necessarily represent a common civic good and often betrayed an ecological one. When human destructiveness overlapped with popular opinion, Earth First! had no compunctions about fighting both.

"THE TYPE OF GOVERNMENT I BELIEVE IN": EARTH FIRST! AND JAMES WATT

Earth First! rebuked the government much more readily than did the Sierra Club or the Wilderness Society, but radicals simply said out loud what establishment environmentalists said quietly to themselves. Even as the sagebrush rebellion pushed mainstream environmentalists to defend public lands and federal management, behind closed doors environmentalists questioned whether their partnership with federal agencies cost more than it paid. The Reagan administration offered environmental organizations an opportunity to split the difference: to repudiate a particular government without dismissing government itself. A hostile administration in Washington, D.C. allowed mainstream environmentalists to challenge federal agencies but avoid rebuffing federal support. Radical environmentalists pushed that skepticism of government past a single election cycle, concerned less with the views of a particular political appointee than with the reliability of the state itself.

Doubts about the federal government began with doubts about the state of the environmental movement. The ten-year anniversary of Earth Day provided an opportunity for taking stock of environmentalism's trajectory. Much of it was grim. "The environmental movement, an important political force during the 1970s, is faltering," *U.S. News & World Report* said. "After a decade of spectacular success, the environmental movement appears to be headed for more perilous times," the *Los Angeles Times* reported. Echoing the same sentiment, the *San Francisco Examiner* asked, "After a decade of turbulent activism, is the environmental movement coming to an end, going the way of previous grass-root political movements in American history?" *Science* described the decline as a long time coming: the 1970s had offered "a large and sobering accumulation of evidence that the environmental movement still has no tried and true strategy for success." All of the assessments pointed to a weakening of federal regulations and, after a decade of economic uncertainty, a renewed concern for economic growth. The end of what *U.S. News & World Report* called "the golden age of environmentalism" began years before the Reagan Era.[22] A sense of decline came from within the movement and from without, a result of both growing opposition to environmental regulation and diminishing returns as a commitment to conventional reform produced ambiguous results like RARE II.

Battle weariness was the mood at a meeting in January 1980 when two dozen environmental leaders, journalists, and federal administrators gathered in Harpers Ferry, Virginia for an "assessment and direction session" about the state of environmentalism. Brock Evans represented the Sierra Club and reported that the meeting had found "certainly evidence of slippage in our movement." Evans described environmentalism as lacking inspiration, bogged down in minutiae, and over-reliant on apathetic federal agencies. Among the problems he identified was the failure of a strategy based largely on federal power: "We thought that we could deal with environmental problems by turning to the government as an interface between us and the industrial corporations," Evans wrote, summarizing the Harpers Ferry discussion. That strategy worked for much of the 1970s but less so by the end of the decade, when the movement's opponents had "seized upon such catch phrases as anti-regulation, anti-federalism, and false trade offs between their values and ours," and those catch phrases "tapped many gut feelings of the American people." The tenor of the meeting, Evans said, was clear: "We need to rekindle the old spark."[23]

The election of Ronald Reagan less than a year later affirmed the view from Harpers Ferry. Reagan, who had cheered the sagebrush rebellion during his campaign, demonstrated little interest in the environmental movement, and his election stirred the hostility toward environmental regulation that major organizations already encountered among politicians. "Because of the November election," one Nevada legislator and sagebrush rebel said soon after Reagan's victory, "it's a whole new ball game."[24] In early 1981 the Sierra Club's Doug Scott warned his colleagues, "There is a strong indication that we will very soon be facing a 'covey' of anti-wilderness/anti-public lands and forests legislation," likely including "nationwide 'release' of National Forest roadless areas (worse than our sufficiency language compromise)." Days later Senator Sam Hayakawa introduced a bill to immediately release for other use all RARE II roadless areas not already proposed as wilderness.[25]

The greatest blow to environmentalists' fortunes in Washington, D.C. came soon after Reagan's inauguration when the president nominated

James Watt for secretary of the interior. Watt had served in the Nixon and Ford administrations and more recently headed the Mountain States Legal Foundation, a nonprofit organization that promoted private enterprise and fought government regulation. In Watt's view federal management of public lands generally did more harm than good, and the national wilderness system was already large enough. He resented environmental organizations and opposed many of their goals, at one point calling them "a left-wing cult which seeks to bring down the type of government I believe in."[26] Within weeks of taking charge at Interior, Watt began relaxing restrictions on strip-mining, offshore oil drilling, and the use of off-road vehicles or snowmobiles on public land. Watt's assault on environmental regulations simultaneously energized his critics and further divided, to differing degrees, mainstream and radical environmentalists from their erstwhile federal allies.

There had been, at Harpers Ferry, the possibility of a more militant environmental establishment. Participants discussed a less amenable, more strident environmentalism, one that inspired greater action from its supporters and consternation from its adversaries. Taking the Civil Rights Movement as a model, representatives at Harpers Ferry had talked about picketing, marches, and street theater as ways to express indignation at lackadaisical federal efforts. "We should get back on the cutting edge where we were ten years ago, and not accept less than the best," Evans said. "We should elevate our issues from the back page to the front page, perhaps through these direct action tactics."[27]

For the major organizations, the possibility of broad-based direct action quickly gave way to a political campaign with a single figure in its crosshairs. Watt fit the role of villain in a way that both clarified and simplified environmentalists' fears. His appointment reinforced the apprehensions mainstream organizations already felt about federal agencies while offering a narrower and much more obvious target. The new secretary of the interior posed a dire threat, and so provided an immediate means of rekindling the "old spark" that Brock Evans found flickering. The press, Scott predicted, would consider the Watt agenda "as a single big issue—basically the tangible expression of the 'Sagebrush Rebellion,' " and that consolidation could invite a unified counterattack, "a really MAJOR campaign on a scale (not unlike Alaska) which can really get grassroots people excited and politically active on a grand scale."[28]

Loud, brash, and unapologetically skeptical of the environmental movement, Watt came to represent federal land mismanagement in its entirety, swelling in size until he took up much of the movement's field of vision. Environmental organizations and especially wilderness advocates depicted Watt as almost singlehandedly bending federal environmental policy away from public sentiment and toward private interests. The Wilderness Society compiled a six-chapter "Watt Book," describing the secretary as tied to corporations and disconnected from popular opinion. Environmentalists represented the views of a majority of Americans, the Watt Book claimed, while Watt fought for the narrow interests of the mining, ranching, lumber, and oil industries.[29] To demonstrate the broad base of anti-Watt sentiment, the Sierra Club gathered over a million signatures for a "Replace Watt" petition that accused the secretary of "sabotaging conservation goals supported by a vast majority of the American people." The signatures, the Club emphasized, came from "all over the country, from Republicans and Democrats, many from people who had never heard of the Sierra Club before."[30] As Scott had predicted, the anti-Watt campaign galvanized concern, more than doubling the Wilderness Society's membership between 1979 and 1983 and nearly doubling the Sierra Club's.

For extractive industries, meanwhile, Watt's tenure signaled a return to what they considered pragmatic, growth-oriented natural resource policies and a measured application of federal oversight. Bronson Lewis, the American Plywood Association's executive vice president, wrote directly to Reagan about the Sierra Club's petition drive and about environmental organizations' "vehement media campaign" against Watt. Lewis assured the president that his "resounding public mandate" signaled "the urgent need to correct policies of the previous Administration [sic] and Congress which sacrificed multiple-use management to the overzealous creation of single-use wilderness."[31] Watt worked with broad public support, industry claimed, and against an aggressive minority. "Predictably," a Mobil Oil ad read, "certain special interest representatives have raised a hue and cry over Mr. Watt's proposals." Even *Newsweek* suggested Watt sought principle more than profit. "He undercuts their basic claim to legitimacy," the magazine argued of Watt's opponents, "which is that they alone are disinterested champions of the commonweal."[32]

Earth First! agreed with industry as much as with mainstream environmental organizations. Yes, Watt was a threat to public lands and natural resources, but not in a way that made him exceptional. Although radical environmentalists never missed an opportunity to mock, disparage, and protest Watt, they insisted the secretary was little different from many other politicians and bureaucrats, and that singling him out was a mistake. "Watt accurately represents the Earth-be-damned attitude of the power establishment in this country," Foreman wrote in the wake of the Sierra Club's anti-Watt campaign, "but he is at least honest about it. . . . In contrast, men like Jimmy Carter and former Secretary of the Interior Cecil Andrus pretended to be friends of the environment but were in reality committed to the same extremist development philosophy that Watt is." Mainstream environmentalists who found fault with Watt and Watt alone failed to see the larger picture: "The petition campaign by the Sierra Club," Foreman continued, "demonstrates that the established conservation groups are committed merely to the reform of the existing system and cannot see that the system itself is responsible for our environmental ills."[33] For Earth First! James Watt was not a distortion of federal management; he was its unbridled realization (see figure 4.1).

Radicals believed not only that Watt was typical in the threat he posed to public lands but also that mainstream environmentalists' response was typically lackluster. For wilderness advocates, Watt's greatest sin was his attempt to expand mineral, gas, and oil exploration in wilderness areas. The Wilderness Act allowed such exploration through the end of 1983 and Watt made it clear he would take advantage of that loophole in ways previous secretaries had not, even proposing an extension of the deadline into the twenty-first century. In response, the Wilderness Society went to the press with a study that showed wilderness could provide only a tiny fraction of the nation's energy needs. Public opposition to Watt's plan grew, and Congress began debating a Wilderness Protection Act that would withdraw all designated wilderness from oil and gas exploration.[34]

Enthusiastic support for the proposed Wilderness Protection Act by groups like the Wilderness Society, according to Earth First!, offered

Figure 4.1 Rallies for (*a*) and against (*b*): Secretary of the Interior James Watt inspired strong feelings of support and opposition. Photos courtesy Dave Foreman.

"further evidence that the environmental movement has gotten too used to scrambling after Wonder Bread crumbs and pretending they're prime rib and artichoke hearts." What, Earth First! asked, would the act do to protect not-yet-designated wilderness left behind by RARE II, like Little Granite Creek in Wyoming's Gros Ventre Range?[35] The Gros Ventres sat astride the overthrust belt running from Canada to Utah where colliding tectonic plates had folded layers of rock on top of each other, producing spectacular mountains and rumors of abundant natural gas. In 1982 Getty Oil applied for a permit to drill at Little Granite Creek, where it held a lease, and the Forest Service accommodated Getty by planning a new road. "Traditional conservation groups . . . will probably sue the feds," Howie Wolke predicted, "but the eventual outcome of this legal action is anybody's guess. Should these legal efforts fail, Earth First! is committed to organizing and carrying out massive civil disobedience, including an occupation of the canyon and rig site, in order to stop this travesty."[36]

Earth First! held its third Round River Rendezvous (the group's annual gathering) in Little Granite Creek on the Fourth of July weekend, 1982. Two of the group's signature tactics made an early appearance: the crowd of nearly five hundred attendees formed a brief, symbolic blockade of the proposed access road, and saboteurs removed several miles of the road crew's survey stakes both before and after the Rendezvous. Earth First! claimed that its Gros Ventre gathering, and the threat of further action, spurred the Wyoming Oil and Gas Commission's denial of Getty's permit as well as the Forest Service's stay on construction of its own road. Equally likely is that the agencies' decisions originated with Bart Koehler's administrative appeal—under the aegis of the Wyoming Wilderness Association—which pointed out that although Getty held a legal claim to the drilling site, it did not yet have the right-of-way required for an access road. Koehler's reasoning led to a similar appeal by the state of Wyoming itself, and it revealed a tenuous alliance of environmentalists, hunters, and Wyoming politicians against outsiders. "We see a multinational corporation and the federal government come in and say they're going to tell us how to run this state," governor Ed Herschler said. "We take the position that Wyoming is not for sale."[37] In this case, Earth First! agreed with Herschler's broad sentiment: extractive industries and the federal government together posed a threat to

Figure 4.2 Earth First!ers tell Getty where to go. Little Granite Creek, Wyoming, 1982. Photo courtesy Dave Foreman.

local interests. Little Granite Creek had to be protected from business and government as usual, not from a rogue bureaucrat (see figure 4.2).

THE USE AND ABUSE OF BUREAUCRACY

"Government is a paradox, but there is no escaping it," Andrew Bard Schmookler wrote in the *Earth First! Journal* in 1986.[38] Schmookler questioned the coherence of anarchy as a political philosophy, and in doing so he called attention to the sometimes mismatch between radical environmentalists' theory and methods. Earth First!'s distrust of federal management ran deep enough that the group nurtured an anarchist spirit. But Earth First! remained committed to and drew from the more traditional conservation movement enough that it often relied on federal agencies and celebrated public lands. Dubious about state power in theory, radicals nevertheless relied on state power in practice. An unapologetic ecocentrism ultimately distinguished radicals from their mainstream counterparts, a distinction that at times mattered little and at times sent Earth First! in directions mainstream groups would not follow.

Radicals looked at the record of federal conservation with bitter regret. "I have heartily supported every law, executive order, and petition to salvage the dwindling biological wealth of the earth," wrote Charles Bowden, a close friend of Edward Abbey and Earth First! "But now I see what happens to every decent impulse in my society: they become that ugly thing, government."[39] The state, radical environmentalists tended to argue, made a blunt tool for protecting the nonhuman world, one that missed as often as it struck. Even the most celebrated pieces of environmental legislation were not exempt from criticism. In 1983, twenty years after passage of the Wilderness Act, Howie Wolke judged the law "seriously and basically flawed" and the nation's total wilderness acreage "a miserable fragment of the system for which early visionaries such as Muir, Marshall, and Leopold had hoped." The wilderness movement's greatest legislative success had accomplished only the bare minimum. "The 'progress'" Wolke wrote, "about which many of our politicians and even some of our alleged colleagues (take note, Bill Turnage) like to brag is illusory."[40]

Earth First! balanced a dwindling faith in state efforts with an expansive view of political philosophy. Many key figures and supporters—most notably Abbey—described themselves as anarchists.[41] Like the crisis environmentalists of the 1970s, radical environmentalists distrusted liberal individualism as a foundation for social policy. The theories, values, and processes that defined conventional American politics offered radicals little hope for the salvation of the natural world. Anarchism, on the other hand, offered a ready-made political philosophy that resonated both in terms of strategy and principle.

Radical environmentalists considered it axiomatic that social hierarchies resting on the concentration of power resulted in the exploitation of the nonhuman world. "A house built on greed cannot long endure," Abbey said. "Whether called capitalism or communism makes little difference; both of these . . . systems are driven by the greed for power over nature and human nature; both are self-destroying." Abbey wrote in response to Schmookler's insistence that "Only government can restrain power in the interests of other values" a claim that made many Earth First!ers bristle.[42] Radical environmentalists shared anarchists' dim view of government as well as anarchists' complaints about the complexity of modern technology; the compromises and corruption of representative democracy; the misguided emphasis on the individual by liberalism; and the exploitative and utilitarian use of the natural world by industrial society. Radical environmentalists thought that anarchists understood modern society's fatal flaws.

The feeling was mutual. When Earth First!er Roger Featherstone visited Chicago's Haymarket International Anarchist Conference in 1986, he didn't have to build many bridges. "It was felt that anarchism may be the only hope for the environment," he reported, "and that present structures are not adequate for the saving of Mother Earth."[43] The affinity Featherstone noted in Chicago had grown during the 1970s and 1980s. The few regular anarchist publications in the United States directed more and more attention toward environmental issues and ecological theory. "The connections, I trust, are clear," Kirkpatrick Sale wrote in 1985. "The subjects are indeed complex, but it seems obvious that the concerns of ecology, appreciated in the full . . . match those of anarchism, particularly in its communal strain."[44] A year earlier John Clark suggested that anarchists were beginning "to see the ecological perspective as the macrocosmic correlate . . . of the libertarian conception of a cooperative, voluntarily organized society."[45] Some anarchists developed specific theories of how anarchism and environmentalism fit together. Sale was one of the most well-known advocates of bioregionalism, an environmentally-based anarchism that stressed small-scale communities organized around ecological features like watersheds and climate. Others simply emphasized connections between environmental and anarchist thought. George Crowder speculated that in any sort of anarchist revival, "The most convincing argument would seek to establish a conceptual link between anarchism and ecological values."[46]

Unlike strict anarchists, however, radical environmentalists could never entirely divorce themselves from the state. Earth First! strategy often revealed the limits of grassroots civil disobedience, the necessity of federal authority, and the important role of even Turnage's Wilderness Society. A few months after Gros Ventre, Earth First! blockaded an illegal road to a drilling site jury-rigged by Yates Petroleum in New Mexico's Salt Creek

Wilderness. With the well two-thirds complete and the protest attracting national attention, a federal judge issued a restraining order forcing Yates to halt its operations.[47] Environmentalists declared victory. "We must have bodies, willing to take the time and energy to watch developers, oil companies, utilities, etc." Kathy McCoy urged after her participation in the Salt Creek blockade, emphasizing the inadequacy of statutory protections. "Without watchdogs, they'll take it all."[48]

At first the Salt Creek blockade stood as an example of bureaucratic failure and the importance of direct action. The oil company had received mixed legal signals; it was granted permission to drill from the State of New Mexico, which owned the subsurface mineral rights, but not from the U.S. Fish & Wildlife Service, which managed the surface. The Department of the Interior informed Yates that despite a temporary congressional ban on drilling in wilderness, it had "no legal objection" to the drill site, but then Fish & Wildlife charged the company with trespassing. Administrative ambiguity left room for creative interpretation. With just hours remaining on its lease, Yates decided that action meant more than regulation and started drilling. Earth First! agreed and stood in the way of Yates drill crews traveling over the illegal road.

What was momentarily a heroic demonstration of civil disobedience soon became an illustration of its limited ambit. Six weeks after the blockade, the government granted Yates a drilling permit. Congress had overturned its own temporary ban, and the Department of the Interior used the opportunity to open up Salt Creek to oil exploration. In his post-mortem on Salt Creek and its disappointing results, Foreman simultaneously criticized and made the case for mainstream environmental organizations: despite an apparent legal victory, Salt Creek suffered the drill "because the rest of the conservation groups did little." Earth First!, Foreman explained, "is not the environmental movement. We are only a part of it. We can only fill a few roles." The Sierra Club, Wilderness Society, and National Audubon Society were necessary and absent, Foreman implied, their importance revealed by their failure.[49]

From its inception Earth First! placed itself sometimes far outside of industrial civilization and liberal democratic thought and sometimes on the fringe of conventional reform. Those two positions were not always mutually exclusive; a narrow ridge connected them, and radicals often walked it. In the mid-1980s the ongoing RARE II fight shifted from a national legal battle over roadless areas to state-by-state wilderness bills. Mainstream groups like the Wilderness Society and the Sierra Club led this strategy, calculating that if they began with West Coast states where the timber industry sought legal clarity on what it could log—and so where environmentalists had more leverage—they could set the terms for future bills and avoid any sweeping release of public lands to industry. Earth First! saw the state-by-state bills as a "lack of vision, courage, and leadership" that would lead to weak initial proposals made even weaker through negotiation. "The forces of industrial tyranny, of humanistic arrogance, sit tall in the saddle," Foreman wrote.[50]

To fight industrial tyranny and human arrogance, Earth First! used a "new weapon": administrative appeals. Earth First! had always found mainstream environmentalists' unwillingness to file suit against RARE II itself one of the great sins of late twentieth-century conservation, one that California Resources Secretary Huey Johnson partially atoned for with *California v. Block*. On Bald Mountain, Earth First! strengthened the case for attacking the Forest Service in court with its own suit, *Earth First! v. Block*, based on Johnson's precedent. A national lawsuit over RARE II would be prohibitively expensive and time-consuming, so Earth First! advocated shelving all wilderness bills until after the 1984 elections and hoping for a more favorable political geography.[51] Administrative appeals drew from the legal authority of *California v. Block* and *Earth First! v. Block*, both of which effectively ruled development activities on RARE II lands in violation of the National Environmental Policy Act. The *Earth First! Journal* published a sample appeals form for readers to file after any announcement of timber sales or development projects in de facto wilderness. "Done at the right time," Earth First! advised in one of the group's milder declarations, "a little piece of paper can temporarily stop the destruction of your roadless area more effectively than anything else."[52]

Using a form that began "Pursuant to 36 C.F.R. §211.18 . . ." as a weapon against modern civilization confirmed Schmookler's description of government as an inescapable paradox. Radicals pointed to the limits of institutional reform only when they weren't busy engaging in it. When Foreman proposed a strategy for a 1980s environmental movement, he both acknowledged and questioned the effectiveness of traditional methods: "The Sierra Club and Wilderness Society lobbyists should keep on wearing their three-piece suits or high heels while playing the game but they should ask for a little more," he wrote. Earth First!, meanwhile, should keep "questioning the very philosophical basis of Western Civilization, and engaging in non-violent direct action to stop the industrial beast whenever necessary"; and anonymous supporters, of their own volition, should continue "spiking trees, closing roads, trashing bulldozers, pulling stakes and what-have-you when the methods of the rest of us fail."[53] Earth First! shifted nimbly between conventional methods and anarchist-inspired resistance, often during the same campaign. Radicals understood and appreciated the federal government's role as steward of the public lands, but they also assumed the state would always fall short of its responsibilities. Federal protections were necessary but never sufficient, and where they flagged, Earth First! picked up the baton.

CAPITALISM AND ENVIRONMENTALISM

In American politics, to be skeptical of public agencies is, generally, to be confident about private enterprise. The Reagan administration argued that federal oversight could be replaced by market incentives and that private property yielded more benefits than did public lands. In 1982 the administration, encouraged by market fundamentalists on the president's Council of Economic Advisors, tried to sell off tens of millions of acres of public land through long-term leases or outright sales. Environmentalists, meanwhile, put even less faith in the market than they did in the government. The Wilderness Society's Bill Turnage called the administration's plan to privatize federal land "pirating the public treasure for private benefit."[54] Environmental opposition to unfettered capitalism was far from absolute, and ideological opposition to environmentalism was never a premise of market fundamentalism, but for the most part environmentalists and capitalists lined up against each other. Paradoxically, it was at their most philosophically uncompromising that they met and that the market seemed to offer environmental protections where the state did not.

An expanding economy divided environmentalists from capitalists. In 1982 an internal Republican Party committee warned colleagues of "the threat that environmental groups represent to natural resource development and economic growth." The committee's report lumped mainstream groups like the Sierra Club, Wilderness Society, National Audubon Society, and Natural Resources Defense Council with "a new revolutionary stream in the environmental movement referred to as 'deep ecology.' "[55] Earth First!, always sensitive to being unfairly associated with environmental moderates, complained that "the Republicans are a little dull when it comes to identifying the environmental 'extremists' they are so actively trying to discredit."[56] But despite the philosophical differences between Earth First! and the Sierra Club, a broad view of American politics would put them side by side on the question of economic growth. The Club was, according to Michael Cohen, inherently "in conflict with the major corporate interests of modern America."[57] In 1971 Club president Philip Berry spoke to the Atomic Industrial Forum about "an end to growth as we have too much known it—growth at the expense of the environment and associated human values."[58]

The opposition of environmentalism and big business after Earth Day was, however, as much a product of industry's attacks on environmentalists as the reverse. At Harpers Ferry in 1980, environmental leaders discussed not just the failures of government but the success of those who worked to undermine governmental regulation. Participants spoke at length about an invigorated effort by industry to weaken federal oversight. This same concern came up at a Conservation Foundation-sponsored meeting of environmental leaders in Estes Park, Colorado three months later, as well as in plans for a series of regional conferences that major environmental groups held in 1981 and 1982. "The corporations, after being caught off guard and set back by us in the early 1970s, seem to have reasserted themselves in their former control of the power structure in the government," Brock Evans reported. "In spite of all the good laws we passed, more and more agencies simply refuse to act to enforce what is there unless they are in turn forced by us, because of this rising counter pressure."[59]

Long before environmentalists had to contend with the Reagan administration's attacks on regulation, they clashed with the regulated industries themselves. Even as environmental organizations celebrated Earth Day and strengthened their hand in Washington, D.C., they heard rumblings of opposition. "The backlash is here," San Francisco's *Clear Creek* reported in 1972.[60] That same year Michael McCloskey talked to the Sierra Club's board about "weathering the full force of industry's counterattack."[61] The Wilderness Society had already warned its members of a "counterrevolution against the environmental movement," offering as evidence a speech that Thomas Shepard, Jr., publisher of *LOOK* magazine, gave to the annual meeting of the Soap and Detergent Association. In its "attempts to destroy our free enterprise system," Shepard said, the environmental movement lied about ecological harms and ignored economic benefits. "To protect some birds, they would deprive mankind of food," he complained. "To keep fish healthy, they would allow human beings to become sick." This "cockeyed set of priorities" was one few Americans would countenance. "So let's start fighting back!"[62]

"Fighting back" involved a combination of diluting and challenging environmental efforts. Industry-sponsored public relations campaigns and public service announcements shifted blame from corporations to consumers by focusing on individual behavior rather than industrial processes. People littered, left lights on, and wasted gasoline, while corporations simply and disinterestedly provided the basic elements of a modern lifestyle. In some cases, utilities advertised electricity as fueling antipollution technologies. Power plants were at once the source of and the solution to the pollution problem. Friend of the Sierra Club Jerry Mander called this doublespeak "eco-pornography."[63] At the same time, those industries most directly saddled with environmental regulation fought back by pushing a cost-benefit language that assumed a zero-sum relationship between economic health and environmental oversight. Such reasoning took root in the stagnant economy of the 1970s. "How can a recession-hit town eject polluting plants at the expense of vitally needed jobs?" *Time* asked.[64]

So successful was this rhetorical attack that the Nixon administration, to address industry concerns about the administration's own National Environmental Policy Act, created a National Industrial Pollution Control Council composed mainly of corporate executives in order to afford industry a voice in the regulatory process. That voice spoke of economic costs, and it led to a "Quality of Life Review" program that evaluated consumer and environmental regulations against potential harm to the private sector. The review process lasted through the Ford administration and served mainly to scrutinize the Environmental Protection Agency. Several weeks before Reagan took office the *New York Times* was already reporting on an "anti-regulatory atmosphere" in New Jersey, where environmentalists "suffered setbacks from business interests on several fronts," including the EPA's decision not to enforce fees on companies dumping sewage in the Atlantic, and Congress's weakening of the Carter administration's "superfund" toxic cleanup act.[65] By then, industry groups simply outspent environmental organizations. "When you talk about environmentalists being on the run," a Carter administration official told the *Los Angeles Times*, "you have to consider that they are being chased by a very well organized, very well financed lobby of some of the biggest corporate names in the country."[66]

The corporate backlash against environmentalism was self-serving, but it was also an expression of a particular philosophy. What environmentalists failed to understand, Thomas Shepard told the Soap and Detergent Association, was that "man must settle for less than perfection, for less than zero risk, if he is to flourish." Modern society, Norman Podhoretz explained in *Commentary*, echoing Shepard's sentiment, involved "a continuing series of bargains—with nature, with the past, with the future—and to make a good life is to make the soundest and fairest bargains we can." Driving these bargains and these balances between risk and flourishing was what Shepard called "progress" and Podhoretz called "restless growth."[67] Material comfort and an expanding economy remained imperative, and were best achieved through market forces made manifest in the choices of consumers and the decisions of chief executives. Government regulation, when it contravened those forces, frustrated modern society's ordered development.

Faith in the market and concern for the nonhuman world were not mutually exclusive, some economists said. No group thought harder about the philosophical relationship between markets and the environment than did a small school of economists who called themselves "free market environmentalists." For most interested parties, the authority of the market moved in and out of environmental debates like a summer storm, dramatic but short-lived. For free-market environmentalists, that authority was a permanent feature of the landscape. Sagebrush rebels and their environmental adversaries summoned market incentives when it was convenient—sagebrushers in protesting what they considered government takings of their property, and environmentalists in accusing ranchers of living off the public dole. Free-market environmentalists' commitment to private property and free enterprise, on the other hand, was doctrinaire and consistent. Free-market environmentalists scoffed at ranchers' subsidized grazing permits just as readily as they complained about publicly funded national parks and forests. Applying libertarian ideas to natural resources, they argued that property owners' economic interests in their investments made them the best conservationists of all: forest owners would always be more concerned with conserving trees and wildlife than would forest visitors and forest managers.

The sagebrush rebellion sprang from a growing partisan divide as Westerners increasingly identified with the Republican Party for a variety of cultural, ideological, and self-interested reasons. Free-market environmentalism emerged out of an intellectual movement closer to the philosophical heart of the New Right. As historian Brian Drake has explained, midcentury academic debates about "externalities"—direct costs of doing business, shouldered by those not receiving direct benefits—produced on the one hand environmental critiques of capitalism by economists like Herman Daly and on the other hand capitalist critiques of environmentalism by neoclassical economists. Libertarians in particular called on the market to solve any and all environmental problems and to illustrate the folly of public land management, claiming that private property regimes offered the best protection for natural resources and national parks. Too many environmental problems, the libertarian magazine *Reason* argued, arose because environmentalists "ignored the way that free markets can cope with shortages by rationing out dwindling supplies and making it profitable to develop substitutes." The New Right's belief in the efficiency and effectiveness of markets over governments applied to the nonhuman world as much as to anything else. "It is the *absence* of the profit system and private property," *Libertarian Review* insisted, "not their *existence*, which causes environmental problems."[68]

Montana State economist John Baden gave institutional form to free-market environmentalism by founding a series of think tanks, beginning with the Center for Political Economy and Natural Resources in the late 1970s and the Political Economy Research Center (PERC—later renamed the Property and Environment Research Center) in 1980. A steady flow of papers and proposals yielded a modest political response when the Reagan administration tried, unsuccessfully, to privatize public lands in 1982. Baden continued to develop his ideas, founding the Foundation for Research on Economics and the Environment in 1985. Never considered part of the recognized environmental movement, free-market environmentalists' views could occasionally accord with those who were. Garrett Hardin's classic essay "The Tragedy of the Commons," one of the canonical examples of 1970s crisis environmentalism, questioned the wisdom of informally shared resources and pointed, ambiguously, toward either greater state control or else privatization. Crisis environmentalists gravitated toward the first choice, but Hardin and Baden gave room to both possibilities in a co-edited volume called *Managing the Commons*. In the book's preface, Hardin and Baden questioned "obsolete sanctions" on the one hand and "independence of individual action" on the other. Aldo Leopold, they pointed out, said that people treated their own property carelessly. Aristotle, they suggested, said the opposite: "What is common to the greatest number gets the least amount of care," Aristotle wrote in *Politics*. "Men pay most attention to what is their own: they care less for what is common."[69]

PRIVATE PROPERTY, PUBLIC LANDS

Baden and his colleagues tried to bring their message of market-based environmentalism to policymakers in state capitals and in Washington, D.C., but it was in the forests and especially on the grasslands of the West that their ideas gained purchase. Environmentalists, increasingly disappointed by public agencies and always skeptical of private industry, at times had to lean toward one or the other. Traditionally, they chose government. On the Great Plains, however, radical environmentalists experimented with the power of the market. Dispirited by the BLM's middling record of defending Western grasslands, Earth First! began to argue that economic competition could achieve what federal agencies could not. Committed to ecocentric rather than to progressive principles, radicals made common cause with market fundamentalists and even, at moments, with the Reagan administration. Earth First!'s rangeland campaigns suggested the group's ideological flexibility. Rangeland activism also suggested how radical environmentalists viewed the natural world in broader and more fluid terms than their critics allowed. Although remote wilderness remained Earth First!'s primary concern, radicals also dedicated themselves to the defense of the working landscapes of the American West.

Whatever line generally existed between private property and public land, between market forces and federal subsidies, disappeared from view behind the rolling hills of the Western range. Although the sagebrush rebellion had concerned grazing permits on public lands, in the rebels' own eyes it was a fight for private property. Grazing permits were tied to private property, and because ranchers factored the permits into the value of their base property, they interpreted an increase in permit fees as a taking without just compensation. Raising fees would lower the value of ranchers' land and so violate their property rights. Adjusting the cost of grazing fees on public lands to fair market value amounted to the seizure of private property by the federal government.

Despite the ambiguities of ownership, the rhetoric remained clear. In the same way that large industries tried to convince Americans that economic well-being was as much a common good as environmental well-being, Western resource users argued that private property was a public interest, and they questioned whether environmentalists were in fact champions of the commonweal. The New Mexico Farm and Livestock Bureau urged ranchers to support the sagebrush rebellion-aligned Mountain States Legal Foundation in its lawsuits against federal land management agencies, warning members of the odds stacked against them. "Over one hundred so-called 'public interest' law centers have been created in order to represent the 'public' in our country's Judicial System," the Bureau explained. Environmental groups, in particular, had "completely ignored private property and individual rights."[70]

In fact, Western livestock was one of the few issues for which environmentalists raised the importance of private property and free enterprise (although not individual rights) as a counterweight against compromised government agencies. When arguing about ranching, everyone became a free-market environmentalist. "We are increasingly convinced that both the environmental and the economic costs of bureaucratic management of natural resources are excessively and unnecessarily high," Baden and PERC co-founder Richard Stroup wrote in 1981. "These social costs are generated by perverse institutional structures that give authority to those who do not bear responsibility for the consequences of their actions."[71] The below-market cost of grazing on the public domain, environmentalists Denzel and Nancy Ferguson wrote two years later, "invites overgrazing and makes profitable the grazing of degraded public lands that could not support grazing in a free-market economy."[72] Baden and Stroup pointed their fingers at federal managers and the Fergusons pointed at ranchers, but all appealed to the logic of the market as a standard against which to judge public programs.

Protecting grasslands from ranching was one of the least glamorous conservation causes of the 1980s but, according to Earth First!'s Don Schwarzenegger, one of the most urgent, "only eclipsed by the threat of a nuclear winter."[73] Denzel and Nancy Ferguson agreed: "Public resources are seldom managed in the public's interest," they wrote in the *Earth First! Journal* in 1984, "and the dismal results are nowhere more evident than in the use of public lands by private stockmen." Cattle ran roughshod over the Western landscape because the ranchers that owned them also owned the agencies managing the public domain. "The industry has held the public land management agencies hostage" the Fergusons explained, "and has dispensed intolerable abuses upon loyal and dedicated federal agencies." In the early 1970s the Fergusons found extensive cattle damage to Oregon's Malheur National Wildlife Refuge, where they managed a field station. They received death threats when they tried to limit grazing at Malheur. That angry response piqued the Fergusons' interest and a decade later they published *Sacred Cows at The Public Trough*, an exposé of how ranching destroyed Western public lands for little obvious benefit.[75] "For any EF!er not to read it is a dereliction," Schwarzenegger advised.[76]

Environmentalists had long been derelict in the attention they paid to the Western range, and Earth First! believed that at the heart of that myopia were anthropocentric values. People could much more easily cherish lush national forests and majestic national parks for aesthetic enjoyment than they could sparse grasslands. Any visitor knew a logged forest when they saw one, the Fergusons pointed out, while few noticed overgrazed grasslands, "yet the end results may be the same."[77] Lynn Jacobs, Earth First!'s grazing task force coordinator, warned against focusing on faraway places to the neglect of "more level, fertile, and well-watered lands . . . where species diversity and wildlife numbers are at their greatest."[78] Although some scholars have accused radical environmentalists of fetishizing spectacular and remote areas, an ecocentric view could easily lead to greater appreciation of more aesthetically mundane landscapes. Earth First!'s commitment to rangelands was a measure of its commitment to an ecological rather than a romantic perspective.

From an ecological perspective ranching presented a series of dire threats to the nation's grasslands. According to the Fergusons, cattle trampled soil and destroyed root systems, contributing to desertification; they clustered in riparian zones, removing vegetation, depositing excrement, and eroding streamsides that provided shaded habitat for fish; they destroyed nesting sites for migratory birds; and they triggered a federal predator control program that intentionally wreaked havoc on populations of coyote, bobcat, mountain lion, and wolf, and unintentionally on those of badger, beaver, fox, raccoon, deer, rabbit, and porcupine. "Suffice it to say" Foreman wrote in agreement, "that the livestock industry has probably done more ecological damage to the western United States than any other single agent."[79]

Addressing this ecological damage meant taking on the ranching industry, and environmentalists waged this fight on two fronts. The first was cultural. The luster of the ranching industry shimmered brightly, and far beyond the plains. "Like other new arrivals in the West," Edward Abbey admitted to a crowd at the University of Montana in 1985, "I could imagine nothing more romantic than becoming a cowboy."[80] Dave Foreman left a brief career as a horseshoer to join the Wilderness Society with his first wife, Debbie Sease. "Our dream, though," he remembered, "was to be cowboys."[81] Challenging the heroic cowboy West was a political risk. The Sierra Club's Brock Evans advised his colleagues against "attacks on either states or states' rights or upon ranchers" when taking on sagebrush rebels, judging those targets "too much a part of the American mythology."[82]

To the Fergusons, reverence for ranching was exactly the problem and had to be revealed as such. "Seldom in history have so many been so thoroughly brainwashed by so few," they wrote of the cowboy myth.[83] Venerated as an example of Western hardihood and individualism, the cowboy was, Abbey finally concluded, "a hired hand. A farm boy in leather britches and a comical hat."[84] The barbed wire fences that historian Walter Prescott Webb once celebrated as an innovation essential to wresting a living from a harsh environment were, for the Fergusons, "a truly alarming cause of wildlife mortality" that tangled pronghorn antelope, bighorn sheep, and moose calves in fatal snares.[85] Ranching destroyed far more than it returned. Environmentalists rattled off the numbers: cattle grazing on public lands produced only 3 percent of the nation's beef supply, cost the treasury twice what it contributed, and disproportionately benefited ranchers with large herds and landholdings. Ranchers were less risk-taking entrepreneurs building a market economy than mooches draining public funds to wreck public lands. "The proud, independent rancher as the paragon of the free enterprise system?" Foreman asked. "Forget it, he's a welfare bum."[86]

The second front, related to the first, was economic. The most vulnerable point in the Western ranching industry's political armor was the below-market grazing fees on BLM land that amounted to public subsidies. In the late 1960s several federal agencies determined that fair market value was five times BLM rates, and in the 1980s the BLM and Forest Service reviewed their fee formulas. Simply raising the rates could drive ranching off public lands, which is exactly what Earth First! wanted. Standard direct-action tactics would be little help in this fight. "Laying down in front of a herd of cows," Schwarzenegger advised, "is just a good way to 'git cow shit on ya.' "[87] Instead, Earth First!ers chose to forego blockades and ally themselves with market forces, becoming fierce advocates of either a competitive bidding process that would help establish a market-based price or, better yet, an open bidding process that would allow environmentalists to bid against ranchers and let the market determine best uses.

"Competitive bidding is the basis of a free-market economy, is democratic, and is standard practice in most federal operations," the Fergusons wrote.[88] In this range war, environmentalists embraced the idea, if only temporarily, that compromised federal agencies managed the public domain for private interests while private enterprise furthered the public interest by conserving resources. Earth First! became a grudging cheerleader for David Stockman, the director of Reagan's Office of Management and Budget, who was willing to wave his cost-cutting axe dangerously close to several political third rails. While in most arenas environmentalists aggressively fought the Reagan administration's budget-cutting and deregulatory approach to government, when it came to ranching on public lands, Schwarzenegger suggested, "the consistent application of 'Reaganomics' could just conceivably bring about the demise of that industry."[89]

Even mainstream environmental groups began to discern the limits of their partnership with the federal government in the 1980s, but radical groups like Earth First! more readily explored other means of staving off industrial development, even if that meant fighting occasional allies and aligning with frequent enemies. Never partisan and rarely ideological other than in its commitment to ecocentrism, Earth First! could find common cause with some conservatives. Radicals' deep skepticism of capitalism as a handmaiden of industrial society prevented any enduring affiliation with the New Right, but frustration with government could make market-based solutions more appealing. In the absence of federal management, markets offered an alternative source of order.

EARTH FIRST! VS. THE FOREST SERVICE

While radical environmentalists chastised the BLM, they saved the lion's share of their anger for the United States Forest Service. Whether because it was responsible for RARE II, or because the clear cuts it sanctioned were such an obvious scar on the land, or because it had a longer and more storied history to betray than any other land management agency, the Forest Service earned as much of Earth First!'s opprobrium as did any extractive industry. "The Forest Service has become a criminal and immoral agency on such a widespread basis," Montana Earth First!er Randall Gloege said, "that any short term victories in the absence of total reformation will likely be temporary, at best."[90]

Radical environmentalists' fury over Forest Service policy was consistent with their view of James Watt as symptom rather than cause. Unlike the BLM, Park Service, and Fish & Wildlife Service, the Forest Service fell under the jurisdiction of the Department of Agriculture and so outside of Watt's purview. And yet, Earth First! argued, the Forest Service epitomized an ethos of reckless industrial growth better than any other federal resource agency. "Although some conservationists believe the Forest Service road building binge to be largely the result of a massive Reagan Administration conspiracy," Wolke wrote, "the fact is that it is actually the result of three quarters of a century's bureaucratic growth," and "an almost religious belief in the anthropocentric idea of 'multiple use.' " Wolke—whose disgust with the Forest Service exceeded that of any five Earth First!ers combined—saw the agency as little more than a means of harvesting natural resources to feed an ever-expanding economy. Environmentalists would have to rede-fine the agency's reason for existence. Short of that, Wolke said, "we're merely pissin' in the wind."[91]

An ethos of industrial growth began with roads, as David Brower rec-ognized in the mid-twentieth century when the Tioga Road fight put him on the path to militancy. Any possibility for development in wilderness started with a road, and a road multiplied such possibilities exponentially. The "road building binge" that Wolke wrote about was a Forest Service plan for 75,000 miles of roads through RARE II roadless areas by the end of the century, roads that would disqualify those areas from wilderness des-ignation. Earth First! regularly called Forest Service employees "Freddies," a derogatory term borrowed from rural Westerners' disdain for all federal agents, but in this case revelations about a massive roadbuilding program came from the Freddies themselves. An anonymous group of foresters known as "Deep Root" warned major media about the Forest Service's pronounced bias toward logging and about the roads that would result. "There's absolutely no question that the reason for all these roads in virgin areas is to make sure the land can never be included in a wilderness," one Deep Root forester from Montana told the *Washington Post*.[92]

The Forest Service's penchant for fragmenting wildlife habitat by build-ing roads into de facto wilderness kept the agency at the top of Earth First!'s enemies list throughout the 1980s. Earth First!ers fought Forest Service logging roads, timber sales, and mineral leases in Oregon's Willamette and Siskiyou Forests, California's Stanislaus and Los Padres Forests, Wyoming's

Bridger-Teton Forest, Montana's Gallatin Forest, Washington's Mount Baker-Snoqualmie Forest, Texas's Sam Houston Forest, and Utah's Dixie Forest, among others. Despite all of these actions and despite mainstream groups like the Sierra Club pushing hard for a reduction in the Forest Service's roadbuilding budget, in late 1986 Congress allocated $229 million for forest roads—$50 million more than the agency itself had requested. Wolke, recently released from several months in prison for pulling up survey stakes on a proposed road in the Bridger-Teton Forest, was livid. "The deeper one delves into the seething caldron of bureaucratic idiocy," he wrote, "the more one is repelled by the stink of the iniquitous. As I continue to learn about the US Forest Service and its roadbuilding mania I am forced to conclude that the major missing ingredient in the battle against the vile agency is *widespread physical resistance.*"[93]

A little over a year later, on John Muir's 150th birthday, Earth First! put Wolke's suggestion into practice. Coordinated by Earth First! stalwart Karen Pickett, the "National Day of Outrage" against the Forest Service on April 21, 1988 consisted of close to one hundred protests from California to New England. Earth First! activists and their friends held rallies outside of Forest Service facilities in big cities and tiny towns. Earth First!er David Barron, dressed as Smokey Bear, offered his resignation to a San Francisco regional office along with 150 other protesters. The Forest Service hid sensitive equipment at some offices, mobilized the Federal Protective Service at others, and in Washington, D.C. put the Department of Agriculture's headquarters on heightened alert.[94]

Direct action was a way to oppose the Forest Service but not necessarily to remake it. That required addressing the presumed shortcomings of public agencies. "The Forest Service is the epitome of all that is wrong with bureaucracy, from the Bureau of Reclamation to the Kremlin," Wolke said.[95] W. Robert Brothers (also known as "Bobcat") called the agency an "entrenched bureaucracy infected with top-level corruption."[96] Requirements for working in the Forest Service, an Earth First!er named "Skoal Vengeance" argued, "should first include a love for the outdoors, and should not include a lust for advancement in a bureaucracy."[97] Earth First!'s view of the Forest Service was not unlike that of free-market environmentalists'. John Baden and Richard Stroup described federal resource agencies as incentivized by little more than protecting individual jobs and agency funding, operating with a lack of accountability in the form of either profits or votes and so with enormous latitude for self-interested decision-making.

Free-market environmentalists prescribed market-based incentives as a cure for bureaucratic inertia, and radical environmentalists seriously considered this view. Wolke and Brothers dismissed the many "obvious anthropocentric analyses" at a forest symposium that featured Stroup and was put on by the forestry consulting firm Cascade Holistic Economic Consultants (CHEC); but Earth First! listened closely to Randal O'Toole, director of CHEC, persistent critic of the Forest Service, and according to Wolke, "a brilliant forest economist."[98] Partial to technical arguments and allergic to sentimental ones, O'Toole spoke a different language than many environmentalists. But when he attacked the Forest Service—as he did in the *Earth First! Journal* and at a Round River Rendezvous—everyone listened carefully. "If the upper echelons of the Forest Service had any pride remaining," Foreman said, "they would be crushed by the detailed criticism their plans receive at the hands of forest economist Randal O'Toole."[99]

The gist of O'Toole's critique of Forest Service timber sales resembled environmentalists' complaints about BLM grazing permits: the sales made little sense economically and a great deal of sense bureaucratically. Although the Forest Service's timber program made money in the aggregate, many individual timber sales amounted to giveaways. The program profited from the cash register forests of the Pacific Northwest and the South while losing money nearly everywhere else. The Wilderness Society made the same argument. "These roads are being built to harvest timber in low-productivity, high-cost areas at a tremendous loss to the taxpayer," the Society's chairman, Gaylord Nelson, said of the Forest Service's massive roadbuilding program.[100] But O'Toole's analysis went further. He argued that economic mismanagement sprang from "budget maximization"—the tendency of bureaucratic agencies to prioritize their own budgets above all other concerns. Because timber programs cost more than recreation and even grazing, because the Forest Service kept more money from timber receipts than any other activity, and because timber production yielded the greatest political returns for those who held the agency's purse strings, "multiple use" meant timber sales first, second, and third. The solution, O'Toole advised, was "marketization": decentralizing the agency, eliminating its congressional appropriations, and allowing forest managers to charge market rates for all resources from timber sales to camping permits.[101]

Earth First!ers tended to agree with O'Toole's criticisms emphatically and with his proposals sporadically. Brothers found environmentalists' discomfort with market incentives antiquated, insisting that because of bureaucratic cost-ineffectiveness, "dollar values have now come over to the side of forest ecology, wilderness and watershed protection."[102] Wolke remained only partially convinced. He supported much of O'Toole's plan but regretted that it was "based on economic, not intrinsic, values" and "would not promote biocentric management in areas where logging really is economically sound."[103]

In fact, environmentalists were gradually winning the fight over forest reform in the 1980s, too gradually for their own tastes and too imperceptibly for many to appreciate. Even more than the BLM, the Forest Service slowly reined in its emphasis on industrial production. The aesthetic appreciation of forests advanced by groups like the Sierra Club, the increasing incidence of and anger over clear cutting, and Nixon-era environmental laws all served as leverage for the application of new ecological ideas about forest management in the late-twentieth century. Scientists emphasized the need for foresters to consider biological and structural diversity, wildlife habitat, and old growth in addition to the maximum sustainable yield of timber. As local and national environmental organizations used ecological insights to criticize federal forest management, foresters entered into a period of soul-searching and forestry schools trained a new generation of ecologically-minded managers. Pressure from outside and inside the Forest Service prompted whistleblowers like Deep Root, groups like Forest Service Employees for Environmental Ethics, and a 1989 forest supervisors conference in Tucson at which supervisors expressed dismay at the agency's stubborn focus on timber.[104]

Still, Earth First! and O'Toole were not wrong in their deprecations against bureaucratic inertia. The transformation of a fixed agency like the Forest Service took decades, the persistent agitation of several organized and vocal stakeholders, and most importantly a coherent set of ideas that could compete with the internal logic already in place. Here environmentalists and economists shared a distrust in public agencies that was the flip side of a greater faith in some larger order. "Marketization" fell several steps behind the privatization pushed by free-market environmentalists, but it rested on the same basic premise as privatization and ecocentric management: reform had to come from without. Politicians, bureaucrats, and their various constituencies often made poor decisions about natural resources and would make similarly poor decisions about structuring any agency in which they remained invested. Remaking the Forest Service depended on some countervailing force—for free-market environmentalists a system of economic incentives, and for radical environmentalists a system of ecological imperatives. In both cases, redemption lay in an order beyond that of central planners and political institutions.

"Indeed," the writer and environmentalist Michael Pollan observes, "the wilderness ethic and laissez-faire economics, antithetical as they might at first appear, are really mirror images of one another."[105] O'Toole agreed: "Although these two groups appear to represent polar extremes," he wrote of PERC and Earth First!, "in fact there are many similarities between them." Both groups shunned interest-group politics, he explained, and both championed decentralization. And although PERC opposed public lands and Earth First! distrusted capitalism, "markets are the key to reforming public land management," O'Toole said, "because they most clearly resemble a natural ecosystem."[106] The free-market environmentalist M. Bruce Johnson liked to point out that the study of interconnectedness in ecology reflected similar interests in economics. "General equilibrium models are a formal way of saying that 'everything depends on everything else,' " he said. Given the similarities, "one wonders why a partnership between the two was not formed in the natural course of events."[107] Lack of faith in government as an expression of a shared ethic led to a conceptual instability that required, for ballast, some larger sense of order, whether of nature or of markets.

The odd correspondence between laissez-faire economic thought and environmentalism arose from a mutual distrust of liberal individualism. Libertarianism is often understood as a philosophy based on reason, individual freedom, and the realization of human potential, but it can just as easily be understood as rooted in the limits of reason and the folly of individuals. This streak of doubt within libertarianism is primarily the legacy of the Austrian School of Economics, whose main exponents—including Ludwig von Mises but in particular Friedrich Hayek and Murray Rothbard—found in the free market an order that countered the limitations of human reason. Hayek was a libertarian not because he had complete faith in individual human freedom, but because he didn't. The point of rules, for Hayek, was to make up for the fact that people did not know enough to make the right decisions all of the time, and the utility of any set of rules was only as sound as the limited knowledge of its authors. The state, therefore, could never regulate deliberately what the market could regulate organically. Hayek called this organic regulation "spontaneous order," and although he believed it arose from the aggregate of choices made by free individuals acting in their own interests, he speculated, as John Gray explains, that it might be found "not only in the population biology of animal species, but in the formation of crystals and even galaxies."[108]

This unease with human design and acceptance of an order beyond human estimation could bring together environmentalism and libertarianism philosophically, despite their profound differences politically. Although they disagreed on nearly all the specifics, both radical and free-market environmentalists subscribed to an order beyond the confines of the human imagination. Ric Bailey gestured toward such an order when he represented Earth First! at a hearing on wilderness held by Oregon's Senator Mark Hatfield and said, "There is more to the scheme of life than the devices of man."[109] Dave Foreman made a similar point by asking, "What right does a man with a life span of seventy years have to destroy a two thousand year old redwood to make picnic tables?"[110] Stephanie Mills reflected more explicitly on human limits after participating in the 1985 Round River Rendezvous, writing, "Some say we are trapped in the solipsism of human consciousness and that there are no absolutes save those we choose. Yet the evidence of ecological destruction that mounts all around us suggests that we may not have infinite latitude for self-definition after all; that, in Paul Ehrlich's mordant phrase, 'Nature bats last.'"[111] Nancy Newhall summarized this sense of order most succinctly in a justification for wilderness that David Brower frequently repeated: "The wilderness holds answers to more questions than we yet know how to ask."[112]

CONCLUSION

Earth First! was never unaware of the complicated and at times contradictory relationship it had with government, bureaucracy, and democracy. In 1985 Mike Roselle, by then the busy center of Earth First!'s direct-action scene, felt aggrieved by the red tape that he encountered when applying for funds from the Earth First! Foundation and entered into an extended argument with some of the Foundation's staff. "I think such conflict is inherent in the situation where an organization deliberately places itself between governmental bureaucracy and an opposing gang of anarchists," observed LaRue Christie, one of the Foundation's creators, "and then arrogantly proposes to use the benefits available through the former to help the latter."[113]

Radical environmentalists' in betweenness was a source of both tension and advantage. Earth First!ers pilloried the Forest Service, the BLM, and even the Wilderness Act itself at the same time as they treated national forests and statutory wilderness as sacrosanct. They lay down in front of bulldozers when federal laws were a hindrance and filed administrative appeals when those laws were a help. And they argued, at turns, that wilderness was either a national inheritance or something beyond nation, law, and even the human capacity to understand. Radicals could not always explain or reconcile their inconsistencies from one case to the next but they rarely lost track of their ultimate commitment to ecocentric principles, even when those principles butted heads with democracy and the state.

Earth First!'s willingness to challenge the state's authority and competence positioned it, at times, alongside conservatives and their own hostility toward centralized power. Environmental anarchists and free-market libertarians could momentarily put aside their considerable differences before a common enemy like the Forest Service. Both groups believed that there was a larger order that called into question a human-devised state order, and even called into question human reason itself, but the different orders to which the groups appealed—a natural one and an economic one—were finally irreconcilable. "Privitization [sic] is not some flimflam scam hatched by Marlboro men in the sagebrush of Nevada," Foreman warned in 1982. "It is a serious thrust launched by neo-conservative intellectuals and free-market economists."[114]

Radical environmentalists' conflicted views about government were exaggerated versions of those held by mainstream environmentalists. As closely tied to federal agencies as mainstream environmentalism became in the 1970s, there was never any essential bond between the movement and the institutions. Environmentalists criticized land management agencies' bias toward industry on grasslands and in forests while relying on regulatory measures rooted in federal power. As Paul Sabin argues, mainstream environmentalists ran hot and cold according to whether they thought federal agencies effectively represented the public interest.[115] Radical environmentalists shifted their stance in similar fashion. But radicals judged federal policy by a broader set of interests, ranging far beyond the human community.

5

Earth First! Against Itself

"I believe that any movement immune from criticism, especially from internal evaluation and analysis, will become uncreative, stodgy, bureaucratic, and undemocratic," Dave Foreman wrote in 1987 with what would prove to be unintended irony.[1] That year, fault lines within Earth First! became unmistakable, and at the end of the decade they began to rupture. The enthusiasm of Earth First! supporters derived from the power and the clarity of the group's animating idea: that protecting wild nature should take priority over all other concerns. By the late 1980s, that idea shifted from an article of faith to a subject of intense debate. Increasingly, dissident voices within Earth First! informed by anarchism, feminism, and a broad sense of social justice insisted on the importance of taking into account social difference, and highlighted the risks of a strictly ecocentric perspective.

Among the greatest risks of an ecocentric perspective was holism, and in particular the view that human beings and nonhuman nature stood across a growing divide. To understand wild nature as existentially threatened by human presence was to understand the two as mutually exclusive. William Cronon has called this view the "central paradox" of the idea of wilderness, "a dualistic vision in which the human is entirely outside the natural."[2] Radical environmentalists could easily fall into this trap, judging nature pure and humans profane and the two forever at odds. "In this era of humanity's suicidal brutality," an Earth First! supporter from Utah said, "any attempt to love Nature by loving mankind is like jumping off a cliff in order to save one's life. Philanthropists ask us to side with the villain in a worldwide conflict. I'll stick with the only side that has any hope of winning in the end."[3] The notion of environmentalism as a "worldwide conflict" between humans and the natural world remained a persistent undertone in Earth First!'s rhetoric, sometimes veering into misanthropy. Like crisis environmentalists, radical environmentalists of the 1980s too often placed the blame for environmental destruction on an undifferentiated human species, refusing to consider relative culpability and the ways that social justice and environmental protection might inform each other. At its worst, this sort of dualism led radicals to advocate reducing the human population through any means and with little regard for who should be left to die.

Critics of Earth First! tended to assume that radical environmentalists embraced this dualistic view always and without qualification, but as readily as radicals spoke of nature's virtues and humanity's vices when they decried environmental destruction, in their own circles they wrestled with how, as Earth First!er W. J. Lines put it, "humans are both inextricably of, and separate from, nature."[4] Behind the occasional declarations of humanity's fundamental corruption was the more common Earth First! view that humans in the modern, industrial world had fallen away from a close and vital relationship with nonhuman nature. "For over 99 percent of our history," Jamie Sayen of Earth First! and Preserve Appalachian Wilderness wrote in 1989, "we have been a part of the wild."[5] In this sense, radical environmentalists differed only in degree and not in kind from more established environmentalists like the Wilderness Society's Howard Zahniser, who said in 1951, "We are a part of the wildness of the universe. That is our nature"; or the Sierra Club's David Brower, who wrote in 1969, "It may seem strange to link a love of the human condition with the wilderness experience, but the two are only different aspects of the same consciousness."[6] At times radical environmentalists dismissed the human species as a purely destructive force. Much more often they struggled to reconcile industrial society's insatiable appetite with humanity's place in the nonhuman world.

The late 1980s were a period of intense political and intellectual conflict for Earth First! As the group enjoyed its greatest renown and influence, antagonists from within the broad environmental movement pointed to the serious limitations of radical environmentalism's perfunctory consideration of social justice. That critique fractured and then changed Earth First! into a group less exclusively dedicated to ecocentrism. Throughout it all, Earth First! and its critics contended with what Cronon calls "the old dilemma about whether human beings are inside or outside of nature," the same dilemma that runs and shifts through all environmentalism.[7]

EDWARD ABBEY

Edward Abbey novels bookended Earth First!'s tenure as the nation's most controversial environmental group. *The Monkey Wrench Gang*, a story of eco-sabotage throughout the Southwest, gained fame just a few years before a band of disaffected conservationists traveled to the Pinacate Desert and imagined a new, more militant environmental group. A sequel, *Hayduke Lives!*, came out in 1990, the year Earth First! began to reorganize and redefine its message and the year after Abbey himself died. Edward Abbey's life and writing intertwined with Earth First! through direct participation and equally direct inspiration. Looking back on his career with Earth First! soon after he left the group, Dave Foreman described one of the initial goals of its founders as "To inspire others to carry out activities straight from the pages of *The Monkey Wrench Gang*."[8] Abbey's novels delineated a view of the relationship between people and their communities, their governments, and their natural environments. In that view, people stood collectively apart from nature, separated by a line between civilization and wilderness. But as individuals they could cross that line and begin to commune with the wild, and to defend it.

Abbey was not a naturalist or "nature-writer" in any conventional sense. "The only birds I can recognize without hesitation are the turkey vulture, the fried chicken, and the rosy-bottomed skinny-dipper," he wrote. "If a label is required say that I am one who loves unfenced country. *The open range.*" It was not just the absence of taxonomical knowledge that distinguished Abbey from more conventional nature writers but also what was present in his work: attitude, opinion, and an argumentative personality. While others concerned with the natural world tried to step out of their readers' way and offer a quiet and unobstructed view, Abbey always remained within sight and within earshot. He was probably the only environmental hero who could get away with writing about tossing empty beer cans out of the window of a moving vehicle (and, by implication, opening full beer cans in a moving vehicle); contemplating wilderness while blasting across a stream in a pickup truck; and disdaining in equal measure tourists, hippies, and park rangers.[9]

"If Abbey is not a naturalist . . . then just what is the place of the environmental theme in his writing?" Donn Rawlings asked Wilderness Society supporters in 1980.[10] The place of the "environmental theme" was at the very center of Abbey's dispute with the modern world. He wrote about nature to make a point. Abbey could write as floridly as John Muir and as contemplatively as Thoreau, but he usually chose not to. Unlike Muir and Thoreau, Abbey relied on humor in his writing, and more than Muir or even Thoreau, he expressed anger. Abbey's fictional characters, as well as the persona he adopted for his personal essays, spoke bitter and profane words. They had little respect for authority of any kind and were generally looking for a fight. Abbey did not concern himself with subtleties and details; he was an advocate of "big nature"—large, wild spaces, *the open range*—and this gave his writing the sort of clarity that comes from a point of view uncomplicated by any concession to nuance. He enjoyed nature on a scale that allowed for an obvious distinction between the civilized and the wild, and he did not spend time exploring the ways that the human and nonhuman worlds ran together, as did nature writers like Edward Hoagland and Wendell Berry. "As I said to Hoagland: 'It is no longer sufficient to *describe* the world of nature. The point is to *defend* it,' " Abbey wrote in his journal in the late 1970s. "He writes back accusing me of trying to 'bully' him into writing in my manner. Which is true, I was. He should."[11] Abbey saw a clear line between the modern, industrialized world and the wild places about which he wrote, and he patrolled that line without apology or ambivalence.

That clear line meant that Abbey took an interest in wilderness above all else. Wilderness for Abbey, and later for Earth First!, stood as the clearest example of not-human, not-technology, not-civilization. This was not an absolutist view. Abbey understood how complicated and subtle an idea wilderness was, and even that it owed a great deal to the human imagination, but to him that made it no less vital or wild. "The boundary around a wilderness area," he wrote, "may well be an artificial, self-imposed, sophisticated construction, but once inside that line you discover the artificiality beginning to drop away; and the deeper you go, the longer you stay, the more interesting things get."[12]

Abbey first drew his line in the sand between wilderness and civilization in Arches National Monument in southern Utah, where he worked for several scattered seasons over the course of a decade as a ranger with the National Park Service. He described his experiences and his thoughts in *Desert Solitaire*, the book that gained him recognition before *The Monkey Wrench Gang* made him famous. *Desert Solitaire* established a set of ideas, principles, and complaints that reappeared in most of Abbey's writing. "There is a cloud on my horizon," he wrote. "A small dark cloud no bigger than my hand. Its name is Progress." Progress, in the immediate sense, took the form of the development of national parks, with roads, power lines, and designated campgrounds. Behind that specific version of progress, though, were a series of assumptions. The starkest and the most explicit was the unquestioning embrace of industrial development. Subtler and more insidious was the view that Abbey attributed to the Park Service: "that although wilderness is a fine thing, certain compromises and adjustments are necessary in order to meet the ever-expanding demand for outdoor recreation." At the base of that view lay the assumption that national parks should be user-friendly, and that an infrastructure built for cars was friendliest to users. "Is this assumption correct?" Abbey asked. "Perhaps. Does that justify the continued and increasing erosion of the parks? It does not."[13]

The essential points Abbey made in his case against "industrial tourism" were the same that David Brower and those closest to him began to make in the 1940s, and that later inspired Earth First! Those points were that unquestioning support of industrial progress was an untenable position; that those government agencies which claimed to protect natural resources and natural places inevitably compromised their principles; that compromise led to the destruction of nature; and that the most popular views were not necessarily the best. Taken together, those principles led to a single conclusion: if development was wrong, if federal protection was weak, and if only a significant minority understood this, then wilderness could be lost forever, "despite the illusory protection of the Wilderness Preservation Act [sic], unless a great many citizens rear up on their hind legs and make vigorous political gestures demanding implementation of the Act."[14] Passive reliance on democratic processes and public agencies would not protect the wild. Only active efforts by dedicated individuals could slow the advance of industrial progress.

ANARCHISM

Abbey's distrust of federal agencies came as much from personal philosophy as from personal experience. He relied on legal protections for public lands but believed those protections emerged despite rather than because of the normal operations of government. Like many in Earth First!, Abbey was a casual anarchist. Anarchist ideas animated the essays and opinion pieces that populated the *Earth First! Journal* alongside action reports and campaign updates. Earth First!'s principles and beliefs, which justified its tactics, grew mostly out of deep ecology but also out of anarchist thought. Although sometimes obscured from view, anarchism provided a crucial framework for the discussions that nourished radical environmentalism early in the 1980s and for the disputes that fragmented it later in the decade (see figure 5.1).

The most fundamental tenets of anarchism are that human freedom is paramount, that institutionalized authority represses that freedom, and that a society without institutionalized authority—in particular, without government—is both feasible and desirable. Government does not foster social harmony; it stifles it. Social harmony is the natural tendency of people left to order their own communities, and formal government takes that initiative, and that tendency, away from people. "Man is born free," Jean-Jacques Rousseau wrote, "and everywhere he is in chains."[15] As soon as a community cedes its decision-making power to a distant government, even a democratic one, it has resigned its members to being governed as abstractions rather than as complete people. The belief that the authority of

Figure 5.1 The Gadsden Flag, a symbol of antigovernment sentiment, often flew at early Earth First! gatherings as a gesture toward the group's frustration with federal land-management agencies and loose affiliation with anarchism. (*a*) Edward Abbey; (*b*) Dave Foreman. Photos courtesy Dave Foreman.

the government derives from the consent of the governed assumes that such consent is granted by every citizen, every minute, regardless of whether citizens were present at the government's founding. According to anarchists, this belief, and the moral authority that it claims, is a fiction.

Whether radical or not, environmentalists had no inherent interest in championing freedom, decrying authority, and dismantling government—the crisis environmentalists of the 1970s found themselves arguing for the exact opposite, at least in the short term—but many of the corollaries to the central tenets of anarchism overlapped with the ethics of radical environmentalism. Most immediately, anarchism offered a cogent critique of conventional democratic procedures. Anarchists found the principle of majority rule baffling. They believed that reason and experience, not the weight of popular opinion, should determine outcomes. The aim should be overwhelming agreement through direct participation rather than a simple show of hands. For radical environmentalists frustrated with the federal agencies in charge of managing public lands and natural resources, anarchism's insistence on more local and more grassroots forms of control were appealing. Although their views of decision-making and especially of human reason differed considerably, anarchists had long made the same complaints about representative democracy that environmentalists began to make in the 1970s: that it granted authority to far-away bureaucrats, that it remained vulnerable to corruption, and that it tended to satisfy no one.[16]

Because they objected to the rule of the majority and to being directed by any institutionalized authority, anarchists often relied on direct action to achieve their ends. Direct action centered on personal decision-making, not on rules from above, and could encompass anything from violence to civil disobedience to cooperative enterprises. The point, for anarchists (as for environmentalists), was to allow individuals and small groups to advance a political position on their own and through their own methods. Whether a sit-down strike in a factory or a tree-sit in a redwood forest, direct action worked on the basis of individual initiative or group consensus, and it avoided immediate participation in the political system it was meant to disrupt.[17]

The most meaningful and the most complicated overlap between anarchism and radical environmentalism, however, was the notion of a natural order. A great deal of distance stood between anarchist and environmental conceptions of it, but that distance shrank considerably when seen from a height that could take in liberal individualism's deep skepticism of natural order. Liberal thinkers generally saw government as a necessary protection against the perils of a state of nature. Anarchists saw government as an obstacle to people's inherent tendency toward social harmony. Rejecting government without eschewing order, anarchists were left in need of a source of structure outside of human invention, one without the authority and hierarchy that inevitably accompanied religion. Many turned instead to an immanent order that included but did not originate with people. "Society," for anarchists, was a product of nature, of the natural order that people were part of when uninhibited by human institutions. Society predated government, and was corrupted by it. "Underlying the perfectionist view," writes George Crowder, referring to the anarchist faith in the human capacity for reason and morality, "is an assumption of ultimate harmony in the universe."[18]

Anarchists' idealized views of a social order rooted in nature have had them perpetually looking over their shoulders at what has already gone by. Despite the reasonable association of anarchists with revolution and with wiping clean the slate, they have often been fixated on long ago. Anarchists' affinity for a natural order, though, is at once focused on the past and also ahistorical. The anarchist conception of long ago is, George Woodcock writes, "a kind of amalgam of all those societies which have lived—or are supposed to have lived—by co-operation rather than by organized government."[19] And this sort of political nostalgia has lent anarchists a kind of "primitivism," an often romantic affection for communities further from the industrial revolution and seemingly closer to nature. The anarchist call for decentralization and for society on a smaller scale has usually been coupled with a call for simplification in terms of technology, social structure, and politics. Generally, the simpler the society the greater the virtue anarchists have found in it. Looking forward, for anarchists, has always meant looking back.

Environmentalists, too, held the distant past in high regard—if not the explicit past then contemporary cultures that suggested to them historical alternatives to modern society. Abbey took the side of Navajo and Hopi traditionalists against the industrial development of reservation land, at least rhetorically. Foreman enthused to Earth First!ers about a speech by American Indian activist Russell Means at the Black Hills International Survival Gathering in 1980. Means criticized the European intellectual tradition—linear, rational, abstract thought, or what Means called "the despiritualization of the universe"—in terms similar to radical environmentalists' own critique. Rationality, Means said, "is a curse since it can cause humans to forget the natural order of things in ways other creatures do not. A wolf never forgets his or her place in the natural order." Against the European mind, Means offered the wisdom of cultures opposed to industrial civilization. "Mother Earth will retaliate, the whole environment will retaliate, and the abusers will be eliminated. Things come full circle, back to where they started. *That's* revolution. And that's a prophecy of my people, of the Hopi people, and of other correct peoples."[20] This cyclical view, in which a better future means a return to tradition and so to the natural order, is as persistent in environmental thought as it is in anarchist thought. Because of this, radical environmentalists embraced traditional cultures, in theory if not always in practice.

MURRAY BOOKCHIN VS. EARTH FIRST!

In bridging anarchist thought and the more radical strains of the environmental movement, there was no thinker more dedicated than Murray Bookchin. In the late 1960s Bookchin's essay "Ecology and Revolutionary Thought" helped bring ecological issues to the New Left. By the 1980s Bookchin had constructed a complex political philosophy called "social ecology," one of the most ambitious attempts to combine anarchist values with environmental concerns. His distrust of mainstream environmentalism and his fidelity to social equality offered a counterpoint to the more single-minded radicalism of Earth First!, and in the late 1980s he became the chief antagonist of deep ecology in general and of Foreman and Abbey in particular. At the heart of Bookchin's complaint lay the issue of human freedom and the way that, according to him, the absence of any social critique impoverished Earth First!'s views. Bookchin's fight with Earth First! became the main event in a larger "social ecology/deep ecology debate" that made clear how relevant social issues remained in discussions of the environment despite Earth First!'s claims otherwise. Bookchin labored to reconcile anarchism's critique of industrialism and sensitivity to the natural world with its commitment to humanism. He convinced few that he had succeeded, but he convinced many that Earth First!'s refusal to try was in itself a kind of failure.[21]

Bookchin grew up in New York surrounded by radical politics; his parents were Russian immigrants and members of the Industrial Workers of the World. As an adolescent he joined the Communist Party, but disillusioned by Stalinism and the Popular Front, he slowly moved away from communism and toward anarchism. At the same time, Bookchin grew interested in the effects of capitalism on the natural and human environment, writing about chemicals and industrial pollutants under the pseudonym "Lewis Herber." In 1962 he published *Our Synthetic Environment*, a study of the environmental consequences of industrial capitalism. Although well received, *Our Synthetic Environment* was overshadowed six months later by Rachel Carson's less far-reaching but more pointed and eloquent *Silent Spring*. At the end of the decade Bookchin founded Ecology Action East in New York City, inspired by the radical politics of Berkeley's Ecology Action.[22]

For years before and after Earth Day, Bookchin's interest in environmental issues grew as a part of his interest in anarchism and social freedom. In 1982 these various tributaries came together in *The Ecology of Freedom*, his major work. The book's central premise was that the domination of nature by humans was a product of the domination of humans by humans. "Indeed, like it or not," Bookchin said, "nearly every ecological issue is also a social issue." The essential problem, according to Bookchin, was not class structure, or impersonal technology, or unjust laws—although these were all part of the problem—but rather the existence of hierarchy. Systems of hierarchy, he believed, structured the way that people thought about each other, about themselves, and about the natural world. Hierarchy nurtured the complementary assumptions that only through authority by some over others could society function, and only through authority of people over nature could society exist. At the root of modern environmental and social problems was the unequal distribution of power among people and between species.[23]

Human society and the natural world, for Bookchin, were in many ways distinct: people had achieved a degree of separation from wild nature that no other species had. But Bookchin also believed that society and nature were not inherently opposed; whatever opposition existed between the human and the natural worlds emerged from hierarchical thought. Much of *The Ecology of Freedom* took up the history and prehistory of this opposition. One of the great conundrums of anarchism was the question of how and why people structured societies along lines of authority and domination if that was not their natural tendency. Bookchin had little new to say about why, but he had a great deal more to say about how.

Like radical environmentalists and his fellow anarchists, Bookchin idealized the distant past. In *The Ecology of Freedom* he celebrated the Neolithic period, or late Stone Age, an era of hunter-gatherer peoples and early agricultural communities. Bookchin called this world "organic society" and praised Neolithic peoples' egalitarianism and rich sense of the natural world. Communal ties guaranteed that all members of a community were provided for, and nature was understood as abundant rather than "stingy" and so something from which sustenance could be coaxed and carefully drawn forth rather than heedlessly and urgently extracted. Neolithic agriculturists did not establish rank or status among each other, Bookchin explained, nor did they assert their own superiority over their surroundings. A sense of mutual benefit within the community encouraged a sense of mutual benefit between the community and its environment. Gradually, however, this balance shifted. "And thence" Bookchin wrote, "came the long wintertime of domination and oppression we normally call 'civilization.' "[24]

How did civilization happen? According to Bookchin, in stages so gradual as to be noticeable only between rather than within generations: Hierarchy first emerged in the form of gerontocracy, a deference toward elders that at least afforded all members of a community the opportunity to achieve superior status. Stratification by gender was more exclusionary and more influential. Conflict between societies led to warrior cultures that privileged men and elevated the civic sphere over the domestic. Not all men joined the warrior class but few if any women could, and so the growing importance of warriors and civic leaders meant the growing subjugation of women. The final and greatest break from organic society was the decline of "the blood oath," an affiliation based on clan, tribe, or village rendered obsolete as urban life minimized familial bonds. The city eclipsed the village, and civic relationships replaced ancestral ties. Communal use of resources declined as private property arose and a system of economic and class relations redefined social life. In the absence of the blood oath, impersonal, economic relations produced the state, "the institutionalized apex of male civilization," and finally capitalism, "the point of *absolute negativity* for society and the natural world."[25]

So deep set was modern society's domination of nature that simple reform was little more than fool's gold. The moderate tone of environmentalism and its tendency toward compromise irritated Bookchin enough that he chose "ecology" rather than "environmentalism" to identify his own philosophy. "Environmentalism, conceived as a piecemeal reform movement," he wrote later, "easily lends itself to the lure of statecraft, that is, to participation in electoral, parliamentary, and party-oriented activities." The mainstream environmental movement participated in the politics of the state and in all of the inherently corrupt and authority-driven practices that such participation meant to an anarchist. Those who succumbed to this temptation were "obliged to function *within* the State, ultimately to become blood of its blood and bone of its bone."[26] Bookchin, in other words, voiced much the same criticism of mainstream environmentalism as did Earth First! and writers who identified as deep ecologists. Earth First!, in turn, frequently pointed to Bookchin as a canonical environmental thinker.

This made it all the more surprising when in the summer of 1987, Bookchin publicly attacked deep ecology, Earth First!, and anyone associated with either, branding them as the most dangerous elements within the broad environmental movement. His keynote speech for the National Green Gathering in Amherst, Massachusetts was largely a denunciation of deep ecology. Bookchin began by applauding the environmental movement's increasing skepticism toward the "shopworn Earth Day approach" of conventional politics. Then he warned that any genuinely radical perspective could not accept the premises of deep ecology. Never one for rhetorical restraint, Bookchin called deep ecology "a black hole of half-digested, ill-formed, and half-baked ideas," an "ideological toxic dump." Its adherents were "barely disguised racists, survivalists, macho Daniel Boones, and outright social reactionaries," and David (Bookchin insisted on the more formal version of his name) Foreman was an "eco-brute." Deep ecology and Earth First! offered one possible road for the environmental movement, Bookchin argued, at the end of which was reaction, xenophobia, and misanthropy.[27]

Earth First! brought Bookchin's anger down on itself. At the Amherst conference, Bookchin responded particularly to public remarks by Foreman and Abbey and to several controversial pieces in the *Earth First! Journal*. In a 1986 interview with Bill Devall, Foreman had suggested that U.S. aid to relieve starvation in Ethiopia was counterproductive and would simply delay the inevitable, leading to even more suffering. The best thing, Foreman said, was to "let nature seek its own balance." In the same interview he advocated immigration restriction because immigrants amounted to "more pressure on the resources we have in the USA."[28] Abbey was famously hostile to immigration from the south as well, not only because of its supposed environmental impact but also its attendant "alien mode of life which—let us be honest about this—is not appealing to the majority of Americans."[29] Most controversial, however, was an article in the *Earth First! Journal* about the AIDS epidemic. "If radical environmentalists were to invent a disease to bring human population back to ecological sanity, it would probably be something like AIDS," wrote the pseudonymous "Miss Ann Thropy." AIDS, the author wrote hopefully, "has the potential to end industrialism, which is the main force behind the environmental crisis."[30] In Bookchin's mind, such remarks captured the callous disregard that was the essence of Earth First!'s uncompromising view.

The controversy highlighted the overlap between crisis environmentalism and radical environmentalism. Both started from the premise that there existed a planetary environmental crisis, and both found a clear path from that premise to various solutions of last resort, including totalitarianism and starvation. Of particular concern was population pressure. The fear of surpassing the planet's carrying capacity had sparked crisis environmentalism in the 1970s and sat at the center of radical environmentalism in the 1980s. This "new Malthusianism" was, to Bookchin, "the most sinister ideological development of all."[31] He had long been wary of the holism that it promoted. Even as he lamented the misguided reformism of mainstream environmentalism in the 1970s, Bookchin made clear that Paul Ehrlich and Zero Population Growth spoke an accusatory language that conflated victims and perpetrators and ignored the role of capitalism in environmental destruction. "This ethos," Bookchin wrote, "already crystallized into the 'life-boat ethic,' 'triage,' and a new bourgeois imagery of 'claw-and-fang' called *survivalism* marks the first steps toward ecofascism."[32] Throughout his career, Bookchin remained committed to the idea that the late twentieth century was a post-scarcity era. In the 1960s this idea buttressed his claim that Marxism was outdated and should make way for a revolutionary politics unbounded by class interest. Two decades later he used the idea of a fecund nature to counter the concept of overpopulation. In the first instance he pointed to technology as the source of abundance and in the second to the cornucopia of nature, but his point remained the same: fear of scarcity was a chain that bound people to a limited set of ideas. In this sense, Bookchin was a rarity in the 1980s—an optimistic environmentalist.

The Amherst speech touched off two years of heated exchange between supporters of Earth First! and supporters of social ecology that poured onto the pages of the mainstream and alternative press. The recriminations flew back and forth. Bookchin repeatedly used the term "eco-fascist" to describe elements within Earth First! R. Wills Flowers of Earth First! called social ecology little more than "a restatement of the old Left/Liberal/Marxist/Progressive social reform ideology," and Bill Devall complained about the "verbal assaults, personal attacks, nonsense, and rubbish" coming from Bookchin and his allies, before stressing the importance of "cordial relationships."[33] The *Utne Reader* quoted Bookchin as saying Garrett Hardin, Edward Abbey, and Earth First! promoted racism. Abbey suggested Bookchin consult a dictionary. Bookchin again called Abbey a racist and a fascist (this time without the modifier), and Abbey called Bookchin a "fat old woman."[34]

Into this already messy fray jumped the editors of *Fifth Estate*. Created in the 1960s as an alternative newspaper based in Detroit, *Fifth Estate* reinvented itself in 1975 as an explicitly anarchist publication. The paper's writers and editors, like earlier anarchists, considered Marxism little better than capitalism in its focus on production, "a rigid fetter on the mind that can only make us shrink from the real potentials of a human existence." Skeptical of the premises underlying both capitalism and Marxism they questioned society's relationship to technology, government, and the natural world.[35] As *Fifth Estate* contributor David Watson wrote in 1981, "The state is only one structural element—albeit an integral one—in a totality which is the bureaucratic-technological megamachine."[36] That "megamachine," an idea borrowed in part from Lewis Mumford, occupied *Fifth Estate's* attention for many years.

Fifth Estate rode a growing wave of frustration with Earth First!'s neglect of social justice. Although Bookchin and the *Fifth Estate* collective frequently clashed, a shared distaste for deep ecology made them intellectual allies. Under the pseudonym "George Bradford," Watson published an extended essay in 1989 summarizing his views on deep ecology. The rhetorical title of Watson's essay, *How Deep Is Deep Ecology?*, left little suspense as to the answer. From the beginning, Watson followed the social ecological critique. Like Bookchin (and Earth First!), he dismissed the mainstream environmental movement as hopelessly compromised. Like Bookchin, he found deep ecology an unacceptable alternative because it ignored social difference and offered "no really 'deep' critique of the state, empire, technology, or capital, reducing the complex web of human relations to a simplistic, abstract, scientist caricature." Like Bookchin, he viewed Foreman's and Abbey's statements about immigration as possibly "fascist," and he rejected crisis environmentalists' belief that overpopulation rather than inequitable distribution caused resource shortages. Much of *How Deep Is Deep Ecology?* in fact refuted William Catton's *Overshoot*, a classic work of crisis environmentalism and a favorite of Earth First! Although more sympathetic to Earth First! than was Bookchin, Watson nevertheless felt that the poverty of the group's ideas outweighed the enthusiasm of its followers.[37]

THE HUMAN AND THE NATURAL

What William Cronon called the "central paradox" of wilderness— the question of whether the human and the natural could be strictly distinguished—always hovered at the edges of debates about Earth First!, anarchism, and justice. When radicals made too-simple statements cleaving people from nonhuman nature, they inadvertently revealed just how intertwined the two actually were. When their critics, including Bookchin, argued that the human and the natural were of a piece, they demonstrated the moral impasses such thinking led to. Like the shoreline and the water's edge, the human and the natural could never be entirely separated or conflated.

The forces that set apart people from nonhuman nature were, for radicals, historical rather than absolute. Earth First! in fact insisted on a fundamental affiliation between humans and nature. Foreman listed "an awareness that we are animals" as a defining principle of the group, and Earth First! saw one of its greatest obstacles as "the bizarre utilitarian philosophy that separates one specie (*Homo sapiens*) from its place in the biosphere and from its relationship with the land community and the life cycles of the entire planet."[38] It was modern society and its attendant beliefs that had wrenched humans away from the nonhuman. The split having taken place, however, radical environmentalists tended to blame a collective "humans" for all of the planet's environmental harms. The sense that people and nature were at odds, even if not inherently, led Earth First! to make the same sort of sweeping accusations against a collective humanity that the crisis environmentalists of the 1970s had leveled. People and nonhuman nature were not sundered forever, but at a great enough distance that radical environmentalists made few distinctions when they cast blame.

Deep ecology, its critics complained, had little to say about class or race or the inequality that global capitalism wrought. And it had little to say about gender, as feminists increasingly pointed out. Lending social ecology's basic argument a more specific valence, "ecofeminists" claimed that the destruction of nature and the oppression of women mirrored each other. Ariel Kay Salleh wrote, "The master-slave role which marks man's relation with nature is replicated in man's relation with woman"; and Ynestra King said, "Deep ecology ignores the structures of entrenched economic and political power within society."[39] Because the purported proximity of women to nature through procreation and childrearing had long been used to restrict women's lives, feminists claimed that any connection between the exploitation of nature and the exploitation of people had to be understood in terms of gender. By associating women with natural cycles, men had historically imagined themselves as rational and disciplined, and women as emotional and instinctual, assumptions that determined men's and women's relative roles in the home, in the community, and in society. Across different eras and different cultures, the closer women were to nature the further they were from autonomy and freedom.

Complicating the feminist critique, another branch of ecofeminism problematically embraced the association of women with nature. Feminists like Mary Daly and Starhawk claimed that women were more directly connected to the natural world and less likely than men to engage in warfare, exploitation, and environmental destruction.[40] If culture and nature stood opposed, women represented the best that nature had to offer against the worst that culture perpetrated. Janet Biehl, Bookchin's longtime companion and intellectual partner, broke with ecofeminism over what she considered its untenable embrace of social categories based in natural processes.[41] But ecofeminists were not alone in wrestling with this problem. Other radical ecological thinkers also turned to nature for moral meaning, if less explicitly. Anarchists spoke of society as natural and spontaneous and stifled by excessive human planning and design. Deep ecologists praised early societies for living in accord with natural cycles and harbored an acute distrust of modern notions of progress. All three groups granted the natural world some degree of order, meaning, and wisdom. Anywhere theories of the human and the nonhuman overlapped, the ground sloped toward essentialism.

In the 1980s and 1990s Bookchin slid down that slope, even as he tried to walk away from it. He moderated his celebration of preindustrial societies and his skepticism of human instrumentalism as he grew more and more frustrated with some ecofeminists and all deep ecologists. He became a defender of human reason. Although Bookchin had always found a central place for people in any conception of an environmentally sound society, his battle with the deep ecologists pushed him into a more robust advocacy of humanism and of people's distinct role as manipulators of the natural world. "Above all," he wrote, "antihumanists deprecate or deny humanity's most distinctive hallmark—reason, and its extraordinary powers to grasp, intervene into, and play a guiding role in altering social and natural reality."[42]

Reason was not just *a* product of nature, Bookchin suggested, but *the* product of nature. Human reason, he implied, might be the manifestation of nature's voice, direction, and meaning, and the product of evolution. "What we today call 'mind' in all its human uniqueness, self-possession, and imaginative possibilities is coterminous with a long *evolution* of mind," Bookchin wrote in *The Ecology of Freedom*. To one degree or another, the subjectivity of the rational mind always inhered in the natural world, culminating in human thought. Nature, then, moved with purpose. "The fact that the natural world is orderly . . . has long suggested the intellectually captivating possibility that there is a logic—a rationality if you will—to reality that may well be latent with meaning." And, Bookchin suggested, that logic and meaning might be readily apparent: "To render nature more fecund, varied, whole, and integrated may well constitute the hidden desiderata of natural evolution."[43] Although he rarely led with this idea, Bookchin often mentioned in his writing at least the possibility that the natural world had a distinct set of goals—fertility, diversity, unity—and that people could be nature's most developed means of achieving those goals.

Bookchin countered deep ecology's calls for a return to wilderness not by claiming human superiority but by claiming that people were nature's means of achieving its own ends and so responsible for improving it. The distinction was lost on Earth First!, and even on Earth First!'s critics. As concerned as those critics remained about Earth First!'s disregard of humans, they also recognized the threat to the nonhuman world posed by conflating people and nature. When Bookchin described people as "literally *constituted* by evolution to intervene in the biosphere," David Watson cried foul, calling such views "a kind of anthropocentric manifest destiny" and Robyn Eckersley read Bookchin's equation of people and nature as the arrogance of humanism in another guise, asking, "Are we really *that* enlightened?"[44]

Like many environmental thinkers, Bookchin tried to steer a course between the permissiveness of judging people a part of nature and the cynicism of judging them apart from it. The former could lead to inaction, or even anti-environmentalism. Some early twentieth-century wilderness advocates embraced progressive evolution and compromised their own activist spirit by believing, as historian Susan Schrepfer writes, that "technology was not a violation of nature but a fulfillment of natural history."[45] Thomas Shepard of *LOOK* magazine took this argument much further. "Man is *part* of nature," he told a roomful of industrialists, explaining the senselessness of the environmental movement. "Anything we do we do as card-carrying instruments of nature."[46] The latter could lead to a poisonous misanthropy, as Bookchin feared and Earth First! demonstrated. "Man has absolute dominion over the earth until he finally will destroy it," one Earth First!er said in a neat summary of the radical environmental view of humanity.[47]

Bookchin struggled to reconcile his fierce loyalty to human freedom and achievement with his deep concerns about environmental destruction. Simply commingling the human and the nonhuman, though, left both constrained. To argue that human beings should follow the dictates of nature was to invite a debate about what those dictates might be, a debate in which the terms "natural" and "unnatural" would be brandished like cudgels. For anyone committed to social justice or human freedom, this would be a debate with no winners. Conversely, to argue that human actions were by definition part of nature was to sanction the very forms of abuse that Bookchin had dedicated himself to fighting. "The fashionable view is that humanity's disruption of the environment is somehow (we know not how) 'natural,' " Earth First!'s Christopher Manes wrote disapprovingly, "since by definition we evolved into the kind of rapacious animals we are."[48] As Joel Kovel suggested, the debate pulled in directions that cut against the grain of what most people believed about human beings: "That is, humans are very much part of nature, but there is also something in us that is never content with nature."[49]

Were people the antithesis of nature or its highest expression? Bookchin and his fellow social ecologists tried to reconcile a commitment to restraining human use of the natural world with a commitment to social justice and human freedom. Social ecologists wanted to satisfy two principles that were in many ways in tension with each other, and so ended up satisfying neither completely. Earth First! tried to ignore one and champion the other, and so ended up supporting positions that most found despicable, like Foreman's solution to starvation, Abbey's statements about immigration, and "Miss Ann Thropy's" comments about AIDS and overpopulation. The logic of social ecology led to impasse; the logic of deep ecology as practiced by Earth First! led to too-simple solutions for complex issues. Earth First! embraced anarchism's critique of modern society but ignored the long-held anarchist commitment to human freedom, a commitment that Bookchin tried for decades to pair with ecological health.

But there was for many an elegance in the simplicity of Earth First!'s politics, and a power in the forthrightness with which the group fought single-mindedly for one cause, never troubling itself with competing moral claims. Because the group had no membership rolls, it is impossible to say how many Earth First!ers there were, but some estimates ran as high as fifteen thousand. By the mid-1980s the group had an international following and reputation and stories about Earth First!'s bravado proliferated in print and on television.[50]

Meanwhile, Murray Bookchin and social ecology remained little known even among environmentalists. There were those who, consciously or not, worked with Bookchin's basic ideas and toward at least his intermediate goals. Most of these people, however, did so within a conventional framework that Bookchin explicitly rejected. They wanted social justice and environmental protection together, and without a fundamental restructuring of society, ignoring Bookchin's view that one depended on the other. Among the radicals to whom Bookchin addressed himself, his many and thoughtful ideas never caught fire. Bookchin's complaints about radical environmentalism were fundamental, prescient, and underappreciated; he anticipated not only some of the particular issues that would divide Earth First! several years later but also the broad issues that would cause concern within mainstream groups. An unconventional anarchist in almost every other way, Bookchin was typical in that his diagnoses rang truer than his prescriptions.

"ALIEN-NATION"

The fierceness of Earth First!'s conviction and the directness of its methods continued to inspire many activists seized by the spirit of radicalism, but the crossed purposes of deep ecology and social justice increasingly vexed others. The roiling of Earth First! in the late 1980s revealed the group's strengths and weaknesses. Internal critics still paid homage to the ethos of Earth First! and often remained convinced that it was the best means of righting the wrongs of industrialism, while at the same time they increasingly rejected the philosophy of Earth First!'s "old guard" with its shades of jingoism and misanthropy. The perception of antihumanism began to cost Earth First! support within its own ranks, and the dissatisfactions pulling at the group's edges came first from the anarchist Left.

One of the earliest signs of irreconcilable differences came during the 1987 Round River Rendezvous in Arizona near the Grand Canyon. At that year's Rendezvous—just a few weeks apart from the National Green Gathering in Amherst—a group of anarchists from Washington engaged Edward Abbey in heated argument. The anarchists set up a table to distribute their literature along with several pieces "for discussion," including copies of an editorial for the *Bloomsbury Review* that Abbey had written a year earlier complaining of high rates of immigration to the United States from Central America. When Abbey approached the table, the anarchists questioned him about his chauvinism and lack of attention to imperialism and inequality. A crowd gathered, and soon the Rendezvous coordinating committee interceded on Abbey's behalf.

Several months later the Washington group published a pamphlet explaining their position under the title "Alien-Nation," and the *Earth First! Journal* reprinted the pamphlet for its readers. The Alien-Nation anarchists explained that they attended the Rendezvous with an open mind but left convinced that Earth First! anarchism was libertarian rather than communalist and that Earth First! espoused a "wild west" image, "extremely right wing, if not decidedly fascist in its orientation." Deep ecology had become "human hating and finally a racist ideal for advanced capitalist countries to maintain their dominance over the rest of the world and its resources." The anarchists' own philosophy was "eco-mutualism, that is, that human society and the natural world are not mutually exclusive." In case it was not entirely clear, the anarchists announced they would no longer associate themselves with Earth First![51]

The impassioned response to Alien-Nation in the *Earth First! Journal* came quickly. Most readers and contributors stridently objected to Alien-Nation. One of the most conciliatory letters was from "Lone Wolf Circles," who described himself as both a deep ecologist and an anarchist. "There will not be any social equality until we are once again small populations of spiritually-aware Earth warriors," he wrote, "conscious of our impact, artisans in lifestyle, spread thin across a globe diverse and wild once again." One of the least conciliatory letters was from Paul Watson, who more than fifteen years earlier had been on the losing side of arguments within Greenpeace over how militant the organization should be. "This is the kind of bullshit that drove David Brower out of Friends of the Earth and hundreds of other people out of groups and movements they founded," he wrote. Watson had no interest in the issues that Alien-Nation raised. "My heart does not bleed for the third world," he wrote. "My energies point toward saving the one world, the planet Earth which is being plundered by one species, the human primate."[52]

Mitch Friedman, one of the coordinators of Washington Earth First!, warned Foreman that the clash between the Washington anarchists and Edward Abbey was symptomatic of greater dissonance within the radical environmental community. Friedman knew and worked with the Alien-Nation anarchists, and although he disagreed with most of their criticisms he recognized that competing views within Earth First! could not be ignored for long. Many local groups handled differences of opinion and approach amicably, but Earth First! had garnered a national reputation, and Friedman understood that on a larger stage personal relationships mattered less. "I'm only concerned that by delaying the problem on the national level," he told Foreman, "it may reach a crisis stage and cause deep rifts."[53]

The rifts opened gradually but steadily. West Coast anarchists came from a younger generation of radicals with their roots in antiauthoritarian politics rather than the conservation politics of Earth First!'s founders. They were deeply committed to preventing environmental destruction, but not exclusively. In 1989 Mikal Jakubal—the original tree sitter—and a group of West Coast anarchists published the first issue of *Live Wild or Die*, a zine that would push past the *Earth First! Journal's* focus on narrowly construed environmental issues. Like Bookchin, Jakubal and his peers saw environmentalism not as an end in itself but as one of the clearest windows onto essential structures of hierarchy and control. "There is an incredible amount of knowledge about the nature of power, revolt, how the system co-opts, organization & the like" Jakubal wrote to Foreman, "that has been developed (& *practiced*, by the way) by the 'anarchist intellectual' community . . . that hasn't even been touched by most of EF!" Jakubal had corresponded with several noted anarchists, including David Watson at *Fifth Estate*. "These folks—though you may not believe it—actually have an almost identical worldview ('deep ecology' if it *must* be labeled) to us but they've come at it from a completely different direction," he told Foreman.[54]

The group behind *Live Wild or Die* emerged from Earth First! but strained against what they perceived to be philosophical limits. "We grew to a certain point under the name Earth First!," *Live Wild or Die* editor Gena Trott wrote to Foreman that summer, "but we won't stop growing if we start to disregard the name—anymore than a baby will stop growing if she stops using the (once beneficial) diaper." The diaper, in fact, had become restrictive. "Surely the battle that Earth First! is fighting is laudable and many of us have learned from it," Trott wrote. "But what was once supposed to be a movement has become self-limiting in its scope."[55] Like Jakubal, Trott had corresponded with the *Fifth Estate* crowd and decided that Earth First!, for all its many strengths, could no longer contain the evolving radical environmental scene on its own (see figure 5.2).

As was the case in the Bookchin/Earth First! debate, questioning environmentalists' most basic goals became a matter of questioning where people ended and nonhuman nature began. Lev Chernyi, pseudonymous editor of *Anarchy*, the magazine that called itself "a journal of desire armed," criticized deep ecology as a moral system that stifled individual freedom. At the center of deep ecology's rigid morality was "nature," Chernyi said, yet another false idol used to control human thought and behavior. Nature could not act as a source of authority. "It is not something to be worshipped," he wrote, "nor is it something for us to serve." Lone Wolf Circles again took up the cause of deep ecology and responded, "Wilderness is the negation of control—it is ultimately radical." Chernyi and Jakubal countered that deep ecology was "false consciousness" and "ideological." Like Bookchin, Chernyi and Jakubal tried to bind human and nonhuman interests in order to reconcile justice and ecology. Nature, they argued, did not constitute a stable reality separate from humanity but rather something each individual defined for herself. "Our own perspectives open out on a natural world, but

Figure 5.2 Although *Live Wild or Die* critiqued Earth First!'s politics, its contributors also embraced Earth First!-style ecotage. From *Live Wild or Die* 1 (1988).

directly because of this fact we thus cannot possibly really see the world from any 'higher' point of view than our own," Chernyi wrote. Any authority external to the individual suppressed that individual's will, Jakubal agreed, whether that authority be Marxism, deep ecology, or "an abstracted idea of Nature itself. These all kill our unruly, natural wild humanity." For Chernyi and Jakubal the only "nature" worth following was an internal one, shaped by an individual's imagination and free will. Like Bookchin, they wondered if the wildest places on the planet might be human minds.[56]

Once the moral authority of nonhuman nature and the objective reality of wilderness lost their moorings, some of environmentalism's most basic claims began to float away. "What a bizarre circumstance," Jakubal wrote, "to be risking injury or imprisonment to defend an idea of nature while killing the real living nature in ourselves!"[57] Trees, mountains, forests, and rivers became ideas, while internal thoughts, impulses, and drives remained real. The new green anarchists, Foreman lamented, were "more interested in the wild within than the wilderness without."[58] Lone Wolf Circles pointed out the risks Jakubal ran: the absence of shared values or an organic order could be used to justify or excuse a great deal. "Is the desire to help someone no greater than the desire to hurt them?" he asked. "The desire to defend the natural world against all odds no 'higher' than the desire to constrain, demean, and destroy it? The bleak and violent history of civilized humanity is all a product of someone's 'armed desire.' "[59]

Deep ecology remained just as ethically problematic. Denying human beings a privileged moral position exposed people (and some more than others) to the same disregard as granting human beings moral superiority exposed nature. David Watson pointed to this dilemma in an exchange with "Miss Ann Thropy." "If we are 'one' with nature," he wrote, "then we are no different than starfish or protomammals, and nature is doing this strange dance with herself, or is *chaos*. If we are a uniquely moral agent, then not only will our intervention reflect *some* kind of stewardship . . . but the question of the configurations of power, domination and alienation *within* human development are key."[60] In all of the debates around Earth First!, the question just out of reach was about the objective and moral limits of people and nature. If nonhuman nature provided an order and stability that humans could violate, environmentalism was an urgent matter of living with restraint. If people were as natural as starfish, environmentalism became primarily a philosophical question about what sort of world the majority of humans wanted.

ENVIRONMENTALISM AND NATIVE SOVEREIGNTY IN THE SOUTHWEST

Radical environmentalists were not averse to working for social justice as long as environmental goals came first. When radicals aligned their cause with social movements, the strict terms of partnership made clear how provisional such alignments were. Environmentalists often found it easiest to affiliate themselves with Native Americans, assuming environmentalism and Native rights to be complementary. Both groups, it was thought, fought to protect and conserve a natural heritage. "What we need to do," Earth First!er Art Goodtimes said in 1986, "is build bridges between natives struggling for sovereignty and deep ecologists struggling for a biocentric paradigm shift away from industrialism's exploitation and desecration of the Mother."[61] Goodtimes saw such bridges as short and sturdy, connecting sister causes against a common enemy. In some cases the connections existed, and environmental and Native groups worked together. But Goodtimes's assumption of shared interests overlooked the ways that environmentalists often considered Native Americans exemplars of a sustainable relationship between people and the nonhuman world, ignoring the more complicated political and social context in which Native peoples fought for sovereignty and for control of their lands.

Radical environmental efforts in the Southwest emerged, in part, from the perception of common ground between environmentalists and Native Americans. That common ground was initially Black Mesa, a coal-rich plateau straddling the Navajo and Hopi reservations in northern Arizona. The fight over Black Mesa coal demonstrated both the powerful rhetoric as well as the risks of political oversimplification in assumptions that Native American sovereignty and environmental protection stood adjacent. In the 1960s a consortium of energy utilities called Western Energy Supply and Transmission (WEST), with plans to build six coal-fired power plants in the Four Corners region of the Southwest, convinced the Hopi and Navajo tribal councils to lease sixty-five thousand acres of Black Mesa to the Peabody Coal Company. The new power plants would feed energy consumption far beyond northern Arizona, turning Black Mesa coal into electricity for Las Vegas, Phoenix, Tucson, and much of Southern California. Peabody's plans to strip mine Black Mesa grew more secure late in the decade when the federal government gained a strong interest in Arizona coal. After the Sierra Club helped defeat the Department of the Interior's proposed Grand Canyon dams, Secretary of the Interior Stewart Udall began to negotiate for a portion of the electricity from WEST's Navajo Generating Station near Page, Arizona. In order to guarantee a steady supply of energy for its Central Arizona Project (CAP), Interior helped WEST construct the legal infrastructure for the generating station and for a railroad to carry Black Mesa coal.[62]

Peabody's Black Mesa and Kayenta mines occupied tens of thousands of acres of the plateau, but their potential environmental effects stretched much further. The rain and snowmelt in drainages that started on the plateau's rim passed through the strip mines, collecting sulfuric acid and then running to nearby farms. Black Mesa Mine used a 275-mile slurry pipeline from the plateau to the Mohave Generating Station near Laughlin, Nevada, carrying 5 million tons of crushed coal a year by pumping 1.4 billion gallons of water through the pipe. That water came from the Navajo Aquifer deep under Black Mesa, a primary source of water for the arid region. Because Black Mesa sat above a basin, lowering the water table there could drain farms and communities for many miles around. Each of the six proposed plants would pump hundreds of tons of sulfur dioxide into the air each day, and several plants would be within just a few miles of each other in a region subject to inversions that trapped warm air and pollutants and kept them stationary for days at a time.[63]

With both public and private interests poised to mine Black Mesa, only Abbey's "citizens on their hind legs" stood in the way. In northern Arizona, at first, these citizens consisted of traditionalist factions within the Navajo and Hopi at odds with their tribal councils, and a handful of amateur conservationists from the Four Corners region. One of those amateurs was Jack Loeffler, a close friend of Abbey's. Loeffler started the Black Mesa Defense Fund in 1970, and both present and future environmental activists moved through its Santa Fe office, including Abbey, the advertising consultant Jerry Mander, and Dave Foreman, who volunteered to stuff envelopes. Black Mesa Defense Fund fought Peabody's plans for the next two years through publicity, public hearings, and occasional clandestine mischief.[64]

Black Mesa Defense Fund made little distinction between environmentalism and traditional Native American culture. "Traditional Indians still live in the Southwest—people who regard themselves as stewards of the Earthmother," Loeffler wrote. "They live by a system of ethics which we seem to have forgotten." Loeffler did not group all Native Americans under a single banner. He sided with the traditionalist factions of the Hopi and Navajo against tribal councils who he believed had betrayed their people. But he and other environmentalists understood Native politics largely through the categories of traditional people and modern, industrial society. "To the Bureau of Reclamation and the power companies, the Southwest is a momentary answer to the energy needs of the West," Loeffler wrote. "To the traditional Indians, to many non-Indians who live there or visit there, the Southwest is the last refuge of peace, beauty and natural balance."[65]

"Natural balance" was not the only issue in the Black Mesa fight, however. Central too was "Navajo nationalism," which historian Andrew Needham calls "the main language by which Navajos sought to alter the dynamics of energy development in the Southwest."[66] The Navajo expressed as great a concern as environmentalists about how Peabody's strip mines would pollute the air and water of northern Arizona, and confronting the ecological consequences of industrial development was an important part of Navajo nationalism. But Navajo nationalism included social and economic dimensions. When voiced by members of the tribal council, Navajo nationalism argued that Native Americans should reap more direct economic benefits from energy development on their land. When articulated by Native activists who doubted their council's leadership, it meant fighting energy development that threatened not just the environment but Navajo culture and political sovereignty. The anti-development version of Navajo nationalism lined up well with environmentalism, pitting both Native Americans and environmentalists against extractive industries. Still, when armed members of the American Indian Movement blocked Peabody mining equipment in 1974, they stood their ground to protect Navajo sheep herds and economic autonomy as much as the plateau itself. In some ways, antidevelopment Navajos and antidevelopment environmentalists even opposed each other. As Navajo activists embraced an anticolonial analysis, Needham explains, they rejected any strict distinction between "civilized" and "primitive" nations, the sort of distinction that radical environmentalists embraced romantically just as easily as developers embraced it disparagingly.[67]

Radical environmentalists' interest in Black Mesa revealed more about their expansive view of nature and environmentalism than about their interest in social justice. A strip mine, like a ranch, was a working landscape and not a wilderness. Needham argues that the Sierra Club's vigorous defense of the Grand Canyon against the threat of dams in the 1960s and less energetic defense of Black Mesa against the threat of mining in the 1970s showcased the Club's tacit categorization of landscapes as either "sacred" or "productive," the one inviolable and the other expendable. The hazard, he suggests, of defining some places as particularly scenic and hallowed was to write off other places to the dirty necessities of industrial production and to ignore the plight of the people who suffered harm. In that case, radical environmentalists held a broader view of what was worth protecting and why.[68] Abbey called Black Mesa "the chief current battleground" in the fight between industrial development and the West.[69] As selectively as radicals sometimes valorized wilderness, their belief in a planetwide fight against the forces of industrialization meant that battles might be fought anywhere. Wilderness areas remained the places most worth protecting, but coal mines and cattle ranches were more immediately threatened, and so they were where activists could most directly engage their opponents.

If the Sierra Club's willingness to cede places like Black Mesa to the imperatives of modern society also meant looking away from the attendant harm to humans living there, radical environmentalists could claim to be the greater populists as well. But that populism remained narrow. The generalizations about people that radical environmentalists relied on meant they shared the cause of traditionalist Native Americans only partially. When Earth First!er George Wuerthner questioned Alaska Natives' relationship to their natural environment in 1987, Lewis Johnson responded, "Since it is my racial group he's attacking, I am on guard and recognize both in his tone and his arguments the kinds of racist statements that are usually made in other contexts, but are made here in defense of ecology—an issue we should be on the same side of."[70]

At times that same side was more obvious, if still conditional. In the mid-1980s Energy Fuels Nuclear proposed several uranium mines near the Grand Canyon, some of which threatened Havasu Canyon on the Havasupai Reservation. In late 1986 Earth First!, the Sierra Club, Canyon Under Siege, and members of the Havasupai held a demonstration at the entrance to Grand Canyon National Park. Several dozen environmentalists and Havasupai then drove thirteen miles to where Energy Fuels Nuclear had begun removing vegetation for its proposed Canyon Mine. The Havasupai offered a prayer and environmentalists replanted sagebrush. "This land which was cursed is now blessed," Earth First!er Roger Featherstone said.[71]

The temporary partnership between Earth First! and the Havasupai arose largely from circumstance. Earth First!ers had been monkeywrenching Grand Canyon mines for months and, along with Mary Sojourner's Canyon Under Siege, fighting federal bureaucracy in general and the Forest Service in particular. "Once again," Earth First!er Ned Powell wrote of the environmental assessment process for mines on Kaibab National Forest land, "the legal process is just a parody of public servants listening to the wishes of the American people."[72] In this case, the American people included Native Americans similarly opposed to uranium mining, and environmentalists welcomed that alliance. Foreman insisted such alliances work primarily on Earth First!'s terms, however. "I would like to see a natural and honest working together between Earth First! and Indians—in mutual respect, without guilt, and with a firm commitment to Earth," he wrote in 1985.[73]

Environmentalists tended to funnel their commitment to Native sovereignty through either romantic generalizations or moral absolutes. In the Southwest, neither environmentalists nor the Navajo could look at Black Mesa without seeing streetlamps and air conditioners in Phoenix, Las Vegas, and Los Angeles. But Navajo activists also saw political and economic inequality, as well as imperialism. Edward Abbey, the Black Mesa Defense Fund, and later Earth First! used fewer and starker categories than did the Navajo to explain energy infrastructure in the Southwest. Those categories were never entirely limited to the human and the nonhuman; radical environmentalists took into account different people's differing relationships to development and Western lands. But radical environmental thought rested on a clear divide between the modern, industrial world and what Loeffler called "the Earthmother," with people lined up on one side or the other.[74]

EMETIC

In the midst of internecine conflicts that pit eco-anarchists and radical and mainstream environmentalists against one another, and that underscored Earth First!'s circumscribed view of social justice, it took the FBI to remind all parties involved that they shared at least some basic aims as well as antagonists. In 1989 federal agents arrested several Earth First!-affiliated activists in Arizona operating under the name EMETIC. Prosecution at the hands of the state bought Earth First! credibility from some of its anarchist critics, and Earth First!ers themselves rallied around their comrades. Attacks from the outside only momentarily muffled what were steadily growing differences within the movement but nonetheless alerted radicals and environmentalists of various stripes to the high stakes for which they fought.

The Evan Mecham Eco-Terrorist International Conspiracy (EMETIC— the name poking fun at Arizona's recently impeached governor) claimed responsibility in the late 1980s for several incidents of sabotage. In 1988 EMETIC damaged or felled several dozen poles supporting power lines that fed Energy Fuels Nuclear's Canyon and Pigeon Mines north of Grand Canyon National Park, temporarily shutting down the mines. In 1987 and again in 1988, the group used acetylene torches to cut ski-lift poles at the Fairfield Snowbowl resort near Flagstaff, writing to the resort to warn of the damage and make clear that repaired poles would be dismantled again.[75]

EMETIC emerged in part from two characteristics of Earth First! activism in the Southwest. The first was a focus on industrial infrastructure. By the time of the 1987 Round River Rendezvous near the Grand Canyon, Earth First! had increased its activities in Arizona significantly, waging battles against a proposed Cliff Dam on the Verde River, a Phelps-Dodge copper smelter in Douglas, and uranium mining near the Grand Canyon.[76]

During the same weekend that Alien-Nation confronted Abbey, one hundred Earth First!ers invaded Pigeon Mine just a few miles away, halting the mine's operations for several hours and landing twenty-one protesters in jail.[77] Focused especially on the energy infrastructure spreading throughout the state, Arizona Earth First!ers hoped eventually to take on the Palo Verde nuclear plant and the Central Arizona Project (CAP) itself.

The second development was the presumed association of environmental activism in the Southwest with Native American rights. The Snowbowl resort sprawled across the San Francisco Peaks and, as EMETIC noted in its letters to the resort's owners, the Hopi and Navajo had long objected to the development of sacred mountains. "The use of this mountain to entertain rich white people by allowing them to slide down without bother of walking up is inappropriate," EMETIC scolded.[78] The eco-activists echoed the Sacred Mountain Defense Fund, a Native group organized to protect the San Francisco Peaks as well as to oppose "colonialism, corruption, waste, rampant unplanned development and nuclear power."[79] Native activists had nothing to do with the Snowbowl sabotage and made no public statements in support or in opposition. EMETIC nonetheless claimed to fight for Native rights, just as it pointed to the rights of the Havasupai in its attacks on the Canyon Mine. The group warned of birth defects and illness from uranium mines and chided Energy Fuels Nuclear, writing, "Perhaps the fact that the victims have mostly been dark skinned children on reservations makes it easier for you to ignore this."[80] Peg Millet of EMETIC said later that she and her fellow activists "were all doing it as a spiritual exercise. Our targets were all sacred lands."[81]

EMETIC was not the same as Earth First! but neither was it entirely distinct. The group emerged from the 1987 Round River Rendezvous. Millett, an Earth First! regular who lived in Prescott, Arizona, volunteered for the Rendezvous organizing committee. Mark Davis, who also lived in Prescott, attended the Rendezvous to learn more about Earth First! and to find some partners in environmental sabotage. He found Millett. She was arrested for the first time at the Pigeon Mine protest and was ready to take even greater risks when Davis revealed his plans for Snowbowl. The pair recruited Ilse Asplund, a close friend of Millett's, as well as a Prescott botanist named Marc Baker.

In late May 1989 Millett, Davis, Baker, and Mike Tait—whom Millett met at the 1988 Round River Rendezvous in Washington—approached a power-line tower feeding energy to a pump station outside of Salome, Arizona, two pieces among thousands that made up the CAP. As they gathered around the tower with a cutting torch, flares suddenly arced above them, illuminating several dozen approaching FBI agents who quickly arrested Baker and Davis. Millett ran into the dark, evading the agents, their tracking dogs, and the searchlight of a Blackhawk helicopter that was scanning the desert. "I did not have an adversarial relationship with the natural world and all of the people who were chasing me did," she explained later.[82] Millett walked sixteen miles through the night, then hitchhiked back into Prescott to the Planned Parenthood office where she worked and where the FBI finally caught up with her. Mike Tait was never arrested. His real name was Mike Fain, and he was an undercover agent who had been infiltrating EMETIC for over a year.

Several hours after Millett eluded capture in the desert, FBI agents burst into Dave Foreman's Tucson home and placed him under arrest. The government charged various combinations of the activists for the attacks on Snowbowl, the uranium mines, and the CAP tower, as well as with conspiracy to destroy an energy facility. The case rested on hundreds of hours of taped conversations gathered by Fain, several paid informers in Prescott and Tucson, and listening devices planted in houses, telephones, and in at least one instance operated by FBI agents in an airplane circling above Foreman and Fain. Among the recorded conversations were discussions between Davis and Fain about the possibility of simultaneously toppling power lines to the Palo Verde nuclear plant in Arizona and the Diablo Canyon nuclear plant in California, as well as to the Rocky Flats nuclear weapons facility in Colorado. The prosecution claimed the CAP action was just practice for the attacks on nuclear facilities, and that although Foreman had not participated in any EMETIC actions he was the group's mastermind and source of funds. Several weeks into the trial the defendants agreed to a plea bargain. The court finally sentenced Davis to six years in prison, Millett to three years, Baker to six months, and Asplund—whom a grand jury indicted on related charges over a year after the initial arrests—to one month. The government's comparatively weak case against Foreman allowed him to plead to a misdemeanor after five years' probation.[83]

The arrests, trial, and sentencing of the "Arizona Five" formed, in many ways, a brief moment of cohesion for an Earth First! that confronted criticisms from within and from without. Friends like David Brower showed up in Prescott to raise support. Gary Snyder, a monkeywrenching skeptic, nevertheless donated money to the activists' legal defense fund.[84] Even recent antagonists pledged their loyalty. "Political differences make little matter to us when the state victimizes those fighting to destroy the megamachine," the editors of *Fifth Estate* wrote. "You are to be congratulated for your efforts, not prosecuted." When the *New York Times* described Murray Bookchin as an Earth First! adversary, he responded, "Whatever my differences with Earth First! and Mr. Foreman, I believe the organization's membership is generally high-minded and deeply concerned with the destruction of the environment. I have contributed to the legal defense fund for the three [sic] who were arrested and urge others to do so." The Sierra Club, which had long kept a safe distance from Earth First!, inched closer. "In its obsession to tie the issue of monkeywrenching to nuclear sabotage," *Sierra* magazine reported, "the FBI had to invent a conspiracy where none existed; whatever 'message' it intended to send was lost along the way."[85]

Earth First!ers urged resolve rather than retreat after the FBI crackdown. Mark Davis, who received the strictest sentence, spoke for himself, refusing to disavow what he had done. "I acknowledge the necessity of courts and laws, and accept my prison term," he said from jail. "But I am not sorry." In fact, he continued to sound an alarm. "We humans are collectively killing this planet and dooming our own children by indulging in an orgy of consumption and denial," he warned, reminding activists of all that he believed remained at stake.[86] Other radicals tried to find in EMETIC inspiration rather than fear. "As I pound away on these keys," Myra Mishkin wrote in a special edition of the *Earth First! Journal*, "it seems that people are carrying on. There are people sitting in Redwoods, others are blockading roads, and meetings go on across the country. The reasons why we each got involved in the first place are still with us."[87] But those reasons—strict ecocentrism or something broader and more capacious—remained at issue, as did Earth First!'s strategy, tactics, and culture.

ECOTOPIA EARTH FIRST!

"Earth First! is alive and well. Earth First! is alive and wild," several of the group's key figures declared in late 1991. "And we must unite as we organize, educate, agitate, and yes, monkeywrench, to defend this Earth."[88] The "statement of solidarity & unity" was an explicit response to the Arizona 5 trial and an implicit acknowledgment of changes arising from Earth First!'s own inner turmoil. Alien-Nation and Murray Bookchin had signaled a larger transformation within Earth First! that would eventually shift the group's philosophy away from deep ecology and toward a more humanistic brand of radicalism; shift the group's tactics away from monkeywrenching and toward civil disobedience; and shift the group's center of gravity away from the Southwest and toward the West Coast. None of these shifts was new. Deep ecology had always been a subject of debate, many of Earth First!'s actions involved sitting in front of bulldozers in the middle of the day rather than sabotaging them at night, and Earth First!ers had always hailed from Oregon and California as much as from New Mexico and Arizona. But by the early 1990s these different approaches had evolved from friendly disagreements to serious doubts about the group's original premises. Despite its decentralized structure and resistance to official hierarchy Earth First! did have a public identity, and a few of its most active chapters moved to redefine that image.

Some of the voices questioning Earth First!'s founding principles were new and distant; others were familiar and close at hand. No voice was more familiar than that of Mike Roselle, who signed the "statement of solidarity & unity" and welcomed a reimagined Earth First! One of the group's founders, Roselle gradually became a stern critic. He came from a different background than the rest of the original Earth First!ers. At the end of the 1970s Roselle had far less exposure to establishment conservation but more experience with radicalism, having spent the early part of the decade as an antiwar activist. He anchored some of the early Earth First! campaigns on the West Coast and remained an active participant throughout the 1980s. By the end of the decade, though, he was increasingly uncomfortable with Earth First!'s sweeping critiques of all people and was interested in building bridges to other progressive movements. In 1990 *The Nation's* Alexander

Cockburn found Roselle during an anti-logging action in California and asked him about the infamous remarks on immigration and starvation by Foreman and Abbey. Roselle complained about Foreman's "dirty laundry" and insisted that most local Earth First! groups were "part of this more progressive movement toward social justice and economic justice as well as environmental sanity." Roselle also discussed his work on a committee charged with overhauling the *Earth First! Journal.* "Discussion of anarchy, animal rights, vegetarianism, racism, and feminism (to name a few) are felt by many to be vital to the health of the movement," the committee's report read.[89] The *Earth First! Journal* had long claimed not to represent any comprehensive view of Earth First! as a movement. Now many felt that it should.

The insurgent feelings within Earth First! coalesced around Judi Bari, who was relatively new to the movement but nonetheless one of its most important figures by the time she signed the statement of solidarity and unity. Originally from Maryland, Bari moved to Northern California in 1979. By the late 1980s she lived in Mendocino County and worked as a carpenter. Her activist background was in organized labor, not environmentalism, but after building houses with thousand-year-old redwood trees, she began thinking and reading about the coastal forests that surrounded her community. Her friend Darryl Cherney, who had moved to California from New York in 1985, convinced her to join Earth First! Very quickly, Bari became one of the most active organizers and key strategists for Earth First! in Northern California. She joined the movement as the logging of old-growth tree stands garnered more and more attention in California and nationwide, and the issue defined her activism (see figure 5.3).

Bari's personal philosophy drew from several influences, and her ease in talking to people with different political commitments made her an especially effective organizer. She was a dedicated environmentalist and considered herself an ecocentric one, although she implied that her ecocentrism differed substantively from that of Earth First!'s old guard. Bari's years as a union organizer gave her a strong sense of loyalty to workers and their communities. During the campaign to save redwoods she tried to ally environmentalists and loggers, constantly reminding both groups that they shared a common enemy in the large corporations profiting off of Northern

Figure 5.3 Judi Bari and her Ecotopia Earth First! championed some radical environmental views while challenging others.

California lumber. Bari also considered herself an ecofeminist, arguing that violence toward nature echoed violence toward women. Her local Earth First! group became gender-balanced while she was part of it and regularly elevated women to leadership positions in its campaigns, a process Bari called "the feminization of Earth First!"[90] And although she never identified as a social ecologist, she often articulated the core claim of social ecology: that social injustice and environmental destruction were bound up with each other, and that neither could be addressed adequately on its own.

Few issues more pointedly captured the differences between the old Earth First! and Bari's Northern California "Ecotopia Earth First!" than the debate over tree spiking, one of radical environmentalism's most controversial tactics. At the core of that debate was the question of whether Earth First! should engage in the sort of sabotage that risked harming people, and whether doing so meant minimizing not just social justice but human welfare. A halting shift away from ecotage and toward civil disobedience was a movement backward along the path Abbey had described at Glen Canyon in 1981: first oppose, then resist, then subvert. Ecotage was— always in symbol and at times in fact—an act of subversion. Civil disobedience was a means of resistance, designed to augment more conventional forms of opposition and to trigger changes in law and public opinion. One tactic sidestepped established institutions; the other at least in part relied on them. Earth First! had long used both tactics, but in Northern California it leaned more and more on civil disobedience alone.

Earth First! civil disobedience in Northern California looked much as it did elsewhere, only more so. Although tree-sits initially grew out of wilderness campaigns in Oregon, the tactic became ubiquitous in California's coastal forests. Starting in 1988, Northern California Earth First!ers climbed trees relentlessly to hang banners over freeways, to attract media attention, and to delay logging. The strategy persisted for the next decade, growing larger in scale and longer in duration. On the ground, activists continued to mount blockades of timber roads. Because blockades were within easy reach of sheriff's deputies, radicals who once simply stood shoulder-to-shoulder now devised increasingly complicated ways of "locking down." Blockaders would, for instance, handcuff themselves to each other after inserting their arms into metal tubes running through concrete-filled barrels half-buried in the ground, a configuration known as the "sleeping dragon." Removing the blockade meant digging up the barrels, breaking apart the concrete, and sawing through the tubes.[91]

While blockades and tree-sits spread as hallmarks of Northern California forest activism, a third tactic—tree spiking—receded. The end goal of tree spiking was the same as tree sitting and blockading: delaying, inconveniencing, and discouraging logging. By driving large nails into trees scheduled to be logged and then informing loggers that an area was "spiked," activists forced the Forest Service to spend time and money walking the forest with metal detectors and removing spikes or else risk breaking expensive mill equipment when saws hit nails. The means, though, were different. Blockading and tree sitting were civil disobedience, publicly staged and demanding recognition. Tree spiking was ecotage, surreptitious and anonymous. Done correctly, tree spiking advocates argued, the risk was minimal. If spikers notified the proper authorities, if those authorities took those notifications seriously, and if the Forest Service or logging companies thoroughly swept the spiked area, then the metal-on-metal hazards of spiked trees could always be avoided. But any missteps in that string of qualifications could lead to a nail striking a mill blade, sending pieces of machinery flying.

Earth First!'s use of tree spiking had always been both tactical and philosophical. Foreman and Bill Haywood recommended non-ferrous hammers for quiet spiking in *Ecodefense: A Field Guide to Monkeywrenching*. The manual also discussed when and where to spike, how high up the tree spikes should be placed, how to enter and exit the forest, and the best types of nails to use. *Ecodefense's* narrow focus on specifics was in the service of broad ideas. "Representative democracy in the United States," Edward Abbey wrote in the book's "Forward!," "has broken down." Even civil disobedience relied too heavily on an established system of reform, he suggested, while ecotage provided a means of directly and immediately confronting industrial development when other means failed. "It is time for women and men, individually and in small groups," wrote Foreman, "to act heroically and admittedly illegally in defense of the wild."[92]

Women and men, individually and in small groups, did exactly that in Earth First!'s early years. In 1983 the "Bonnie Abzug Feminist Garden

Club"—named after one of the members of Abbey's Monkey Wrench Gang—spiked a stand of trees in Oregon's Willamette National Forest, and the following year the "Hardesty Avengers" notified the Willamette Forest supervisor that a proposed timber sale in the Hardesty Mountain roadless area contained sixty-three pounds of spikes.[93] In both instances the Forest Service spent time and money de-spiking the sales. Over the next seven years, tree spikers struck repeatedly in Oregon, Washington, and British Columbia. Gradually the practice spread to other states too. In 1989 there were a dozen incidents in Northern California alone.[94]

Tree spiking was the most unequivocal statement of Earth First!'s militancy. By booby-trapping the forest, Earth First! edged toward an armed defense of wilderness and seemed willing to risk human well-being for the sake of trees. The backlash came quickly. In the late 1980s tree spiking became the easiest way to turn public opinion against Earth First! In Oregon, the Forest Service offered $5,000 for information about tree spikers.[95] Oregon congressman Bob Smith described tree spiking as "a radical environmentalist's version of razor blades in Halloween candy."[96] Hal Salwasser, a Forest Service researcher, called Earth First! "criminally insane." Louisiana-Pacific's managers began calling tree spikers "environmental terrorists."[97]

In May 1987, a Louisiana-Pacific band saw at a mill in Cloverdale, California hit a spike in a redwood log and shattered. Pieces of the saw flew across the room, one of them hitting a mill worker named George Alexander in the head, shattering his plastic shield. Alexander ended up in the hospital with a broken jaw, missing teeth, and major lacerations. It was the first injury attributed to tree spiking. There was evidence that the Cloverdale incident had nothing to do with Earth First!, but it nevertheless demonstrated the possibility of what spiking trees could lead to, scaring loggers and giving some Earth First!ers pause.[98] Criticism of radical environmentalism from politicians, the timber industry, the Forest Service, and the public grew louder. One year later senators from Idaho and Oregon attached a rider to a drug enforcement bill that made tree spiking a felony. A year after that, FBI and Forest Service agents in Montana subpoenaed several Wild Rockies Earth First!ers for a grand jury regarding a tree-spiking incident in Idaho.[99]

Tree spiking put mainstream environmentalists in an awkward position, at a distance and yet never separate from radicals. The easiest response was simple condemnation. Doug Scott, the Sierra Club's associate executive director, said, "Action in the night is on a slippery slope down toward terrorism, and that is a slippery slope that I abhor." And yet the tactic was on a slope and not off of a cliff; even established groups could see a winding path from lobbying to some forms of ecotage. "Boy, I could probably put cement in a bulldozer," one "high-ranking staffer at a Washington environmental group" told a New York Times reporter under cover of anonymity. More forthrightly, the National Audubon Society's Brock Evans told the Los Angeles Times, "I honor Earth First! for having the guts to do the things they do."[100]

In late 1988, at the height of the tree-spiking controversy, Wilderness Society staffers felt pulled in two directions. Pointing to the increasing association of established conservation groups with "more fringe and radical activist groups," a staff member distributed a memorandum recommending a clear public statement of disapproval and a small contribution to a tree-spiking fund in Oregon that the Bureau of Land Management used for information leading to arrests. One staffer responded, "Before we attack another environmental group in such an aggressive way, we'd better be damn sure it's a good idea." Another agreed. "The time to talk about tree spiking is if we are asked or if someone tries connecting us to this practice," she wrote. The tree-spiking fund, she pointed out, was associated with the local timber industry, and it was likely that "the same companies who have practiced their own form of violence against people engaged in peaceful civil disobedience are contributing to the fund." Reminding the other staff members of a recent incident in which a logger almost felled a tree with a protester on it, she concluded, "If this logger or his employer is contributing to the tree spiking fund, I for one would not want [the Wilderness Society] on record in support of the effort."[101]

Radicals themselves never shied from debating the merits and failings of tree spiking. Earth First! recognized that many within its own ranks remained uncomfortable with ecotage, whether for moral or strategic reasons. Public attacks by a U.S. congressman led some Montana Earth First!ers to distance themselves from the tactic. "Neither I nor anyone else that I know of affiliated with Montana Earth First! has ever spiked trees," insisted Montana Earth First! coordinator Gary Steele.[102] In Oregon, Earth First!ers created the Cathedral Forest Action Group in part to deemphasize ecotage. "The dignity of people outside CFAG is recognized by following a nonviolent code," explained Mary Beth Nearing and Brian Heath, two stalwarts of the old-growth fights. "For us, that eliminates tree spiking and survey stake pulling—either individually or as a group."[103] But through many fierce arguments about ecotage—one of them leading to the resignation of the *Earth First! Journal*'s editor—Earth First!'s basic stance remained the same. The group did not explicitly endorse ecotage but celebrated the efforts of those who engaged in it on their own initiative. "We are not terrorists," Foreman insisted. "But we are militant. We are radical. . . . We will not officially spike trees or roads but we will report on the activities of those who do. They are heros [sic]."[104]

That basic stance began to falter in 1990 when Judi Bari and Ecotopia Earth First! disavowed tree spiking more forcefully than had any Earth First!ers. Tree spiking, Bari argued, didn't work. Despite dozens of recorded instances of spiked tree stands, most of those stands ended up cut. Those that remained were more likely saved by legislative activity or public pressure than by sabotage. If the goal of tree spiking was to cost timber companies money then the reasoning behind it was flawed, Bari pointed out, as it was the tax-funded Forest Service that generally absorbed the cost of removing spikes. In addition, spiking trees stoked the anger of loggers and sheriffs and put activists engaging in civil disobedience at risk of retribution. Finally, it was inherently dangerous. Although it was likely that no Earth First! tree-spike had ever hurt any person, the risk remained. "The point is," Bari wrote, "that if you advocate a tactic, you had better be prepared to take responsibility for the results."[105] Was Earth First!'s commitment to ecocentrism firm enough to put human life at risk?

At the heart of Bari's rejection of tree spiking was her sense of social justice and her desire to build an alliance with loggers. Bari tried to reconcile her ecocentric views with her background in labor organizing, and Northern California forest activism offered her an opportunity. Because Earth First! had operated almost entirely on public lands in the 1980s it tended to view the Forest Service as its main antagonist. Pacific Lumber, Ecotopia

Earth First!'s longtime adversary, was a private company logging private land, where trees were a capital investment and so the imperative to log them was much greater. Here, Bari's experience targeting corporate management rather than public agencies proved especially useful. She worked toward partnerships with timber workers by telling them that Pacific Lumber executives were their real enemies. Loggers remained unconvinced by Bari's overtures as long as they felt threatened by spikes, so spiking had to end. Gene Lawhorn, a timber worker and environmentalist from Oregon who first challenged Bari to speak out against tree spiking, insisted that the practice was dangerous for loggers, bad publicity for environmentalists, and an effective wedge issue which timber companies could use to prevent environmentalist-logger alliances. "Renouncing tree spiking is not a compromise," Lawhorn said, "but a move forward."[106]

Many within Earth First! remained unmoved. Some simply resented what they considered a compromise, telling Ecotopia Earth First! to "go back to the Sierra Club."[107] Paul Watson was as usual the most strident, and he zeroed in on Bari's core concern. "Those anthropocentric socialistic types—whose hearts bleed for the antiquated rights of the workers—were won over," he wrote of Ecotopia Earth First!'s stance. Loggers, Watson believed, were guilty by association. "Certainly they are being exploited by the companies," he wrote, "but they have made the decision to be exploited. The trees have not." Civil disobedience, meanwhile, was of only limited utility. "Redwood Summer is not an Earth First! type of action," Watson said of Bari's 1990 old-growth campaign. "The establishment loves CD. The authorities are trained to deal with it. There are no surprises."[108]

Nonetheless, Ecotopia Earth First! had reached a decision. In its public announcement it called its renunciation "not a retreat, but rather an advance that will allow us to stop fighting the victims and concentrate on the corporations themselves."[109] In a memo to the broader Earth First! Movement, Bari claimed that in Northern California, "Earth First! has been so successful in working & strategizing with timber workers that the alienation caused by tree spiking, not to mention the danger, be it real or imagined, was harming our efforts to save this planet."[110]

The tree-spiking debate changed Earth First! and radical environmentalism, although not decisively. The abandonment of tree spiking and eventually of ecotage by Earth First! did not fundamentally transform the group or its relationships with allies and antagonists. Bari's attempts at logger-environmentalist alliances never fully materialized.[111] And mainstream organizations, although they publicly disparaged tree spiking, continued to hold some sympathy for radical activism and for the risks that radicals took to defend forests. Within Earth First!, arguments about strategy and tactics raged on. A year after Ecotopia Earth First!'s moratorium on spiking and days before he began a weeks-long jail sentence for protesting the construction of an astronomical observatory on Arizona's Mt. Graham, Erik Ryberg posed the same questions about civil disobedience that Bari had about tree spiking. Echoing Abbey, Watson, and other proponents of ecotage, Ryberg asked whether civil disobedience had become "nothing more than a ritual of dissent which raises *no* questions, a game which holds *no* surprises, a compulsive societal twitch that confuses no one, subverts nothing, and which in practice does as much to legitimize power as it does to undermine it?"[112]

Nevertheless, after Judi Bari's declaration Earth First! became increasingly committed to traditional civil disobedience, while monkeywrenchers carried out their activities without the Earth First! stamp. Bari's critique had suggested the limits of ecotage to the point that even Foreman began to express doubts. "But is tree spiking really effective?" he asked in 1991. "Is it of significant value in stopping the logging of our forests? Probably. In some cases. But . . . I dunno. It's like a tough piece of jerky being chewed around the campfire. You chew and you chew and you chew and nothing much happens. You work up a lot of spit, but you still have a big glob in your mouth. I dunno."[113]

Foreman's opaque analogy considered tree spiking's effectiveness as opposed to its morality, but the two could not be separated. Earth First! was willing to try many tactics of dubious utility, but few produced the sort of soul-searching that tree spiking did. If tree spiking was in fact explicitly violent, it was for many a bridge too far. Advocating violence to achieve political ends meant rendering a final judgment on the legitimacy of the liberal democratic procedures that Earth First! criticized and circumvented but never entirely gave up. Further, it meant declaring the battle against not just institutions but the modern world itself, and drawing a bright line between people and nonhuman nature. Earth First! let others take up that fight. "It's time to leave the night work to the elves in the woods," Bari advised in 1994.[114] The "elves in the woods" were anonymous members of the Earth Liberation Front, an Earth First!-inspired group of saboteurs who in the 1990s began using tree spiking and arson to combat logging, recreational development, suburban sprawl, and genetic engineering.[115] Even more radical, ELF took up where Earth First! left off. Tree spiking represented the horizon of Earth First!'s willingness to judge nature above all human interest.

REDWOOD SUMMER

Bari spent less time than many other prominent Earth First!ers spelling out her views in detail. She was primarily an activist, and her actions spoke clearly and consistently. In 1989 she assisted employees at a Georgia-Pacific lumber mill as they filed claims with the Occupational Safety and Health Administration after a dangerous chemical spill, and later she helped workers at a Pacific Lumber mill publish an underground newsletter, *Timber Lyin'*, challenging the official company newsletter, *Timberline*. Her organizing around redwoods culminated in an event called "Redwood Summer," which brought over three thousand people to the hills and mountains of Northern California in 1990 for a series of marches, rallies, and direct actions from early June through August. Ecotopia Earth First! organized blockades, tree-sits, picket lines, and demonstrations at corporate offices. Whenever the opportunity presented itself, Ecotopians held impromptu discussions between activists and loggers. Although many staunch Earth First!ers viewed any cooperation with loggers, miners, or dam-builders as a form of capitulation to industrial society, Bari argued that the modern world could only be changed from the inside out.[116]

Bringing several thousand activists into the woods and logging towns of Northern California for weeks of marches and direct actions was a dangerous proposition for all involved, and Bari tried to defuse the possibility of violence through her tree-spiking moratorium. But violence was already a part of old-growth activism. In 1989, outside of Whitehorn on the Humboldt-Mendocino border, a group of Earth First!ers confronted the

Lancasters, a family that ran a small logging company that had been violating its timber harvest plan. The confrontation erupted into a fist fight. A fifty-year-old activist named Mem Hill tried to intercede and got knocked unconscious. A shotgun blast into the air finally sent the environmentalists running.[117] In 1991, near Boonville in Mendocino County, two Earth First! activists chained themselves to a cattle guard to blockade a road until a court order took effect halting nearby logging. A local man and his wife nearly ran over the activists, stopping their truck only when a sheriff's deputy reached through the window and grabbed the keys.[118] Soon after the Whitehorn incident, Bari, Cherney, a friend, and several children skidded off the road when a logging truck hit Bari's station wagon from behind, slamming it into a parked vehicle. Bari assumed the collision was an accident until she realized that she and Cherney had blockaded the same driver and truck a day earlier.[119]

Bari was both the Earth First!er most associated with opposing potential violence and the most notable victim of it. On May 24, 1990 Bari and Cherney drove from Oakland to Berkeley to pick up their musical equipment for an afternoon show in Santa Cruz promoting Redwood Summer. They had stopped in the East Bay to meet with Seeds of Peace, a group helping Earth First! prepare for the summer's actions. As Bari's Subaru station wagon approached Interstate 580 at Park and Thirty-Fourth Street in Oakland, a ball bearing rolled into place and completed an electrical circuit, triggering the detonation of an eleven-inch pipe bomb under the driver's seat. The explosion warped the front end of the car, blew out the windshield, and collapsed the passenger compartment. Cherney suffered minor injuries, while Bari took the brunt of the blast and had to be extracted from the car by emergency responders. Within an hour, a dozen FBI agents began an investigation. Normally the Bureau of Alcohol, Tobacco and Firearms would have jurisdiction in a bombing case, but because Earth First! was on the FBI's list of domestic terrorist groups, the ATF handed the case over to the special agents on the scene. The FBI briefed the Oakland Police Department on Bari and Cherney, explaining that they were part of a terrorist organization, some members of which had recently been arrested in Arizona for attempting to destroy a power line and plotting to cut off power to several nuclear facilities. Later that afternoon the police arrested both

Cherney and Bari on charges of illegally transporting a bomb. The police moved Cherney to the downtown jail and posted several officers outside of Bari's room at Highland Hospital.[120]

Bari remained in the hospital for the next two months before moving back to Mendocino County to further recuperate. She never regained the full use of her right leg. Gradually, mainstream environmental organizations rallied to Bari's and Cherney's defense. Greenpeace, which had suffered its own bombing in 1985 when French commandos attached mines to the Greenpeace ship *Rainbow Warrior*, put up one million dollars in bail for Bari and Cherney. Along with Friends of the Earth, Greenpeace helped convince the Sierra Club and the National Audubon Society to publicly question the FBI's investigation.[121]

Although Bari spent Redwood Summer in the hospital, she insisted that it should continue without her. Cherney remained involved in the summer's activities and several other Northern California Earth First!ers stepped into Bari's place. Redwood Summer and the bombing made Ecotopia Earth First! one of the most talked about Earth First! groups in the nation. Bari, however, remained skeptical of radical environmentalism's culture and politics. She embraced the idea of ecocentrism and the strategy of direct action, but she rejected blanket attacks on humanity along with the single-minded defense of wilderness despite any social costs. Bari's criticisms were not new, but she did more than just voice them; she inculcated activists in one of the most dynamic Earth First! regions to her way of thinking. By 1990 Earth First! was stretched to the point of breaking between the intermountain West and the West Coast.

The break came as Redwood Summer wound down. The *Earth First! Journal* devoted its September issue to what some considered the splintering of Earth First! and others considered the group's maturation. Most of the journal's staff announced their respective resignations, and several prominent articles discussed the battle between the "new guard" and the "old guard," the place of social context in wilderness campaigns, and the growing influence of California Earth First! groups. Howie Wolke expressed his dismay at the infighting and wondered if he was still a part of Earth First!. "Wilderness is the real world," he wrote, making clear his fundamental concern, "and its importance dwarfs all human demons, real and imagined."[122]

Dave Foreman and his professional and personal partner, Nancy Morton, wrote what they called a "Dear John" letter to Earth First! "We feel like we should be sitting at the bar of a seedy honky-tonk," they began, "drinking Lone Star, thumbing quarters in the country-western jukebox, and writing this letter on a bar napkin." They emphasized their pride in the group's accomplishments and their confidence that it would continue to do good work. "But we cannot escape the fact that we are uneasy with much in the current EF! movement," they wrote. In particular they worried about "an effort to transform an ecological group into a Leftist group." Earth First!, they explained, was always a wilderness preservation group before and above anything else, and its proponents followed that principle: "We are biocentrists, not humanists." Calling their departure a "no-fault divorce," they declared their separation from what Earth First! had become.[123]

"I feel like I should be sitting around base camp listening to Bob Marley, smoking a hooter, and writing this on the back of a rolling paper," Bari responded, emphasizing the cultural distance between the Southwest and the West Coast. She made clear her respect for Foreman, "for introducing me and many others to the idea of biocentrism, and for the decentralized, non-hierarchical non-organization he helped set up in EF!" But she also expressed her approval of Foreman's departure, because of his unwillingness to support the changes within Earth First! A narrow focus on wilderness preservation to the exclusion of any other forms of activism could not last, she felt; Earth First! had to concern itself with changing the way people thought and behaved, so that wilderness preservation would become a priority for society as a whole. "In other words, Earth First! is not just a conservation movement," Bari wrote, "it is also a social change movement."[124] With those words Bari neatly summarized what was for some in Earth First! an obvious statement and for others a betrayal of the group's most essential principle.

CONCLUSION

After the shakeup of 1990, Earth First! remained a conflicted group but one gradually moving toward a more ecumenical style of environmentalism. That new style allowed Earth First! more allies, more supporters, and for many a more palatable sense of ends to work toward and means to get there. What got lost was the clarity and purposefulness of an Earth First! that claimed to represent, almost alone, strictly nonhuman interests. An ecocentric view—and its implicit skepticism toward humanism—was Earth First!'s great strength and weakness. The strength came from a single and undeniably radical idea that, like a lighthouse, cut through the fog of competing interests and values. At a time when the mainstream, national environmental groups entrenched themselves in Washington, D.C. and fixed on technical legislative battles, Earth First! championed unqualified resistance to industrial development through direct action. Mikal Jakubal admitted as much to skeptical *Fifth Estate* readers, writing that "it is the heartfelt desire to act on one's beliefs that deeply infuses EF! and lends the movement a vitality and spirited sense of purpose and humor not often found in activist milieus today."[125] For environmental activists who believed that the gradualism and moderation of conventional democratic reform could not possibly address what was a clear and growing crisis, Earth First! offered the possibility of an energetic, grassroots alternative. For those who believed that liberal humanism itself lay at the root of the environmental crisis, only groups like Earth First! offered a commensurate response.

Ecocentrism's great weakness was that it risked advocating simplistic and myopic ideas. The same sort of holism that could focus a collective effort on a single goal could also reduce complicated questions to deceptively easy solutions. Painting all people with a broad brush was not only counterintuitive but often counterproductive. As Bari pointed out, sabotaging bulldozers did little to hurt large lumber corporations, which contracted out logging operations to smaller companies that actually owned the equipment. More fundamentally, Earth First!'s broad condemnations ignored profound social differences and glossed over the divergent roles that different people played in the transformation of the natural world. "While the split is truly a multiple fracture," Estelle Fennell wrote of Earth First!'s travails in *Fifth Estate*, "the major conflict can be boiled down to a difference of opinion over whether radical environmentalism can be effective without supporting social justice issues."[126] Too often ecocentrists began conversations by pointing an accusatory finger at everyone in the room, uninterested in their particular stories.

Anarchism provided an alternative to the complete rejection of liberal humanism. Disavowing unqualified individualism, anarchists instead advocated small-scale, decentralized communities, a careful regard for natural order, and an end to industrialization. In these ways anarchists and radical environmentalists were allied, and Alien-Nation, Murray Bookchin, and Earth First! could speak the same political language. But anarchists held a strong faith in human nature as well, and sought various forms of social justice. Although they readily admitted the persistence of human folly—most notably in the form of the state—they believed a desire for freedom and justice ran like a current through history, ready to be released in the service of a better society. People always stood at the center of the anarchist ideal, and here anarchism and radical environmentalism parted ways.

Radical environmentalists had few satisfying answers for the criticisms that Bookchin, Bari, ecofeminists, and green anarchists voiced, but radical environmentalism's critics did not have entirely satisfactory answers themselves. In part the ongoing argument was the familiar one about radicalism and reform. Soon after Redwood Summer, one of the *Fifth Estate's* readers complained about the paper's favorable coverage of Bari's signature campaign. "The Redwood Summer cover story refers to the summer's actions as the 'environmental equivalent of the 1964 voter registration campaign in Mississippi,' " wrote J.B. "Since when do anti-industrial anarchists support either voting or environmentalism or reproductions of '60s liberal reform?"[127] The same crucial questions that Bari asked about monkeywrenching's effectiveness could be applied to her own strategies. Redwood Summer almost certainly affected the debate over reform of forest management in California, but many complained that in immediate terms it did not save a single tree.

More fundamentally, Earth First! and its critics contended with the distinction—if any—between human beings and nonhuman nature. Recoiling from environmental misanthropy, some critics of radical environmentalism risked muddying the waters so much that it became hard to know what counted as a wrong committed against nonhuman nature. Radical environmentalists at times erred in the other direction, blaming an abstract "humanity" for anything that wild nature might not somehow sanction. Connecting these two extremes was what the biologist Stephen Jay Gould once called "an essential and unresolvable tension between our unity with nature and our dangerous uniqueness."[128] Earth First! never stopped struggling with that tension. "We are creatures of the earth and we participate in the great mysteries of the earth," Earth First!er James Berry said of humans. "While we are each different we share an identity."[129] The overly generalized "we" led radicals in many troubling directions, but it also led to a sense of communion with the natural world and an appreciation of people's place in it.

Edward Abbey depicted the internecine fights at Earth First! gatherings in a chapter of *Hayduke Lives!* The scene is a Round River Rendezvous, at which a single character—"Bernie Mushkin," a social ecologist from Berkeley—represents both Murray Bookchin and Alien-Nation. As Dave Foreman speaks to the crowd, Mushkin calls him a "fascist," "racist," "terrorist," and "eco-brutalist." Then Mushkin takes the stage and delivers a screed against all assembled, accusing them of setting the environmental movement back several decades. Mushkin is a comical character, and although Abbey allows him a reasonable approximation of Bookchin's actual criticisms, Abbey generally leaves him flustered and ineffective.[130]

But even Abbey could not completely discount Bookchin's respect for human dignity. Abbey, amid all his complaints about people, and his claims to prefer deserts to human society, was given to rare moments of reverence for the human. In *Desert Solitaire*, Abbey describes finding the dead body of a tourist at the edge of the canyonlands. He notes how easy it is to joke about the anonymous death, and how a dead person is simply an example of natural cycles that keep the planet habitable. And then he points out how insufficient this impersonal perspective is. "A part of our nature rebels against this truth and against that other part which would accept it," he writes, searching out the limits of his own radical beliefs. "A second truth of equal weight contradicts the first, proclaiming through art, religion, philosophy, science and even war that human life, in some way not easily definable, is significant and unique and supreme beyond all the limits of reason and nature. And this second truth we can deny only at the cost of denying our humanity."[131]

6

The Limits and Legacy
of Radicalism

Earth First! reached the limits of radicalism in the 1990s. Those limits were
not absolute, but they forced the Earth First! movement to change—in the
minds of some, to change enough that Earth First! became something else
entirely. Direct action was still radical environmentalists' defining tactic,
but the tree-spiking debate had already limited the role of ecotage and elevated the importance of civil disobedience. Ecocentrism remained the philosophical core of Earth First!-style radical environmentalism, but it was an
ecocentrism tied more and more to scientific justifications. Ecology gradually migrated to the center of the conservation movement over the course
of the century and has always been at the heart of radical environmentalism. By the 1990s, though, some Earth First!ers had aligned themselves
almost completely with conservation biology, a mission-driven scientific
field that bridged empirical claims and passionate activism. Wilderness also
remained a fundamental category for radicals, but the dynamics of wilderness advocacy shifted. One of the most important environmental battles of
the 1990s—over Northern California's Headwaters Forest—took place on
private land, helping to revise an understanding of "wilderness" that had
long rested on public agencies and public lands.

At the same time, radical environmentalism changed the environmental movement as a whole. What had once been extreme was now mainstream. This was especially the case at the Sierra Club, where a ballot system and direct election of the board of directors allowed members to push for rapid change. On logging, on dam removal, and on ambitious wilderness bills, pressure from grassroots members and from newly elected directors pushed the Club to take positions that just a decade earlier had defined the movement's outer fringe. The legacy of radical activism also shook the Club in a years-long fight over immigration restriction, a controversy that suggested not only the persistence of radicals' subordination of social difference and social justice but also how that subordination had long been part of the mainstream movement as well.

The fragmenting of Earth First!-style activism in the 1990s and the speed with which its signature issues appeared among mainstream organizations made clear how close radical and mainstream environmentalists always were. Their differences were significant but their commonalities were more so. As Earth First! absorbed less criticism, its struggle to weigh environmentalism against industrial society and liberal humanism belonged to the movement as a whole.

THE REDWOOD FORESTS

In their broad, philosophical writings, radical environmentalists often used abstract terms like "civilization," "the environment," and "the natural world." In their own personal experiences these abstractions took concrete form. "Civilization" was most immediately a shopping mall, a dam, a strip mine, or a nuclear reactor. Similarly, "nature" at its most meaningful was a nearby river, a threatened desert, an endangered species, or a high mountain lake. The passion with which radical environmentalists fought against development ran strongest when it cohered around a particular place. And for many radicals in the late 1980s and 1990s, no place meant more than the old-growth forest stands of the Pacific Northwest.

The most immediately distinct characteristic of the West Coast's temperate rainforests—stretching from Northern California through Oregon and Washington and into Canada—is their size. With the exception of junipers, the forests are home to the largest species within each conifer genus that grows there, including Douglas firs, noble firs, sugar pines, ponderosa pines, Sitka spruce, and Port Orford cedars. Each of these species is capable of growing higher than the tallest trees in the eastern United States, and some can reach nearly twice the height of any tree east of the Mississippi. Looming above all of them are the redwoods, the tallest trees in the world. At their greatest height, coast redwoods begin to approach four hundred feet, taller by far than the Statue of Liberty from the base of the foundation to the tip of the torch.[1]

Coast redwoods grow so high that their canopies remained unexplored until the 1990s. Scientists expected to find a "redwood desert"—a mass of branches and foliage, and little else—but found instead a redwood forest. Redwood trunks and branches are capable of producing "reiterated trunks" that sprout dozens or hundreds of feet above the ground, growing alongside the main bole. At the point where the trunks meet, as well as on large branches, soil can collect. These patches of "canopy soil" can become several feet deep, hundreds of feet in the air. Epiphytes—plants that live on other plants—spring from the canopy soil. Ferns and shrubs flourish high up in redwood crowns, as do other trees: firs, hemlocks, and spruce can be found growing in redwood canopies.

Redwoods' ecological relationships reach beyond surrounding plants and into the clouds. Redwood trees transport water from the ground to hundreds of feet above it, but they also drink from the coastal fog of Northern California summers. Stripped of redwoods, a forest stand might lose close to a third of its water gain because of increased solar radiation, accelerated evaporation, and the loss of moisture that redwoods harvest from foggy days and transfer to the forest floor. Even more sensitive to climate and geography than the lesser giants around them, redwoods range only from Big Sur halfway up the California coast to just a few miles over the Oregon border.

Tall as they are, coastal conifers may be even more impressive for their longevity. Most of their ages are measured in centuries; some are measured in millennia. The redwoods, again, are exceptional, and are among the oldest trees in the world. Redwoods grow about fifty feet in their first couple of decades and usually reach maximum height sometime during their eighth century. Young redwoods that find themselves surrounded by taller trees and trapped in shadow stop growing for many years. With what humans can only describe as patience, they wait until a big tree falls and a shaft of light breaks through, and then they sprout rapidly. Scientists cannot tell exactly how old most redwoods are because so many of them have been hollowed out by fire and lost their rings, but they estimate that the largest—called "giants" or "titans"—are well over two thousand years old. The numbers are big enough that redwoods' ages often require points of reference; they are described as trees that began growing during the reign of Julius Caesar, that reached full height during the middle ages, that already constituted old growth by the time Columbus arrived in the Americas.

Logging in Northern California started when many of these trees were into their second or even third centuries. Cutting began at lower elevations, near the coast, where the soil was more productive and the trees closer to market. Forests withdrawn for public lands were higher and still mostly uncut by the middle of the twentieth century. But while the timber industry had until then lobbied to keep public forests off of the market in order to keep prices high, the housing boom of the 1950s and 1960s led to greater demand and increased logging on federal land. By the 1980s almost all of the unprotected lower elevation old growth was gone and what remained further inland fell to the saw at a faster and faster clip.

Those forests did not vanish without a fight. When Earth First! took up the cause of Northern California redwoods, it joined a long list of conservation organizations and a century-old concern for the survival of the state's most iconic tree. "No tree species in modern U.S. history," writes Jared Farmer, "has inspired more passion and controversy than the coast redwood."[2] In the late nineteenth century the Sierra Club and the Sempervirens Club called attention to redwood logging in the Santa Cruz Mountains south of San Francisco, attention that led to the establishment of the California Redwood Park (later renamed Big Basin Redwoods State Park). In the 1900s William Kent, a businessman who later served in Congress and helped create the National Park Service, donated a grove of the Bay Area's last old-growth redwood to the federal government with the understanding that Theodore Roosevelt would then designate it Muir Woods National Monument. In the mid-twentieth century conservationists looked north to Humboldt and Del Norte counties, where logging companies gained access to once remote forests, prompting the newly formed Save the Redwoods League and the Sierra Club to campaign for what would eventually become Redwood National Park. Still, the modest successes of West Coast conservationists were anomalies. Because old growth is difficult to define there is no precise account of how much disappeared, but by any reasonable estimate the vast majority has been logged. By the 1990s old-growth redwood forests were likely reduced by 95 percent from what stood before European settlement.[3]

For some environmentalists it was rivers, or deserts, or mountains that came to represent the mystery and majesty of nature. For many of the most confrontational activists of the 1990s it was thousand-year-old trees. For these activists, the size and age of old-growth forests moved them to humility before something so unfathomable, and left them full of shame at the ease with which people destroyed it. And shame could very easily become anger that, when combined with a sense of urgency, offered a justification for uncompromising positions and radical tactics.

OLD GROWTH, SPOTTED OWLS,
AND CONSERVATION BIOLOGY

In the 1980s and 1990s activists paired awestruck reverence of nature with scientific arguments for the importance of biological complexity and diversity. The broader conservation movement had relied on sentiment since the late nineteenth century, and then increasingly on technical knowledge in the late twentieth. The two approaches were distinct but never entirely; the mechanics of ecological processes might arouse as much wonder as the sight of a majestic tree, and scientific justifications for conservation were usually packaged with an emotional appeal. Forest activism required reaching people both in their hearts and in their heads.

Scientific research could provide a counterweight to the sort of economic demands that informed the profession of forestry. Decades of orthodoxy had taught foresters to aim for "regulated" forests where young trees predominated rather than "overmature" forests where annual decay canceled out annual growth. As timber, young trees were productive while old trees were wasted space. This philosophy put a premium on logging and in the short term maximized lumber yield. When the Forest Service took the approach to its logical conclusion, allowing extensive clear-cutting in order to meet midcentury demand for timber, forest visitors cried foul for aesthetic and then ecological reasons. Clear-cuts were jarring scars on a green mountainside, and they also destabilized slopes, disrupted watersheds, and fragmented wildlife habitat.[4]

Environmental organizations put pressure on land management agencies to adopt new scientific approaches to their work, a pressure sometimes matched from within the agencies themselves. This was especially true of the Forest Service. In the 1980s, agency foresters like Jerry Franklin pushed for "new forestry" practices that would balance timber production with ecosystem management and timber sale planner Jeff DeBonis created a group called the Association of Forest Service Employees for Environmental Ethics to criticize his own agency's fixation on logging.[5] "Ecological forestry," as the historian Samuel Hays calls it, treated the forest as a whole rather than as a sum of its parts.[6] Forests provided habitat for wildlife and so the protection of biodiversity, a buffer for riparian areas and so the protection of watersheds, and nutrients for soil and so the protection of loamy ground and all that grew from it. Long trained in silviculture, federal foresters increasingly brought to bear ecological sciences as well. In the early 1990s John Mumma, the first biologist ever to rise to the position of regional forester, resigned after refusing to contravene environmental laws in order to meet congressionally imposed timber targets. By then Paul Hirt was willing to suggest, in the pages of the *Earth First! Journal*, that "we appear to be in the midst of a major, historic revolt within the Forest Service."[7]

Chief among the new ideas that began to reframe forestry and land management was conservation biology. Conservation biologists took the insights of island biogeography—especially the relationship between the size and relative isolation of island habitats on the one hand, and species and genetic diversity on the other—and applied them to islands of wildlife in a sea of civilization. Habitat fragmentation, they argued, whether caused by four-lane highways or clear-cut forests, jeopardized biodiversity. The size of habitats mattered as did ease of migration between them, so that wildlife preserves should be large and interconnected. Led initially by the ecologist Michael Soulé, the field of conservation biology translated scientific research directly into policy prescriptions.[8]

Conservation biology drew from a spirit of urgency and intervention, pairing research and advocacy. In 1980, long before he began working with conservation biologists, Dave Foreman wrote, "Someone needs to forcefully state the importance of preserving the biological/ecological diversity of our planet."[9] Although Foreman did not know it, Soulé was doing just that, describing conservation biology as "a mission-oriented discipline" aimed at conserving biodiversity. By 1986, when the ecologist Reed Noss attended the National Forum on Biodiversity on behalf of Earth First!, science and politics mixed easily. Soulé spoke at the Forum, as did Paul Ehrlich, David Ehrenfeld, the biologist E.O. Wilson, and the paleontologist Stephen Jay Gould, all of them as interested in outcomes as in data. "[M]ore and more academic scientists are becoming angry enough about the loss of biodiversity to speak eloquently in its defense," Noss reported. This was not science for the sake of knowledge but for the sake of arresting an extinction crisis, one that conservation biologists believed people caused and people could prevent.[10]

Just as some scientists embraced advocacy in the mid-1980s, many activists made greater use of scientific research. In the *Earth First! Journal*, colorful descriptions of protesting and monkeywrenching gradually made room for sober articles about the plight of the Atlantic salmon or the Coeur d'Alene salamander. Mitch Friedman described conservation biology as "a welcome advance in conservation, where biological considerations have tended to be overcome by political and economic forces, in part due to a relative lack of solid data on which to base decisions."[11] As crucial as empirical research was becoming to conservation, though, its authority remained limited by the inevitable ambiguity of its theories and models. "Diversity" for instance, the term at the very center of conservation biology, was never an unalloyed good. Noss warned that when environmentalists stressed the importance of species diversity they risked playing into the hands of the logging industry. Measured simply as the total number of species present, diversity could serve as a justification for clear-cuts, because although clear-cuts fragmented habitat for the forest's longtime inhabitants, they also created habitat for those species that thrived in early successional environments. And clear-cuts created zones where different habitats met, providing simultaneously for adjacent sets of inhabitants as well as species that specialized in straddling—a set of circumstances that ecologists called "the edge effect."[12] In this sense biodiversity could be a relatively weak argument against clear-cuts in the short term, although in the long term, high edge-interior ratios did tend to reduce overall biodiversity. Scientific arguments relied on interpretation and political acumen.

Because the technical language of science remained politically muted, environmentalists had to speak in more lyrical terms as well, and here ambiguity was a boon. Much of the debate about forestry practice concerned old growth. The term "old growth" was not a technical one, or at least not very specific. Its exact definition shifted from region to region and even from forest to forest. Generally it involved a forest's size, estimated age, canopy, undergrowth, and ecological complexity. For decades the Forest Service had thought of old growth as little more than old trees, valuable for the wood they could provide and the space their removal would open up. In the 1970s and 1980s, research began to point to old growth as a key element in forest health. Old trees amplified structural diversity, contributing to a greater variety of habitats and a richer set of ecological processes. Cutting down old trees jeopardized those habitats and processes and so jeopardized the forests themselves. "In the rush to turn public and private forests into agricultural tree farms," Earth First!'s George Wuerthner warned, "we may be ripping apart ecological relationships which hold all forest ecosystems together."[13]

In 1986, after several years of study, a Forest Service Old-Growth Definition Task Group concluded that old-growth forests were "too complex in structure and composition to allow simple characterizations."[14] A year later, as environmentalists ratcheted campaigns to protect aged stands in the Pacific Northwest, the Wilderness Society was still reaching for a workable definition. The timber industry exploited this uncertainty, calling into question large discrepancies between Forest Service and Wilderness Society estimates of remaining old growth. The Northwest Forest Resource Council, an industry-affiliated trade group, claimed that the nation's forests were still flush. "Most of the mature forests in the national forests of the

Pacific Northwest," the council said, "are old growth under one definition or another."[15]

But if old growth could not be clearly defined, it could still be movingly described. Forest activists experimented with terms like "virgin" and "primeval." They settled on "ancient forests," a phrase that had the virtues of both accuracy and poetry, suggesting the complex whole that might be lost and also how trees that took centuries to grow were, in human terms, irreplaceable.[16] Rebranded, the fight to protect old growth continued under new banners. A coalition of grassroots and national environmental groups— including the Sierra Club, the Wilderness Society, and the National Audubon Society—loosely coordinated their efforts as the Ancient Forest Alliance. A group of philanthropic foundations provided funds for a new organization called the Western Ancient Forest Campaign, built with local activists from the Pacific Northwest. A congressman from Indiana named Jim Jontz introduced the Ancient Forest Protection Act, a bill calling for the designation of ecologically significant forest reserves. And a rotating crew of activists led by Earth First!'s Mitch Friedman organized an Ancient Forest Rescue Expedition, a weeks-long educational tour of the nation in a flatbed truck carrying a 730-year-old Douglas fir that Friedman and Ric Bailey bought from a wood products firm in Port Angeles, Washington.[17] "Old growth, or 'ancient forest,' " Friedman said after a Wilderness Society old-growth strategy conference in 1988, "is now a national issue."[18]

Just as the ancient forest campaign gained traction, the spotted owl controversy of the 1980s and 1990s tested environmentalists' use of both science and sentiment. Northern spotted owls nested in Pacific Northwest old growth, and the more that old growth fell to the saw, the fewer owls survived. As early as the 1970s, biologists asked the Forest Service to avoid cutting old growth near owl nests. By the 1980s spotted owl populations were in precipitous decline and environmentalists began filing lawsuits. Protecting the owls, they knew, was a way of protecting forests. Several laws offered leverage, including the National Forest Management Act (NFMA), which required the Forest Service to safeguard a diversity of plant and animal species as well as "viable populations" of vertebrate species; the National Environmental Policy Act (NEPA), which directed federal agencies to consider the environmental impact of their actions; and the Endangered Species Act (ESA), which had the power to stop logging trucks in their tracks if they threatened the extinction of an officially listed species. Lawsuits based on the NFMA in particular led a federal judge to issue an injunction in 1989 severely restricting logging in Oregon and Washington. Timber companies fought back, accusing environmentalists of privileging wildlife over livelihoods and landing the spotted owl on the cover of *Time* magazine.[19]

"When we try to pick out anything by itself," John Muir wrote, "we find it hitched to everything else in the universe."[20] Few things validated Muir's sense of interconnectedness more than did the spotted owl. Because the spotted owl thrived in old growth, it acted as a kind of scientific metonym for both the forests and the complex ecological relationships the forests housed, and even Forest Service biologists considered the owl an "indicator species" whose own health tracked the health of forest habitats. But the owl's connectedness was political as well as ecological. The Ancient Forest Alliance knew that the plight of the spotted owl could come to represent far more than the constitution of forests. Fairly or not, the owl could also signal environmentalists' dismissive attitude toward the economic well-being of entire communities. Owl protection coincided with declining economic fortunes in Pacific Northwest logging towns, making it easy to blame the one for the other. The timber industry estimated that owl protection would cost the region 50,00 to 100,000 jobs. Environmentalists claimed the industry blamed owl protection for job losses that were in fact the result of mechanization and the exporting of American logs. "In fact, then," the Wilderness Society's George Frampton wrote, "while this previously obscure, shy and attractive little creature may have hastened change, it simply accelerated trends that were driven and inevitable."[21]

Whether or not they were inevitable, the changes that swept through Pacific Northwest logging towns in the 1970s and 1980s were jarring, and by the late 1980s logging communities increasingly pinned declines in logging and milling work on spotted owl protection. Aware of this political context, the Ancient Forest Alliance hemmed and hawed over whether to continue its legal assault. The top-down approach that legal challenges entailed, with federal judges dictating policy for entire forests, did not endear environmentalists to logging communities. Pressure built within the environmental

community, however, and by 1992 environmentalists had not only forced the U.S. Fish & Wildlife Service to list the owl as endangered but also won an injunction under NEPA against logging old growth on Bureau of Land Management lands.[22] Pacific Northwest towns that had once allied themselves with environmental organizations now turned away. As the historian Erik Loomis has shown, timber industry labor unions in Washington and Oregon spent much of the twentieth century concerned about workplace safety (including chemical exposure among timber workers) and the protection of natural resources that logging towns relied on.[23] Conservationists and environmentalists were obvious partners in these concerns, and the AFL-CIO worked with the Sierra Club to compensate workers who lost jobs because of public lands conservation. Late twentieth-century economic contractions strained such partnerships, pitting environmentalists against jobs in loggers' eyes. By the 1980s loggers saw environmentalists as sacrificing local paychecks for the sake of an odd-looking bird.

Environmentalists had a harder time touting intact ancient forests when they stood just miles away from disintegrating logging towns. Whatever the relationship between the two, simple emotional appeals for one grew more fraught because of the other. Scientific data became all the more important, but even biological research remained a moving target. In the 1970s and 1980s biologists learned not only that the owl depended on old-growth forest but also that it ranged widely. As scientists discovered more and more nesting sites and longer and longer flight patterns, the forest preserves they recommended for spotted owl protection ballooned from three hundred to ten thousand acres each.

These sorts of uncertainties complicated policy debates. Spotted owl talk dominated Washington Earth First!'s Regional Rendezvous in 1986, where local Earth First!ers discussed a Forest Service plan to protect 550 pairs of owls in habitat areas of 2,200 acres per pair spaced roughly twelve miles apart. The Audubon Society, meanwhile, recommended protection for 1,500 pairs in habitat areas of anywhere from two thousand to six thousand acres, close together and connected by habitat corridors. The Forest Service claimed its plan would adequately protect a viable owl population, while the Audubon Society argued that 550 pairs was too few and that the islanded habitats envisioned by the Forest Service would create edge areas that would encourage competition and predation by barred and great horned owls.[24] Scientific findings were rarely definitive. What had been a battle of words became a battle of numbers.

The increased prominence of biological science in land management policymaking constituted one of the great environmental victories of the 1980s, but research went only so far without determined political support. U.S. district court judge William Dwyer's 1989 temporary injunction on all logging in western Washington and western Oregon found that, according to scientists, the Forest Service had not satisfied the requirements of the NFMA. In response, U.S. senators Mark Hatfield of Oregon and Brock Adams of Washington, both allies of the timber industry, bypassed the court with a spending bill rider that released more than a billion board feet from Dwyer's injunction and exempted future timber sales from legal challenge. Although Vermont Senator Patrick Leahy was preparing to enlist environmentalists in killing the rider, Sierra Club and Wilderness Society lobbyists withdrew their opposition when Hatfield agreed to include language acknowledging the ecological value of old growth. Having decided that the simple recognition of scientific findings constituted a victory, environmentalists gave up the political fight. Earth First!, meanwhile, held protests at Hatfield's Portland and Salem offices and accused the Club of betraying the Ancient Forest Alliance. "The rider from hell," as environmentalists called it once its consequences became clear, led to more than six hundred timber sales, many of them involving clear-cuts and most of them in spotted owl habitat.[25]

Judge Dwyer maintained jurisdiction over the spotted owl controversy even after the rider from hell, and the Forest Service knew that in order to satisfy the judge it would have to work with the best science available. The Forest Service hired Jack Ward Thomas, an agency biologist from Oregon, to head three separate scientific committees in the late 1980s and early 1990s. All of Thomas's committees advanced the idea of "ecosystem management"—that forests should be managed as a whole and not for the protection of any single species or for the harvesting of a single resource. Thomas used the research of conservation biologists to argue that protecting the spotted owl under the ESA necessarily meant protecting old-growth forests and thousands of species that inhabited them.

The Thomas committees also understood the political imperative of allowing logging on national forests at a level that could sustain the Pacific Northwest timber industry. In 1993, in the wake of newly elected president Bill Clinton's "timber summit" in Portland, the third Thomas committee released a Northwest Forest Plan that satisfied the environmental regulations the Forest Service had long neglected while still allowing over a billion board feet of timber, including logging in old-growth reserves.[26] Heartened at the prominent role of scientists in a Forest Service initiative and worried that the Northwest Forest Plan might be the last chance to exercise leverage, organizations like the Wilderness Society and Sierra Club Legal Defense Fund gave their support. "Mainstream Groups Sell Out," ran the headline on page one of the *Earth First! Journal*.[27]

Two years later the Sierra Club echoed Earth First!'s skepticism. Jack Ward Thomas had become Clinton's chief forester and continued to champion ecosystem management. Done right, *Sierra* magazine allowed, the approach could transform Forest Service practice. "At worst, however, Ecosystem Management serves as a smarmy justification for the same old abusive logging, a theoretical beauty strip around the clearcut."[28] The spotted owl debate tested and tried environmentalists' justifications for protecting old-growth forest, making clear that the balance between moral claims, scientific findings, and political muscle needed constant adjustment. Appeals to meaning and value on their own were at times shortsighted and too readily dismissed; research and data without political advocacy were too often manipulated. For radical environmentalists, this meant drawing more and more on the work of conservation biology while remaining committed to bedrock ecocentric principles and direct-action tactics, as well as taking into account the views of those who lived and worked alongside the land at risk.

PACIFIC LUMBER AND THE TIMBER WARS

Earth First! reimagined its political relationship to wilderness during the "timber wars," a series of battles over old growth in Northern California. The timber wars would eventually become the most visible environmental controversy in the country, drawing in several members of Congress, the governor of California, and the president of the United States. In the early 1980s, though, two environmental groups led the way among the redwoods: Earth First! and the Environmental Protection Information Center (EPIC), a tiny organization based in the town of Garberville just a few dozen miles south of Scotia. EPIC and Earth First! shared the same goals, but because EPIC consisted mainly of professional and amateur lawyers working within strict legal boundaries, the two groups maintained a comfortable distance in public. Operating apart, Earth First!'s brash direct actions and EPIC's methodical legal actions nonetheless worked in concert and set a template for forest activism.

Activists and logging companies fought the timber wars in Mendocino and Humboldt counties, north of the San Francisco Bay Area.[29] Initially environmentalists tried to limit the cuts of logging companies like Georgia-Pacific (G-P) and Louisiana-Pacific (L-P), high-volume timber companies known for clear-cutting their land down to the smallest commercially viable trees. On its own land in coastal Mendocino County, G-P clear-cuts decimated old-growth redwood and crept closer and closer to the borders of Sinkyone Wilderness State Park. Trees fell at Hotel Gulch, Dark Gulch, and Anderson Gulch. EPIC drew the line at a grove of trees next to Little Jackass Creek, an area that environmental activists—worried that its name would not inspire affection—called "Sally Bell Grove" after a Sinkyone Indian who had still lived on the rugged coast in the early twentieth century. EPIC spent the first years of the decade working through the state assembly to little effect, and in 1983 Earth First! entered the forest. Radical activists readied to stall logging while EPIC prepared a lawsuit against the California Department of Forestry (CDF) and the Save the Redwoods League and the Trust for Public Land began negotiating a purchase of Sally Bell Grove. In October EPIC posted an alert—"G-P Cutting Sinkyone"—on a Garberville theater marquee, and fifty Earth First!ers rushed into action, lying on the ground where trees might fall and forcing a halt to logging while EPIC convinced a judge to grant a temporary restraining order. "Once again," Mike Roselle concluded, "nonviolent direct action proved effective and essential in helping to protect our natural heritage."[30]

In 1985 EPIC, with the support of the International Indian Treaty Council and the Sierra Club, won its suit alleging that CDF approval of G-P's timber harvest plan violated the California Environmental Quality Act by not sufficiently seeking public input, neglecting the impact of logging on the creek's hillside, and failing to consult the Native American Heritage Commission.[31] The following year, G-P agreed to sell seven thousand acres to the Trust for Public Land and the Save the Redwoods League. The Trust for Public Land donated half, including Sally Bell Grove, to Sinkyone Wilderness State Park, and years later donated the other half to an Inter-Tribal Sinkyone Wilderness. The Sally Bell fight looked much like other Earth First! efforts in that activists placed themselves between chainsaws and old growth, but Sally Bell Grove was private land owned by a private company and environmentalists protected it by applying laws more often associated with public lands and, finally, purchasing the land and transferring it to public hands. They pursued the same strategy on a much larger scale a decade later.

By the 1990s the timber wars centered on the smallest of the "big three" timber companies and the one that, for many years, seemed least likely to anger environmentalists. Pacific Lumber, which operated almost entirely in Humboldt County, spent much of the twentieth century exercising restraint. The company practiced "selective cut" and "sustained yield," removing only 70 percent of mature trees and cutting no more in total wood than could grow back each year. It avoided the sort of clear-cuts that other companies practiced regularly. These policies were a matter of economy as much as ecology. Clear-cuts left soil loose and mobile and ready to wash into streams and rivers under heavy rains, and less soil on the forest floor meant less nutrients for second-growth trees and so less timber over time. In the early 1980s Pacific Lumber was neither the biggest nor the wealthiest company cutting trees in Northern California, but it possessed more high-value old growth than any other and 70 percent of all remaining privately held ancient redwood.[32]

In 1985 Pacific Lumber seemed a good example of the claims made by free-market environmentalists. A year later it became a cautionary tale about profligate use of resources in private hands. In 1985 the company owned 190,000 acres of land and the trees on it and, as free-market environmentalists suggested, ownership bred careful conservation. Sustained yield harvesting allowed modest profits while the company's thousand-year-old assets steadily increased in value. But the very qualities that made Pacific Lumber profitable, sustainable, and solvent over the long term left it vulnerable to exploitation. Because Pacific Lumber had protected its old-growth redwood groves, it had practically cornered the market for some of the most valuable wood in the industry. As investors soon realized, that same old growth could produce record profits in the short term through maximizing the timber harvest and clear-cutting big trees.

Charles Hurwitz was one of those investors. A corporate raider from Texas, Hurwitz owned several companies including the Houston-based Maxxam. Normally, exploiting a company like Pacific Lumber would be prohibitively difficult because of the cost and the reluctance of shareholders and the board of directors to sell. But in the 1980s both problems could be overcome through hostile takeovers using leveraged buyouts: deals financed with high-risk, high-yield securities (often "junk bonds"), the securities collateralized with assets from the soon-to-be purchased company. Maxxam's raid of Pacific Lumber featured some of the best-known names in 1980s corporate takeovers, including Michael Milken, Ivan Boesky, and the investment bank Drexel Burnham Lambert. By the time the Pacific Lumber board of directors realized what was happening there was little they could do but negotiate. In early 1986 they sold at $40 a share.[33]

The historian Darren Speece has made clear that Hurwitz did not single-handedly transform Pacific Lumber.[34] Years before Maxxam's takeover, an executive named John Campbell had already pushed the board of directors to increase the annual harvest and return to clear-cutting. But Hurwitz catalyzed Campbell's aggressive business plan and swept away whatever restraints still stood at Pacific Lumber's headquarters in San Francisco or in Scotia, its company town. Pacific Lumber under Hurwitz and Campbell turned into one of the most voracious timber companies on the West Coast, hiring hundreds of new employees and increasing shift lengths at its mills in order to more than double production. And it zeroed in on some of the oldest and biggest stands of redwood in Humboldt County and so in the world. Maxxam had incurred $795 million in debt to buy Pacific Lumber. To pay it off, Hurwitz sold most of Pacific Lumber's holdings not directly related to timber production and accelerated logging on some of the company's most valuable land, speeding the annual rate of cut from 140 million board feet in 1985 to 330 million in 1988.

For environmentalists like Darryl Cherney and Greg King, Pacific Lumber came to represent the worst of the Northern California timber industry. Cherney had been the frenetic center of Earth First! in Northern California before Judi Bari assumed the role in 1988, and he and Bari worked together closely in the 1990s. King had written about the lumber industry as a Sonoma County journalist and gave up reporting on logging in order to campaign against it. Having read about Pacific Lumber under Maxxam, King convinced Cherney that local Earth First!ers should focus their energy on the company's redwood stands. The two founded the Earth First! Redwood Action Team for that purpose.

King often snuck onto private land to explore old-growth forests. In March 1987, he searched for two parcels of old growth included in timber harvest plans Pacific Lumber had recently filed with the state. The parcels sat deep in the woods at the headwaters of Salmon Creek and the Little South Fork of the Elk River. Logging companies assigned parcels numbers, and environmental activists personalized them by giving parcels evocative names. King passed through a threatened stand that the Redwood Action Team called All Species Grove. Beyond All Species Grove, and deeper into the forest than he had ever penetrated, King found a stand of redwoods where the undergrowth was so thick he could barely move forward. He had wandered onto several thousand acres of the largest remaining stand of old-growth redwood on private land. The parcels he was searching for were 87–240 and 87–241. He named the whole area Headwaters Forest. The subsequent campaign against Maxxam remained a fight against logging old growth throughout Northern California and even the entire Pacific Northwest, but the Headwaters Forest was often figuratively and sometimes literally at the center of that fight.[35]

FORESTS FOREVER?

In late August 1987, Greg King and Jane Cope sat on platforms suspended 130 feet above the Headwaters Forest floor. When Humboldt County sheriff's deputies and Pacific Lumber security accused King and Cope of trespassing, King replied that Pacific Lumber's logging practices invalidated whatever claims the company held to the forest. Owning forestland that was also interconnected wildlife habitat did not, King suggested, exempt owners from responsible management. "I feel that Maxxam has abrogated its right to private property by its total destruction of it," he later told the press.[36]

Forest activists refined their views of ownership and stewardship in their fight against Pacific Lumber. The spotted owl controversy in the Pacific Northwest encouraged Earth First! to pivot toward a greater emphasis on ecological arguments, rooted in the work of conservation biologists, pairing radical environmentalists' core ecocentric beliefs with scientific research. In Northern California, meanwhile, following biological studies and ecocentric principles led radicals away from their longtime commitment to public lands and toward the defense of old-growth in forests owned by private companies. When scientific and moral considerations were paramount, legal and administrative boundaries meant less. In 1988 Howie Wolke recommended that Earth First!ers should "force the big timber companies to practice sustained yield on their private lands."[37] At that point forest activists were already beginning to push further. When they realized that some of the most intact stands of old growth grew in privately held forests, they began agitating for an end to logging in those stands. The fight over private forestry culminated in the Headwaters Forest. As increasingly ambitious strategies met with increasingly formidable obstacles, activists adapted with novel approaches and evolving ideas about where wilderness began and ended, yielding new legal and political conceptions of wilderness in a democratic society.

By 1990 both EPIC and Earth First! were stretched thin as legal and extralegal tactics began to stall. EPIC had become unshakably effective in its legal maneuvers, successfully arguing suit after suit charging that a given Pacific Lumber timber harvest plan violated state or federal environmental laws. But despite increasing legal help from the Sierra Club, the arduous work fell mostly to a handful of people, especially EPIC co-founder Robert Sutherland, known to all as "The Man Who Walks in the Woods" or more commonly "Woods," and Cecelia Lanman, an ex-labor organizer and veteran of the Sinkyone fight. For every suit that Woods, Lanman, and their colleagues filed based on a particular timber harvest plan, Pacific Lumber could draw up a dozen more plans for environmentalists to review. In between the filing of a suit and the granting of an injunction, Pacific Lumber might cut as many trees as it could manage unless Earth First!ers stood in the way. EPIC's work slowly eroded the rubber-stamp relationship between the CDF and the timber industry that Darren Speece has called "industrial corporatism."[38] But old growth continued to fall.

California's ballot initiative system offered the chance of a more enduring proscription. A few hundred thousand signatures earned any initiative a place on the statewide ballot and, if voters saw fit, the force of law. EPIC and its grassroots allies put together a thorough forest management reform package inspired in part by the "new forestry" of Jerry Franklin, banning nearly all clear-cutting, heavily restricting logging near riparian zones, requiring sustained-yield practices, creating a compensation and retraining fund for loggers, and authorizing a $750 million bond to purchase biologically significant old growth starting with Headwaters Forest. Soon large environmental organizations like the Sierra Club and the Natural Resources Defense Council joined the effort. When the initiative received enough votes, it officially became Proposition 130, but its backers made sure it was better known as "Forests Forever."

The gambit failed by a slim margin, polling at 56 percent a week before voting but earning only 48.5 percent on election day. The reasons for the defeat were varied. Voters were confused by another measure—Proposition 128 or "Big Green"—assembled by the California Public Interest Research Group. Big Green focused less on old growth, addressing clear-cutting but also greenhouse gasses and pesticide use. The Sierra Club supported both propositions, but Pacific Lumber described Forests Forever as a radical, Earth First!-inspired measure. And Pacific Lumber agreed to a voluntary moratorium on clear-cuts in old growth (although not on selective cutting) provided several key legislators refuse to support Forests Forever. In addition, the election came amid the 1991 Gulf War, pushing environmental issues down on voters' list of priorities. Hundreds of hours and millions of dollars' worth of reform effort yielded almost no tangible results as voters rejected both Forests Forever and Big Green.[39]

While EPIC tried to save the forest Earth First! defended the trees, meeting logging companies on the ground. Redwood Summer and the bombing of Bari and Cherney had already focused national attention on Northern California old growth. Freshly arrived activists like Alicia Littletree Bales staged dozens of actions on the coast and in the Headwaters Forest.[40] Then in the summer of 1995 another rider to another appropriations bill again pushed environmentalists back on their heels. The Republican wave election of 1994 put in power a House of Representatives hostile to environmental regulation, and in 1995 the House attached a "salvage logging" rider to a bill providing emergency funds for the victims of the Oklahoma City bombing. The rider ostensibly allowed timber companies to salvage dead trees before they lost value but was written broadly enough that just a handful of sick trees cleared the way for logging anywhere nearby. President Clinton initially vetoed the bill but then signed it under political pressure. Months later he called the bill "a mistake."[41]

The salvage rider infuriated activists and underscored the need for a long-term remedy. In Oregon's Willamette National Forest, an arson-caused fire opened up spotted owl habitat to salvage logging, and Earth First!ers mounted a fort complete with a moat and drawbridge on a logging road leading to Warner Creek. The Warner Creek blockade lasted a year, canceled the timber sale, and inspired similar stand-offs throughout the Pacific Northwest. But the overall effect of the salvage rider was bruising. "Each year," the environmental group Earth Island Institute wrote to its donors about ongoing activism to protect Headwaters Forest, "this coalition of activists and attorneys have managed to block the logging, but this year the salvage rider has created a whole new set of rules. The tactics of the past have been significantly weakened."[42]

To the chagrin of some activists, the tactics of the future involved relying on the federal government. Environmental activism on private land proved as difficult as it was urgent. Endangered species crossed legal boundaries all the time, and so efforts to preserve biodiversity had to cross those boundaries as well. But while legal distinctions meant little for wildlife, they meant a great deal for activists. "Private lands, where endangered species' habitats generally do not receive legal protection," Reed Noss wrote about his home state of Florida, "are simply not being managed in a way that will maintain red-cockaded woodpeckers, black bears, or Florida panthers."[43] The short-term answer was Earth First!-style activism; one long-term answer was making private lands public. "Ideally," George Wuerthner wrote, "our public and private lands should both be managed with ecological processes in mind. However, this would require a complete change in our attitudes about private property and what constitutes responsible stewardship."[44] Forest activists were gradually learning to craft approaches that could stretch across both public and private lands, a strategy that a group called the Wildlands Project would soon champion. In the pitched battle over the Headwaters, that sort of nuance remained out of reach.

Earth First!ers knew that conservation work on private property presented serious legal obstacles, and so they had long considered the possibility of a federal purchase of Headwaters. In 1993 Darryl Cherney began pushing a "debt-for-nature" plan in which Pacific Lumber would hand the Headwaters Forest to the federal government in exchange for forgiveness of several hundred million dollars of claims against Hurwitz related to management of United Savings Association of Texas, one of many Savings and Loans that the government had to bail out in the late 1980s.[45] By 1995 the Sierra Club's Ed Wayburn began discussing the same idea with California senators Dianne Feinstein and Barbara Boxer.[46]

Pacific Lumber itself drew the federal government in further. In 1996 the Ninth Circuit U.S. Court of Appeals ruled in favor of EPIC when it upheld an injunction on logging Owl Creek in Headwaters Forest because of the threat that logging posed to the endangered marbled murrelet. Pacific Lumber immediately filed a "takings" suit against the government, claiming that under the Fifth Amendment private property owners were due compensation if regulatory action deprived them of their property's value.

As the presidential election of 1996 approached, the Clinton administration was under fire from environmentalists for its acquiescence to the salvage logging rider and under the threat of Pacific Lumber's takings suit. Eager to defuse the suit and win back the green vote, the administration hoped to broker a deal that would save Headwaters and satisfy Hurwitz. Both sides steadily applied more pressure. Pacific Lumber threatened to begin salvage logging in Headwaters. Earth First! gathered thousands of protesters for a rally in the mill town of Carlotta and assembled a massive tree-sit at Owl Creek, where four hundred square feet of netting connected six redwoods. Behind the scenes, the Clinton administration spoke with senators Feinstein and Boxer, California governor Pete Wilson, and Pacific Lumber management.[47]

In late September, Feinstein announced what would soon be called "the Deal." The federal government would pay $250 million and the state of California $130 million for roughly 7,500 acres of Pacific Lumber land, including part of Headwaters Forest along with a thin buffer zone. The money would also facilitate the transfer of several thousand acres of non-old growth from another timber company to Pacific Lumber. Additionally, Pacific Lumber would file a Habitat Conservation Plan (HCP) and California Sustained Yield Plan for its remaining lands, and drop its takings suit.

The Deal satisfied no one fully, and many not at all. Ironing out the details took several more years, during which Earth First! continued to stage direct actions in the woods and outside the offices of politicians and executives. The Headwaters Forest Coordinating Committee—a coalition of groups whose key representatives ranged from longtime Sierra Club redwood activist Kathy Bailey to Earth First!er Karen Pickett—pushed to expand the protected acreage. David Brower, now the chairman of Earth Island Institute, was among the environmentalists who called Pacific Lumber's HCP "even worse than expected." HCPs had been added to the Endangered Species Act in 1982 as a way of giving property owners the flexibility to destroy endangered species and their habitats provided they offset that destruction by improving habitat elsewhere. Brower called it "the Headwaters hoax."[48] Environmentalists managed to strengthen the HCP's protections of coho salmon and marbled murrelet habitat, but not to everyone's satisfaction. Nonetheless, in 1999 Pacific Lumber, the federal government, and the state of California finalized the Deal, tacking on an extra $100 million for 1,600 more acres of old growth, much of it in Owl Creek.

As the Deal neared its final negotiations, Carl Pope, the Sierra Club's executive director, took stock of the Club's approach to private forestland. Moral hazard, Pope made clear, was one of the most vexing concerns about conservation through the purchase of private land. "They do not believe," he wrote of the Deal's environmental critics, "that public aquisition [sic] of the groves is sufficiently important to justify paying Hurwitz an inflated price and giving him the additional financial resources to purchase additional timber lands." The politics of purchasing private land twisted some of the Club's basic strategies. Building a legislative majority would no longer guarantee success, "because the landowner will always have a veto." Appealing to the public could have perverted consequences, since generating concern and anger were "the very actions that increase the landowners leverage and jack up the price." And there was added pressure for environmental organizations to complete a deal, given how challenging was activism on private lands. "There is little precedent for preventing all logging on such a valuable piece of private timberland for such an extended period of time," Pope noted. "Only public ownership has proven a reliable way of exercising public control over this kind of a resource."[49]

And yet purchasing land or land rights had long been a basic tool of the conservation movement. The Save the Redwoods League had relied on it. Muir Woods, one of the most visited stands of protected redwoods, gained recognition only after switching from private to public hands. Stephen Mather and the Sierra Club purchased the Tioga Road for Yosemite National Park. There was not only a federal program—the Land and Water Conservation Fund—dedicated to the acquisition of ecologically significant private lands, but also an entire sector of the conservation movement—land trusts—that rested on purchase power. Land trusts, which protected threatened places by buying them outright or buying rights to them, stretched back in one form or another to the eighteenth century but grew especially important in the late twentieth century through the work of groups like the Nature Conservancy and the Trust for Public Land.[50]

Protection-through-purchase and protection-through-easement had always been accepted tactics, even for Earth First! A decade before the Deal and just a few dozen miles south of Headwaters Forest, Earth First! created the conditions for the Save the Redwoods League and the Trust for Public Land to save Sally Bell Grove by paying for it. During the 1980s, Earth First!ers discussed the possibility that conservationists might protect grasslands by simply buying ranchers' grazing permits. By the 1990s, land purchases and conservation easements gained influence as activists followed endangered species onto private lands and ecological imperatives demanded not just representative samples of particular landscapes but large and intact ecosystems.

In the 1980s and 1990s environmentalists began to question the effectiveness of islanded reserves in public parks and public forests. More and more, wilderness advocacy involved not just the solid blocks on maps that represented Forest Service or Park Service holdings, but a legal patchwork stitched together to make a messy whole—what some scholars have called "mosaics on the land." The idea of wilderness was moving away from the clear boundaries suggested in the Wilderness Act and toward a piecemeal definition that might yield larger swaths through which a mountain lion could safely roam. For activists pushing once-radical ideas in novel directions, this strategy became the basis for a new approach to wilderness.[51]

THE LEGACY OF RADICAL ENVIRONMENTALISM: THE WILDLANDS PROJECT

No organization better represented the new approach to wilderness than the Wildlands Project (TWP). The conversation that would become the Wildlands Project began in Ann Arbor, Michigan in 1988 when Barbara Dugelby, a onetime Texas Earth First!er who had moved to Michigan to study with Michael Soulé, brought Dave Foreman and David Brower to campus and took them and Soulé out to breakfast. TWP took firmer shape after a 1991 meeting of veteran Earth First! activists and supporters including Foreman, Soulé, Rod Mondt, Mitch Friedman, Roz McClellan, John Davis, George Wuerthner, Jamie Sayen, and Reed Noss.[52] The group met in San Francisco at the house and at the behest of Doug Tompkins, the founder of the clothing brands Esprit and The North Face. TWP shared many basic commitments with Earth First!, notably an ecocentric philosophy and a sense of planetary crisis fueled by the sixth great extinction. But TWP was not a direct-action organization. Its staff took less interest in the spirited defense of particular places than in formulating blueprints for large-scale land management and convincing policymakers and stakeholders that what might sound idealistic was not only realistic but also imperative.[53]

"The U.S. conservation movement has been in a period of identity crisis since the late 1980s," Friedman wrote to the TWP board and staff in 1997, "when the tactical 'vision' of Earth First! and the science-based 'vision' of conservation biology combined to challenge the traditionally incremental approaches to wildlands protection."[54] That identity crisis was an opportunity for remaking. TWP used it to argue in favor of continental wildlands planning—vast areas created and managed "based on the needs of all life, rather than just human life." Dismissing existing parks, wildlife refuges, and wilderness areas as little more than "islands of nature in a sea of development," TWP encouraged greater purpose and ambition. Such ambition began with Earth First!'s central goal: protecting de facto wilderness. "Not one more acre of old-growth or substantially natural forest should be cut," TWP's mission statement made clear. "Not one more mile of new road bladed into a roadless area."[55] It ended with the restoration of a considerable chunk of the continent to a wild state. Not a static state, but rather one that Foreman hoped would allow "the process of evolution, of speciation, of seral changes in ecosystems," and that Noss described simply as "adaptable to a changing environment."[56, 57]

Conservation on this scale meant reaching far beyond public lands, and figuring out how to create buffer zones in which limited human activity existed alongside wildlife. TWP's carefully sketched plans for massive nature reserves looked like jungle camouflage, with differently shaded blobs that demarcated degrees of use nudging and penetrating one another. The Sky Islands/Greater Gila Nature Reserve Network included low and moderate use "stewardship zones" that could be public or private land and on which people might hunt, log, or even graze cattle.[58] TWP's David Johns described the Yellowstone to Yukon Network, perhaps the most ambitious conservation effort of all, as "politically complex, subject to the jurisdiction of at least three states, two provinces, two territories, two central governments, international treaties, several Native peoples' governments, multinational corporations and many local governments."[59] Under these conditions wilderness advocacy no longer involved just one agency or even government, nor did it involve drawing strict boundaries between wild and domesticated places. "How do we integrate Wildlands objectives with traditional uses of the land—ranching, farming, hunting, fishing, etc.—while encouraging sustainable, wildlife-friendly practices on private lands?" TWP asked its supporters.[60] Harvey Locke, a TWP director and Yellowstone to Yukon founder, encouraged conservationists to adapt. "We need to think how the landscape lives," Locke said, "not how we draw lines."[61]

In many ways this was simply an extension of what Earth First! had always advocated. From its earliest years Earth First! drafted and redrafted its own wilderness preserve system, sized to nearly ten times the existing system in order to "allow meaningful wildness to coexist with human civilization on the North American continent."[62] And Earth First! had always advocated restrained use of working landscapes. Looking back in 1995, Foreman explained, "We have fought for Wilderness Areas, yes; we have also fought like hell for sensible, sensitive, sustainable management of other lands," from agricultural valleys to rangelands. *"We have fought for good management of the matrix."*[63]

In another sense, TWP's work constituted a significant next step. Earth First! was a form of resistance, while TWP was a means of planning for a possible future. Even more than Earth First!, TWP emphasized the "science-based 'vision' of conservation biology."[64] Emphasizing science meant that TWP insisted on what conservation biologists called "cores, corridors, and carnivores"—large, core reserves of wilderness; areas outside of wilderness through which wildlife could easily travel from one core to another; and the presence of keystone species, most often large predators.[65] TWP worked to push cores, corridors, and carnivores to the top of conservationists' agendas. "TWP is a lonely hearts club for conservation biologists," Foreman said. "We're like a computer dating service to introduce them to conservation groups who want to use their knowledge and expertise." Emphasizing "vision" meant describing a world in which human self-restraint might permit sufficient habitat for wildlife. Allowing himself more hope than he ever had in his Earth First! days, Foreman wrote, "It is only by rewilding and healing the ecological wounds of the land that we can learn humility and respect; that we can come home, at last."[66]

The Wildlands Project did not sit in or spike trees, did not block logging roads, did not even picket Forest Service offices, but it nevertheless demonstrated some of the successes of Earth First!-style radicalism. First, by imagining wildlands protection on a large scale, TWP inspired or furthered projects in which conservationists began with the assumption that wildlife deserved room to thrive as much as people did. Those projects ranged from Reed Noss's attempts to create a regional reserve network for panthers in Florida; to the Southern Rockies Ecosystem Project's efforts to protect bears, lynx, wolves, and bighorn sheep across the Southwest; to Mitch Friedman's work on the Greater North Cascades Ecosystem, straddling the U.S.-Canadian border; to the Sky Islands/ Greater Gila Nature Reserve Network, stretching from northern Mexico to northern New Mexico.[67]

Second, by stressing conservation biology, TWP inadvertently made clear how important were Earth First!'s moral claims. Appeals to what was good or right, on their own, tended to convince only those who were already persuaded, and it was partly for this reason that wilderness advocates increasingly relied on scientific research. "I don't know if science alone can help us rise above deep-rooted social conflict," Amy Irvine of the Southern Utah Wilderness Alliance said. "But I do have faith that solid research and facts strengthen our philosophical assertions that we need more wilderness."[68] Still, science never remained beyond doubt; and in fact, some TWP projects tested hypotheses as much as they applied theories. The Sky Islands/Greater Gila project was, in part, an investigation into whether "umbrella species"—species that ranged especially widely each day, month, or season—could serve as indicators for a reserve system.[69] The biologist Daniel Simberloff raised doubts about whether conservationists could even be sure that cores, buffers, and corridors were the best approach to wildlife preservation. For Simberloff, though, this was beside the point. "In your past writings," he told Foreman, "you have been enormously effective *not* by being science-based, but by articulating visions of conservation and human activities conducive to conservation, and by inspiring people to work towards those visions even without necessarily thinking about all the details . . ."[70] The National Audubon Society's Brock Evans agreed, writing to *Wild Earth*, TWP's partner journal, "For all the important discussions about biology and biodiversity, about ecosystems and change of life, we should never forget the spiritual and aesthetic part of our forests, too."[71] Earth First!'s clenched fist remained a vital part of wilderness work even when it emerged from the sleeve of a lab coat.

THE LEGACY OF RADICAL ENVIRONMENTALISM:
THE SIERRA CLUB

"If you were effective, baby, the dreaded U.S.-sector secret police would have put a bomb in your car just as they did with effective environmentalists Judi Bari and Darryl Cherney," Keith Lampe/Ro-Non-So-Te/Ponderosa Pine wrote to David Brower in 1994. "If you were effective, you'd have spent a few years in prison because of lies about you uttered before a lackey judge by paid members of that same secret police. That's exactly what happened to effective environmentalists Marc Baker, Mark Davis and Peg Millett of Earth First!"[72] In 1985 Lampe had attended an Earth First! and Rainforest Action Network road show in San Francisco, focused on Central American deforestation. He brought a version of the show to a community center in Bolinas and wrote to Brower, "Earth First! has done our dirty work long enough. It's time for us to take on the cutting-edge chores and let them kick back awhile."[73] A decade later, frustrated by Brower's lack of interest, Lampe accused him of ineffectiveness and "speechifying."

For Lampe, Earth First!'s radicalism took its most meaningful shape as direct action and complete opposition to the establishment. Anything less was mere "speechifying." Some Earth First!ers likely agreed with him but most did not. Earth First! had always operated in tension but in tandem with established environmental organizations. A sympathetic gadfly, Earth First! worked with groups that ranged from militant to milquetoast and had a hand in founding several new groups that rabble roused without risking arrest, including the Wildlands Project, the Rainforest Action Network, and the Center for Biological Diversity.

One of the clearer signs of Earth First!'s enduring legacy, however, was how it helped shape the Sierra Club, a group that Earth First!'s John Davis described in 1990 as "in need of infiltration and radicalization" and Brower accused of being "so eager to compromise" that it undercut grassroots activists.[74] Although mainstream groups had embraced conventional reform and negotiation since the early 1970s, their cause retained the potential for a fundamental critique of modern society. Even at its meekest, environmentalism whispered questions about the reasonableness of unending industrial growth, the wisdom of technological progress, and the assumptions of liberal individualism. The differences between radical and mainstream environmentalists were real and significant, but never absolute. Some of the policy debates that had been taking place at Earth First! gatherings migrated—in a somewhat more moderate form—into the conference rooms of the established organizations. This was especially the case at the Sierra Club, where members elected the board of directors and could amend the Club's official positions through ballot initiatives. In the 1990s, Sierra Clubbers inspired by the no-compromise environmental politics of the 1980s led the Club to tougher positions on several key issues.

Despite the general opposition of its leadership, in 1996 the Club voted to endorse an end to all commercial logging on national forests, a policy that the Sierra Club officially called "no commercial logging" to make clear that cutting by individuals and families was exempted, but which most environmental activists knew by its catchier name, "zero cut."[75] Overriding Club leadership had required a lengthy campaign. Zero cut emerged years earlier and hundreds of miles away from the timber wars of the West Coast, at the meetings of an Indiana environmental group called Protect Our Woods (POW). Focused on the tiny and fragmented Hoosier National Forest in southern Indiana, POW initially fought off-road vehicles and clear-cuts and by 1987 called for an end to commercial logging in the Hoosier. When POW's Andy Mahler learned that most national forest timber sales made little economic sense, he founded a new organization called Heartwood to push for zero cut throughout the national forest system. Heartwood started its work in 1991, soon after Earth First! and local activists completed an eighty-day occupation of a logging road into Illinois's Shawnee National Forest.[76] Back on the West Coast, a frustrated Sierra Club volunteer in Oregon named Tim Hermach started a group called the Native Forest Council (NFC) after butting heads one too many times with Club leadership. When NFC pursued an end to the logging of old-growth forests and roadless areas, Hermach found himself tangling once again with the Club and several other environmental organizations worried about the political fallout from NFC's doggedness. Like Earth First!, NFC's frustrations with mainstream groups pushed it to take even stronger stances and soon it supported zero cut in all national forests.

The Club's calculated moderation risked discouraging its most dedicated members. Two in particular, Margaret Hays Young and David Orr, created the Association of Sierra Club Members for Environmental Ethics (ASCMEE) to push the Club away from compromise and toward a hard-line stance on wilderness. Young's and Orr's complaints echoed those of Earth First!, which Orr had worked with in Texas before volunteering for the Club. The established environmental groups made decisions "in private, by a small number of very powerful people," Young wrote in *Wild Earth*. "Individual members' opinions do not enter into their political calculations, because they feel we are not as well informed and we don't have 'political expertise.'" The result, Young explained, was that the established organizations settled on positions weaker than those of their own chapters or of local environmental groups.[77] In 1994 ASCMEE—relabeled the "John Muir Sierrans" after the Club threatened to sue over the use of its name—put a proposal on the Club ballot that the Sierra Club endorse zero cut. Nearly two-thirds of the membership voted against it. In 1996 the John Muir Sierrans tried again. This time two-thirds of the Club's membership voted in favor.

The two years between the two votes witnessed changes outside and inside of the Club. Outside, the new Republican majority in the House of Representatives convinced President Clinton to sign the salvage rider that put forest activists in Northern California and the Pacific Northwest on the defensive. Grassroots activists, sensing that the major organizations' clout in Washington, D.C. yielded only limited returns, tried to put in place sturdier statutory restrictions. "Without an offense, we are destined to always be pushed backwards," the zero cut campaign insisted. "The recent passage of the horrible 'salvage logging' rider, which suspended our public forest protection laws nationwide, is a grim example of this."[78] Although zero cut would have no direct effect on private forestlands like that of Pacific Lumber, it would erase any room for negotiation or maneuver on the nation's public forests. By its nature, zero cut was a policy of no compromise.

Inside the Club, the insurgency grew. Chad Hanson, a member of the Los Angeles chapter, began writing articles in the *Earth First! Journal* about the Club's failure to take a stand on logging, and soon he received an invitation to join the John Muir Sierrans. In 1995 Hanson took charge of the zero cut effort for the 1996 ballot. The John Muir Sierrans gathered their two thousand signatures and started sending letters to each of the individual chapters, using the addresses on the back of each chapter's newsletter. Club leadership notified the John Muir Sierrans that the chapter addresses were proprietary and that their use would disqualify the ballot initiative. So Hanson and Orr spent the next two months driving all across the United States, talking to chapter leaders in person and sleeping on volunteers' floors.[79]

The insurgency outran even those who might be most expected to support it. When the *Earth First! Journal* asked Brower for his views on zero cut in 1995 he advised against it, arguing that it would protect new growth on public lands at the expense of old growth on private lands.[80] Dave Foreman opposed zero cut because he considered it ecologically unsound (preventing necessary logging in monocultural second-growth stands that replaced clear-cuts) and strategically unwise (risking a backlash at the moment that environmentalists were trying to reverse the salvage logging rider).[81] Hermach and Hanson finally convinced Brower to support zero cut. Foreman remained opposed to zero cut as national Club policy but supported a forest-by-forest approach.

"By adopting such a stringent and ill-conceived posture, the normally mainstream environmental group has joined the ranks of the radical extremist groups like Earth First! and Greenpeace," wrote environmental critic Karl Drexel in an opinion piece for the *Christian Science Monitor* soon after the Sierra Club announced its support for zero cut.[82] This was overstatement, but the success of the John Muir Sierrans did show how mainstream groups could be pushed by those activists who had embraced the no-compromise culture of groups like Earth First! The Club, for its part, tried to downplay the extremism of zero cut. Hanson and Carl Pope responded to Drexel by explaining that 95 percent of the nation's original forest was gone; that the federal logging program was essentially a massive subsidy to the timber industry; that a Forest Service poll showed a majority of Americans opposed to resource extraction on public lands; and that only 12 percent of the national timber supply came from public lands. "What is the more 'radical' position?" they asked.[83]

Activists had only begun to push the Club in more militant directions. In 1995 both David Brower and Dave Foreman won election to the Sierra Club board of directors. From 1994 to 2000, the John Muir Sierrans ran candidates for each board election, achieving a brief majority in 1999. Even after the adoption of zero cut, the policy's advocates within the Club continued to push for further action on logging and then on other issues. Several years after the zero cut victory, Club members solicited enough signatures for an ultimately unsuccessful "zero cud" initiative advocating an end to commercial grazing on public lands, a position that Earth First! had urged the Club to adopt as early as 1988.[84]

Brower recommended several changes to Club strategy. Among them were partnering with the Wildlands Project, "the most promising of efforts to determine now what we hope America will look like fifty years from now," and supporting a five-state wilderness bill called the Northern Rockies Ecosystem Protection Act (NREPA).[85] Inspired by the reintroduction of gray wolves to Yellowstone in 1987, and the epitome of the cores, corridors, and carnivores philosophy that lay at the heart of the Wildlands Project, NREPA was a vast wilderness reserve that would encompass over sixteen million acres of public land. It was, according to Foreman, "the strongest and most visionary wilderness legislation since the Alaska National Interest Lands Conservation Act."[86] TWP championed NREPA, as did the Alliance for the Wild Rockies. But the Club's national office as well as its Montana chapter considered NREPA unrealistic, and not only fought against the proposed legislation but also nearly suspended Margaret Hays Young's Atlantic Chapter for its support.[87]

In 1993 the Montana Chapter held a special meeting to consider censuring and even disbanding Bozeman's Headwaters Group of the Sierra Club (named after the headwaters of the Missouri River) for its continued support of NREPA despite Club opposition. "The continued existence of the Headwaters Group is in considerable jeopardy," the chapter chair warned.[88] Brower, the Wildlands Project, and the Alliance for the Wild Rockies continued to press the issue, and the Club grew increasingly uncomfortable with the infighting. Realizing that the grassroots would not easily fall in line, the Club pivoted grudgingly and then enthusiastically in favor of NREPA. By the time the bill reached the House floor in 1994, the Club called it a "visionary proposal" and sent its legislative director, Debbie Sease, to testify in favor.[89] Thanking Brower for his consistent support, Brooks Martin of the Headwaters Group summarized the conflict just as Earth First! might have. "We learned to stick firm against not only anti-environmentalists," he wrote, "but also against the compromise-compromise conservation community."[90]

Brower had always served as a bridge between the mainstream environmental movement and its radical critics, commanding respect from the environmental establishment while championing grassroots and radical groups, even when the organizations he worked for—and the organizations he founded—did not. In 1993 he sent a check to Mark Davis of EMETIC at a federal prison in California after Davis appealed for funds in the pages of the *Earth First! Journal*. The prison sent the check back to Brower, along with a note from Davis. "I am taken care of for the moment, and I know that you could do better things with the money," the Arizona Five conspirator wrote. "But I thank you very sincerely for the thought. And while I'm at it, thanks for how you've lived your life. I don't think there is much hope of keeping the industrial death machine from it's [sic] apocalyptic and pyrrhic 'victory' over nature, but you sure have been an inspiration to try."[91]

As he reached his eighties Brower kept trying, at times to the Club's consternation. If Bill Clinton's greatest sin for conservationists was the salvage logging rider, his support of free-trade policies that rolled back environmental regulations was a close second. "To let loose corporations on a global marketplace without adherence to minimum global environmental laws will reverse almost every conservation gain made this century," Brower warned.[92] Hundreds of environmental groups opposed the North American Free Trade Agreement (NAFTA) as well as the updated General Agreement on Tariffs and Trade (GATT). "Economic growth under such circumstances—however vibrant, however sustained—can never translate into economic and environmental health," Carl Pope wrote of NAFTA's effects on the U.S.-Mexico border.[93]

Discouraged with Clinton's first term, Brower wrote an opinion piece in the *Los Angeles Times* citing the salvage logging rider, NAFTA, and GATT, and declaring that he could not support Clinton's re-election. Coming just as the Club was considering a second Clinton endorsement, Brower's piece sparked a vigorous round of emails among staffers about principle and practicality. "The Brower Op-Ed plants the seeds of discouragement for this election season among environmentalists," Julie Beezley wrote. "Frankly," Paul Hendricks wrote of Clinton, "right now we need him more than he needs us." Leslie Reid, on the other hand, called Clinton's record a "betrayal of the Sierra Club" and claimed an endorsement would cost the Club credibility among younger members.[94] Chad Hanson said that an endorsement "would be disastrous for morale in the Club."[95]

Club president Adam Werbach stepped in to calm nerves, explaining that Brower had told him the opinion was Brower's own and had nothing to do with the Club's endorsement. Brower remained pragmatic enough to understand the Club's reasons for supporting Clinton but angry enough about the salvage rider and NAFTA that he could not bring himself to do so too, and he wanted the president to know it. For Tim Hermach, however, it was the Clinton endorsement that pushed him out the door after years of challenging the Club's leadership. "President Clinton sees our movement as little more than a political expediency," Hermach wrote to his friends and colleagues, "and he has used our good will to break the back of many of our environmental and social justice efforts." Hermach finally quit the Sierra Club, "in resignation and disgust."[96]

Brower preferred to work from the inside, pushing and cajoling the Club toward a harder line. In 1996 he coaxed the Club to adopt the policy proposal closest to his and many radical environmentalists' hearts: tear down Glen Canyon Dam. Unlike Abbey and Earth First!, Brower did not mean this literally. The dam, he pointed out, could remain standing, while its diversion tunnels let 200,000 cubic feet of water per second through the end of the canyon, effectively draining Lake Powell and revealing Glen Canyon once again. Brower, activist Katie Lee, and longtime Club director Martin Litton created the Glen Canyon Institute to develop a restoration plan. In November 1996, the Club's board unanimously supported removal.[97]

Brower's proposal was, by 1996, slightly less inconceivable than it had once been. As hundreds of dams came due for licensing renewal in the 1990s, a combination of economic sense and political will put greater pressure on dams than did the water they impounded. Dams threatened more and more fish populations along with the livelihoods of fishing communities; agricultural regions began to find alternative sources of water; and Secretary of the Interior Bruce Babbitt took dam removal seriously. A surge in dam removal was limited to smaller structures, however, making the Glen Canyon bypass a long shot. When Congress's Subcommittee on National Parks and Public Lands held hearings on the Sierra Club's proposal, the tone of lawmakers' comments ranged from skeptical to hostile. Even with the Club's backing, the idea of draining Lake Powell never had much chance.[98]

Even if Glen Canyon Dam held fast, the Club's proposal had consequences. The Sierra Club made several pragmatic arguments for draining Lake Powell: the lake was becoming smaller and smaller through a combination of sedimentation and evaporation; its value in storing water was negligible other than in case of severe drought; and Glen Canyon Dam generated a relatively insignificant amount of power. For Brower, however, the most important arguments remained philosophical. "Beginning with the Industrial Revolution," he wrote to Club members about his proposal, "people have been forgetting to ask what progress costs the earth and the future."[99] Decommissioning Glen Canyon Dam made economic and ecological sense, but it also served as a symbol of the anti-industrial ethos that radicals had been using for years to criticize the moderate politics of established groups. By the turn of the century the Club trumpeted that ethos itself, at least rhetorically. Among five "bold ideas for the new century" named by *Sierra* magazine were both zero cut and the end of Glen Canyon Dam. "In Edward Abbey's eco-classic *The Monkey Wrench Gang*," the magazine noted, "a band of nature-loving malcontents plots to restore the Colorado River by blowing up Glen Canyon Dam. The Sierra Club has the same goal of rescuing rivers across the country (minus the outlaw pyrotechnics)."[100] In advocating the removal of Glen Canyon Dam, the Sierra Club also advocated the removal of part of what stood between radical and mainstream environmentalism (see figure 6.1).

Figure 6.1 Katie Lee and Dave Foreman in Durango, Colorado. Lee helped found the Glen Canyon Institute, which advocated the removal of Glen Canyon Dam. Photo courtesy Dave Foreman.

THE LEGACY OF RADICAL ENVIRONMENTALISM:
IMMIGRATION

Among the legacies of Earth First!-style radicalism was the sort of holism that amounted to a bleak view of people. The very idea of the destruction of nature, where "nature" was the nonhuman world, rested on the belief that humans were invariably the destructive force. The greater the crime that humanity committed against the planet, the less germane were distinctions between different people and their relative degrees of guilt. Radical groups made explicit what established organizations kept tacit. Just as radical environmentalists' campaigns against industrial society grew from the seed of an idea already present in the mainstream movement, radicals' disregard for social difference was an extreme version of what could already be found among mainstream environmentalists. Radical or not, environmentalists could easily miss the people for the planet.

The environmental justice movement made this point most forcefully, admonishing established groups in the same way social ecologists admonished radical groups.[101] Environmental justice activism was at least as old as environmental activism and arguably older. Pollution was a local issue, disproportionately affecting particular communities, long before it was a national and international concern. As the environmental movement garnered attention in the 1960s and 1970s, antitoxics activists in groups like the Citizens' Clearinghouse for Hazardous Wastes, the Urban Environment Conference, the Association of Community Organizations for Reform Now, and many smaller groups fought the effects of industrial pollution in low-income communities. But there was little sense of a coherent movement based around issues of the environment, race, and class until the late 1980s. In 1987 the Commission for Racial Justice of the United Church of Christ issued a report called *Toxic Wastes and Race in the United States*, which helped define the range and the pervasiveness of what became known as "environmental racism." Soon after, sociologist Robert Bullard examined how siting decisions for dumps and industrial pollution disproportionately harmed minority neighborhoods in *Dumping in Dixie*. Environmental justice activists fought against industrial pollution on a neighborhood-by-neighborhood basis, preventing toxic dumping through countless local battles. This strategy was as much a function of limited resources as it was of effective organizing, as the movement had few allies in Washington, D.C. That absence, to environmental justice advocates, was in part a failure of the mainstream environmental groups.

In 1990 ten of the largest mainstream environmental organizations received two letters, one from the Gulf Coast Tenant Leadership Development Project and the other from the Southwest Organizing Project, both signed by many other local groups and individual activists. The letters pointed out the mainstream environmental movement's failure to address pollution as it affected working-class communities and communities of color, and the lack of representatives from those communities on the boards and staffs of all of the national organizations. In 1991 environmental justice activists held the First National People of Color Environmental Leadership Summit in Washington, D.C. Three hundred grassroots activists attended the first day of the Summit. On the second day, 250 additional attendees joined, some of them from mainstream environmental groups. The mainstream leaders who spoke at the Summit confessed to their organizations' conspicuous absence from environmental justice campaigns, and promised a stronger effort to address environmental justice issues and to hire more diverse staffs.

The mainstream environmental groups and the environmental justice movement approached each other haltingly. A year and a half after established leaders promised a new commitment to issues of justice, that pledge remained largely unfulfilled. The Environmental Careers Organization released a report on diversity within environmental groups, concluding that the broad environmental movement remained overwhelmingly white. And although many established groups quickly launched environmental justice programs in the wake of the two 1990 letters and the 1991 summit, most of those programs would come from new grant proposals. Few groups committed significant existing funds to issues of social justice.

Environmental justice advocates, meanwhile, wrestled with some of the thornier implications of all environmental activism. Mark Dowie has chronicled the evolution of environmental justice from NIMBY ("not in my backyard") to NIABY ("not in anybody's backyard").[102] Campaigns based on NIMBY tended to simply push pollution from one neighborhood to another. Activists tried to address this problem by opposing pollution on a wider scale and preventing the dumping of waste in any economically marginal community. As corporations began to export their waste to poorer countries around the world, environmental justice activists began to talk of a third acronym: NOPE ("not on planet earth"). The Reverend Benjamin Chavis, one of the most influential proponents of environmental justice, insisted that the movement did not seek to simply relocate toxic facilities. "You can't get justice by doing an injustice on somebody else," he said. "When you have lived through suffering and hardship, you want to remove them, not only from your own people but from all peoples."[103] This was a radical proposition. To demand an end to industrial byproducts anywhere on earth was to demand an end to industry itself, or at least a dramatic scaling back. Environmental justice activists rarely followed this line of thought to its ultimate conclusion; like mainstream and radical environmentalists, they never fully reconciled means with ends.

Whatever its own limits, the environmental justice movement made clear how environmental organizations struggled to balance a commitment to protecting particular resources with a broader concern for social justice. No single issue dragged this struggle onto a public stage more than did the issue of immigration. The immigration debate exploded in the 1990s, but even in the 1970s immigration had been a vital piece of population politics. While most crisis environmentalists sounded alarms about drowning in a planetwide sea of people, some of them—notably Garrett Hardin—warned that waves of humanity would soon crash over national borders. Hardin's "lifeboat ethics" required severe immigration restrictions. More and more people piling into lifeboat nations, Hardin argued, would eventually sink everyone.[104]

The Sierra Club often stood at the center of the conversation about immigration and the environment. At one of the Club's 1972 board meetings, director Sidney Liebes, a member of the board's population committee, pointed to immigration's contribution to overall population growth in the United States and recommended the Club declare an official policy on immigration. At least one board member objected, and the board president referred the idea to several other committees for consideration.[105] Five years later the population committee offered concrete changes to the Club's population policies, including a call for an end to illegal immigration and a gradual reduction of legal immigration.[106] A year after that, the population committee had backed off those specific goals and instead proposed an examination of federal immigration laws, foreign policy, and the root causes of immigration to the United States.[107] The Club adopted the proposal as policy, and then in 1988 called on the federal government to seek immigration levels that would not destabilize the nation's population.[108]

In 1993, as the Club finished celebrating its centennial, the population committee drafted a comprehensive population plan that included among its recommendations a reduction in net immigration to the U.S. and Canada and that claimed immigration rates led to significant environmental harm. The draft plan struck many desks with the force of controversy and sparked several years of debate. Vivian Li, chair of the Club's Ethnic and Cultural Diversity Task Force—created in the wake of the environmental justice movement's criticisms—expressed "anger and rage" at the plan's premises. "The debate" Julie Beezley said a year and a half later, "has been contentious and exhausting."[109]

Although immigration policies concerned national borders, the fight over those policies often unfolded in California. Along with the Ethnic and Cultural Diversity Task Force the draft plan's most persistent critic was the Club's Angeles chapter, representing greater Los Angeles. Soon after the draft plan's release, the Angeles chapter passed a resolution recommending the Club take an explicitly neutral position on immigration control. The chapter warned the national office that anything short of a neutral position would risk painting the Club as bigoted, xenophobic, and provincial, and could alienate large communities in diverse areas like Southern California.[110] Immigration politics threatened to further entrench the prejudices that environmental justice advocates had pointed to only a few years earlier.

That threat grew even greater in mid-1994 when anti-immigration activists put Proposition 187 on the state ballot, a measure that would deny public services to undocumented immigrants. Among Proposition 187's supporters was the Federation for American Immigration Reform (FAIR), an anti-immigration organization started by John Tanton. In the 1970s Tanton had served as president of Zero Population Growth and chair of the Club's population committee. By the 1990s he cared less about protecting natural resources than about protecting a social order. Wealthy nations like the United States, he wrote to the *Atlantic*, "are being selected against in the great reproductive sweepstakes and will gradually be replaced (become extinct, in Johnson's and Darwin's term) *unless* they control entry into their living space. It's that simple."[111]

The Club's board tried to end the debate in 1996, resolving that no one speaking for the Club could take a position on immigration policy. "The Club remains committed to environmental rights and protections for all within our borders," the resolution read, "without discrimination based on immigration status."[112] But the politics of population and immigration had already ranged too far to be contained by one proclamation. As soon as the board declared neutrality, a group of Sierra Club members began to agitate for an explicit Club policy that called for comprehensive population stabilization through a drop in both natural increase and net immigration. They formed a group, Sierrans for U.S. Population Stabilization (SUSPS), led by Ohio Sierra Club volunteer Alan Kuper.[113] SUSPS succeeded in putting its proposal on the Sierra Club ballot in 1998. The Club's board, overwhelmingly against the proposal, put a counter-proposal on the ballot calling for the Club to reaffirm its neutral stance on immigration policy. SUSPS argued that reducing consumption in the United States was important but not adequate; only by reducing both consumption and population could the American environment be saved. The board insisted that the Club should both think and act globally and address root causes such as poverty and the restriction of human rights, of which immigration was only a symptom.[114]

Whichever proposal received the most votes would have no legal weight, no immediate impact beyond the Club itself, and likely no effect on U.S. policy—and yet the vote raised concern throughout the environmental community. The National Audubon Society and the environmental journalist Bill McKibben supported the board's position;[115] Earth Day founder Gaylord Nelson and Harvard biologist E.O. Wilson supported the SUSPS proposal. California State Senator Hilda Solis wrote to Carl Pope to warn of the vote's corrosive effects. "It is imperative," Solis wrote, "for [the Club's] members to realize how divisive and potentially harming a position against immigration would be to the organization."[116] The tension within the Club pulled at longtime loyalties. Anne Ehrlich, Paul Ehrlich's wife, colleague, and frequent co-writer, emailed Kuper to withdraw her and her husband's endorsement. Although the Ehrlichs generally supported any discussion of population politics, in this case they felt the debate had become so contentious as to take away from the Club's overall mission.[117]

Although both sides fought for his support, Brower waffled. He had always insisted on the centrality of overpopulation to environmental politics and the relevance of immigration to both, but he was as concerned with root causes as with policies at the border. Brower believed that free trade agreements and the influence of corporate agriculture on nearby nations contributed to unduly high rates of immigration. NAFTA, Brower argued, both incentivized immigration and encouraged rampant consumerism. Julie Beezley, worried that Brower might support the SUSPS proposal and reminding him that he had insisted on the importance of root causes at a recent board meeting, told him that the board's proposal sought to address exactly those concerns. SUSPS felt a similar claim to Brower's vote. "Dave," Alan Kuper urged, "we can't silently acquiesce to endless rapid U.S. population growth and also 'protect and preserve' much of anything. The credibility of the Sierra Club is at stake."[118]

The credibility of the Sierra Club amid a protracted fight worried Dave Foreman and led him, at first, to grudgingly advise that Kuper drop his campaign. "I think a battle over immigration will be even more emotionally divisive than zero cut or a Clinton endorsement," he told Kuper in 1996.[119] Eventually though, Foreman offered his support for the SUSPS proposal. It was an odd endorsement given the ways in which his new organization, the Wildlands Project, built coalitions and pushed beyond national boundaries. Several of TWP's reserves straddled the United States' southern or northern borders and involved working with Canadian and Mexican conservationists and landowners. "Understanding the culture and cultural differences of the region provides us with the means of connecting to people," TWP's David Johns wrote of the countless communities that lived within the vast sweep of the Yellowstone to Yukon reserve.[120] The conservation work of TWP depended on crossing political boundaries and on treating people as not just raw numbers but distinct parties with distinct but overlapping interests. "Thus," one internal memo about working with Native peoples read, "the question to TWP should not be whether, but how to include most effectively other cultures whose knowledge and political clout are critical to our long-term success."[121]

The approach that TWP increasingly represented, one based on hazy borders and hard-won partnerships, carried the day at the Sierra Club when 60 percent of members voted for the board proposal. But the fight reminded all involved of the delicate balance between curtailing human impacts and protecting human freedoms. Although they differed in their solutions, the most reasonable advocates on both sides of the Club's immigration debate agreed that the core of the problem was more and more people consuming at an American pace. In 1994 the Angeles chapter warned that support of immigration restriction would put "blame for our environmental problems on immigrants while not taking responsibility for our own U.S. consumptive lifestyles."[122] In 1997 Ric Oberlink, an SUSPS supporter, said simply, "The larger the U.S. population, the more havoc we cause."[123] The immigration debate demonstrated the slow emergence of social politics and coalition-building in an environmental movement that had long neglected both. It also demonstrated how the freedom of people—and particularly of Americans—to amass and consume remained a central concern for the environmental movement.

WILDERNESS REVISITED

Wilderness remained at the center of philosophical and political disputes in which radical ideas persisted. Even as the Wildlands Project moved away from an exclusive focus on strictly bounded wilderness and toward a mosaic of different land uses, it defended the core philosophical commitments of traditional wilderness advocacy. In the late 1990s environmentalists clashed publicly over wilderness as an idea even as they achieved political victories that protected wilderness acreage. Wilderness remained a contentious issue in environmental thought and activism, a key measure of what environmentalists hoped to achieve.

A debate about the meaning of wilderness among environmentalists and philosophers gathered momentum in the mid-1990s when the University of California's Humanities Research Institute launched a three-year project on "Reinventing Nature," comprising conferences in Berkeley, San Diego, and Davis, and a semester-long residential seminar in Irvine. Conservation biologists and wilderness advocates grew interested and wary when they heard about the effort. Michael Soulé and the philosopher Gary Lease held their own conference in Santa Cruz—partially under the auspices of the Reinventing Nature project—in order to examine what they considered a "tense but unavoidable relationship" between a human-focused "constructionism" and a nature-focused "essentialism."[124]

The tense relationship grew more so when the *New York Times Magazine* published "The Trouble with Wilderness," an essay by William Cronon that grew out of the Reinventing Nature seminar. Pointing to Earth First! in particular, Cronon presented the idea of wilderness as not only essentialist but also exclusionary and ahistorical. The essay did not take issue with the National Wilderness Preservation System itself but with a particular understanding of wilderness that, Cronon wrote, "is entirely a creation of the culture that holds it dear, a product of the very history it seeks to deny." To the degree that wilderness served as a bedrock idea for much of the environmental movement—and Cronon believed it to be a high degree—its limitations suffused much of what environmentalists fought for.[125]

Cronon's essay and its reprinting in several magazines and newspapers raised hackles at *Wild Earth*. "We've decided to devote much of the winter '96 issue of *Wild Earth* to defenses of wilderness—the concept as well as the areas—against the latest philosophical onslaught," editor John Davis wrote to Gary Snyder. "In particular, *WE* will challenge William Cronon's problems with wilderness."[126] The winter 1996 issue devoted several dozen pages to aggressive critiques of "The Trouble with Wilderness," most of them accusing Cronon of reckless relativism. Lost in the salvos was the common ground on which each side had at least one foot. "In the wilderness," Cronon wrote, neatly summarizing a tenet of ecocentrism, "we need no reminder that a tree has its own reasons for being, quite apart from us."[127] In *Wild Earth*, ecologist Don Waller granted Cronon's central claim that wilderness was in large part a cultural product. Waller turned to "wildness" instead and, echoing Cronon's and TWP's pivot away from strict wilderness, wrote, "We must recognize that *degrees of wildness exist.*"[128]

As Cronon's essay and *Wild Earth*'s reaction to it made clear, wilderness remained a critical idea and a sensitive subject for many environmentalists, a classification that carried a great deal of conceptual weight even as it changed from decade to decade. Wilderness also did crucial political work. TWP fought to protect "de facto wilderness"—roadless areas without official wilderness designation—as "cores," largely undeveloped land surrounded by nested degrees of wildness. Bill Clinton, the subject of so much discord at the Sierra Club, became an unlikely hero in the protection of de facto wilderness. Pressured by environmentalists and frustrated by the House of Representatives, Clinton looked to achieve a conservation legacy and increasingly relied on administrative authority. In 1997 Clinton and Forest Service chief Mike Dombeck announced a science-based effort to reform roadless area management. After three years of political wrangling, that reform took shape as a roadless rule that would prohibit roadbuilding and commercial logging on nearly 59 million acres of national forest roadless areas, while still allowing some grazing, mining, and motorized recreation.[129] "The Clinton ruling is perhaps the best example of how a continually evolving concept of wilderness has influenced on-the-ground policy and management," Foreman later wrote.[130] In 2004, as the Bush administration fought to prevent the rule's enactment, it looked as though the achievement would come to nothing. Foreman remarked that the Clinton rule "ranks with the passage of the Wilderness Act as a landmark conservation victory—had it been successfully implemented."[131] But the legal battle continued well into the Obama administration, and although lawsuits scaled back the acres protected, for the most part the Clinton roadless rule survived intact. From a policy perspective it was one of the most far-reaching legacies of Earth First!-style wilderness advocacy.

CONCLUSION

Earth First! emerged in 1980 as an oppositional group, against industrial society, against human-centeredness, and against the incrementalism of the mainstream environmental movement. But as much as they badgered mainstream organizations, radicals never entirely abandoned them. Earth First!'s founders always argued that they could push the movement away from compromise and toward more robust protection of wilderness by making the established groups look moderate. In 1980 they created a shadow group called La Manta Mojada ("the wet blanket"), made up of eight counselors from national organizations charged with preventing Earth First! from acting completely at odds with the larger movement.[132] La Manta Mojada did not last long, and soon Earth First! abandoned any formal attempt to work with established organizations. But radicals never abandoned the goal of coaxing the national groups a little further down the path that Earth First!ers had already walked.

There was, through the 1980s and 1990s, much straddling and shuffling between mainstream and radical circles. Widely read writers like George Wuerthner and Jamie Sayen also wrote for the *Earth First! Journal*. Respected scientists like Reed Noss and Michael Soulé conspired with radical activists. Federal land management employees like Denzel and Nancy Ferguson and Jeff DeBonis contributed to radical critiques. And conservation legends like David Brower and Brock Evans decided that Earth First! was vital, the one immediately and the other eventually.

As much as anyone else, Bart Koehler embodied the bridge between radical and reformist environmental work. Frustrated with new and in his mind timid leadership at the Wilderness Society in the late 1970s, Koehler quit and helped found Earth First! For several years he was the heart of Earth First!'s early demonstrations and its "road show" recruitment efforts as Johnny Sagebrush, "legendary outlaw country singer." But Koehler was also an experienced grassroots strategist and by the middle of the decade he had left Earth First! to work with the Southeast Alaska Conservation Council (SEACC), a local organization working through Congress to protect Alaska's Tongass National Forest. SEACC's work in the 1980s culminated in the Tongass Timber Reform Act of 1990, which protected nearly one million acres of forest from logging. In the late 1990s Koehler joined wilderness advocates Brian O'Donnell and Melyssa Watson to work on the Wilderness Support Center, a training and troubleshooting group for wilderness campaigns around the country. The Support Center needed financial and institutional assistance, and found it in a newly grassroots-friendly Wilderness Society under the leadership of Bill Meadows. Nearly two decades after he left it, Koehler returned to a Wilderness Society reinvested in the sort of ground-level work that he felt it had forsaken in the 1970s. Having given full rein to his radical ideals, Koehler also stepped back toward the sort of gradual reform that Earth First! had long questioned. "Battling for the freedom of the wilderness in the halls of Congress is one of the purest forms of Democracy that there is," Koehler wrote in an essay for a Wilderness Support Center manual, stressing the civic-mindedness of wilderness advocacy. After expounding on the importance of working within the political system, Koehler ended by quoting Edward Abbey—"A patriot must always be ready to defend his country against his government"—and winking at his own more radical days, when wilderness activism ended with an exclamation mark and began with a sense of fighting for what was most vital in the world.[133]

Conclusion

In December 2008, the outgoing Bush administration held an auction in Salt Lake City for oil and gas drilling rights on thousands of acres of public land in the West. As the Southern Utah Wilderness Alliance protested outside, a University of Utah student named Tim DeChristopher entered the federal building with a vague plan to deliver an impromptu speech about fossil fuels and climate change. Someone asked him if he was there to bid, and he quickly responded that he was. Soon DeChristopher had won drilling rights worth nearly two million dollars on twenty-two thousand acres of land. Bureau of Land Management officials abruptly ended the auction and interrogated DeChristopher, who admitted that he had placed bids only to interfere with an auction that he believed threatened the planet.[1]

Charged with disrupting the auction and making false statements, DeChristopher tried to employ a "choice of evils" or "necessity" defense, a legal strategy that would allow him to argue that the imminent catastrophe of climate change required that he choose a lesser evil—breaking the law—in order to prevent a much greater harm. The judge did not allow the defense and sentenced DeChristopher to nearly two years in prison. An environmental movement ever more focused on climate change embraced DeChristopher's actions and the urgency behind them, and in 2013 he emerged from prison a hero to many organizations and activists.[2]

DeChristopher's appeal to necessity assumed the need for an extralegal response to an impending crisis in a way that echoed Earth First! In 1984, when thirty-four activists with the Earth First!-affiliated Cathedral Forest Action Group were arrested for protesting logging upriver from the Middle Santiam Wilderness in Oregon's Willamette National Forest, several employed the necessity defense.[3] Earth First!er Cecelia Ostrow reminded the jury that governments often sanctioned injustice, leaving citizens with an obligation to break the rules. Ostrow based her ultimately unsuccessful bid on the belief that moral imperatives could eclipse legal strictures. She assumed that laws were always imperfect and in flux, as did Mike Roselle, who tried to use the necessity defense several times. "When the system fails, and everyone admits that it does fail occasionally," Roselle wrote, "an individual has only his or her conscience to consult for guidance."[4] Radical environmentalists' consciences told them that human institutions remained limited and fallible, and that environmental crises demanded action that might outpace legal progress.

The necessity defense's implied critique of conventional reform, established institutions, and common wisdom was at once what separated and connected radical and mainstream environmentalists. The separation began in the 1970s. Convinced of an already unfolding crisis and frustrated by creeping professionalism and a culture of compromise among mainstream groups, radicals turned their backs on traditional reform and the political and philosophical commitments it entailed. They adopted a strategy of direct action, from civil disobedience to sabotage. They advocated an eco-centric philosophy, ascribing to the natural world a moral standing equal to that of the human world. And they argued that wilderness remained the most significant measure of the chances that one world would survive the other. Seeing in the mainstream movement a capitulation to liberal humanism and its anthropocentric values, radicals took a separate stand against the ills of modern, industrial civilization.

But while radical and mainstream environmentalists defined themselves against each other in the 1980s, they sprouted from the same seed. "What you gentlemen have been discussing is profoundly radical and subversive in the context of the present political, economic and technological paradise," Raymond Sherwin remarked after a panel on population and wilderness preservation at the Sierra Club's 1969 wilderness conference, pointing to environmentalism's unwelcome message.[5] Two years later, and still nearly a decade before the emergence of Earth First!, Sierra Club president Phil Berry described the conservation movement as "fundamentally at odds" with industrial society. "No responsible conservationists advocate violence and certainly I don't," he said, "but it is worth noting that if we fail in our efforts, others who might assume leadership in the conservation field would be unwilling to work through existing institutions."[6]

In its message and at times in its methods, the environmental movement questioned basic premises. Environmentalists felt impelled to push back against a press of humanity moving toward bigger economies, more consumption of natural resources, and an escape from earthly limits. That impulse could encourage holism, the treatment of all people as a consentient mass acting against the nonhuman world. To embrace holism was to ignore social difference and flatten social inequality, to indict all people regardless of their particular actions, experiences, and identities. Especially when expressed by radicals, environmental holism imagined the combination of consumerism, individualism, and liberal humanism as a near universal problem that led to the privileging of people and their interests over biodiversity and intact ecosystems. This modern condition, some environmentalists argued, afflicted nearly everyone. Loggers, ranchers, shoppers, executives, the rich and the poor, all shared complicity in the destruction of nonhuman nature. This was an unconditional view that risked essentializing that which was wild and vilifying all that was not.

Further, such a view risked a questioning of human wants and needs that could easily appear to be a form of misanthropy. At times it was. Dave Foreman's remarks about ending foreign aid for the good of the planet were condemnable but not exceptional. Long before Earth First! existed, the Sierra Club considered whether foreign aid should be restricted solely to programs that limited human numbers. The Club's board discussed how foreign aid for "seemingly humanitarian purposes" in fact competed with the need to limit population growth.[7]

But misanthropy was never fundamental to radical or mainstream environmentalism, nor was the belief that people were antithetical to the nonhuman world. It has become reflexive for critics of environmentalism to insist that humans are a part of nature, even though a strict separation between the two has never been among the central claims of mainstream or radical environmentalism. Many environmentalists, in fact, worried that modern humans recklessly ignored their essential connection to the nonhuman world. In 1983 Friends of the Earth considered whether to change the name of its newsletter, *Not Man Apart*. The odd-sounding and, for many, sexist name came from the poet Robinson Jeffers, who wrote, "The greatest beauty is organic wholeness," and advised, "love that, not man apart from that." In defense of the newsletter's name, David Brower, Tom Turner, and Connie Parrish described organic wholeness and the connection between people and nature as "the most important part of the conservation ethic." Jeffers's line was, they insisted, "properly critical of people who, in their escape from humility, try to separate humanity from the wholeness it is dependent on."[8]

A call for humility, restraint, and a sense of connectedness was in fact at the heart of the environmental movement. This call could come in many forms: a skepticism toward material and technological progress, a belief in limits to human reason and knowledge, and an insistence on the inherent value of nonhuman life. At its most oppositional—David Ehrenfeld's declamations against the "arrogance of humanism," Paul Ehrlich's taunting "Nature bats last," or Earth First!'s tree spikes—it could hint at or veer into antihumanism. Mostly, however, it was the conviction that human beings as a whole should exercise precaution in their dealings with an unfathomably complicated nonhuman world. That sort of forbearance could be its own reward. Modesty, deep ecologists Bill Devall and George Sessions claimed, was a byproduct of "ecological resistance" and "a virtue nearly lost in the dominant technocratic-industrial society."[9] It could even be liberatory. "The ability to accept freedom within the limits of the natural world," Brower suggested, clarified rather than constrained. "In understanding those limits we define ourselves, and by that definition we can finally understand what our real possibilities are," he wrote. "We are set free to act in a truly human way by our comprehension of the whole within which we exist."[10]

Although it points in the direction of misanthropy, holism does not have to lead there. Understood as a functional although always incomplete way of looking at the world, it can instead lead toward questions that grow more and more vital in the age of climate change. The historian Dipesh Chakrabarty acknowledges the profound limitations of any uniform conception of people, but he also believes the scope of climate change transcends familiar historical narratives and explanations and pushes toward broad categorizations that "scale up our imagination of the human." Chakrabarty calls this scaled-up imagination "species thinking."[11] It is more an abstract than a lived reality; capitalism, the legacy of imperialism, and many forms of inequality necessarily structure how climate change unfolds and reshapes people's lives. Within the terms set by planetary climate there are diverse and contingent human experiences. But the terms remain nonetheless.

Among the insights of species thinking may be a different understanding of human freedom. Various conceptions of freedom since the Enlightenment, Chakrabarty says, have all concerned oppressions and injustices at the hands of people and systems of people's devising. Those conceptions have never in any direct sense taken into account the conditions of the natural world, he points out, although post-Enlightenment thought overlaps with the accelerating use of coal, oil, and gas as forms of energy. "The mansion of modern freedom stands on an ever-expanding base of fossil-fuel use," Chakrabarty writes. "Most of our freedoms so far have been energy-intensive." The abstract ideals to which liberal thought are committed have rested, precariously, on the demands of growth liberalism. There is a complicated correlation between the politics of the modern, industrial world and that world's environmental repercussions, and so Chakrabarty asks whether the vast scale of those repercussions may be "the price we pay for the pursuit of freedom."[12]

For the novelist and literary scholar Amitav Ghosh, it is the inequalities through which climate change unfolds that connect the particular to the general, the unevenness of the world to Chakrabarty's species-thinking. European imperialism concentrated the use of fossil fuels in the West by monopolizing the production and consumption of resources—especially oil—that were available elsewhere. The consequences, Ghosh explains, included not only a stratification of wealth and power but also a staggered progression toward fully industrialized economies on the Asian continent and, now, billions of people on the cusp of fossil-fuel driven wealth and material comfort at the very moment that such wealth and comfort has reached a point of crisis. "Asia's historical experience demonstrates that our planet will not allow these patterns of living to be adopted by every human being," Ghosh writes. "Every family in the world cannot have two cars, a washing machine, and a refrigerator—not because of technical or economic limitations but because humanity would asphyxiate in the process." Environmental holism, in other words, stands against a less obvious because more widely embraced holism, what Ghosh calls "the universalist premise of industrial civilization" as well as "a hoax."[13] It may be that the age of climate change is stretched between these two forms of holism. "So it looks as if we are faced with an impasse," writes Jeremy Davies. "Justified hostility to the claim that 'we're all in it together' versus justified recognition that fossil-fueled prosperity for everybody appears ecologically impossible."[14]

Responding to climate change must involve a recognition of inequity and history and an aspiration toward justice, and an understanding of how limits to growth are produced by politics and human decisions as much as by material absolutes. For Davies this means a turn to "plural ecologies"—varied movements and strategies that respond to common concerns in different ways.[15] As environmentalists have insisted, though, any response should include a chastening of modern exuberance. Ghosh, concerned especially with literature and storytelling, doubts the 2015 Paris climate agreement's "expression of faith in the sovereignty of Man and his ability to shape the future," preferring the more diffident view of humankind in Pope Francis's *Laudato Si'*. "Insofar as the idea of the limitlessness of human freedom is central to the arts of our time," Ghosh writes, "this is also where the Anthropocene will most intransigently resist them."[16]

The most essential message of ecocentric environmentalism was always a call for humility, precaution, and the inclusion of nonhuman interests in human decision-making. "Humility" is a near-meaningless concept when taking into account the diversity and inequity of human experience, but a meaningful one when considering humanity in the most general terms. Ecocentric radicals were saying in a much more pointed way what the environmental movement as a whole has long suggested: that, as Ghosh writes of human affairs and nonhuman subjects, "conversations among ourselves have always had other participants."[17] At its most pointed this message spoke of ideals like freedom and liberal individualism as defined and delimited by a green planet and everything it sustains.

In 1987 Mike Roselle and four Greenpeace activists tried to hang a banner protesting acid rain over the faces of Mt. Rushmore. Park rangers arrested them before they could get the entire banner unfurled. They spent a month in a Rapid City jail. Roselle, when he realized that he would have to submit to random searches of his home and person in order to be released on probation, decided to spend three additional months in confinement instead. He wrote a statement that he hoped to read to the judge who had sentenced him. The judge's ruling, Roselle explained, ignored both free speech and Native American treaty rights. "As for the protest, in your Honor's words, being a 'violation' of the Shrine of Democracy," Roselle wrote, "I can only say, that in all due respects to the cherished ideals that the carved heads of the 4 former Presidents represent, the sculpture itself is a violation of the mountain into which they have been dynamited."[18]

In 2007 Roselle helped found a new group, Climate Ground Zero (CGZ), to fight the dynamiting of different mountains.[19] Based in West Virginia, CGZ wages Earth First!-style campaigns against mountaintop removal mining. Roselle has spent years living among coal miners and their families, convinced that activism works best when it is embedded in the specifics of particular communities and their circumstances. CGZ's broad goals, though, reach far beyond West Virginia. Roselle considers mountaintop removal mining the most destructive and carbon-intensive method of getting coal, and ending coal burning the necessary first step in fighting climate change.

Balanced precariously between determination and resignation, Roselle has immersed himself in the particulars of Appalachian coal communities while doubting whether the human species can survive its own folly. He continues to wrestle with the questions that environmentalists of all stripes have confronted, however incompletely: the limits of human freedoms and ambitions, the relationship between the human and the natural, and the intersection of social justice and environmental resilience. They will be reasked and reanswered on a changing planet.

Notes

MANUSCRIPT COLLECTIONS

ACR   Alaska Coalition Records, Conservation Collection, Denver Public Library, Denver, Colorado

DRB   David Ross Brower Papers, Bancroft Library, University of California, Berkeley

DF   Dave Foreman personal papers, Albuquerque, New Mexico

EA   Ecology Action Records, Bancroft Library, University of California, Berkeley

EW   Edgar Wayburn Papers, Bancroft Library, University of California, Berkeley

GN   Gaylord Nelson Papers, State Historical Society of Wisconsin, Madison, Wisconsin

GS   Gary Snyder Papers, Special Collections, University of California, Davis

PE   Paul Ehrlich Papers, University Archives, Stanford University, Stanford, California

ROC   Richard O. Clemmer Papers, Special Collections, University of California, Davis

SCMP   Sierra Club Members Papers, Bancroft Library, University of California, Berkeley

SCNLOR   Sierra Club National Legislative Office Records, Bancroft Library, University of California, Berkeley

SCOED   Sierra Club Office of the Executive Director Records, Bancroft Library. University of California, Berkeley

SCR   Sierra Club Records, Bancroft Library, University of California, Berkeley

SCSW   Sierra Club Southwest Office Records, Bancroft Library, University of California, Berkeley

KL   Keith Lampe Column, Special Collections, University of California, Santa Barbara

SPC   Social Protest Collection, Bancroft Library, University of California, Berkeley

WSR   Wilderness Society Records, Conservation Collection, Denver Public Library, Denver, Colorado

PREFACE

1. William Cronon, "The Trouble with Wilderness; or, Getting Back to the Wrong Nature," in Cronon, ed., *Uncommon Ground: Rethinking the Human Place in Nature* (New York: Norton, 1995), 69.

2. Cronon, "The Trouble with Wilderness," 80. For collections of familiar writings about wilderness and responses to recent reinterpretations—most notably Cronon's—see J. Baird Callicott and Michael Nelson, eds., *The Great New Wilderness Debate* (Athens: University of Georgia Press, 1998); and *The Wilderness Debate Rages On: Continuing the Great New Wilderness Debate* (Athens: University of Georgia Press, 2008). For a useful overview of the wilderness debate, see Paul Sutter, *Driven Wild: How the Fight Against Automobiles Launched the Modern Wilderness Movement* (Seattle: University of Washington Press, 2002), 7–18. The most important popularizer of these ideas is Michael Pollan, whose work is committed to the idea that nature and culture are intermingled so deeply that one cannot understand either on its own. The garden is Pollan's example and metaphor for this claim, a place "where nature and culture can be wedded in a way that can benefit both," and a metaphor that "may be as useful to us today as the idea of wilderness has been in the past." See Pollan, *Second Nature: A Gardener's Education* (New York: Grove, 1991), 5.

3. Richard White, "From Wilderness to Hybrid Landscapes: The Cultural Turn in Environmental History," *The Historian* 66, no. 3 (September 2004), 562.

4. William Cronon, *Nature's Metropolis: Chicago and the Great West* (New York: Norton, 1991), xvii.

5. See, for instance, Louis Warren, *The Hunter's Game: Poachers and Conservationists in Twentieth-Century America* (New Haven: Yale University Press, 1997); Karl Jacoby, *Crimes Against Nature: Squatters, Poachers, Thieves, and the Hidden History of American Conservation* (Berkeley: University of California Press, 2003); Mark Spence, *Dispossessing The Wilderness: Indian Removal and the Making of the National Parks* (New York: Oxford University Press, 1999); and Jake Kosek, *Understories: The Political Life of Forests in Northern New Mexico* (Durham: Duke University Press, 2006). See also Richard White, " 'Are You an Environmentalist or Do You Work for a Living?': Work and Nature," in Cronon, ed., *Uncommon Ground*. On cities and nature see Michael Rawson, *Eden on the Charles: The Making of Boston* (Cambridge: Harvard University Press, 2010); Matthew Klingle, *Emerald City: An Environmental History of Seattle* (New Haven: Yale University Press, 2007); Richard Walker, *The Country in the City: The Greening of the San Francisco Bay Area* (Seattle: University Of Washington Press, 2007); Catherine McNeur, *Taming Manhattan: Environmental Battles in the Antebellum City* (Cambridge: Harvard University Press, 2014); and Dawn Beihler, *Pests in the City: Flies, Bedbugs, Cockroaches, and Rats* (Seattle: University Of Washington Press, 2015). On suburbs see Adam Rome, *The Bulldozer in the Countryside: Suburban Sprawl and the Rise of American Environmentalism* (New York: Cambridge University Press, 2001); and Christopher Sellers, *Crabgrass Crucible: Suburban Nature and the Rise of Environmentalism in Twentieth-Century America* (Chapel Hill: University of North Carolina Press, 2012).

6. Paul Sutter, "The World with Us: The State of American Environmental History"; and "Nature Is History," all in *Journal of American History* 100, no. 1 (June 2013), 97, 147.

7. A rich meditation on the multiple uses of "natural" is Kate Soper, *What is Nature?: Culture, Politics and the Non-Human* (Oxford: Blackwell, 1995).

8. For a sense of ecocentrism's centrality to environmental philosophy, see the journal *Environmental Ethics*, in particular during the 1980s and 1990s.

9. William Cronon, "Modes of Prophecy and Production: Placing Nature in History," *Journal of American History* 76, no. 4 (March 1990), 1129.

10. Sutter, "The World with Us," 119.

11. "Mr. Reagan v. Nature," *Washington Post*, October 10, 1980.

12. Llewellyn Rockwell, Jr., "An Anti-Environmentalist Manifesto," *From the Right* (1990), 4, 6; and "The sky is not falling," advertisement, *New York Times*, September 28, 1995.

13. Rob Nixon, *Slow Violence and the Environmentalism of the Poor* (Cambridge: Harvard University Press, 2011), 21–22. For a discussion of the claim that climate change is "natural," see Jeremy Davies, *The Birth of the Anthropocene* (Oakland: University of California Press, 2016), 23–24.

14. Sutter, "The World with Us," 97. Sutter believes that anxiety is an essential part of environmental history too. "So angst it is—existential fear tinged with hope," he writes. "How can anyone do environmental history without it?" See Sutter, "Nature Is History," 148.

15. Jedediah Purdy, *After Nature: A Politics for the Anthropocene* (Cambridge: Harvard University Press, 2015), 285.

16. Cronon, "The Trouble with Wilderness," 70, 80, 87.

INTRODUCTION

1. Nicholas Kristof, "Forest Sabotage Is Urged by Some," *New York Times*, January 22, 1986.

2. Max Oelschlaeger describes the distinction between "biocentrism" and "ecocentrism" as a concern for living beings on the one hand and a concern for natural systems (including non-living nature) on the other. Although radical environmentalists used the terms interchangeably, "ecocentrism" best captures radicals' focus on species and ecosystems rather than on individuals. See Max Oelschlaeger, *The Idea of Wilderness: From Prehistory to the Age of Ecology* (New Haven: Yale University Press, 1991), 292–301.

3. Alan Wolfe, *The Future of Liberalism* (New York: Vintage, 2009), 11. "Although liberalism comes in many stripes," Douglas Kysar writes, "at the core of liberal theories tends to be a belief that the individual is, if not ontologically prior to social groups and orderings, then at least normatively privileged in the sense of providing the proper vantage point from which to consider government obligations to protect and provide." See Kysar, *Regulating from Nowhere: Environmental Law and the Search for Objectivity* (New Haven: Yale University Press, 2010), 151. C. B. MacPherson describes key elements of liberal democracy as civil liberties, equality before the law, protection of minorities, and "a principle of maximum individual freedom consistent with equal freedom for others." See MacPherson, *The Life and Times of Liberal Democracy* (Ontario: Oxford University Press, 1977), 7. For useful discussions of environmentalism's commitment to ends, and

liberalism's commitment to means, see Mark Sagoff, *The Economy of the Earth: Philosophy, Law, and the Environment* (Cambridge: Cambridge University Press, 1988), 146–170; and Andrew Dobson, *Green Political Thought*, 4th ed. (New York: Routledge, 2007), 149–158. See also Matthew Alan Cahn, *Environmental Deceptions: The Tension Between Liberalism and Environmental Policymaking in the United States* (Albany: State University of New York Press, 1995).

4. Environmentalism's skeptical stance toward humanism has been much criticized. For a liberal's call for an environmentalism that celebrates rather than denigrates people, and that embraces human potential rather than criticizes human actions, see Alan Wolfe, "Liberalism, Environmentalism, and the Promise of National Greatness," in Neil Jumonville and Kevin Mattson, eds., *Liberalism for a New Century* (Berkeley: University of California Press, 2007). Similarly, the self-described liberal environmentalist Martin Lewis criticizes the antihumanist strain within environmentalism and calls for a "Promethean environmentalism" that seeks to prevent environmental destruction by harnessing human ingenuity through technological progress. See Lewis, *Green Delusions: An Environmentalist Critique of Radical Environmentalism* (Durham: Duke University Press, 1992).

5. On environmentalism as opposed to individualism, see Thomas Borstelmann, *The 1970s: A New Global History from Civil Rights to Economic Inequality* (Princeton: Princeton University Press, 2012), 231–247; and Jefferson Cowie and Nick Salvatore, "The Long Exception: Rethinking the Place of the New Deal in American History," *International Labor and Working-Class History* 74 (2008), 23.

6. See Robert Collins, *More: The Politics of Economic Growth in Postwar America* (New York: Oxford University Press, 2000); and Lizabeth Cohen, *A Consumer's Republic: The Politics of Mass Consumption in Postwar America* (New York: Vintage, 2003).

7. For an example of how environmental commitments can be broad but shallow, see Michael Bess, *The Light-Green Society: Ecology and Technological Modernity in France, 1960–2000* (Chicago: University of Chicago Press, 2003).

8. Rob Nixon, *Slow Violence and the Environmentalism of the Poor* (Cambridge: Harvard University Press, 2011), 253–254 and 288n47. Two key scholarly critiques of deep ecology from the 1980s and 1990s are Ramachandra Guha, "Radical American Environmentalism and Wilderness Preservation: A Third World Critique," *Environmental Ethics* 11 (Spring 1989); and William Cronon, "The Trouble with Wilderness; Or, Getting Back to the Wrong Nature," in William Cronon, ed., *Uncommon Ground: Rethinking the Human Place in Nature* (New York: Norton, 1995). Another influential criticism is George Bradford, *How Deep Is Deep Ecology?* (Ojai: Times Change Press, 1989). For the techno-thriller view of radical environmentalists as both naïve and lethal, see Tom Clancy, *Rainbow Six* (New York: Penguin, 1998); and Michael Crichton, *State of Fear* (New York: HarperCollins, 2004).

9. For overviews of the environmental movement, see Samuel Hays, *A History of Environmental Politics Since 1945* (Pittsburgh: University of Pittsburgh Press, 2000); Hal Rothman, *Greening of a Nation? Environmentalism in the United States Since 1945* (New York: Harcourt Brace, 1998); Kirkpatrick Sale, *The Green Revolution: The American Environmental Movement, 1962–1992* (New York: Hill and Wang, 1993);

and Philip Shabecoff, *A Fierce Green Fire: The American Environmental Movement* (New York: Hill and Wang, 1993). On environmental historians and the sources of modern environmentalism, see Roderick Nash, *The Rights of Nature: A History of Environmental Ethics* (Madison: University of Wisconsin Press, 1989); Samuel Hays, *Beauty, Health, and Permanence: Environmental Politics in the United States, 1955–1985* (Cambridge: Cambridge University Press, 1987); and Adam Rome, *The Bulldozer in the Countryside: Suburban Sprawl and the Rise of American Environmentalism* (Cambridge: Cambridge University Press, 2001). Nash argues that environmentalism is part of a long tradition of extending rights to long-ignored groups (in this case, parts of nature). Donald Worster has reiterated this view, writing, "We have not fully appreciated how much the protection of wild nature owes to the spread of modern liberal, democratic ideals and to the support of millions of ordinary people around the world." See Worster, "Nature, Liberty, and Equality," in Michael Lewis, ed., *American Wilderness: A New History* (New York: Oxford University Press, 2007), 263. Hays's and Rome's important works are the classic explanations of how middle-class affluence led to environmentalism. More recently, Rome has written about Earth Day and considered the various roles of liberals and the New Left. Although Rome does not focus on ideology, he offers a strong sense of Earth Day's ideological diversity. See Rome, *The Genius of Earth Day: How a 1970 Teach-In Unexpectedly Made the First Green Generation* (New York: Hill and Wang, 2013). Christopher Sellers has argued that suburban environmentalism was not just a middle-class phenomenon but also a cross-class and multiracial movement. See Sellers, *Crabgrass Crucible: Suburban Nature and the Rise of Environmentalism in Twentieth-Century America* (Chapel Hill: University of North Carolina Press, 2012). Paul Sabin is concerned with how environmentalism became partisan in the 1970s and 1980s, reflecting broader philosophical stances for both parties. See Sabin, *The Bet: Paul Ehrlich, Julian Simon, and Our Gamble Over Earth's Future* (New Haven: Yale University Press, 2013). Andrew Kirk has considered the relationship between counterculture environmentalism and market-centered libertarianism in Kirk, *Counterculture Green: The Whole Earth Catalog and American Environmentalism* (Lawrence: University Press of Kansas, 2007). Frank Zelko has also examined countercultural environmentalism, mostly in terms of how it never realized its political ideals. See Zelko, *Make It a Green Peace!: The Rise of Countercultural Environmentalism* (New York: Oxford University Press, 2013). An early work that looks carefully at radical environmental thought is Robert Gottlieb, *Forcing the Spring: The Transformation of the American Environmental Movement*, rev. ed. (Washington, D.C.: Island Press, 2005). For recent works that deal seriously with radical activism, see Thomas Robertson, *The Malthusian Moment: Global Population Growth and the Birth of American Environmentalism* (New Brunswick: Rutgers University Press, 2012); James Morton Turner, *The Promise of Wilderness: Environmental Politics Since 1964* (Seattle: University of Washington Press, 2012); Douglas Bevington, *The Rebirth of Environmentalism: Grassroots Activism from the Spotted Owl to the Polar Bear* (Washington, D.C.: Island Press, 2009); and Darren Speece, *Defending Giants: The Redwood Wars and the Transformation of American Environmentalism* (Seattle: University of Washington Press, 2016). Political philosophers have been more interested in radical environmental thought. One of the standard texts is Dobson, *Green Political Thought*, a good summary of much other work and a rich discussion in its own right. For political philosophers' views, see also Robyn Eckersley, *The Green State: Rethinking Democracy and Sovereignty* (Cambridge: MIT Press, 2004); Brian Doherty and Marius De Geus, eds., *Democracy and Green Political Thought: Sustainability, Rights, and Citizenship* (London: Routledge, 1996); Tim Hayward, *Ecological Thought: An Introduction* (Cambridge: Polity Press, 1995); Marcel Wissenburg, *Green Liberalism: The Free and the Green Society* (London: UCL Press, 1998); Marcel Wissenburg and Yoram Levy, eds., *Liberal Democracy and Environmentalism: The End of Environmentalism?* (London: Routledge, 2004); Andrew Dobson and Paul Lucardie, eds., *The Politics of Nature: Explorations in Green Political Theory* (London: Routledge, 1993); Andrew Dobson and Robyn Eckersley, eds., *Political Theory and the Ecological Challenge* (Cambridge: Cambridge University Press, 2006); and John Barry and Robyn Eckersley, eds., *The State and the Global Ecological Crisis* (Boston: MIT Press, 2005). Many of these authors are in direct conversation with one another. Their concern is usually more political than historical, focused on technical questions like whether environmentalism is an ideology in its own right. Another important work in this field is Robert Paehlke, *Environmentalism and the Future of Progressive Politics* (New Haven: Yale University Press, 1989). See also David Pepper, *Modern Environmentalism: An Introduction* (London: Routledge, 1999); and Bob Pepperman Taylor, *Our Limits Transgressed: Environmental Political Thought in America* (Lawrence: University Press of Kansas, 1992). Historians of religion are well versed in taking extreme ideas seriously. For excellent recent examples, see Darren Dochuk, *From Bible Belt to Sunbelt: Plain-Folk Religion, Grassroots Politics, and the Rise of Evangelical Conservatism*; and Molly Worthen, *Apostles of Reason: The Crisis of Authority in American Evangelicalism* (New York: Oxford University Press, 2014).

10. One of the most influential early examples of environmental optimism was Michael Shellenberger and Ted Nordhaus, "The Death of Environmentalism: Global Warming Politics in a Post-Environmental World," originally distributed as a pamphlet but widely available online. The essay was expanded into a book, Nordhaus and Shellenberger, *Breakthrough: From the Death of Environmentalism to the Politics of Possibility* (New York: Houghton Mifflin, 2007). For further examples, see Stewart Brand, *Whole Earth Discipline: Why Dense Cities, Nuclear Power, Transgenic Crops, Restored Wildlands, and Geoengineering Are Necessary* (New York: Penguin, 2009); and Emma Marris, *Rambunctious Garden: Saving Nature in a Post-Wild World* (New York: Bloomsbury, 2011). For a useful discussion of the competing philosophies at work as they relate to public lands, see Ben Minter and Stephen Pyne, eds., *After Preservation: Saving American Nature in the Age of Humans* (Chicago: University of Chicago Press, 2015).

11. Naomi Klein, "Capitalism vs. The Climate," *The Nation* (November 28, 2011), 14. For an extended version of this argument, see Klein, *This Changes Everything: Capitalism vs. The Climate* (New York: Simon & Schuster, 2014), 56–58.

12. Martha Nussbaum, *Political Emotions: Why Love Matters for Justice* (Cambridge, MA: Harvard University Press, 2013), 383.

1. ECOLOGY AND REVOLUTIONARY THOUGHT

1. On the Sierra Club's democratic structure, see William Devall, "The Governing of a Voluntary Organization: Oligarchy and Democracy in the Sierra Club," (unpublished dissertation, University of Oregon, 1970); and Michael Cohen, *The History of the Sierra Club, 1892–1970* (San Francisco: Sierra Club, 1988), 395–406. Cohen's is the best and most complete history of the Sierra Club. On the Club in the mid-twentieth century, see also Tom Turner, *David Brower: The Making of the Environmental Movement* (Berkeley: University of California Press, 2015).

2. Stephen Fox, *The American Conservation Movement: John Muir and His Legacy* (Madison: University of Wisconsin Press, 1985 [1981]), 115.

3. Fox, *The American Conservation Movement*, 182.

4. Cohen, *The History of The Sierra Club*, 51–52. On the role of private wealth in the early National Park Service, see Susan Schrepfer, *The Fight to Save The Redwoods: A History of Environmental Reform*, 1917–1978 (Madison: University of Wisconsin Press, 1983), 20

5. On the Sierra Club in the 1960s, see Michael McCloskey, *In the Thick of It: My Life in the Sierra Club* (Washington, D.C.: Island, 2005), 52–55.

6. On Rosalie Edge and Paul Sears, and on working behind the scenes, see Fox, *The American Conservation Movement*, 110, 334.

7. Fox, *The American Conservation Movement*, 267.

8. James Morton Turner, *The Promise of Wilderness: American Environmental Politics Since 1964* (Seattle: University of Washington Press, 2012), 28. Schrepfer describes the early Save the Redwoods League as "both zealous in its privatism yet democratic in its spirit." Schrepfer, *The Fight to Save the Redwoods*, 36.

9. Fox, *The American Conservation Movement*, 112.

10. On Farquhar and for Leonard quote, see Cohen, *The History of the Sierra Club*, 151–154.

11. Paul Sutter establishes the many connections between outdoor recreation and conservation in Sutter, *Driven Wild: How the Fight Against Automobiles Launched the Modern Wilderness Movement* (Seattle: University of Washington Press, 2002). See also Marguerite Shaffer, *See America First: Tourism and National Identity*, 1880–1940 (Washington, D.C.: Smithsonian, 2001).

12. Schrepfer, *The Fight to Save the Redwoods*, 88.

13. David Brower, *Environmental Activist, Publicist, and Prophet* (Regional Oral History Office, Bancroft Library, University of California-Berkeley, 1980) 56.

14. Bestor Robinson (written anonymously), "San Gorgonio: Another Viewpoint," *Sierra Club Bulletin*, January 1947, 5.

15. David Brower, "San Gorgonio Auction: Going, Going, —," *Sierra Club Bulletin*, January 1947, 9, 13. On the San Gorgonio debate, see Cohen, *The History of The Sierra Club*, 82–89. Brower was a skier himself and not opposed to the sport; see Brower and Richard Felter, "Surveying California's Ski Terrain," *Sierra Club Bulletin*, March 1948.

16. Brower, "How to Kill a Wilderness," *Sierra Club Bulletin*, August 1945, 3–4. On Brower's military service, see Brower, *For Earth's Sake: The Life and Times of David Brower* (Salt Lake City: Peregrine Smith, 1990), 87–128.

17. Sutter, *Driven Wild*, 53.

18. On the Tioga Road fight, see Cohen, *The History of The Sierra Club*, 89–100, 134–142.

19. For the Club's views on Tioga and roadbuilding in general, see Harold Bradley and David Brower, "Roads in the National Parks," *Sierra Club Bulletin*, June 1949.

20. David Brower, "WE Interview," *Wild Earth*, Spring 1998, 36.

21. On Ansel Adams's resignation and telegrams, see Adams, *Conversations with Ansel Adams* (Regional Oral History Office, Bancroft Library, University of California-Berkeley, 1978), 634.

22. Ethan Carr, *Mission 66: Modernism and the National Park Dilemma* (Amherst: University of Massachusetts Press, 2007).

23. Cohen, *The History of The Sierra Club*, 100. For a sense of fears among Club leaders about crowds in parks, see William Colby, "Yosemite's Fatal Beauty," *Sierra Club Bulletin*, March 1948.

24. Marc Reisner, *Cadillac Desert: The American West and its Disappearing Water* (New York: Penguin, 1986), 140.

25. See Russell Martin, *A Story That Stands Like a Dam: Glen Canyon and the Struggle for the Soul of the West* (New York: Henry Holt, 1989); Cohen, *The History of The Sierra Club*, 143–186; and Brower, *Environmental Activist*, 111–137.

26. On Leonard and Dinosaur, see "Board of Directors Meets at Norden," *Sierra Club Bulletin*, September 1950.

27. Edgar Wayburn, *Sierra Club Statesman, Leader of the Parks and Wilderness Movement: Gaining Protection for Alaska, the Redwoods, and Golden Gate Parklands* (Regional Oral History Office, Bancroft Library, University of California-Berkeley, 1985), 49.

28. Fox, *The American Conservation Movement*, 279.

29. On Brower and compromise, see Michael McCloskey, *In the Thick of It: My Life in the Sierra Club* (Washington, D.C.: Island, 2005), 89–90. On the Grand Canyon dams battle, see Reisner, *Cadillac Desert*, 283–290; Cohen, *The History of The Sierra Club*, 352–365; and Brower, *For Earth's Sake*, 325–370.

30. Fox, *The American Conservation Movement*, 272.

31. On substituting coal for hydropower, see Reisner, *Cadillac Desert*, 290; Brower, *Environmental Activist*, 140–141; and Andrew Needham, *Power Lines: Phoenix and the Making of the Modern Southwest* (Princeton, NJ: Princeton University Press, 2014), 185–212. Tom Turner suggests the causal relationship between Grand Canyon dams and the power plant was less than clear, as did the Club's Southwest Representative John McComb, who in 1970 argued that energy needs so dwarfed the output of the proposed dams that power plants were an inevitability. See Turner, *David Brower*, 127–128, and McComb, letter to the editor, *Arizona Daily Star*, April 5, 1970.

32. Aldo Leopold, *A Sand County Almanac: And Sketches Here and There* (New York: Oxford University Press, 1949).

33. Eliot Porter, *The Place No One Knew: Glen Canyon on the Colorado* (San Francisco and New York: Sierra Club/Ballantine, 1963), 5.

34. Porter, *The Place No One Knew*, 6.

35. Brower, *Environmental Activist*, 142.

36. Porter, *The Place No One Knew*, 6;

37. David Brower, "Conservation and the American Conscience," carton 9, folder 12, DRB.

38. Brower, "Foreword," in Brower, ed., *Wildlands in Our Civilization* (San Francisco: Sierra Club, 1964), 17.

39. Brower, "The Citizen Acts—As Lobbyist," carton 9, folder 46, DRB.

40. Brower, *Environmental Activist*, 142.

41. Among the classic interpretations of the modern environmental movement are Samuel Hays, *Beauty, Health, And Permanence: Environmental Politics in the United States, 1945–1985* (New York: Cambridge University Press, 1987), and Robert Gottlieb, *Forcing the Spring: The Transformation of the American Environmental Movement* (Washington, D.C.: Island, 1993). See also Philip Shabecoff, *A Fierce Green Fire: The American Environmental Movement* (New York: Hill and Wang, 1993), and Kirkpatrick Sale, *The Green Revolution: The American Environmental Movement, 1962–1992* (New York: Hill and Wang, 1993). On the suburban origins of environmentalism, see Adam Rome, *The Bulldozer in The Countryside: Suburban Sprawl and the Rise of American Environmentalism* (New York: Cambridge University Press, 2001), and Christopher Sellers, *Crabgrass Crucible: Suburban Nature and the Rise of Environmentalism in Twentieth-Century America* (Chapel Hill: University of North Carolina Press, 2012). For environmentalism as less a response to industrial technology and more a response to corporate capitalism, see Thomas Jundt, *Greening the Red, White, And Blue: The Bomb, Big Business, and Consumer Resistance in Postwar America* (New York: Oxford University Press, 2014).

42. Rice Odell, *Environmental Awakening: The New Revolution to Protect the Earth* (Cambridge, MA: Harper & Row, 1980), 4.

43. Board of directors meeting minutes, September 20–21, 1969, carton 4, folder 9, SCR.

44. Board of directors meeting minutes, May 2–3, 1970, carton 4, folder 10, SCR.

45. Charles Reich, *The Greening of America* (New York: Random House, 1970), 4.

46. Charles Reich, *The Greening of America*, 15.

47. James Miller, claims that the New Left's commitment to participatory democracy was "America's last great experiment in democratic idealism." Van Gosse similarly argues that the New Left achieved a "new democratic order" in which hierarchies of race, gender, and sexuality were no longer widely accepted. David Barber is much more critical, arguing that the white New Left, represented by SDS, failed to achieve radical change because it cleaved to traditional notions of nationalism, gender roles, and especially racial hierarchy. Neither celebratory nor critical is Doug Rossinow, who finds that the New Left was primarily an existential search for authenticity that experimented with radical politics and settled on reform liberalism. See James Miller, *Democracy Is in the Streets: From Port Huron to the Siege of Chicago* (New York: Simon & Schuster, 1987), 16; Van Gosse, *Rethinking the New Left: An Interpretive History* (New York: Palgrave Macmillan, 2005), 208; David Barber, *A Hard Rain Fell: SDS and Why It Failed* (Jackson, MS: University

Press of Mississippi, 2008); and Doug Rossinow, *The Politics Of Authenticity: Liberalism, Christianity, and the New Left in America* (New York: Columbia University Press, 1998). Understandably, none of these works—with the exception of a few pages in Rossinow—discusses environmentalism. For broader overviews of the decade that put the New Left and environmentalism in some conversation with each other, see Terry Anderson, *The Movement and The Sixties: Protest in America From Greensboro to Wounded Knee* (New York: Oxford University Press, 1995); and Mark Hamilton Lytle, *America's Uncivil Wars: The Sixties Era from Elvis to the Fall of Richard Nixon* (New York: Oxford University Press, 2006).

48. Todd Gitlin, "Theses for the Radical Movement," *Liberation*, May–June, 1967, 34–36.

49. Paul Booth, "Facing the American Leviathan: Convention Working Paper," *New Left Notes*, August 24, 1966, 27.

50. *The Port Huron Statement* is available widely, online and in published form, including as an appendix to Miller, "Democracy Is in the Streets," 329–374.

51. Tom Hayden, *Revolution in Mississippi* (New York: Students for a Democratic Society, 1962), 5. On participation in SNCC by white, non-Southern students, see Anderson, *The Movement and the Sixties*, 43–57; Gitlin, *The Sixties*, 81–85; and Clayborne Carson, *In Struggle: SNCC and the Black Awakening of the 1960s* (Cambridge: Harvard University Press, 1981), 51–55.

52. Arthur Schlesinger, Jr., "The New Liberal Coalition," *The Progressive*, April, 1967, 15. Todd Gitlin responded, "The differences between the New Left and Schlesinger's liberalism could occupy many volumes," carefully specifying that "Schlesinger's liberalism" was only one version. Gitlin found the spirit of Schlesinger's appeal to human reason unobjectionable since, in 1967, the New Left was making the same appeal. See Todd Gitlin, letter to the editor, *The Progressive*, May, 1967, 38.

53. *America and the New Era* (Chicago: Students for a Democratic Society, 1963). Michael Kazin notes that the *Port Huron Statement* had no mention of environmentalism, feminism, and conservatism. See Kazin, "The Port Huron Statement at Fifty," *Dissent*, Spring 2012, 88.

54. *New Left Notes*, July 10, 1967.

55. "Calls for Radical Reconstruction," *New Left Notes*, April 22, 1966, 5.

56. Todd Gitlin, *The Sixties: Years of Hope, Days of Rage* (New York: Bantam, 1987), 232.

57. On the Democratic National Convention, see Kirkpatrick Sale, *SDS* (New York: Random House, 1973), 473–477, and David Farber, *Chicago '68* (Chicago: University of Chicago Press, 1988); on radicalism within the antiwar movement, see Anderson, *The Movement and the Sixties*, 145–147.

58. Carl Oglesby, "Notes on a Decade Ready for the Dustbin," *Liberation*, August–September, 1969, 7.

59. "Vote No on Survival," *The Fifth Estate*, February 19–March 4, 1970.

60. "Eco-Shuck," *Berkeley Tribe*, April 17–24, 1970, 15.

61. "Hold it Right There, Sam! Have You Heard About Ecology?" *Rat*, December, 1969, 10. On the history of the Underground Press Network, the Liberation News Service, and the alternative press generally, see Abe Peck, *Uncovering the Sixties: The Life and*

Times of the Underground Press (New York: Pantheon, 1985); Roger Lewis, *Outlaws of America: The Underground Press and its Context* (London: Heinrich Hanau, 1972); and Raymond Mungo, *Famous Long Ago: My Life and Hard Times with Liberation News Service* (Boston: Beacon, 1970).

62. On the mainstream media see, for instance, Gladwin Hill, "Environment May Eclipse Vietnam as College Issue," *New York Times*, November 30, 1969; Gladwin Hill, "Youth and Environmental Reform," *New York Times*, November 24, 1969; and "New Bag on Campus," *Newsweek*, December 22, 1969, 72.

63. "Editorial," *Ramparts*, May 1970, 2–4.

64. "Too Many People?" *New Left Notes*, May, 1970, 8.

65. "A Letter from an Angry Reader," *Northwest Passage*, May 18, 1970, 12.

66. Connie Flateboe, memorandum to board of directors, December 6, 1969, carton 4, folder 9, SCR.

67. Ron Eber to student contacts, October 12, 1971, carton 116, folder 20, SCMP.

68. Connie Flateboe, memorandum to Lone Star Chapter, November 14, 1970, carton 22, folder 48, SCR.

69. "Protest!" *Sierra Club Bulletin*, December 1969, 11.

70. Paul Brooks, "Notes on the Conservation Revolution," *Sierra Club Bulletin*, January 1970, 16–17.

71. Ronald Eber and Shelley McIntyre to Sierra Club Board of Directors, February 3, 1972, carton 22, folder 48, SCR.

72. On Livermore, see Cohen, *The History of The Sierra Club*, 121–126.

73. On Zahniser and the Wilderness Society, see Brower, *Environmental Activist*, 180.

74. Ansel Adams, *Conversations with Ansel Adams* (Regional Oral History Office, Bancroft Library, 1978), 683.

75. On the Wilderness Act, see Edgar Wayburn, *Sierra Club Statesman*, 28, 158–159, and "About the Wilderness Conference," carton 133, folder 15, SCMP.

76. On the 1959 conference, see Cohen, *The History of The Sierra Club*, 232–233; and "How Dense Should People Be?" *Sierra Club Bulletin*, April 1959.

77. Cohen, *The History of The Sierra Club*, 233.

78. Schrepfer, *The Fight to Save The Redwoods*, 129.

79. On Brower, Muir, and Smokey Bear, see Brower, *Environmental Activist*, 164. The classic work on the history of ecological thought is Donald Worster, *Nature's Economy: A History of Ecological Ideas* (New York: Cambridge University Press, 1977). See also Sharon Kingsland, *The Evolution of American Ecology*, 1890–2000 (Baltimore: The Johns Hopkins University Press, 2005).

80. On Darwin, Eiseley, and the Club, see Schrepfer, *The Fight to Save The Redwoods*, 79–102. See also Cohen, *The History of The Sierra Club*, 345–350. Cohen emphasizes the critical view of humankind in the poetry of Robinson Jeffers, increasingly present in Club materials and a source of controversy for the board.

81. Schrepfer, *The Fight to Save The Redwoods*, 236;

82. James Morton Turner, *The Promise of Wilderness: American Environmental Politics Since 1964* (Seattle: University of Washington Press, 2012), 120.

83. Press clippings about the wilderness conference are in carton 123, folder 15, SCR, and carton 133, folder 16, SCMP.

84. Hardin, "We Must Earn Again for Ourselves What We Have Inherited," in Maxine McCloskey, ed., *Wilderness: The Edge of Knowledge* (San Francisco: Sierra Club, 1970).

85. Robinson, "San Gorgonio: Another Viewpoint," 13.

86. Dan Luten to Stewart Udall, January 29, 1969, carton 133, folder 10, SCMP.

87. Hardin, "We Must Earn Again for Ourselves What We Have Inherited," 260.

88. McCloskey, ed., *Wilderness: The Edge of Knowledge*, 41, 212, 216–217, 245.

89. Garrett Byrnes, "The Sierra Club: Explore, Enjoy, Protect . . .," *The Providence Journal*, March 14, 1969, carton 123, folder 15, SCR.

90. McCloskey, ed., *Wilderness: The Edge of Knowledge*, 116.

91. McCloskey, ed., 254–255.

92. "Smokey The Bear Sutra," at Snyder's direction, "may be reproduced free forever" and is widely available online. The Forest Service mascot's official name is "Smokey Bear."

93. On Snyder, see Rasa Gustaitis, "We Have Met the Enemy and He is Us," *Los Angeles Times*, November 30, 1969.

94. Keith Lampe, "Last Chance for Our Species," *Berkeley Barb*, March 21–27, 1969. For more on Lampe, see Rasa Gustaitis, *Wholly Round* (New York: Holt, Rinehart and Winston, 1973), 218–264. On the Pentagon, see Lampe to Snyder, July 23, 1967, carton 102, folder 62, GSP.

95. For an overview of the relationships between these various groups and movements nationally, see Adam Rome, *The Genius of Earth Day: How a 1970 Teach-In Unexpectedly Made the First Green Generation* (New York: Hill and Wang, 2013), 9–56.

96. Fred Bunnell and Cliff Humphrey, "A Unifying Theme," *Ecology Action*, 1971, carton 4, folder 10, EA, 6.

97. Cliff Humphrey, "Student Strife on a Befouled Planet"; "Radical Politics—June 1968"; and Eugene Anderson, "The Uptight Politics of Conservation," all in carton 24, folder 14 (reel 89) SPC.

98. Anderson, "The Uptight Politics of Conservation."

99. Bunnell and Humphrey, "A Unifying Theme," 5.

100. Humphrey, "Student Strife on a Befouled Planet," 2–3.

101. Eugene Anderson to "people," n.d., carton 1, folder 1, EA.

102. Peace and Freedom Park petition, carton 7, folder 54, EA. On the history of Ecology Action and Herrick Peace and Freedom Park, see Mary Humphrey, "History and Evolution of Ecology Action as Indicated by Early Leaflets and Essays—With Comments by an Insider," *Ecology Action*, (1971), carton 4, folder 10, EA, 14–19.

103. This account of People's Park is taken largely from W. J. Rorabaugh, *Berkeley At War: The 1960s* (New York: Oxford University Press, 1989), 124–166, and Jon David Cash, "People's Park: Birth and Survival," *California History 88*, no. 1 (2010), 8–55.

104. Robert Scheer, "Dialectics of Confrontation: Who Ripped Off the Park," *Ramparts*, August, 1969, 43.

105. Winthrop Griffith, "People's Park—270' by 450' of Confrontation," *New York Times Magazine*, June 29, 1969, 5;

106. Val Douglass, "What Has Happened to Our City," *The Black Panther*, May 31, 1969, 14;

107. Lawrence Davies, "Reagan Links 'People's Park' Battle to Politics," *New York Times*, June 14, 1969.

108. "From Occupied Berkeley," *New Left Notes*, May 30, 1969, 1; see also "The Berkeley Massacre," *New Left Notes*, May 20, 1969, 1. For a more conservative critique written around the same time, see William O'Neill, *Coming Apart: An Informal History of America in the 1960s* (New York: Times, 1971), 260–261. Many histories of the 1960s barely mention People's Park, and when they do generally associate it with New Left militancy rather than with environmentalism. One exception is Mark Hamilton Lytle, *America's Uncivil Wars*, 329–331.

109. Tom Hayden and Frank Bardacke, "Free Berkeley," *Berkeley Tribe*, August 22–29, 1969, 13–16.

110. Keith Lampe, "The Real Dirt on People's Park," *Berkeley Tribe*, August 29–September 4, 1969, 10.

111. "We Will Be the Earth," *Berkeley Barb*, May 30–June 5, 1969, 2; and "Never Forget," *Berkeley Barb*, 2.

112. ". . . And but for the sky there are no fences facing. . . " *Berkeley Tribe*, March 13–20, 1970, 13–16.

113. On the various post-People's Park actions and events, see Earth Read-Out 2, May 29, 1969, KLCS; "Earth Read-Out," *The Fifth Estate*, June 12–25, 1969, 10; "Eco-Tripping," *Berkeley Tribe*, September 5–12, 1969, 7; "Extinction Fair—Dig?" *Berkeley Barb*, June 6–12, 1969, 13; "Ecolibrium," *Berkeley Tribe*, February 6–13, 1970, 13; and "Tree Conspiracy Spreads," *Berkeley Tribe*, January 16–23, 1970, 7.

114. "The Trees Are Our Allies," *The Fifth Estate*, October 30–November 12, 1969, 8.

115. "Lumpy Wavy and the Five Days of Styrofoam," *Seed*, November 7–20, 1969, 8.

116. Todd Gitlin, "Earth and Politics," *Space City News*, July 17–August 28, 1969, 19.

117. Keith Lampe, "Earth Read-Out," *Berkeley Tribe*, November 27–December 5, 1969, 18.

118. "Radical Conservation, Part I: Technology & Environment," *Rag*, June 26, 1969, 3.

119. "Earth Revolts: Man Victim," *Rat*, July 9–23, 1969, 14.

120. Anderson to "People," n.d., carton 1, folder 1, EA;

121. Philip MacDougal, "The Helicopter and the Green Balloon," *Despite Everything*, December, 1969, in carton 7, folder 54, EA, 2. The article is only attributed to "P. M.," but it is reasonable to assume that it is MacDougal. On *Despite Everything*, see Rorabaugh, *Berkeley At War*, 126.

122. Eldridge Cleaver, "On Meeting the Needs of the People," *The Black Panther*, August 16, 1969, 4.

123. MacDougal, "An I-Told-You-So Introduction to the Second Printing," *Despite Everything* (December, 1969), vii-viii. Rorabaugh claims that Bobby Seale did show up at People's Park, but there is no evidence of this in *The Black Panther*. MacDougal reports, "No Panthers ever appeared at the Park. . . ." See Rorabaugh, *Berkeley At War*, 157; and MacDougal, "An I-Told-You-So Introduction to the Second Printing," viii.

124. "Earth Revolts: Man Victim," *Rat*, July 9–23, 1969, 14.

125. For a collection of Boockhin's most important essays from the period, see Murray Bookchin, *Post-Scarcity Anarchism* (Edinburgh: AK, 2004).

126. Murray Bookchin, "Ecology and Revolutionary Thought," *The Fifth Estate*, April 2–April 15, 1970, 9.

127. "The Politics of Ecology," *Rat*, August 12–26, 1969, 12.

128. "The Roots of Ecology," *The Old Mole*, April 3–16, 1970, 12.

129. Michael McCloskey, "Editorial," *Sierra Club Bulletin*, June 1970, 2.

130. McCloskey, "Editorial," 2.

2. CRISIS ENVIRONMENTALISM

1. Gladwin Hill, "Ecology Emerges as Issue in Many of Nation's Races," *New York Times*, September 27, 1970. On the importance of Earth Day in establishing environmentalism's broad reach, see Adam Rome, *The Genius of Earth Day: How a 1970 Teach-In Unexpectedly Made the First Green Generation* (New York: Hill and Wang, 2013).

2. Cliff Humphrey, "Sweeping Social Change Is on the Way: Why It Must Be a Cultural Transformation and Why It May Be a Violent Revolution," 1969, 1, carton 5, folder 10, EA.

3. Humphrey, "Sweeping Social Change," 2.

4. David Bird, "Muskie Tells Conservationists Economic Growth Must Go On," *New York Times*, April 19, 1970.

5. Michael McCloskey, "Sierra Club Executive Director: The Evolving Club and the Environmental Movement, 1961–1981," oral history by Susan Schrepfer, 1981 (Regional Oral History Office, The Bancroft Library, University of California, Berkeley), 149–152.

6. Brock Evans to Arthur Magida, January 29, 1976, carton 201, folder 37, SCR.

7. Margot Hornblower, "Environmental Movement Has Grown a Sharp Set of Teeth," *Washington Post*, June 2, 1979.

8. On the Club's tax battle, see Michael Cohen, *The History of the Sierra Club, 1892–1970* (San Francisco: Sierra Club, 1988), 163–166; see also Michael McCloskey, *In the Thick of It: My Life in the Sierra Club* (Washington, D.C.: Island, 2005), 146–149. On Brower's later objections to Washington, D.C. and on grassroots environmentalists "unhappy with the movement's new emphasis on lobbying and legislation," see Lucy Howard, "Environmentalists in a Family Fight," *Newsweek*, January 27, 1986.

9. On Wayburn, see Michael Cohen, *The History of the Sierra Club, 1892–1970* (San Francisco: Sierra Club, 1988), 277.

10. Scott Thurber, "Tax Crackdown 'Helps' Sierra Club," *San Francisco Chronicle*, March 11, 1968.

11. On other organizations' reactions, see Robert Mitchell, "From Conservation to Environmental Movement: The Development of the Modern Environmental Lobbies," in Michael Lacey, ed., *Government and Environmental Politics: Essays on Historical Developments Since World War II* (Washington, D.C.: The Wilson Center, 1989), 103–104.

12. On NEPA, see Robert Gillette, "National Environmental Policy Act: How Well Is It Working?" *Science*, April 14, 1972, 146–150; and Gillette, "National Environmental

Policy Act: Signs of Backlash are Evident," *Science*, April 7, 1972, 30–33. See also Serge Taylor, *Making Bureaucracies Think: The Environmental Impact Statement Strategy of Administrative Reform* (Stanford, CA: Stanford University Press, 1984).

13. On Nixon and environmentalism, see J. Brooks Flippen, *Conservative Conservationist: Russell E. Train and the Emergence of American Environmentalism* (Baton Rouge: Louisiana State University Press, 2006); Bruce Schulman, *The Seventies: The Great Shift in American Culture, Society, and Politics* (Cambridge, MA: Da Capo, 2001), 30–32; and Rick Perlstein, *Nixonland: The Rise of a President and the Fracturing of America* (New York: Scribner, 2008), 460–462. Flippen and Perlstein argue that Nixon passed environmental laws to gain political advantage, not realizing—or not caring—how consequential those laws would be. Schulman goes further, arguing that Nixon passed laws he knew to be relatively weak in order to appear friendly to environmentalism while in fact undermining its legal basis. Schulman does not explain, however, how his argument takes into account the consistent and widespread use of Nixon-era laws by environmental groups ever since.

14. On the Ford Foundation and environmental law, see Christopher Bosso, *Environment, Inc.: From Grassroots to Beltway* (Lawrence: University Press of Kansas, 2005), 39–40; and Paul Sabin, "Environmental Law and the End of the New Deal Order," *Law and History Review* 33, no. 4 (November, 2015). See also Don Harris, "Conservation and the Courts," *Sierra Club Bulletin*, September 1969.

15. On the gradual shift from lobbying for new legislation in the 1970s to enforcing existing legislation through lawsuits in the 1980s (and an attendant shift from national to local groups), see Cody Ferguson, *This Is Our Land: Grassroots Environmentalism in the Late-Twentieth Century* (New Brunswick, NJ: Rutgers University Press, 2015).

16. On the number of lobbyists in Washington, see Mitchell, "From Conservation to Environmental Movement," 104; and Rome, *The Genius of Earth Day*, 215–216.

17. On membership numbers, see James R. Wagner, "Washington Pressures—Environment Groups Shift Tactics from Demonstrations to Politics, Local Action," *National Journal*, July 24, 1971, 1557–1564.

18. Arthur Magida, "Environment Report—Movement Undaunted by Economic, Energy Crises," *National Journal*, January 17, 1976.

19. Michael McCloskey, "Are Compromises Bad?" *Sierra Club Bulletin*, February 1977, 20–21.

20. Brock Evans, "New Life for the Old Cause," *Sierra Club Bulletin*, April 1975, 19.

21. William Futrell, "Editorial: The Environment and the Courts," *Sierra Club Bulletin*, May 1973, 18. On the environmental bill of rights generally, see Carole Gallagher, "The Movement to Create an Environmental Bill of Rights: From Earth Day, 1970 to the Present," *Fordham Environmental Law Journal* 9, no. 1 (Fall 1997), 107–154. On the Sierra Club's involvement, see Nancy Mathews to Michael McCloskey, May 6, 1968, carton 117, folder 29, SCR; and McCloskey, "Keynote address of Michael McCloskey," carton 132, folder 24, SCR, in which McCloskey concluded with a call for a "bill of environmental rights."

22. McCloskey, "Are Compromises Bad?."

23. McCloskey, *In the Thick of It*, 108.

24. The literature on Zero Population Growth is limited; there is not yet a full study of the organization. The best places to start for ZPG and population politics in the 1960s are Thomas Robertson, *The Malthusian Moment: Global Population Growth and the Birth of American Environmentalism* (New Brunswick, NJ: Rutgers University Press, 2012); Derek S. Hoff, *The State and the Stork: The Population Debate and Policy Making in U.S. History* (Chicago: University of Chicago Press, 2012); and Paul Sabin, *The Bet: Paul Ehrlich, Julian Simon, and Our Gamble over Earth's Future* (New Haven: Yale University Press, 2013).

25. On eighteenth-century discussions of population, see Hoff, *The State and the Stork*, 14–43. On global overpopulation and its many connections, in particular in Europe and Asia, see Alison Bashford, *Global Population: History, Geopolitics, and Life on Earth* (New York: Columbia University Press, 2014).

26. On Leopold and carrying capacity, and on Vogt and Osborn, see Robertson, *The Malthusian Moment*, 23–29, 36–60, 170–171.

27. Rasa Gustaitis, "We Have Met the Enemy and He Is Us," *Los Angeles Times*, November 30, 1969. On Mills more generally, see Rome, *The Genius of Earth Day*, 184–190; on the Bay Area and population, see Robertson, *The Malthusian Moment*, 132–136.

28. On Brand, see Gustaitis, "We Have Met the Enemy and He Is Us."

29. On Reynolds, "I Sing a Song of Living," *ZPG National Reporter*, November 1970, 9.

30. For Berry quote, see board of directors' meeting minutes, exhibit A, May 1970, carton 4, folder 10, SCR; see also National Population Committee memo to "chapter and group population committees," n.d., carton 91, folder 8, SCNLOR.

31. For a sketch of the Club's various population activities in the 1960s, and for Nichols's warnings, see Louise Nichols memo to Chuck Clusen, December 28, 1973, carton 5, folder 9, SCR. For one of the Club's early population policy statements, see "Population and the Sierra Club," June 1975, carton 91, folder 8, SCNLOR. On the "Office of Population Policy," see "Statement of Judith Kunofsky," March 11, 1982, carton 285, folder 124, SCR.

32. Member Kenneth Kraft wrote to several Society officials all at once. See Kenneth Kraft to James Marshall, Kenneth Kraft to Stewart Brandborg, and Kenneth Kraft to John Oakes, all March 24, 1969, and James Marshall to Kenneth Kraft, March 28, 1969, all in box 43, folder 14, WSR.

33. Morris Udall to Stewart Brandborg, July 31, 1969, box 43, folder 14, WSR.

34. "Statement Concerning the Need for a National Population Policy," box 43, folder 19, WSR.

35. Robertson, *The Malthusian Moment*.

36. "Zero Population Growth Inc., Plans and Perspectives," box 1, folder 6, PE.

37. Letters to the editor, *ZPG National Reporter*, April, 1971, 23.

38. Carl Pope memo to ZPG board including draft "population policy document" by Pope, Judy Senderowitz, and others, n.d., 21, box 1, folder 2, PE.

39. Clifford Humphrey, "From Institutionalized Inaction to Action Institutions," box 5, folder 13, EA, 4.

40. Apocalyptic environmentalism in the 1970s has received increasing attention from environmental historians, most notably in Hoff, *The State and the Stork*, and Robertson, *The Malthusian Moment*. Samuel Hays gives a broad overview of concerns about overpopulation, diminishing resources, and limits to growth in Hays, *Beauty, Health, and Permanence*, chap. 7. Frederick Buell gives more specifics and argues that a palpable sense of crisis in the 1970s had not diminished two decades later, but had become so embedded in everyday politics and culture that it was unexceptional; see Buell, *From Apocalypse to Way of Life: Environmental Crisis in the American Century* (New York: Routledge, 2003). Political scientists have also paid attention to these environmentalists. See, for instance, Bob Pepperman Taylor, *Our Limits Transgressed: Environmental Political Thought in America* (Lawrence: University Press of Kansas, 1992), chap. 2; and Robert Paehlke, *Environmentalism and the Future of Progressive Politics* (New Haven: Yale University Press, 1989), chap. 3.

41. I am using the term "crisis environmentalism"—my own—to refer both to the advocates of a steady-state economy (people like Herman Daly, Kenneth Boulding, and E. F. Schumacher) as well as to the "neo-Malthusians" like Garrett Hardin and William Ophuls who argued for the necessity of scaling back civil liberties. These two groups did not necessarily consider themselves a coherent school of thought, but they were both animated by the same belief in an imminent crisis that both American society and the major environmental groups were either underestimating or ignoring entirely, and they were both willing to question received values to a degree that the mainstream movement was not. For an example of Daly and Ophuls making similar arguments against a common adversary, see "Economic Growth" in letters to the editor, *Science*, August 8, 1975, 410–414. For a treatment of the two groups as aligned against Lockean liberalism, see Susan M. Leeson, "Philosophic Implications of the Ecological Crisis: The Authoritarian Challenge to Liberalism," *Polity* 11, no. 3 (Spring 1979), 303–318. The great exception to this description of "crisis environmentalism" was Barry Commoner, who was second to no one in his sense of urgency about impending ecological catastrophe but who had very different views from Hardin and Ophuls about the best solutions. Where Hardin and Ophuls thought that environmentalism trumped all other issues, Commoner argued that protecting the environment and promoting social justice were deeply connected; where Hardin and Ophuls believed that avoiding crisis would mean scaling back democracy, Commoner insisted that only through more democratic processes could the public hold private interests accountable and reduce pollution. Paul Ehrlich, however, was Commoner's primary opponent. Commoner argued that Ehrlich overemphasized and oversimplified the role of overpopulation in the environmental crisis. See Michael Egan, *Barry Commoner and the Science of Survival: The Remaking of American Environmentalism* (Cambridge: MIT Press, 2007).

42. Paul Ehrlich, *The Population Bomb* (New York: Ballantine, 1971 [1968]); and Thomas Malthus, *An Essay on the Principle of Population* (New York: Oxford University Press, 1993).

43. Donella Meadows, et al., *The Limits to Growth: A Report for the Club of Rome's Project on the Predicament of Mankind* (New York: Universe Books, 1973 [1972]), 23. On the

reception to this thesis, see Robert Reinhold, "Mankind Warned of Perils in Growth," *New York Times*, February 27, 1972; Robert Gillette, "The Limits to Growth: Hard Sell for a Computer View of Doomsday," *Science*, March 10, 1972; B. Bruce Briggs, "Against the Neo-Malthusians," *Commentary*, July 1, 1974; William Tucker, "Environmentalism and the Leisure Class," *Harper's*, December 1977; Anthony Lewis, "Ecology and Politics: 1," *New York Times*, March 4, 1972; "On Reaching A State of Global Equilibrium" *New York Times*, March 13, 1972; and "A Blueprint For Survival," *New York Times*, February 5, 1972. For further critiques, see John Maddox, *The Doomsday Syndrome* (London: MacMillan, 1972); Wilfred Beckerman, *Two Cheers for the Affluent Society: A Spirited Defense of Economic Growth* (New York: St. Martin's, 1974); and Peter Passell and Leonard Ross, *The Retreat from Riches: Affluence and Its Enemies* (New York: Viking, 1973). For a historian's consideration at the end of the decade, see Samuel Hays, "The Limits-To-Growth Issue: A Historical Perspective," *Explorations in Environmental History: Essays by Samuel Hays* (Pittsburgh: University of Pittsburgh Press, 1998).

44. Edward Goldsmith, et al., *Blueprint for Survival* (Boston: Houghton Mifflin, 1972), 3, 8. On the decline of establishment population concerns, see Hoff, *The State and the Stork*, 195–218, and on the "shot in the arm," see Hoff, 222.

45. Herman Daly, "The Steady-State Economy: Toward a Political Economy of Biophysical and Moral Growth," in Herman Daly, ed., *Toward a Steady-State Economy* (San Francisco: W.H. Freeman, 1973), 149–174. On "ecological economics" and environmentalism, see Hoff, *The State and the Stork*, 175–187.

46. E. F. Schumacher, *Small Is Beautiful: Economics as if People Mattered* (New York: Harper & Row, 1973), 50, 54, 57.

47. Daly, "The Steady-State Economy," 149–150.

48. Schumacher, *Small Is Beautiful*, 27.

49. Schumacher, 17.

50. Daly, "The Steady-State Economy," 150–151.

51. Cliff Humphrey, "Sweeping Social Change Is on the Way," 4, carton 5, folder 10, EA.

52. Humphrey, "From Institutionalized Inaction to Action Institutions," 5.

53. Rome, *The Genius of Earth Day*, 38.

54. "The Environmental Research (Survival) Committee Report to the Sierra Club Board of Directors," April, 1972; Richard Cellarius to committee members—n.d., but likely November 15, 1972; Richard Cellarius to committee members, December 27, 1972, all in carton 53, folder 21, SCR.

55. Phillip Berry, "Sierra Club Leader, 1960s-1980s: A Broadened Agenda, A Bold Approach," oral history by Ann Lage, 1981, 1984 (Regional Oral History Office, The Bancroft Library, University of California, Berkeley), 59–61. Berry stated that the Club's energy and population committees resulted in part from discussions in the survival committee; the Sierra Club had been working on issues of population and energy for several years, however, before the survival committee was organized.

56. John Fischer, "The Easy Chair: Survival U.," *Harper's*, September 1, 1969, 14, 22. Fischer declared that he had found "Survival U." two years later. See Fischer, "The Easy Chair: Survival U. is Alive and Burgeoning in Green Bay, Wisconsin," *Harper's*, February 1, 1971.

57. Paul Ehrlich, Douglas Daetz, Robert North, and Dennis Pirages, "A Proposal to Establish a Program in Social Ecology at Stanford University," February, 1972, box 4, folder 9, PE, 1, 5, 19.

58. Ehrlich, *The Population Bomb*, xi. Ehrlich claimed that even if his predictions proved false, his prescriptions would leave people better fed and housed. Sabin, *The Bet*, 98.

59. Jay Forrester, "Counterintuitive Behavior of Social Systems," *ZPG National Reporter*, June, 1971.

60. "Editorial," *ZPG National Reporter*, June, 1971, 8. Ehrlich's interest was reciprocal; Dennis Meadows told Ehrlich that his *Population, Resources, Environment* was "required reading for anyone joining our group," and in late 1971 Ehrlich arranged for Donella and Dennis Meadows, along with Princeton professor of international law Richard Falk, to participate in several seminars with Stanford faculty and students. See Meadows to Ehrlich, January 19, 1971; Ehrlich to Meadows, January 27, 1971; and "Schedule for Meadows-Falk Visit," n.d., all in box 4, folder 43, PE.

61. David Runciman, *The Confidence Trap: A History of Democracy in Crisis from World War I to the Present* (Princeton, NJ: Princeton University Press, 2013), 204. According to Ira Katznelson, the 1930s and 1940s was the greatest test of democracy in the twentieth century, a period that "witnessed the disintegration and decay of democratic and liberal hopes." See Ira Katznelson, *Fear Itself: The New Deal and the Origins of Our Time* (New York: Liveright, 2013), 12. Anne Kornhauser argues that democracy was to some degree sacrificed as the United States created "a level of bureaucracy that threatened popular sovereignty"; see Anne Kornhauser, *Debating the American State: Liberal Anxieties and the New Leviathan, 1930–1970* (Philadelphia: University of Pennsylvania Press, 2015), 4–5.

62. Garrett Hardin, "The Tragedy of the Commons," in Garrett Hardin and John Baden, eds., *Managing the Commons* (San Francisco: W. H. Freeman, 1977), 20.

63. William Ophuls, "Leviathan or Oblivion?" in Daly, *Toward a Steady-State Economy*, 225. By 1977, Ophuls had moderated his views on authoritarianism only a little. Whereas four years earlier he had written, "Only a Hobbesian sovereign can deal with this situation effectively," in 1977 he said, "Only a government possessing great powers to regulate individual behavior in the ecological common interest can deal effectively with the tragedy of the commons." His terminology was not as stark, but his basic claim had not changed: although a steady-state society did not necessarily need to involve "dictatorial control over our everyday lives," it certainly would have to "encroach upon our freedom of action." The only alternatives to a self-imposed loss of freedom were "the coercion of nature" or "an iron regime." See William Ophuls, *Ecology and the Politics of Scarcity: Prologue to a Political Theory of the Steady State* (San Francisco: W. H. Freeman, 1977), 152–156.

64. Robert Heilbroner, *An Inquiry into The Human Prospect* (New York: Norton, 1974), 110.

65. Robert Heilbroner, "Second Thoughts on the Human Prospect," *Futures*, February 1975, 36, 40; and Ophuls, *Ecology and the Politics of Scarcity*, 152–156. On the crises of the 1970s and the Trilateral Commission, see Runciman, *The Confidence Trap*, 184–224. On the sense of crisis and environmentalism, see Robertson, *The Malthusian Moment*, 186–190; and Hoff, *The State and the Stork*, 211–230. Crisis environmentalists' critique

of democracy was a longstanding one. Robert Dahl has written that the two strongest critiques of democratic principles have always been anarchism and "guardianship" (Dahl's term for an enlightened form of authoritarianism). Despite their differences, anarchists and guardians both argue that what the majority wants is not necessarily what is best. See Robert Dahl, *Democracy and Its Critics* (New Haven: Yale University Press, 1989). No crisis environmentalist welcomed the idea of an authoritarian state. Both Heilbroner and Ophuls, for instance, believed in small-scale, decentralized alternatives but did not think them possible in the short-term. Heilbroner valorized the Greek polis and Ophuls favored a "frugal sustainable state" committed to conservation and oriented around "humane values" rather than industrial growth. See Heilbroner, *An Inquiry into the Human Prospect*, 134–141; and Ophuls, "The Politics of the Sustainable Society," in Dennis Pirages, ed., *The Sustainable Society: Implications for Limited Growth* (New York: Praeger, 1977), 157–172.

66. Kingsley Davis, "Zero Population Growth: The Goals and the Means," in Mancur Olson and Hans H. Landsberg, eds., *The No-Growth Society* (New York: Norton, 1973), 21, 28.

67. "In This Issue," *ZPG National Reporter*, August 1970, 3. See also "Compulsory Pregnancy Criminal Laws," *ZPG Communicator*, March 1969, 3, box 1, folder 7, PE.

68. Shirley Radl to Paul Ehrlich, April 2, 1970, box 1, folder 1, PE.

69. Shirley Radl to Edgar Chasteen, (n.d.), box 1, folder 1, PE.

70. "Plans and Perspective," box 1, folder 6, PE.

71. On the film, see Hal Seielstad, "Zealot Paramount Gambles," *ZPG National Reporter*, April 1972, 3.

72. Hal Seielstad, confidential memo of February 8, 1972, box 1, folder 1, PE.

73. Harold Seielstad, "Crisis Alert," February 17, 1972, box 3, folder 7, PE.

74. On ZPG's legal proceedings and leafleting efforts, see Board of Directors Fortnightly Report, February 16–29, 1972; Board of Directors Fortnightly Report, March 16–31, 1972, box 1, folder 1, PE; and Hal Seielstad, "ZPG Sues Paramount," *ZPG National Reporter*, March 1972, 3. On ZPG's polling, see Board of Directors Monthly Report, December 1972, box 1, folder 1, PE.

75. See Richard Bowers, letter to the editor, *Wild Earth* (Winter 1991/1992), 9.

76. Hal Seielstad, "Executive Director's Report," *ZPG National Reporter*, May 1972, 16.

77. "ZPG: Too Many People?" *New Left Notes*, May 1970, 8. By "ZPG," *New Left Notes* generally meant the movement, not the organization; all of its specific criticisms were against Ehrlich and *The Population Bomb*. By 1970, *New Left Notes* was a publication of the "Progressive Labor" faction of Students for a Democratic Society and no longer represented SDS as a whole.

78. On Ehrlich and Commoner, see Egan, *Barry Commoner*; on Ehrlich and Simon, see Sabin, *The Bet*.

79. Robert Collins, *More: The Politics of Economic Growth in Postwar America* (New York: Oxford University Press, 2000), 61.

80. Lizabeth Cohen, *A Consumer's Republic: The Politics of Mass Consumption in Postwar America* (New York: Vintage, 2003), 127. See also Robertson, *The Malthusian Moment*. For a discussion of three major phases of liberalism in the United States,

see Alan Brinkley, *The End of Reform: New Deal Liberalism in Recession and War* (New York: Vintage, 1995), 3–14. Meg Jacobs traces "economic citizenship" back to the early twentieth century and emphasizes the fight to achieve "purchasing power" and restrain inflation. Like Collins and Cohen, she connects consumption to political identity. See Meg Jacobs, *Pocketbook Politics: Economic Citizenship in Twentieth-Century America* (Princeton, NJ: Princeton University Press, 2005).

81. Hoff, *The State and the Stork*, 92.

82. Environmental Research Committee on Survival meeting minutes, November 6–7, 1971, carton 34, folder 12, SCR.

83. Carl Pope memo to ZPG Board, (n.d.), 17–20, box 1, folder 2, PE.

84. George Mumford to Paul Ehrlich, April 14, 1970, box 10, folder 19, PE.

85. Keith Lampe, *Earth Read-Out 5*, July 10, 1969, 3, KL.

86. "Editorial: On Population," Ecology (n.d.), carton 4, folder 10, EA, 21.

87. "A Center for Growth Alternatives," September 6, 1973, carton 117, folder 23, DRB.

88. Carl Pope memo to ZPG Board, (n.d.), box 1, folder 2, PE, 21–23.

89. Rhonda Levitt and Madeline Nelson, "Editorial," *ZPG National Reporter*, May 1971, 12.

90. Planned Parenthood Federation of America Annual Report 1974, carton 35, folder 30, DRB, 1.

91. "In This Issue," *ZPG National Reporter*, August 1970, 3. See also *ZPG National Reporter*, July–August 1971.

92. On World Population Day, see Judy Kunofsky, memorandum and report, November 4, 1974, carton 120, folder 12, SCMP. On *Roe v. Wade* anniversary, see January 1975 letter to Congress, carton 91, folder 2, SCNLOR.

93. On both the partnership of ZPG and Planned Parenthood and the eventual split of population activists and feminists, see Robertson, *The Malthusian Moment*, 157–160, 190–194; and Hoff, *The State and the Stork*, 188–189. On *The Birth Control Handbook* and ZPG, see Christabelle Sethna, "The Evolution of the Birth Control Handbook: From Student Peer-Education Manual to Feminist Self-Empowerment Text, 1968–1975," *Canadian Bulletin of Medical History* 23 (2006); and "Letters," *ZPG National Reporter* July–August 1971, 26.

94. Ehrlich, *The Population Bomb*, 1–2.

95. Hank Lebo, "Revolutionary Chicken," *Clear Creek*, June 1972, 10.

96. See Hays, "The Limits-To-Growth Issue."

97. On African American objections to ZPG and population politics, see Robertson, *The Malthusian Moment*, 171–175, 178–181, 190–194.

98. "A Comment on LIFE's Coverage of ZPG," *ZPG National Reporter*, May 1970, 13. On Ehrlich, see Robertson, *The Malthusian Moment*, 171–175.

99. "Letters," *ZPG National Reporter*, August 1970, 36.

100. Hal Seielstad, "Zero Consumption Growth," *ZPG National Reporter*, April 1972, 12.

101. Lewis Perelman, "Towards Global Equilibrium," *ZPG National Reporter*, June 1972, 8.

102. On population politics and genocide, see Hoff, *The State and the Stork*, 149–157. On Council on Population & Environment, see Janet Malone to Michael McCloskey, July 30, 1971, carton 91, folder 3, SCNLOR. On local effects, "In This Issue,"

ZPG National Reporter, September 1970, 3. On suburbs, see Bicky Dodge, "The Road to Hell Is Paved with Good Inventions," *ZPG National Reporter*, September 1971, 1. For local growth resolution, see ZPG Board of Directors meeting minutes, October 19, 1974, box 1, folder 2, PE, 9.

103. Keith Lampe, *Earth Read-Out 17*, November 26, 1969, 4, KL.

104. Jean Weber to Paul Ehrlich, November 4, 1972, box 2, folder 10, PE. See also Robin Daniels to Paul Ehrlich, September 20, 1972, box 2, folder 10, PE.

105. On the history of the Sierra Club and immigration, see Louise Nichols to Chuck Clusen, December 28, 1973, carton 5, folder 9, SCR.

106. Memo from Carl Pope to ZPG board on population policy committee (n.d.), box 1, folder 2, PE, 26.

107. On ZPG's policies, see ZPG: Recommendations for a New Immigration Policy for the United States, box 3, folder 4, PE.

108. Gerda Bikales, "Immigration Policy: The New Environmental Battlefield," *National Parks & Conservation Magazine*, December 1977, carton 91, folder 5, SCNLOR, 16.

109. For Tanton's affiliations, see Tanton, "Testimony prepared for the Commission on Population Growth and the American Future," carton 285, folder 122, SCR.

110. Louise Nichols to Chuck Clusen, December 28, 1973, carton 5, folder 9, SCR.

111. Tanton to Ehrlich, September 17, 1974; and Ehrlich to Tanton, July 25, 1974, both in box 3, folder 1, PE.

112. Jason DeParle, "The Anti-Immigration Crusader," *New York Times*, April 17, 2011. See also "English Spoken Here, But Unofficially," *New York Times*, October 29, 1988.

113. Bookchin's response to "Four Changes" was published in *Earth Read-Out* 13, October 30, 1969, 2, KL.

114. Timothy O'Riordan, *Environmentalism* (London: Pion, 1976), 36.

3. A RADICAL BREAK

1. Letter to the editor, *Earth First!*, June 21, 1983, 3. The publication had different names at different moments but was generally known as the *Earth First! Journal*. For convenience, though, in the notes I refer to it simply as *Earth First!*, which is often how the name appeared on the journal's front page.

2. D. H., letter to the editor, *Earth First!*, June 21, 1982, 2.

3. The exception to "major groups" avoiding strict ecocentrism was Greenpeace in its earliest days. See Frank Zelko, *Make It a Green Peace!: The Rise of Countercultural Environmentalism* (New York: Oxford University Press, 2013), 195–197.

4. Michael Cohen, *The History of The Sierra Club: 1892–1970* (San Francisco: Sierra Club, 1988), 128.

5. Board of Directors annual meeting minutes, May 6–7, 1972, exhibit F, carton 4, folder 12, SCR; and David Brower and Richard Felter, "Surveying California's Ski Terrain," *Sierra Club Bulletin*, March 1948.

6. Board of Directors annual meeting minutes, May 1–2, 1965, carton 4, folder 4, SCR, 13–14. For background on Mineral King, see Cohen, *The History of the Sierra Club*, 339–345.

7. Michael McCloskey to John Leasher, July 16, 1974, carton 3, folder 19, SCLDF. "Sierra Club Proclamation on Wilderness," Exhibit F, board of directors annual meeting minutes, May 2–3, 1970, carton 4, folder 10, SCR.

8. Christopher Stone, *Should Trees Have Standing?: Toward Legal Rights for Natural Objects* (Los Altos, CA: William Kaufman, 1974).

9. Stone, *Should Trees Have Standing*, 44.

10. Stone, 75. On Harry Blackmun's separate dissent, see Stafford Keegin, "Top of the Seventh: Mickey Mouse-1, Sierra Club-0," *Clear Creek*, July–August, 1972.

11. "Ecology Conference: Birds and Trees Speak Up in S.F.," *San Francisco Examiner*, n.d., box II: 103, folder 3, GS. For the larger legal discussion of the "rights of nature," see Martin Krieger, "What's Wrong with Plastic Trees?" *Science* 179, no. 4072 (February 2, 1973); Laurence Tribe, "Ways Not to Think About Plastic Trees: New Foundations for Environmental Law," *Yale Law Journal* 83, no. 7 (June 1974); Mark Sagoff, "On Preserving the Natural Environment," *Yale Law Journal* 84, no. 2 (December 1974); and Tribe, "Environmental Foundations to Constitutional Structures: Learning from Nature's Future," *Yale Law Journal* 84, no. 3 (January 1975).

12. Keith Lampe to "Allen," June 25, 1970, box II: 102, folder 66, GS. See also Rasa Gustaitis, "They Didn't Laugh at Ro-Non-So-Te," *Washington Post*, March 11, 1971.

13. Lampe, "An Open Letter to Readers of the Old Earth Read-Out," Spring 1972, box II: 102, folder 85, GS. Of Living Creatures Associates, Buckminster Fuller said, "A nice manifest of man's consciousness. Their effectiveness approximately zero," in Rasa Gustaitis, *Wholly Round* (New York: Holt, Rinehart and Winston, 1973), 264.

14. Press release, San Francisco Ecology Center, August 4, 1978, box II: 103, folder 3, GS.

15. Lampe to Gary Snyder, June 27, 1983, box II: 103, folder 4, GS.

16. Keith Lampe to Tom Hayden, July 18, 1975, box II: 102, folder 90, GS.

17. Debra Weiners, "Biocentrics: This Is the Latest Trend in the Ecology Movement," *San Francisco Examiner*, October 4, 1975, box II: 103, folder 3, GS.

18. Debra Weiners, "Biocentrics."

19. Arne Naess, "The Shallow and the Deep, Long-Range Ecology Movement: A Summary," *Inquiry* 16 (1973), 100. On what was most influential from Naess's original article, see Bill Devall and George Sessions, *Deep Ecology: Living as if Nature Mattered* (Salt Lake City: Peregrine Smith, 1985), 65–77. See also Max Oelschlaeger, *The Idea of Wilderness: From Prehistory to the Age of Ecology* (New Haven: Yale University Press, 1991), 281–319.

20. Arne Naess, "The Shallow and the Deep," 95–100.

21. On Devall and Sessions and their embrace of deep ecology, as well as their important publications, see Warwick Fox, *Toward a Transpersonal Ecology: Developing New Foundations for Environmentalism* (Boston: Shambhala, 1990), 60–70. As Fox points out, several thinkers discussed anthropocentric vs. non-anthropocentric environmentalism before or around the same time as Naess, including Leo Marx, Theodore Roszak, Timothy O'Riordan, and Murray Bookchin. Fox offers three possible reasons for why deep ecology took root in a way that these other thinkers' ideas did not: that deep ecology came first (which Fox shows to be inaccurate); that deep ecology had better and more determined boosters than any similar school of thought

(which Fox agrees was at least part of the story); and that deep ecology was substantially different from other forms of non-anthropocentrism in ways that made it more intellectually attractive (which Fox argues was the case). Fox places far more weight on deep ecology's psychological dimension (Naess's interest in gaining an appreciation of symbiosis and interconnectedness through 'self-realization') than on its 'popular' interpretation (what Naess sometimes called 'biocentric egalitarianism'). But for radical environmental groups like Earth First!, the 'popular' interpretation was the more relevant. Earth First!ers and similar radical activists had little to say about the dissolution of the ego and the discovery of nature through psychological awareness, and much to say about the hierarchy of values that privileged the human over the natural. See Fox, *Toward a Transpersonal Ecology*, 26–40, 55–77.

22. John Tanton, "Testimony Prepared for the Commission on Population Growth and the American Future," April 15, 1971, carton 285, folder 122, SCR, 3–4.

23. On Commoner and Lappé among other critics, see Thomas Robertson, *The Malthusian Moment: Global Population Growth and the Birth of American Environmentalism* (New Brunswick: Rutgers University Press, 2012), 176–200.

24. Robert Carter and David Lasenby, "Values and Ecology: Prolegomena to an Environmental Ethics," *Alternatives*, Winter 1977, 40.

25. Richard Bond, "Salvationists, Utilitarians, and Environmental Justice," *Alternatives*, Spring 1977, 41, 42.

26. Janet Besecker and Phil Elder, "Lifeboat Ethics: A Reply to Hardin," *Alternatives*, December 1975, p. 23; see also Jeffrey O'Hearn, "Beyond the Growth Controversy: An Assessment of Responses," *Alternatives*, Summer 1978.

27. On Friends of the Earth and the 'conserver society,' see "Editorial," *Alternatives*, Summer/Fall 1979, p. 2; and Arthur Cordell, "Another Look at . . . the Conserver Society," *Alternatives*, Winter 1980, 4–9.

28. Richard Watson, "A Critique of Anti-Anthropocentric Biocentrism," *Environmental Ethics* 5, no. 3 (Fall 1983), 251. Although Watson never uses the term "deep ecology," preferring "anti-anthropocentric biocentrism," he identifies Sessions and especially Naess as chief offenders, making clear that he is writing about deep ecology and its followers. See also Watson, "Comment: A Note on Deep Ecology," *Environmental Ethics* 6, no. 4 (Winter 1984), in which Watson accuses deep ecologists of utopianism and argues that there is little hope for human civilization to ever consciously live in balance with nature for an extended period of time.

29. Arne Naess, "A Defence of the Deep Ecology Movement," *Environmental Ethics* 6, no. 3 (Fall 1984).

30. David Ehrenfeld, *The Arrogance of Humanism* (New York: Oxford University Press, 1978), 240. Like all polemics, Ehrenfeld's book tended toward simplification and overstatement. As Milton Snoeyenbos pointed out, it was difficult for an environmentalist to attack human reason, technology, and science, given the central role that those things played in identifying environmental problems. "In short," Snoeyenbos wrote, "it is reason that enables us to recognize reason's horizons." Radical environmentalism had an ambivalent relationship with science and technology, on the one hand relying

on scientific expertise to prove the ill effects of industrial civilization, and on the other hand blaming scientific expertise for creating those ill effects. But few environmentalists—radical or not—were willing to denounce science and technology without reservation. For most, the problem was one of degree: the modern world, they argued, fostered an unquestioning belief in scientific progress's inherent good, a belief that deserved greater skepticism. See Milton Snoeyenbos, "A Critique of Ehrenfeld's Views on Humanism and the Environment," *Environmental Ethics* 3, no. 3 (Fall 1981), 234.

31. Ehrenfeld, *The Arrogance of Humanism*, 202, 208.

32. J. Baird Callicott, "Animal Liberation: A Triangular Affair," *Environmental Ethics* 2, no. 4 (Winter 1980), 337. Regarding Leopold's hunting, the apparent exception that in the end proves to be the rule is the wolf that Leopold describes killing and in whose eyes a "fierce green fire" dies as he reaches her. The wolf, Leopold makes clear, represents a natural order and is important less as an individual than as part of an interconnected world. See Aldo Leopold, *A Sand County Almanac, and Sketches Here and There* (London: Oxford University Press, 1949), 130. The animal liberation/land ethic debate is deeply complicated with differences of philosophical opinion even within the animal rights community. The debate ranged across the pages of *Environmental Ethics* for the journal's first several years. A useful summary of one side of the debate by the journal's editor is Eugene Hargrove, ed., *The Animal Rights/Environmental Ethics Debate: The Environmentalist Perspective* (Albany: State University of New York Press, 1992). See also Anthony Povilitis, "On Assigning Rights to Animals and Nature," *Environmental Ethics* 2, no. 1 (Spring 1980); Tom Regan, "Animal Rights, Human Wrongs," *Environmental Ethics* 2, no. 2 (Summer 1980); Tom Regan, "The Nature and Possibility of an Environmental Ethic," *Environmental Ethics* 3, no. 1 (Spring 1981); and Edward Johnson, "Animal Liberation versus the Land Ethic," *Environmental Ethics* 3, no. 3 (Fall 1981). One of the founding texts of animal liberation is Peter Singer, *Animal Liberation* (New York: HarperCollins, 2002 [1975]). All of this only scratches the surface.

33. Callicott, "Animal Liberation: A Triangular Affair," 326.

34. Paul Watson, *Earthforce!: An Earth Warrior's Guide to Strategy* (Los Angeles: Chaco, 1993), 37, 24, 18.

35. See "Wilderness Preserves" in *Earth First!*, a pamphlet and 'guide' to the group produced by the *Earth First! Journal* and undated, but published sometime in the late 1980s—probably 1987, DF.

36. Michael McCloskey, "Wilderness Movement at the Crossroads," *Pacific Historical Review* 41, no. 3 (August, 1972), 352.

37. Paul Sutter, *Driven Wild: How the Fight Against Automobiles Launched the Modern Wilderness Movement* (Seattle: University of Washington Press, 2002), 80.

38. James Morton Turner, *The Promise of Wilderness: American Environmental Politics Since 1964* (Seattle: University of Washington Press, 2012), 28. Sutter and Turner have delved deeper into the political meaning of wilderness than any recent historians. The classic work on the meaning of American wilderness is Roderick Nash, *Wilderness and the American Mind* (New Haven: Yale University Press, 1967).

39. This description of Alaskan wilderness politics is drawn largely from Julius Duscha, "Setting the Crown Jewels: How the Alaska Act Was Won," *The Living Wilderness*, Spring 1981, 4–9; Nash, *Wilderness and the American Mind*, 272–315; and Turner, *The Promise of Wilderness*, 141–181. See also a series of updates by Edgar Wayburn, including "Alaska: President Carter to the Rescue," *Sierra*, January/February 1979, 22; "Alaska 1979," *Sierra*, March/April 1979, 25; "Alaska in the House: The Last Act?" *Sierra*, May/June 1979, 54–55; and "Alaska Lands Bill in the Senate: Slowdowns and Showdowns," *Sierra*, September/October 1980, 36–39.

40. Edgar Wayburn, "Alaska: An Act of History," *Sierra*, January/February 1981, 5. On the Alaska Coalition's origins in the battle over the Trans-Alaska Pipeline, see Peter Coates, *The Trans-Alaska Pipeline Controversy: Technology, Conservation, and the Frontier* (Fairbanks: University of Alaska Press, 1993 [1991]), 217–220.

41. White House Press Office, "Alaskan Lands Endangered Again," April 26, 1979, box 1, folder 1, ACR.

42. "The Alaska Lands Issue in 1979," January 1979, box 1, folder 1, ACR.

43. "Two Alaskan Perspectives: 17 National Monuments Proclaimed; Congress Has Unfinished Business," *The Living Wilderness*, October/December 1978, 20.

44. Edgar Wayburn, "Alaska Lands Bill in the Senate," 38; Wayburn, "Alaska: An Act of History," 5.

45. Chuck Clusen, "Viewpoint," *The Living Wilderness*, Spring 1981, 3. On the role of ecology in the Alaska campaign more generally, see Turner, *The Promise of Wilderness*, 146–148. The campaign that resulted in ANILCA was hugely influential but not the first to use ecological arguments. On the ecological arguments made in establishing the Arctic National Wildlife Range two decades earlier, see Roger Kaye, *The Last Great Wilderness: The Campaign to Establish the Arctic National Wildlife Refuge* (Fairbanks: University of Alaska Press, 2006), 213–225.

46. One of the best histories of the Forest Service's wilderness policies throughout the twentieth century is Dennis Roth, *The Wilderness Movement and the National Forests* (College Station, TX: Intaglio, 1988). The best political history of RARE II is Turner, *The Promise of Wilderness*, 183–224. See also Tim Mahoney and Jody Bolz, "RARE II: A Test for Forest Wilderness," *The Living Wilderness*, April/June 1978.

47. On RARE I, see Roth, *The Wilderness Movement and the National Forests*, 37–45; and James Risser, "The Forest Service and its Critics," *The Living Wilderness*, Summer 1973.

48. Board of directors annual meeting minutes, May 6–7, 1972, 3, carton 4, folder 12, SCR.

49. The acreage under consideration for RARE II was considerably more than RARE I because RARE II used different systems of analysis to determine what lands qualified, left aside the Forest Service's restrictive "purity policies," and gave greater consideration to Eastern forests. See Turner, *The Promise of Wilderness*, 190.

50. Turner, 129. On Brandborg's enthusiasm and eventual firing, see Turner, 101–104, 128–133.

51. On the Society's internal problems and the firing of Brandborg, see Turner, 131–133; and "Resolution of the Governing Council of the Wilderness Society," July 28, 1975, box 16, folder 12, WSR.

52. Celia Hunter to "Friend of Wilderness," (n.d.), folder 30, box 6, WSR.

53. Celia Hunter to Clif Merritt, September 9, 1977. box 37, folder 25, WSR.

54. Clif Merritt to Celia Hunter, September 23, 1977, box 37, folder 25, WSR.

55. Clif Merritt to Bill Turnage (n.d., but in response to August 30, 1978 memo from Hunter), box 17, folder 6, WSR.

56. Bart Koehler activity reports, July 1977 and April 1978, box 37, folder 22, WSR.

57. Bob Langsenkamp activity reports, June 1978 and October 1978, box 37, folder 23, WSR.

58. Howie Wolke to Jeff Knight and Rafe Pomerance, (n.d., but sometime in fall 1978), carton 26, folder 1, DRB.

59. On the firing of Koehler and Carter, see Ann Schimpf, "Wilderness Society Fires Key Utah Environmentalist," *High Country News*, July 27, 1979. On Turnage generally, see Turner, *The Promise of Wilderness*, 202–210.

60. Minutes, executive committee, December 14 and 15, 1979, 14, box 17, folder 6, WSR.

61. Foreman, "Making the Most of Professionalism," *Earth First!*, August 1, 1984, 16.

62. Michael McCloskey, "Wilderness Movement at the Crossroads, 1945–1970," Pacific Historical Review 41, no. 3 (August 1972), 354.

63. Foreman, "Making the Most of Professionalism," 16.

64. Meeting minutes, Sierra Club Board of Directors, May 5–6, 1979, carton 4, folder 18, SCR.

65. Sherry Howman, "RARE II Touches off Stormy Debate," (fact sheet attached to Environmental Study Conference briefing paper), February 5, 1979, box 160, folder 33, GN. On the Club's role in the Environmental Study Conference, see minutes of the annual board of directors meeting, May 3–4, 1975, 18–19, carton 4, folder 15, SCR.

66. See series of bulletins from the Sierra Club and the Wilderness Society: "RARE-II: A Citizen's Handbook for the National Forest Roadless Area Review and Evaluation Program: 1977–1978," May 1978, carton 224, folder 19, SCR; "RARE-II: A Citizen's Handbook . . .," December 1978, carton 224, folder 21, SCR; and "RARE II: A Raw Deal for Wilderness," February 1979, carton 235, folder 34, SCR.

67. Press release (n.d.), box 11, folder 3, WSR.

68. "Tim, John" to "Chuck, Bill," April 6, 1979, box 11, folder 3, WSR.

69. "Tim, John" to "Chuck, Bill," April 6, 1979, annotated by William Turnage, box 11, folder 3, WSR.

70. Dave Foreman memo to "the leading intellectual and literary lights of EARTH FIRST," September 1, 1980, DF.

71. Huey Johnson, "The Flaws of RARE II," *Sierra*, May/June 1979, 10. On the response to RARE II and to the Johnson suit, see Roth, *The Wilderness Movement and the National Forests*, 53–55; Susan Zakin, *Coyotes and Town Dogs: Earth First! and the Environmental Movement* (New York: Viking, 1993), 93–100; Robert Jones, "Plan to Open Million Acres of Forest Blocked," *Los Angeles Times*, January 9, 1980; and Robert Day, Jr., "California v. Bergland," *Journal of Forestry* 78, no. 4 (April 1980).

72. On the aftermath of RARE II, see Turner, *The Promise of Wilderness*, 183–224; Roth, *The Wilderness Movement and the National Forests*, 56–60; and John McComb to Senator Jesse Helms, April 4, 1981, carton 52, folder 1, SCNLOR.

73. Dave Foreman, *Confessions of an Eco-Warrior* (New York: Crown, 1991), 13–14.

74. Turner, *The Promise of Wilderness*, 68, 5.

75. The most complete version of the Pinacate Desert story is told by Susan Zakin in *Coyotes and Town Dogs*, 115–134. Foreman references the Wyoming campfire in "Earth First!" *The Progressive*, March 1981.

76. Edward Abbey, *Beyond the Wall: Essays from the Outside* (New York: Holt, Rinehart and Winston, 1984), 151.

77. On the arid conditions of the desert West and the consequent political and industrial infrastructure, see W. Eugene Hollon, *The Great American Desert: Then and Now* (New York: Oxford University Press, 1966). The literature on water in the West is huge. One of the best—and most fun—overviews is Marc Reisner, *Cadillac Desert: The American West and its Disappearing Water* (New York: Penguin, 1986).

78. The story of Glen Canyon Dam is told in Russell Martin, *A Story That Stands Like a Dam: Glen Canyon and the Struggle for the Soul of the West* (New York: Henry Holt, 1989).

79. For some of Abbey's more politic views on Glen Canyon Dam, see "The Damnation of a Canyon," in Abbey, *Beyond the Wall*. Abbey's thoughts about blowing up the dam appear in fictional form in *The Monkey Wrench Gang* (New York: Perennial Classics, 2000 [1975]). See also "Down the River," in Abbey, *Desert Solitaire: A Season in the Wilderness* (New York: Simon & Schuster, 1990 [1968]).

80. Foreman, "Earth First!," 42.

81. "The Wilderness Society Supports Logging and Mining in Montana Roadless Areas??!" *Earth First!*, August 1, 1984, 7; See also "Kill the Bills," *Earth First!*, November 1, 1983, 1.

82. Peter Coppelman and Bill Devall, Exchange, *Earth First!*, December 21, 1984, 18.

83. Dave Foreman, "Earth First!" *Earth First!*, February 2, 1982, 5.

84. "Sierra Club Proclamation on Wilderness," exhibit F, board of directors annual meeting minutes, May 2–3, 1970, carton 4, folder 10, SCR.

85. "Statement of David Brower," August 5, 1971, carton 91, folder 1, SCNLOR, 1.

86. Earth First!, a pamphlet and 'guide' to the group produced by the *Earth First! Journal* and undated, but published sometime in the late 1980s—probably 1987, DF.

87. Emma Marris, *Rambunctious Garden: Saving Nature in a Post-Wild World* (New York: Bloomsbury, 2011), 24–25, 52.

88. William Cronon, "The Trouble with Wilderness; or, Getting Back to the Wrong Nature," in Cronon, ed., *Uncommon Ground: Rethinking the Human Place in Nature* (New York: Norton, 1995), 79.

89. David Brower, ed., *Wildlands in Our Civilization* (San Francisco: Sierra Club, 1964), 146–151.

90. Turner, *The Promise of Wilderness*, 72–90.

91. Pamela Rich to Harold Sparck, January 28, 1977, carton 40, folder 36, DRB.

92. Bill Cunningham, "Grazing in Wilderness," July 30, 1980, carton 20, folder 17, SCSW.

93. Howie Wolke, "Dismantle the Wilderness Act!" *Earth First!*, March 21, 1983, 11. See also Sutter, *Driven Wild*, 71, on Aldo Leopold's non-purist definition of wilderness.

Conservationists often fought to relax classification standards. While arguing that the Sweetwater River should be awarded Wild and Scenic River status, Wolke complained to the Bureau of Outdoor Recreation: "It seems that you are bound up by the term 'outstandingly remarkable.' I don't know who in Congress cooked-up that descriptive term, but your interpretation strikes me as meaning 'one of a kind.' Standard dictionary definitions refute that meaning." See Wolke to B.O.R., July 7, 1977, box 37, folder 22, WSR.

94. "The Other Side of the Bioregion," *Siskiyou Country*, February/March 1984, 2.

95. George Wuerthner, "The Natural Role of Humans in Wilderness," *Earth First!*, December 21, 1989, 25. On rewilding, see, for instance, "Wilderness Recovery Areas," *Earth First!*, February 2, 1984, 7.

96. Reed Noss, "Recipe for Wilderness Recovery," *Earth First!*, September 23, 1986, 22.

97. Aldo Leopold, *A Sand County Almanac* (New York: Ballantine, [1949] 1966), 197.

98. Howie Wolke, "Editorial," *Earth First!*, March 20, 1982, 4–5.

99. Tony Moore, "Editorial," *Earth First!*, May 1, 1982, 5.

100. Mike Roselle, "Guest Editorial: Nomadic Action Group," *Earth First!*, September 23, 1987, 3.

101. Turner, *The Promise of Wilderness*, 68.

102. Roselle, "Nomadic Action Group," 3.

103. Abbey, *The Monkey Wrench Gang*, 68.

104. *Express Times* article reprinted as "PG&E Saboteur, Still at Large, Tells How He Did It," *Rat*, June 1–14, 1968, 8;

105. "The Eco-Guerillas Are Coming," *Harry*, April 24–May 7, 1971, 9; "Eco-Guerillas," *Northwest Passage*, August 16–September 5, 1971.

106. "The 'True' Adventures of Billie Board," *Argus*, June 1971, 6–7.

107. On the Eco-Commando Force '70, see "Eco-Guerillas," and Allyn Brown, "Ecology Commandoes Strike at Dawn," *Coronet*, May 1971, 73–77. Subversive actions by environmentalists were so popular after Earth Day that the student group Environmental Action held an "ecotage" award ceremony, handing the top honor to Eco-Commando Force '70. See Stewart Udall and Jeff Stansbury, "Ecotage," press release, January 26, 1972, carton 167, folder 15, SCR.

108. Frank Zelko, *"Make It a Green Peace!": The Rise of Countercultural Environmentalism* (New York: Oxford University Press, 2013).

109. This description of the origin of Greenpeace and the Amchitka campaign is drawn from Robert Hunter, *Warriors of the Rainbow: A Chronicle of the Greenpeace Movement* (New York: Holt, Rinehart & Winston, 1979); and Zelko, *"Make It a Green Peace!"* The literature on Greenpeace includes many first-person accounts besides Hunter's, including Rex Weyler, *Greenpeace: How A Group of Journalists, Ecologists, and Visionaries Changed the World* (Emmaus, PA: Rodale, 2004). The major scholarly treatment is Zelko, *"Make It a Green Peace!"* See also Paul Wapner, "In Defense of Banner Hangers: The Dark Green Politics of Greenpeace," in Bron Taylor, ed., *Ecological Resistance Movements: The Global Emergence of Radical and Popular Environmentalism* (Albany: State University of New York Press, 1995); and Ronald Shaiko, "Greenpeace U.S.A.:

Something Old, New, Borrowed," *Annals of the American Academy of Political and Social Science* 528 (July 1993).

110. R. B. Weeden, memorandum, September 17, 1969, carton 14, folder 13, SCNLOR.

111. James Moorman, memorandum, September 19, 1969, carton 14, folder 13, SCNLOR.

112. On the "legal guerilla actions," see Lloyd Tupling to Walter Hickel, September 29, 1969.

113. David Brower to Walter Hickel, September 29, 1969; "Sierra Club Challenge Use of Wildlife Refuge as Site for Nuclear Bomb Test By AEC," press release, October 1, 1969, all in carton 14, folder 13, SCNLOR.

114. On Committee for Nuclear Responsibility, see Robert Fleisher, press release, July 8 (year unknown), carton 14, folder 13, SCNLOR.

115. Hunter, *Warriors of the Rainbow*, 52.

116. Mark Long, "Campaign in Spain," *Greenpeace Examiner*, Winter 1980, 18.

117. Eric Schwartz, "Ecologists Escalate Fight Over Nature," *Chicago Tribune*, May 30, 1981. There are several useful books on Watson and Sea Shepherd, all of them largely descriptive and all of them with combative titles that contrast sharply with the pacific name of Watson's group. See Paul Watson and Warren Rogers, *Sea Shepherd: My Fight for Whales and Seals* (New York: Norton, 1982); Paul Watson, *Ocean Warrior: My Battle To End the Illegal Slaughter on the High Seas* (Toronto: Key Porter, 1996); David Morris, *Earth Warrior: Overboard With Paul Watson and the Sea Shepherd Conservation Society* (Golden, CO: Fulcrum, 1995); and Peter Heller, *The Whale Warriors: The Battle at the Bottom of the World to Save the Planet's Largest Mammals* (New York: Free Press, 2007). See also Raffi Khatchadourian, "Neptune's Navy: Paul Watson's Wild Crusade to Save the Oceans," *The New Yorker*, November 5, 2007.

118. W. B. Rood, "Army Hunts Reservoir Foe," *Los Angeles Times*, May 25, 1979. For a complete account of Friends of the River, see Tim Palmer, *Stanislaus: The Struggle for a River* (Berkeley: University of California Press, 1982).

119. Schwartz, "Ecologists Escalate Fight Over Nature," 11.

120. Robert Hunter, "Eco-Violence," *New Age*, October 1980, 51.

121. Dave Foreman to editor of *New Age*, (n.d.), DF.

122. On the Pacific forest, see David Rains Wallace, *The Klamath Knot: Explorations of Myth and Evolution* (San Francisco: Sierra Club, 1983); and Catherine Caufield, "The Ancient Forest," *New Yorker*, May 14, 1990.

123. On the history of the Kalmiopsis, see Chant Thomas, "Kalmiopsis/Bald Mountain Background," *Earth First!*, May 1, 1983; and "Oregon RARE II Suit Filed," *Earth First!*, February 2, 1984.

124. On the Bald Mountain blockades, see "Kalmiopsis Blockade Begins," *Earth First!*, May 1, 1983; and "Wilderness War in Oregon" and "Blockade Personal Accounts," *Earth First!*, June 21, 1983. On the G-O Road, see "Gasquet-Orleans Road," *Earth First!*, May 1, 1982; "The Siskiyous and the G-O Road," *Earth First!*, May 1, 1983; and Peter Matthiessen, Indian Country (New York: Viking, 1984), 167–199. On the lawsuit, see "Sue the Bastards," *Earth First!*, June 21, 1983. See also Zakin, *Coyotes and Town Dogs*, 228–272.

125. Molly Campbell, Ric Bailey, et al., "Blockade Personal Accounts," *Earth First!*, June 21, 1983.

126. Karen Pickett, "Blockade #7," *Earth First!*, September 23, 1983, 4.

127. See George Draffan, "Cathedral Forest Action Group Fights for Oregon Old Growth," *Earth First!*, June 20, 1984.

128. On the summer blockades, see Draffan, "Cathedral Forest Action Group Fights for Oregon Old Growth," *Earth First!*, June 20, 1984; Mike Roselle, "Middle Santiam Heats Up: 15 Arrested—More to Come," *Earth First!*, June 20, 1984; Matt Veenker, "Blockaders Roughed Up in Middle Santiam," *Earth First!*, August 1, 1984; and Mike Roselle, "Middle Santiam Struggle Continues," *Earth First!*, August 1, 1984. On the office occupation see Mike Roselle, "*Earth First!* Takes Regional Forester's Office," *Earth First!*, November 1, 1984.

129. On tree sits, see Ron Huber, "Tree Climbing Hero" *Earth First!*, June 21, 1985; Aries, "Go Climb a Tree!," *Earth First!*, June 21, 1985; Ron Huber, "Battle for Millenium Grove: Giant Crane Attacks Tree Sitter" *Earth First!*, August 1, 1985; and Mike Roselle, "Oregon Overview: Squaw Creek Action," *Earth First!*, August 1, 1985. See also Zakin, *Coyotes and Town Dogs*, 260–261.

130. For comments from other environmentalists about Earth First! see Elizabeth Kaufman, "Earth-Saving: Here Is a Gang of Real Environmental Extremists," *Audubon*, July 1982, 116–120; and Ann Japenga, "Earth First! A Voice Vying for the Wilderness," *Los Angeles Times*, September 5, 1985.

131. Bill Devall and George Sessions, "Direct Action," *Earth First!*, November 1, 1984, 19.

132. Greg King, "Roselle Does Two Weeks," *Earth First!*, September 23, 1987, 8. For a useful summary of Kalmiopsis actions, see Karen Wood, "North Kalmiopsis Threatened," *Earth First!*, August 1, 1991. On Lou Gold, see Lou Gold and T. A. Allen, "Lou Gold Escapes Bald Mountain," *Earth First!*, November 1, 1987. See also Chant Thomas, "Return to Bald Mountain," *Earth First!*, March 21, 1987.

133. Eugene Hargrove, "Ecological Sabotage: Pranks or Terrorism?" *Environmental Ethics* 4, no. 4 (Winter 1982), 291–292.

134. Edward Abbey, Dave Foreman, and Eugene Hargrove, "Exchange," *Environmental Ethics* 5, no. 1 (Spring 1983), 94–96.

4. PUBLIC LANDS AND THE PUBLIC GOOD

1. On the Grand County incident, see R. McGreggor Cawley, *Federal Land, Western Anger: The Sagebrush Rebellion and Environmental Politics* (Lawrence: University Press of Kansas, 1993), 4–9.

2. Recent literature that complicates late twentieth-century political oppositions includes Matthew Lassiter, *The Silent Majority: Suburban Politics in the Sunbelt South* (Princeton: Princeton University Press, 2007); Robert Self, *All In the Family: The Realignment of American Democracy Since the 1960s* (New York: Hill and Wang, 2012); Thomas Borstelmann, *The 1970s: A New Global History from Civil Rights to Economic Inequality* (Princeton, NJ: Princeton University Press, 2012); Michael Stewart Foley,

Front Porch Politics: The Forgotten Heyday of American Activism in the 1970s and 1980s (New York: Hill and Wang, 2013); Jefferson Cowie, *Stayin' Alive: The 1970s and the Last Days of the Working Class* (New York: New Press, 2010); and Jefferson Cowie and Nick Salvatore, "The Long Exception: Rethinking the Place of the New Deal in American History," *International Labor and Working-Class History* 74 (2008). Several environmental historians have recently given Reagan's election significant weight. See Paul Sabin, *The Bet: Paul Ehrlich, Julian Simon, and Our Gamble over Earth's Future* (New Haven: Yale University Press, 2013), 137–152; Thomas Robertson, *The Malthusian Moment: Global Population Growth and the Birth of American Environmentalism* (New Brunswick: Rutgers University Press, 2012), 218–220; Darren Frederick Speece, *Defending Giants: The Redwood Wars and the Transformation of American Environmental Politics* (Seattle: University of Washington Press, 2017), 122–123; and Patrick Allitt, *A Climate of Crisis: America in the Age of Environmentalism* (New York: Penguin, 2014), 156–165. Cody Ferguson tells a somewhat different story in which the shift from the 1970s to the 1980s was not just ideological but technical, as environmentalists focused more on enforcing than passing legislation. See Cody Ferguson, *This Is Our Land: Grassroots Environmentalism in the Late Twentieth Century* (New Brunswick: Rutgers University Press, 2015). For a discussion of environmentalism that focuses on partisanship but downplays Reagan, see James Morton Turner, " 'The Specter of Environmentalism': Wilderness, Environmental Politics, and the Evolution of the New Right," *Journal of American History* 96, no. 1 (June 2009).

3. Paul Sabin, "Environmental Law and the End of the New Deal Order," *Law and History Review* 33, no. 4 (November 2015), 968, 1000. For a discussion of the uneven history of liberal skepticism about state power, see Anne Kornhauser, *Debating the American State: Liberal Anxieties and the New Leviathan, 1930–1970* (Philadelphia: University of Pennsylvania Press, 2015).

4. The literature on the New Right has been growing rapidly in recent years. For general works focusing especially on politics and ideas, see Rick Perlstein, *Before the Storm: Barry Goldwater and the Unmaking of the American Consensus* (New York: Hill & Wang, 2001), and *Nixonland: The Rise of a President and the Fracturing of America* (New York: Scribner, 2008); Godfrey Hodgson, *The World Turned Right Side Up: A History of the Conservative Ascendancy in America* (New York: Houghton Mifflin, 1996); Laura Kalman, *Right Star Rising: A New Politics, 1974–1980* (New York: Norton, 2010); Daniel Rodgers, *Age of Fracture* (Cambridge: Belknap, 2011); and Bruce Shulman and Julian Zelizer, *Rightward Bound: Making America Conservative in the 1970s* (Cambridge, MA: Harvard University Press, 2008). The classic work is George Nash, *The Conservative Intellectual Movement in America Since 1945* (New York: Basic, 1976).

5. "Conservation: High Priority," *National Review*, January 27, 1970, 70–72.

6. Jim Merkel, "Environmental Control: The Conservative Imperative," *The New Guard*, April 1970, 14–16. On the New Right and social politics (but not environmentalism), see Lassiter, *The Silent Majority*; Self, *All in the Family*; Lisa McGirr, *Suburban Warriors: The Origins of the New American Right* (Princeton: Princeton University

Press, 2001); and Kevin Kruse, *White Flight: Atlanta and the Making of Modern Conservatism* (Princeton: Princeton University Press, 2007). On environmentalism and the New Right, see Brian Allen Drake, *Loving Nature, Fearing the State: Environmentalism and Antigovernment Politics before Reagan* (Seattle: University of Washington Press, 2013); and Turner, " 'The Specter of Environmentalism.' "

7. Robert Bailey, "As Radicals Work to Seize Control of Ecology Movement," *Human Events*, April 4, 1970, 12–13.

8. John Chamberlain, "Are We Being Too Tough on Pesticides?" *Human Events*, March 7, 1970, 17; James Jackson Kilpatrick, "Pause Needed in Ecological Binge," *Human Events*, February 14, 1970, 13.

9. Randal Cornell Teague, "Environmental Pollution and YAF," *The New Guard*, April 1970, 9–10.

10. Norman Podhoretz, "Reflections on Earth Day," *Commentary*, June 1970, 28.

11. Norman Podhoretz, "Doomsday Fears and Modern Life," *Commentary*, October, 1971, 6. See also, for instance, Gertrude Himmelfarb, "A Plague of Children," *Commentary* April, 1971; Rudolf Klein, "Growth and its Enemies," *Commentary*, June, 1972; and B. Bruce-Briggs, "Against the Neo-Malthusians," *Commentary*, July, 1974.

12. A. C. Wilkerson, "Rancher Speaks Out Against Environmentalists," *Vernal Express*, February 9, 1978, carton 20, folder 25, SCSW. On FLPMA and the BLM wilderness review see John McComb, "The BLM Begins Its Wilderness Review," *Sierra*, January/February 1979, 46; and James R. Skillen, *The Nation's Largest Landlord: The Bureau of Land Management in the American West* (Lawrence: University Press of Kansas, 2009), 120–131. Western distrust of the federal government might also owe much to nuclear testing and the Atomic Energy Commission. See Leisl Carr Childers, *The Size of the Risk: Histories of Multiple Use in the Great Basin* (Norman: University of Oklahoma Press, 2015), 69–102.

13. The most comprehensive study of the sagebrush rebellion is Cawley, *Federal Land, Western Anger*. Also important are William Graf, *Wilderness Preservation and the Sagebrush Rebellions* (Savage, MD: Rowman & Littlefield, 1990); and Karen Merrill, *Public Lands and Political Meaning: Ranchers, The Government, and the Property Between Them* (Berkeley: University of California Press, 2002). Skillen, *The Nation's Largest Landlord* is the best work on the BLM and includes a useful discussion of the sagebrush rebellion. On the wilderness movement and the sagebrush rebellion, see James Morton Turner, *The Promise of Wilderness: American Environmental Politics Since 1964* (Seattle: University of Washington Press, 2012), 225–262; and William Robbins and James Foster, eds., *Land in The American West: Private Claims and the Common Good* (Seattle: University of Washington Press, 2000). The primary legal argument used by the sagebrush rebels was a challenge to the legality of the "disclaimer clause" under which most Western states were admitted to the Union and which required each state to disclaim any right to unappropriated public land. The Northwest Ordinance of 1784, which contained the disclaimer clause, also contained an "equal footing doctrine" under which new states were to be admitted on an equal footing with the original states. Sagebrush rebels argued that the clause violated the

doctrine, since the original states had not been forced to disclaim public lands. Legal precedent offered little support for this argument. See Cawley, *Federal Land, Western Anger*, 96–101. On the flagging popularity of the rebellion, see Dan Balz, "Once Riding High, Sagebrush Rebels Turn in Midstream," *Washington Post*, April 10, 1982; and Sara Terry, "Sagebrush Rebellion Becomes Newest Bad Guy Out West," *Christian Science Monitor*, August 5, 1981.

14. Nevada's Select Committee on Public Lands, "Questions and Answers on the 'Sagebrush Rebellion,'" February 22, 1980, folder 2, carton 139, SCNLOR; Don Young to "Colleague," January 25, 1977, folder 36, carton 40, DRB. On antistatism and the late twentieth century West, and particularly the role of Barry Goldwater, see Lisa McGirr, *Suburban Warriors*; Rick Perlstein, *Before the Storm: Barry Goldwater and the Unmaking of the American Consensus* (New York: Hill and Wang, 2001); and Drake, *Loving Nature, Fearing the State*.

15. "The Public Land Grab—An Exercise in Greed," February, 1981; and Debbie Sease, memorandum, August 26, 1979; both in box 44, folder 17, WSR.

16. Skillen, *The Nation's Largest Landlord*, 111;

17. Richard McArdle, "Multiple Use—Multiple Benefits," *Journal of Forestry* 51 (May 1953), 325. On the expanding definition of multiple use, see Childers, *The Size of the Risk*, especially 121–123. For a discussion of the tension between the public interest and pluralism, see Kornhauser, *Debating the American State*, 29–40.

18. William Voigt, Jr., *Public Grazing Lands: Use and Misuse by Industry and Government* (New Brunswick: Rutgers University Press, 1976).

19. On Brower and the park and forest services, see Tom Turner, *David Brower: The Making of the Environmental Movement* (Berkeley: University of California Press, 2015), 86–89; and Michael Cohen, *The History of the Sierra Club, 1892–1970* (San Francisco: Sierra Club, 1988), 190–191.

20. "Sagebrush Rebellion Succeeds!" *Earth First!*, November 1, 1980, 6. Scholars take seriously the claim that the sagebrush rebellion was more about influence than legislative change. See for instance Sandra Davis, "Fighting over Public Lands: Interest Groups, States, and the Federal Government," in Charles Davis, ed., *Western Public Lands and Environmental Politics* (Boulder, CO: Westview Press, 1997), 21.

21. Dave Foreman, "Editorial—Timid Environmentalism," *Earth First!*, December 21, 1980, 5.

22. "Hard Times Come to Environmentalists," *U.S. News & World Report*, March 10, 1980; Robert Jones, "U.S. Environmental Efforts Face Erosion," *Los Angeles Times*, November 25, 1979; Peter Bernstein, "Whatever Happened to Ecology Movement?" *San Francisco Examiner*, April 20, 1980; Luther Carter, "Environmentalists Seek New Strategies," *Science* 208 (May 2, 1980); all in carton 246, folder 7, SCR. See also Bill Stall and Anne E. Baker, "The Revolutionary Years," *The Living Wilderness*, Fall 1981; and Brock Evans, "The New Decade—Dawn or Dusk?" *Sierra*, January/February 1980.

23. Brock Evans, memorandum, January 11, 1980, carton 246, folder 7, SCR. Antienvironmentalists agreed with his sentiments. Well before Reagan's election, the National Association of Property Owners told its members that the environmental

movement's success in Alaska was a "high water mark" and would result in "severe backlash." See "NAPO Fact Sheet," carton 20, folder 25, SCSW.

24. " 'Sagebrush Rebels' are Reveling in Reagan," *New York Times*, November 24, 1980.

25. Doug Scott, memorandum, March 26, 1981, carton 52, folder 1, SCNLOR. On the Hayakawa bill, see Turner, *The Promise of Wilderness*, 198–202.

26. Dale Rusakoff, "Watt and His Opponents Love Their Mutual Hate," *Washington Post*, March 23, 1982. On the Reagan administration's response to environmental issues generally, see Samuel Hays, *Beauty, Health, and Permanence: Environmental Politics in the United States, 1955–1985* (Cambridge: Cambridge University Press, 1987), 491–526. On Watt, see Cawley, *Federal Land, Western Anger*, 110–122; and Turner, *The Promise of Wilderness*, 232–238. For a hagiographical take on Watt, see Ron Arnold, *At the Eye of The Storm: James Watt and the Environmentalists* (Chicago: Regnery Gateway, 1982).

27. Brock Evans, memorandum, January 11, 1980, carton 246, folder 7, SCR.

28. Doug Scott, memorandum, March 26, 1981, carton 52, folder 1, SCNLOR.

29. "The Watt Book," carton 131, SCMP; press release, April 16, 1981, carton 131, folder 14 SCMP.

30. "More than a Million Americans Sign for the Environment," carton 131, folder 15, SCMP. On the response to the anti-Watt campaign, see Turner, *The Promise of Wilderness*, 236.

31. Bronson Lewis to President Reagan, May 12, 1981, carton 131, folder 14 SCMP.

32. "A Plug for Mr. Watt," carton 131, folder 14 SCMP; Jerry Adler, "James Watt's Land Rush," *Newsweek*, June 28, 1981, 22.

33. "Earth First! Opposes Watt Removal Drive," press release, April 23, 1981, DF.

34. On Watt's attempts to expand energy exploration and Congressional action in response, see Turner, *The Promise of Wilderness*, 234–237.

35. "Editorial: The Wilderness Protection Act," *Earth First!*, September 21, 1982, 2.

36. Howie Wolke, "Little Granite Rig Gets Green Light!" *Earth First!*, May 1, 1982, 1.

37. Dale Russakoff, "Unlikely Wyoming Posse Saddles Up for Energy Fight," *Washington Post*, August 27, 1982. On the Rendezvous, see Bart Koehler and Pete Dustrud, "Earth First! Tells Getty Where to GO," and "Little Granite Stakes Pulled—Again," both in *Earth First!* August 1, 1982; and Susan Zakin, *Coyotes and Town Dogs: Earth First! and the Environmental Movement* (New York: Viking, 1993), 216–221.

38. Andrew Bard Schmookler, "Schmookler on Anarchy," *Earth First!*, May 1, 1986, 22.

39. Charles Bowden, *Blue Desert* (Tucson: The University of Arizona Press, 1988 [1986]), 34.

40. Howie Wolke, "Dismantle the Wilderness Act!" *Earth First!*, March 21, 1983, 11.

41. For a rich discussion of Abbey and anarchism, see Drake, *Loving Nature, Fearing the State*, 139–178.

42. Edward Abbey, "A Response to Schmookler on Anarchy," *Earth First!*, August 1, 1986, 22; Andrew Bard Schmookler, "Schmookler on Anarchy," *Earth First!*, May 1, 1986, 22. See also Schmookler, "Schmookler Replies to the Anarchists," *Earth First!*, December 21, 1986, 24; Schmookler, "Schmookler Replies to Anarchists' Replies to Schmookler's Reply to the Anarchists," *Earth First!*, September 23, 1987, 26; and

Schmookler, *The Parable of the Tribes: The Problem of Power in Social Evolution*, 2nd ed. (Albany: State University of New York Press, 1995).

43. Roger Featherstone, "Report from The Midwest," *Earth First!*, June 21, 1986, 9.

44. Kirkpatrick Sale, "Anarchy and Ecology—A Review Essay," *Social Anarchism* 10 (1985), 15.

45. John Clark, *The Anarchist Moment: Reflections on Culture, Nature and Power* (Montreal: Black Rose, 1984), 28.

46. George Crowder, *Classical Anarchism: The Political Thought of Godwin, Proudhon, Bakunin, and Kropotkin* (New York: Oxford University Press, 1991), 195. See also Kingsley Widmer, "Natural Anarchism: Edward Abbey, and Gang," *Social Anarchism* 15 (1990). On bioregionalism, see Sale, *Dwellers in The Land: The Bioregional Vision* (San Francisco: Sierra Club, 1985). For more on the connection between anarchism and environmentalism, see Graham Purchase, *Anarchism and Ecology* (Montreal: Black Rose, 1996).

47. "Judge Bars Drilling in Wilderness Area," *Washington Post*, November 13, 1982.

48. Kathy McCoy, "A Trip to Salt Creek," *Earth First!*, December 21, 1982, 10. See also Bart Koehler, "The Battle of Salt Creek," *Earth First!*, December 21, 1982.

49. Dave Foreman, "Editorial: The Lessons of Salt Creek," *Earth First!*, March 21, 1983, 2. See also Dale Russakoff, "Firm Gets Approval to Drill in Refuge," *Washington Post*, December 28, 1982.

50. Dave Forman, "Editorial: Shipwrecked Environmentalism," *Earth First!*, March 20, 1984, 2. On the state-by-state strategy, see Turner, *The Promise of Wilderness*, 217–222.

51. Dave Foreman, "Editorial: Kill the Bills," *Earth First!*, September 23, 1983, 2.

52. "Appeal the Bastards!" *Earth First!*, May 1, 1984, 1.

53. Dave Foreman, "An Environmental Strategy for the '80s," *Earth First!*, September 21, 1982, 7.

54. On the privatization initiative and Turnage's response, see Philip Shabecoff, "U.S. Plans Biggest Land Shift Since Frontier Times," *New York Times*, July 3, 1982; see also Cawley, *Federal Land, Western Anger*, 123–142. On the response of sagebrush rebels, see William Schmidt, "West Upset by Reagan Plan to Sell Some Federal Lands," *New York Times*, April 17, 1982.

55. Republican Study Committee, "The Specter of Environmentalism: The Threat of Environmental Groups," February 12, 1982, carton 267, folder 52, SCR.

56. "An 'F' for the Republicans," *Earth First!*, May 1, 1982, 6.

57. Cohen, *The History of The Sierra Club*, 441.

58. Philip Berry, "No Growth, Zero Growth, Limited Growth," October 21, 1971, carton 282, folder 157, SCR, 2.

59. Brock Evans, memorandum, January 11, 1980, carton 246, folder 7, SCR. On the Estes Park meeting, see Neal Pierce, "Ecologists Facing Image Problem," *Sacramento Bee*, April 20, 1980, carton 246, folder 7, SCR; and Carter, "Environmentalists Seek New Strategies." On the regional meetings, see Ann Sweazey, memorandum, August 14, 1981, and Chuck Clusen, memorandum, September 23, 1981, both in box 8 folder 14, WSR.

60. Roger Lubin, "Ecology Backlash: The Selling of the Environment," *Clear Creek*, March 1972, 26.

61. Minutes of the Sierra Club board of directors meeting, May 6–7, 1972, carton 4, folder 12, SCR, 3.

62. "The Counterrevolution," *The Living Wilderness*, Summer 1971, 2; and Thomas Shepard, Jr., "The Case Against 'The Disaster Lobby,' " *The Living Wilderness*, Summer 1971, 28–30.

63. On public service announcements and individual behavior, see Finis Dunaway, *Seeing Green: The Use and Abuse of American Environmental Images* (Chicago: University of Chicago Press, 2015), 64–120. On electric utilities and Jerry Mander, see Joe Greene Conley II, "Environmentalism Contained: A History of Corporate Responses to the New Environmentalism," (PhD Dissertation, Princeton University, 2006), 75–79.

64. "The Rise of Anti-Ecology," *Time*, August 3, 1970, 43.

65. Leo H. Carney, "For Environmentalists, the Battle Goes On," *New York Times*, January 4, 1981; On the Quality of Life Review program, see Conley, "Environmentalism Contained," 159–167.

66. Jones, "U.S. Environmental Efforts Face Erosion."

67. Shepard, Jr., "The Case Against 'The Disaster Lobby,' " 29–30; Podhoretz, "Doomsday Fears and Modern Life," 4–6.

68. Robert Poole, Jr., "There's A New Age Dawning," *Reason*, April 1979, 16; Jeff Riggenbach, "Free Market Conservation," *Libertarian Review*, February 1979, 6. See also C. R. Batten, "The Second Battle of the Redwoods," *Reason*, October 1979, 23; Jeffrey Sanchez, "A Pollution Revolution," *Libertarian Review*, October/November 1980, 55; and Robert Smith, "Conservation and Capitalism," *Libertarian Review*, October 1979, 25. The best summary of free-market environmentalism's history is Brian Drake, *Loving Nature, Fearing the State*, 114–138; the best summary of its ideas is Terry Anderson and Donald Leal, *Free Market Environmentalism*, rev. ed. (New York: Palgrave, 2001). Libertarianism has a complicated relationship to the broader conservative movement. On the Libertarian Party, see Jennifer Burns, "O Libertarian, Where Is Thy Sting?" *Journal of Policy History* 19, no. 4 (2007); on libertarianism more generally, see Brian Doherty, *Radicals for Capitalism: A Freewheeling History of the Modern American Libertarian Movement* (New York: PublicAffairs, 2007). On the role of free market thought in the rise of the New Right, see Angus Burgin, *The Great Persuasion: Reinventing Free Markets Since the Depression* (Cambridge, MA: Harvard University Press, 2012).

69. Garret Hardin and John Baden, eds., *Managing the Commons* (New York: W. H. Freeman, 1977), x–xi.

70. A.W. Langenegger to Farm Bureau members, n.d., carton 131, folder 15, SCMP. Skillen, *The Nation's Largest Landlord*, 73–77. Ranchers' association of permits with private property was in part a product of the complicated legislative history of range ownership in the West. For a useful discussion, see Childers, *The Size of the Risk*, 20–30.

71. John Baden and Richard Stroup, *Bureaucracy vs. Environment: The Environmental Costs of Bureaucratic Governance* (Ann Arbor: University of Michigan Press, 1981), 1.

72. Denzel Ferguson and Nancy Ferguson, *Sacred Cows at the Public Trough*, (Bend, OR: Maverick Publications, 1983), 202.

73. Don Schwarzenegger, "Beyond Sacred Cows at the Public Trough . . . Or Heading to the Last Roundup . . . (With Any Luck at All)," *Earth First!*, November 1, 1984, 22.

74. Denzel Ferguson and Nancy Ferguson, "Sacred Cows at the Public Trough," *Earth First!*, August 1, 1984, 14.

75. Ferguson and Ferguson, *Sacred Cows at The Public Trough*, 199.

76. Schwarzenegger, "Beyond Sacred Cows," 22.

77. Ferguson and Ferguson, *Sacred Cows*, 90.

78. Lynn Jacobs, "The Howling Wilderness?" *Earth First!*, March 20, 1986, 17.

79. Dave Foreman, "My Heroes Have Always Been Cowboys," *Earth First!*, February 2, 1986, 18.

80. Edward Abbey, "Free Speech: The Cowboy and His Cow," in Abbey, *One Life at A Time, Please* (New York: Henry Holt and Company, 1988), 9.

81. Foreman, "My Heroes Have Always Been Cowboys," 18.

82. Brock Evans, memorandum, November 26, 1980, carton 22, folder 28, SCSW.

83. Ferguson and Ferguson, *Sacred Cows at the Public Trough*, 3, 122.

84. Abbey, "Free Speech," 17.

85. Walter Prescott Webb, *The Great Plains* (Lincoln: University of Nebraska Press, 1981 [1931]), 295–318.

86. Foreman, "My Heroes Have Always Been Cowboys," 18.

87. Schwarzenegger, "Beyond Sacred Cows at the Public Trough," 22. On permit rates, see Skillen, *The Nation's Largest Landlord*, 75.

88. Ferguson and Ferguson, *Sacred Cows at the Public Trough*, 206.

89. Don Schwarzenegger, "Free Enterprise Threatens Welfare Ranchers," *Earth First!*, May 1, 1985, 14. On various bidding schemes, see Lynn Jacobs, "Free Our Public Lands!" *Earth First!*, September 23, 1987.

90. "Forest Debate Heats Up," *Earth First!*, March 20, 1984, 7.

91. Howie Wolke, "Road Frenzy," *Earth First!*, June 21, 1985, 1; "Forest Debate Heats Up," 7. See also Wolke, "The Grizzly Den," *Earth First!*, December 21, 1984, 11. Historians do not disagree with Wolke's assessment. See Paul Hirt, *A Conspiracy of Optimism: Management of the National Forests Since World War Two* (Lincoln: University of Nebraska Press, 1994).

92. T. R. Reid, "Guerrilla War for the Wilderness," *Washington Post*, November 25, 1984. See also "30,000 Miles of Roads in RARE II Areas," *Earth First!*, December 21, 1984.

93. Howie Wolke, "Editorial: Do It!" *Earth First!*, December 21, 1986, 5.

94. See "Smokey the Bear Has a Bone to Pick," *Los Angeles Times*, April 22, 1988; and Karen Pickett, "Day of Outrage Shakes Forest Service Nationwide!" *Earth First!*, June 21, 1988.

95. Howie Wolke, "Stop the Forest Service!" *Earth First!*, February 2, 1988, 1.

96. Bobcat, "Everything You Ever Wanted to Know About the US Forest Service—But Were Afraid to Ask," *Earth First!*, August 1, 1984, 13.

97. Skoal Vengeance, "Burn Down the Façade!" *Earth First!*, June 21, 1988, 28.

98. Howie Wolke, "Don't 'Marketize' the Priceless!" *Earth First!*, June 21, 1988, 28. On the CHEC symposium, Michael, "Freddies and Environmentalists Talk (But What About the Trees?)," *Earth First!*, February 2, 1985, 6. On O'Toole, see Kathie Durbin, *Tree Huggers: Victory, Defeat and Renewal in the Northwest Ancient Forest Campaign* (Seattle: The Mountaineers, 1996), 38–40.

99. Dave Foreman, "Hands-On Forest Planning," *Earth First!*, August 1, 1985, 24.

100. Gaylord Nelson, letter to the editor, *New York Times*, November 17, 1984.

101. Randal O'Toole, *Reforming the Forest Service* (Washington, D.C.: Island, 1988).

102. Bobcat, "Everything You Ever Wanted to Know . . .," 11.

103. Wolke, "Save Our National Forests!" (insert) *Earth First!*, March 20, 1988.

104. On changes in forestry and the Forest Service, see Samuel Hays, *Wars in the Woods: The Rise of Ecological Forestry in America* (Pittsburgh: University of Pittsburgh Press, 2007). For a perspective from inside the agency, see Jim Furnish, *Toward A Natural Forest: The Forest Service in Transition* (Corvallis: Oregon State University Press, 2015).

105. Michael Pollan, *Second Nature: A Gardener's Education* (New York: Dell, 1991), 223.

106. O'Toole, *Reforming the Forest Service*, 185, 193.

107. M. Bruce Johnson, "Concluding Thoughts on Earth Day Reconsidered," in John Baden, ed., *Earth Day Reconsidered* (Washington, D.C.: Heritage Foundation, 1980), 106. This alignment of environmentalism and economics has roots in classical economic theory, which took the limits of the natural world as absolute and so understood the study of economics and the study of nature as overlapping. According to Margaret Schabas, the decoupling of economics from the natural sciences—the "denaturalization of the economic order"—was recent and incomplete. Only in the late-nineteenth century, she argues, did economists begin to measure the influence of human agency as equal to or above the influence of natural phenomena. See Schabas, *The Natural Origins of Economics* (Chicago: University of Chicago Press, 2005). Lisa McGirr argues that despite the many disagreements between libertarians and social conservatives, they joined forces because libertarians' belief in property rights as fundamental to ordering the human world was equivalent to the transcendent moral authority of religion. See McGirr, *Suburban Warriors*, 163–165.

108. John Gray, *Hayek on Liberty* (Oxford: Basil Blackwell, 1984), 29. On libertarian distrust of human reason and even reservations about the moral basis of capitalism, see Burgin, *The Great Persuasion*, 32–38, 108–116, 188–192. According to Alexander Shand, Hayek considered the market an organic system of protocols arising from collective and unconscious knowledge that operated by "the same fundamental principle of natural selection found in the mechanism of Darwinian evolution." See Shand, *Free Market Morality: The Political Economy of the Austrian School* (London: Routledge, 1990), 54, 66–68.

109. "Oregon Wilderness Hearing," *Earth First!*, September 23, 1983, 21.

110. Dave Foreman, "Dreaming Big Wilderness," *Earth First!*, August 1, 1985, 18.

111. Stephanie Mills, "Thoughts from the Round River Rendezvous," *Earth First!*, February 2, 1986, 25.

112. David Brower, *For Earth's Sake: The Life and Times of David Brower* (Salt Lake City: Peregrine Smith, 1990), 287.

113. LaRue Christie, memorandum, August 20, 1985, DF.

114. Dave Foreman, "Around the Campfire," *Earth First!*, September 21, 1982, 2. Presumably Foreman meant "neoliberals."

115. Sabin, "Environmental Law and the End of the New Deal Order."

5. EARTH FIRST! AGAINST ITSELF

1. Dave Foreman, "Around the Campfire," *Earth First!*, March 20, 1987, 2.

2. William Cronon, "The Trouble with Wilderness: Or, Getting Back to the Wrong Nature," in Cronon, ed., *Uncommon Ground: Rethinking the Human Place in Nature* (New York: Norton, 1995), 80.

3. Leslie Lyon, letter to the editor, *Earth First!*, December 22, 1987, 22.

4. W. J. Lines, "Is 'Deep Ecology' Deep Enough?" *Earth First!*, May 1, 1987, 31.

5. Jamie Sayen, "Thoughts on an Evolutionary Ethic," *Earth First!*, June 21, 1989, 26.

6. Howard Zahniser, "How Much Wilderness Can We Afford to Lose?" in David Brower, ed., *Wildlands in Our Civilization* (San Francisco: Sierra Club, 1964), 48; David Brower, "Foreword," in Maxine McCloskey and James Gilligan, eds., *Wilderness and the Quality of Life* (San Francisco: Sierra Club, 1969), vii.

7. Cronon, "The Trouble with Wilderness," 80.

8. Dave Foreman, *Confessions of an Eco-Warrior* (New York: Crown, 1991), 18. On Edward Abbey, see James Cahalan, *Edward Abbey: A Life* (Tucson: University of Arizona Press, 2001); and Brian Drake, *Loving Nature, Fearing the State: Environmentalism and Antigovernment Politics Before Reagan* (Seattle: University of Washington Press, 2013), 139–178. Also helpful are James Bishop, Jr., *Epitaph for A Desert Anarchist: The Life and Legacy of Edward Abby* (New York: Atheneum, 1994); James Hepworth and Gregory McNamee, eds., *Resist Much, Obey Little: Remembering Edward Abbey* (San Francisco: Sierra Club, 1996); and Bill McKibben, "The Desert Anarchist," *New York Review of Books*, August 18, 1988.

9. Edward Abbey, *The Journey Home: Some Words in Defense of the American West* (New York: E. Dutton, 1977), xi–xiii. On Abbey and nature writing, see Cahalan, *Edward Abbey*, 274–275. For Abbey's various adventures in his own words, see "The Second Rape of the West," in Abbey, *The Journey Home*, 158; "How It Was," in Edward Abbey, *Beyond the Wall: Essays from the Outside* (New York: Holt, Rinehart & Winston, 1984), 60–61; and "Return to Yosemite: Tree Fuzz vs. Freaks," in Abbey, *The Journey Home*, 138–145.

10. Donn Rawlings, "Abbey's Essays: One Man's Quest for Solid Ground," *The Living Wilderness*, June, 1980, 45.

11. Edward Abbey, *Confessions of A Barbarian: Selections from the Journals of Edward Abbey, 1951–1989* (New York: Little, Brown & Company, 1994), 264–265.

12. Edward Abbey, "Freedom and Wilderness, Wilderness and Freedom," in Abbey, *The Journey Home*, 230.

13. Edward Abbey, *Desert Solitaire: A Season in the Wilderness* (New York: Simon & Schuster, 1968), 42–51. "On wilderness preservation: Don't rely on the Park Service," Abbey wrote in his journal in 1956. See Abbey, *Confessions of a Barbarian*, 132.

14. Abbey, *Desert Solitaire*, 47. On David Brower's battle with the Park Service over its "Mission 66" program to encourage car-friendly parks, see Tom Turner, *David Brower: The Making of the Environmental Movement* (Berkeley: University of California Press, 2015), 86–88.

15. Jean-Jacques Rousseau, "On the Social Contract," in Rousseau, *The Basic Political Writings* (Indianapolis: Hackett, 1987), 141. There is a large literature on classical anarchist history and theory. An essential introduction is George Woodcock, *Anarchism: a History of Libertarian Ideas and Movements* (New York: Meridian, 1962). A more recent synthesis is Peter Marshall, *Demanding the Impossible: A History of Anarchism* (New York: HarperCollins, 1991). See also James Joll, *The Anarchists* (New York: Grosset & Dunlap, 1964); Gerard Runkle, *Anarchism: Old and New* (New York: Delacorte, 1972); Irving Horowitz, ed., *The Anarchists* (New York: Dell, 1964); Alan Ritter, *Anarchism: A Theoretical Analysis* (Cambridge: Cambridge University Press, 1980); and George Crowder, *Classical Anarchism: The Political Thought of Godwin, Proudhon, Bakunin, and Kropotkin* (New York: Oxford University Press, 1991). Rousseau's relationship to anarchism is fraught. Joll points to Rousseau's valorization of nature and "primitive" societies as well as to his emphasis on education and reason, writing, "It is Rousseau who created the climate of ideas in which anarchism was possible" (*The Anarchists*, 30). But while anarchists adopted Rousseau's criticisms of modern society, they rejected his prescriptions. According to Runkle, "Rousseau, whose celebration of the simple life and whose praise for the natural goodness and equality of man make him a hero of sorts for many anarchists, is nevertheless a flawed hero" (Runkle, *Anarchism*, 43). Rousseau, after all, argued for a social contract that would bind all people and even generations not yet born. As Woodcock writes, anarchists' belief in the natural origin of society set them against any structured system contrived by people, and "has made almost every anarchist theoretician, from Godwin to the present, reject Rousseau's idea of a Social Contract" (Woodcock, *Anarchism*, 23).

16. "The anarchist is beguiled by neither the practice nor theory of democracy," Gerald Runkle writes in *Anarchism* (4–5). See also Robert Dahl, *Democracy and Its Critics* (New Haven: Yale University Press, 1989), 37–51.

17. On direct action, see Woodcock, *Anarchism*, 32–33; and Runkle, *Anarchism*, 95.

18. Crowder, *Classical Anarchism*, 13. The belief in a natural order, always just out of reach, has taken on different forms in anarchist thought but has remained foundational. The British proto-anarchist William Godwin distinguished between justice and human law, the former arising from unchanging moral truths, the latter from easily corrupted human decisions. The French anarchist Pierre Proudhon believed that personal relationships, unregulated by government, inevitably produced a balanced social structure. But it was the Russian anarchist Peter Kropotkin who first connected his social beliefs directly to the natural world. "Science loudly proclaims that the struggle of each against all is the leading principle of nature," he wrote, "and of human societies as well," when in fact, he argued, the opposite was true. Against a crude Darwinism, Kropotkin claimed animals of the same species survived and evolved by assisting one another, and that cooperation rather than self-interest was the basic principle of nature. (*Mutual Aid: A Factor of Evolution* [Mineola, NY: Dover Publications, 2006], 188). Kropotkin's ethics were "empirical," according to Runkle, their justification found "in nature itself" (*Anarchism: Old and New*, 59–60). As Woodcock points out, this is one of the fundamental problems with anarchist theory: anarchists reject authority and champion

freedom, but they believe in a well-ordered society. "Indeed," Woodcock writes, "the general anarchist tendency to rely on natural law and to imagine a return to an existence based on its dictates leads by a paradoxical logic toward determinist conclusions which, of course, clash in a very obvious way with the belief in the freedom of individual action" (*Anarchism*, 70). Alan Ritter tries to reconcile this difficulty by arguing that anarchists advocate "communal individuality," in which greater freedom for individuals leads to greater awareness by individuals of their social situatedness and so a greater appreciation of community (*Anarchism: A Theoretical Analysis*, 25–39). The point is that individual freedom, on its own, is not enough for anarchists; the important thing is what results from that freedom. See also L. Susan Brown, "Anarchism, Existentialism and Human Nature: A Critique," *The Raven*, June 1988; Michael Duane, "Anarchism and Nature: 1," *The Raven*, June 1988; and David Morland, "Anarchism and Nature: 2," *The Raven*, July 1989.

19. Woodcock, *Anarchism*, 25–27; see also John Clark, *The Anarchist Moment: Reflections on Culture, Nature and Power* (Montreal: Black Rose, 1984), 15.

20. "For Your Information," *Earth First!*, December 21, 1980. Means's speech is reprinted in several periodicals, including as an insert titled "On the Future of The Earth" in *The Fifth Estate*, December 1980. Foreman saw Earth First! as allied with bioregionalism, an anarchistic movement for simplified technology and decentralized political structures shaped to ecological regions. "Bioregionalism," he wrote, "is what we are working for—the future primitive." See Dave Foreman, "Reinhabitation, Biocentrism and Self Defense," *Earth First!*, August 1, 1987, 22. For a more complete version of the environmentalist veneration of traditional cultures, see Paul Shepard, *The Tender Carnivore and the Sacred Game* (Athens: University of Georgia Press, 1998 [1973]).

21. Bookchin has never received the attention he deserves. The literature on Bookchin is limited and not at all proportional to the richness of his writing, and as a result he became his own greatest promoter. In addition to Bookchin's own voluminous works, see Janet Biehl, *Ecology or Catastrophe: The Life of Murray Bookchin* (New York: Oxford University Press, 2015). For a collection of mostly critical essays about Bookchin and social ecology, see Andrew Light, ed., *Social Ecology After Bookchin* (New York: Guilford, 1998). For another critical treatment, by a frequent antagonist and sometimes admirer of Bookchin, see David Watson, *Beyond Bookchin: Preface for a Future Social Ecology* (New York: Autonomedia, 1996). For defenses of Bookchin, see Andy Price, *Recovering Bookchin: Social Ecology and the Crises of Our Time* (Norway: New Compass, 2012); and John Clark, ed., *Renewing the Earth: The Promise of Social Ecology: A Celebration of the Work of Murray Bookchin* (London: Green Print, 1990).

22. On the early years of Bookchin's career, see Murray Bookchin, *Anarchism, Marxism, and the Future of the Left: Interviews and Essays, 1993–1998* (San Francisco: AK, 1999), 15–58; on the origins of Bookchin's interest in environmentalism and on Ecology Action East, see Biehl, *Ecology or Catastrophe*, 52–99, 131–137; see also Murray Bookchin, "When Everything Was Possible," *Mesechabe*, September/October 1991.

23. Murray Bookchin, *The Ecology of Freedom: The Emergence and Dissolution of Hierarchy* (Oakland: AK, 2005), 32, 68. Bookchin's other major works on social ecology include

The Rise of Urbanization and the Decline of Citizenship (San Francisco: Sierra Club, 1987), an explanation of an anarchist approach to city life called "libertarian municipalism"; *Remaking Society: Pathways to a Green Future* (Boston: South End, 1990), a condensed description of both social ecology and libertarian municipalism; and *The Philosophy of Social Ecology: Essays in Dialectical Naturalism* (Montreal: Black Rose, 1996), a more theoretical treatment of social ecology.

24. Bookchin, *The Ecology of Freedom*, 129. On organic society more broadly, see 109–129.

25. Bookchin, *Remaking Society*, 66, 94. On hierarchy more generally, see Bookchin, *The Ecology of Freedom*, 130–190.

26. Murray Bookchin, *Remaking Society*, 160.

27. Murray Bookchin, "Social Ecology versus 'Deep Ecology': A Challenge for the Ecology Movement," *Green Perspectives*, Summer 1987. The text reprinted in Green Perspectives is a longer version of the remarks Bookchin made at Amherst and was distributed to the audience. On the subsequent debate between Bookchin and Earth First!, see Mark Stoll, "Green versus Green: Religions, Ethics, and the Bookchin-Foreman Dispute," *Environmental History* 6, no. 3 (July 2001); and Steve Chase, "Introduction: Whither the Radical Ecology Movement?" in Chase, ed., *Defending the Earth*.

28. On the Foreman interview, see Foreman, "Second Thoughts of an Eco-Warrior," in Chase, ed., *Defending the Earth*, 107–109; for a more complete version of Foreman's early views on immigration, see Foreman, "Is Sanctuary the Answer?" *Earth First!*, November 1, 1987.

29. Edward Abbey, "Immigration and Liberal Taboos," in Abbey, *One Life at A Time, Please*, 43.

30. Miss Ann Thropy, "Population and AIDS," *Earth First!*, May 1, 1987, 32. "Miss Ann Thropy" was the pseudonym of Earth First! stalwart Christopher Manes. See also Daniel Conner, "Is AIDS the Answer to an Environmentalist's Prayer?" *Earth First!*, December 22, 1987.

31. Bookchin, *Remaking Society*, 11.

32. Bookchin, *The Ecology of Freedom*, 140 (emphasis in original). On Bookchin's critiques of Ehrlich and ZPG, see Biehl, *Ecology or Catastrophe*, 148–150; and for a sense of Bookchin's original arguments about post-scarcity society, see Bookchin, *Post-Scarcity Anarchism*.

33. R. Wills Flowers, "Of Old Wine in New Bottles: Taking Up Bookchin's Challenge," *Earth First!*, November 1, 1987, 19; Bill Devall, "Deep Ecology and Its Critics," *Earth First!*, December 22, 1987, 18. On the term "eco-fascist," see Michael Zimmerman, *Contesting Earth's Future: Radical Ecology and Postmodernity* (Berkeley: University of California Press, 1994), 166–183.

34. Brad Edmonson, "Is AIDS Good for The Earth?" *Utne Reader*, November/December 1987, 14; letters, *Utne Reader*, January/February 1988; letters, *Utne Reader*, March/April 1988. For a description of much of this exchange, see Kirkpatrick Sale, "Deep Ecology and Its Critics," *The Nation*, May 14, 1988; and Bookchin, letter to the editor, *The Nation*, October 10, 1988.

35. "Marx: Good-By to All That," *Fifth Estate*, March 1977, 7. For a detailed defense of the newspaper's anti-technological stance, see T. Fulano, "Uncovering a Corpse: A Reply to the Defenders of Technology," *Fifth Estate*, November 1981.

36. George Bradford, "Marxism, Anarchism and the Roots of the New Totalitarianism," *Fifth Estate*, July 1981, 10.

37. George Bradford, *How Deep Is Deep Ecology?* (Ojai: Times Change, 1989), 10, 35. On Catton, see, for instance, Bill Devall and George Sessions, "The Books of Deep Ecology," *Earth First!*, August 1, 1984, 18; and William Catton, *Overshoot: The Ecological Basis of Revolutionary Change* (Urbana: University of Illinois Press, 1980). Catton responded that the problem was not capitalism but "industrialism, capitalist or non-capitalist." See Catton, Bill McCormick, and George Bradford, "Was Malthus Right? An Exchange on Deep Ecology and Population," *Fifth Estate*, Spring 1988, 9.

38. Dave Foreman, "Whither Earth First!?" *Earth First!*, November 1, 1987, 21; on "bizarre utilitarian philosophy," see "Wilderness Preserve System," *Earth First!*, June 21, 1983, 9.

39. Ariel Kay Salleh, "Deeper Than Deep Ecology: The Eco-Feminist Connection," *Environmental Ethics* 6, no. 4 (Winter 1984), 340, 344; Ynestra King, letter to the editor, *The Nation*, December 12, 1987. One of the most important essays on this subject is Sherry Ortner, "Is Female to Male as Nature is to Culture?" in Michelle Rosaldo and Louise Lamphere, eds. *Woman, Culture, and Society* (Stanford: Stanford University Press, 1974); on the assumed opposition of nature and culture, see Carole Pateman, " 'The Disorder of Women': Women, Love, and the Sense of Justice," *Ethics* 91, no. 1 (October 1980).

40. See Mary Daly, *Gyn/Ecology: The Metaethics of Radical Feminism* (Boston: Beacon Press, 1978); Starhawk, *The Spiral Dance: A Rebirth of the Ancient Religion of the Great Goddess* (New York: Harper & Row, 1979).

41. Janet Biehl, *Rethinking Ecofeminist Politics* (Boston: South End, 1991). On the split between "nature feminists" and "social feminists," see Joan Griscom, "On Healing the Nature/History Split in Feminist Thought," and Ynestra King, "Feminism and the Revolt of Nature," both in *Heresies*, 1981. See also Marti Kheel, "The Liberation of Nature: A Circular Affair," *Environmental Ethics* 7, no. 2 (Summer 1985).

42. Murray Bookchin, *Re-enchanting Humanity: A Defense of the Human Spirit Against Antihumanism, Misanthropy, Mysticism and Primitivism* (London: Cassell, 1995), 4. By the 1990s, Bookchin expressed regret over his earlier "excessive criticism of the Enlightenment." See Biehl, *Ecology or Catastrophe*, 289.

43. Bookchin, *The Ecology of Freedom*, 320, 319, 441.

44. Bookchin, *Remaking Society*, 71–72; Watson, *Beyond Bookchin*, 17; and Robyn Eckersley, "Divining Evolution and Respecting Evolution," in Light, ed., *Social Ecology After Bookchin*, 71.

45. Susan Schrepfer, *The Fight to Save the Redwoods: A History of Environmental Reform, 1917–1978* (Madison: University of Wisconsin Press, 1983), 87.

46. Thomas Shepard, Jr., "The Case Against 'The Disaster Lobby,' " *The Living Wilderness*, Summer 1971, 30.

47. Tom Stoddard, "Wilderness and Wildlife," *Earth First!*, December 22, 1983, 11.

48. Christoph Manes, "On Becoming Homo ludens," *Earth First!*, November 1, 1988, 27.

49. Joel Kovel, "Negating Bookchin," in Light, ed., *Social Ecology After Bookchin*, 49.

50. For the estimate of Earth First! followers, see Douglas Bevington, *The Rebirth Of Environmentalism: Grassroots Activism from the Spotted Owl to the Polar Bear* (Washington, D.C.: Island, 2009), 33. On Earth First!'s notoriety, see Stewart McBride, "The Real Monkey Wrench Gang," *Outside*, December/January 1983; "Dave Foreman: The Plowboy Interview," *Mother Earth News*, January/February 1985; Ken Slocum, "Radical Ecologists Pound Spikes in Trees to Scare Loggers and Hinder Lumbering," *Wall Street Journal*, November 14, 1985; Ann Japenga, "Earth First! A Voice Vying for the Wilderness," *Los Angeles Times*, September 5, 1985; James Coates, "'Bears' Monkey with Yellowstone Intruders," *Chicago Tribune*, August 20, 1985; Ronald Taylor, "Pranks and Protests Over Environment Turn Tough," *U.S. News & World Report*, January 13, 1986; and Kirkpatrick Sale, "The Forest for The Trees," *Mother Jones*, November 1986.

51. Alien-Nation, "'Dangerous' Tendencies in Earth First!?" *Earth First!*, November 1, 1987, 17–18. As much as "Alien-Nation" sounded like a restatement of social ecology, Earth First! reported that the Washington anarchists considered Bookchin's effort a failure.

52. For Lone Wolf Circles see letters to the editor, *Earth First!* December 22, 1987, 21; Paul Watson, "Paul Watson Replies to Alien-Nation, *Earth First!*, December 22, 1987, 20.

53. Mitch Friedman to Dave Foreman, September 23 (no year given, but almost certainly 1987), DF. On Friedman's tenure with Earth First!, see William Dietrich, *The Final Forest: Big Trees, Forks, and the Pacific Northwest* (Seattle: University of Washington Press, 2010), 159–173.

54. Mikal Jakubal to Dave Foreman (n.d.), DF.

55. Gena Trott to Dave Foreman, May 12, 1989, DF. For a preview of *Live Wild or Die* as "a forum for activists feeling a bit alienated from the workings of the [*Earth First! Journal*]," see Mikal Jakubal, "'Live Wild or Die'—The Other EF!," *Fifth Estate*, Winter 1988, 10.

56. Lev Chernyi, "Biocentrism: Shackler of Desire," *Anarchy: A Journal of Desire Armed*, March/April 1989, 19; Lone Wolf Circles, "The Freedom of Biocentrism: A Poem"; and Lev Chernyi, "If Nature Abhors Ideologies . . . Biocentrism is no Exception," both in *Anarchy: A Journal of Desire Armed*, Fall/Winter 1988, 19; and Mikal Jakubal, "Biocentrism: Ideology Against Nature," *Anarchy: A Journal of Desire Armed*, May/July 1989, 21. See also Feral Faun, "Not Guilty," *Anarchy: A Journal of Desire Armed*, March/April 1989, 18; and Feral Faun, "The Iconoclast's Hammer: Nature as Spectacle," *Anarchy: A Journal of Desire Armed*, Summer 1991, 28. Despite intellectual clashes, the anarchists continued to participate in Earth First! actions. See Mikal Jakubal, "Stumps Suck! on the Okanogan"; and Lev Chernyi, "Notes from The California Earth First! Rendezvous," both in *Anarchy: A Journal of Desire Armed*, Fall/Winter 1988; and Orin Langelle, "Timber Sale Halted in the Shawnee," *Anarchy: A Journal of Desire Armed*, Autumn 1990.

57. Jakubal, "Biocentrism: Ideology Against Nature," 21.

58. Estelle Fennell, "The Split in Earth First!" *Fifth Estate*, Winter 1990/1991, 5.

59. Lone Wolf Circles, "Earth Jazz: Bear Scat and Deep Ecology Licks (More Poet-Tree)," *Anarchy: A Journal of Desire Armed*, March/April 1989, 18.

60. George Bradford to Christoph Manes, March 20 (no year, although likely 1986 or 1987), DF.

61. Art Goodtimes, letter to the editor, *Earth First!*, June 21, 1986, 9. On the perception of environmentalism and Native Sovereignty as aligned, see Paul C. Rosier, "'Modern America Desperately Needs to Listen': The Emerging Indian in an Age of Environmental Crisis," *Journal of American History* 100, no. 3 (December 2013).

62. On Black Mesa and Peabody Coal, see Rosier, "Modern America Desperately Needs to Listen"; Judith Nies, "The Black Mesa Syndrome: Indian Lands, Black Gold," *Orion*, Summer 1998; Andrew Needham, *Power Lines: Phoenix and the Making of the Modern Southwest* (Princeton, NJ: Princeton University Press, 2014); and James Robert Allison III, *Sovereignty for Survival: American Energy Development and Indian Self-Determination* (New Haven: Yale University Press, 2015), 37–60.

63. See William Brown, "The Rape of Black Mesa," *Sierra Club Bulletin*, August 1970; and Melissa Savage, "Black Mesa Mainline: Tracks on the Earth," *Clear Creek*, May 1972.

64. On Black Mesa Defense Fund, see Susan Zakin, *Coyotes and Town Dogs: Earth First! and the Environmental Movement* (New York: Viking, 1993), 45–62.

65. Jack Loeffler, "Editorial"; and Loeffler, "The Southwest As Symbol," both in *Clear Creek*, May 1972, 12.

66. Needham, *Power Lines*, 213.

67. On Navajo nationalism generally, see Needham, *Power Lines*, 213–245; and Rosier, "Modern American Desperately Needs to Listen," 728–733. Navajo activists, Allison explains, developed a "colonial critique" that "blamed bad energy deals on an imperialist federal government intent on 'modernizing' (that is, anglicizing) the 'savage.'" See Allison, *Sovereignty for Survival*, 59.

68. Needham, *Power Lines*, 201–212.

69. Abbey, "The Second Rape of the West," 158–162.

70. Lewis Johnson, letter to the editor, *Earth First!*, June 21, 1987, 3.

71. Lew Kemia, "Havasupais and Earth First!ers Restore the Canyon," *Earth First!*, December 21, 1986, 7.

72. Ned Powell, "Grand Canyon Uranium Mine Update," *Earth First!*, May 1, 1986, 11. On mine monkeywrenching, see Hayduchess, "Mining the Grand Canyon," *Earth First!*, May 1, 1985; and Mary Sojourner, "Grand Canyon Uranium Mine Protested," *Earth First!*, September 22, 1985.

73. Dave Foreman, "Around the Campfire," *Earth First!*, September 22, 1985, 2.

74. For an account of how environmental harm, race, class, and gender have inevitably interwoven in the Southwest, see Traci Brynne Voyles, *Wastelanding: Legacies of Uranium Mining in Navajo Country* (Minneapolis: University of Minnesota Press, 2015).

75. On EMETIC's various actions near the Grand Canyon and at Snowbowl, see "Dear Ned Ludd," *Earth First!*, November 1, 1988; and "Monkeywrenching News from Around the World," *Earth First!*, February 2, 1989.

76. John Davis, "Arizona Earth First! Defends on a Broad Front," *Earth First!*, September 22, 1985.

77. Michael Robinson, "21 Arrested in Uranium Mine Takeover," *Earth First!*, August 1, 1987.

78. Leslie James Pickering, *The Evan Mecham Eco-Terrorist International Conspiracy* (Portland: Eberhardt, 2012), 7.

79. *Sacred Mountain Notes*, fall 1979, box 3, folder 4, ROC.

80. David Quammen, "Reckoning," *Outside*, November 1990, 54.

81. Peg Millett, "Interview with Peg Millett," in Pickering, *The Evan Mecham Eco-Terrorist International Conspiracy*.

82. Millett, "Interview with Peg Millett," 47. On the FBI operation and EMETIC, see Zakin, *Coyotes and Town Dogs*, 316–341; and Dale Turner, "FBI Attacks Earth First!" *Earth First!*, June 16, 1989.

83. On the trial, see Michael Lerner, "The FBI vs. the Monkeywrenchers," *Los Angeles Times Magazine*, April 15, 1990; and Karen Pickett, "Arizona Conspiracy Trial Ends in Plea Bargain," *Earth First!*, September 23, 1991.

84. On Brower, see Zakin, *Coyotes and Town Dogs*, 429; on Snyder, see Daniel Conner to Gary Snyder, July 15, 1989, box II: 49, folder 13, GS.

85. The Fifth Estate staff, letter to the editor, *Earth First!*, June 21, 1989, 3; Murray Bookchin, letter to the editor, *New York Times*, July 27, 1989; Christine Keyser, "Compromise in Defense of Earth First!," *Sierra*, November/December 1991, 47. See also "Gov't Attacks Earth First!" *Fifth Estate*, Summer 1989. Bookchin and Foreman later made peace; see Chase, ed., *Defending the Earth*.

86. Mark Davis, "Wake Up!" *Earth First!*, November 1, 1991, 1.

87. Myra Mishkin, "Keep One Keeping On," *Earth First!* Special Edition, June 16, 1989, np.

88. Mike Roselle, Judi Bari, et al., letters to the editor, *Earth First!*, November 1, 1991, 31.

89. Alexander Cockburn, "Beat the Devil" *The Nation*, July 16/23, 1990, 79; G.T., "A Report from the Journal Advisory Committee," *Earth First!*, September 22, 1990, 4. On Mike Roselle's career more generally, see Roselle, *Tree Spiker: From Earth First! To Lowbagging: My Struggles in Radical Environmental Action* (New York: St. Martin's, 2009). Roselle was central not only to Earth First! and Greenpeace but to the Rainforest Action Network and, later, the Ruckus Society.

90. Judi Bari, "The Feminization of Earth First!" *Ms.*, May 1992. See also Bari, *Timber Wars* (Maine: Common Courage, 1994); and Zakin, *Coyotes and Town Dogs*, 342–396. On Bari's political views generally, see "Earth First! in Northern California: Interview with Judi Bari," *Capitalism, Nature, Socialism* 4, no. 4 (December 1993).

91. On tree-sits, see Greg King, "New Battles in Maxxam Campaign," *Earth First!*, June 21, 1988; Greg King, "Anti-MAXXAM Warriors Climb Back into the Trees," *Earth First!*, June 21, 1989; and Judi Bari, "Californians Start a New Fad: Tree-Sitting Becomes a Pastime," *Earth First!*, September 22, 1989. On lock-box tactics, see Bevington, *The Rebirth of Environmentalism*, 63, 133–134; and Mike Roselle, *Tree Spiker: From Earth First! to Lowbagging: My Struggles in Radical Environmental Action* (New York: St. Martin's, 2009), 88.

92. Dave Foreman, and Bill Haywood, eds., *Ecodefense: A Field Guide to Monkeywrenching* (Tucson: Ned Ludd, 1990 [1985]), 14.

93. Zakin, *Coyotes and Town Dogs*, 259–260; and "Hardesty Avengers Spike Trees," *Earth First!*, November 1, 1984, 1.

94. Trip Gabriel, "If a Tree Falls in the Forest, They Hear It," *New York Times Magazine*, November 4, 1990, 58.

95. Ken Slocum, "Radical Ecologists Pound Spikes in Trees to Scare Loggers and Hinder Lumbering," *Wall Street Journal*, November 14, 1985.

96. Bob Smith, see "Radicals Hard as Nails About Trees," *Chicago Tribune*, June 22, 1988.

97. Michael Lerner, "The FBI vs. the Monkeywrenchers," *Los Angeles Times Magazine*, April 15, 1990, 16.

98. See Dave Foreman, *Confessions of an Eco-Warrior* (New York: Crown, 1991), 149–152; and Mike Roselle, *Tree Spiker*, 124–126. The spiked tree was a thin, second-growth redwood logged outside of wilderness, from an uncontroversial timber sale, and had been spiked only after logged, all of which suggested the spiker was not affiliated with Earth First!.

99. Dale Turner, "Montana Earth First!ers Get Federal Subpoenas," *Earth First!*, November 1, 1989.

100. Gabriel, "If A Tree Falls in The Forest," 58–59; Lerner, "The FBI vs. the Monkeywrenchers," 21.

101. Rich to Mary, et al., August 11, 1988; and Deanne to Rich, et al., August 12, 1988, both in box 47, folder 14, WSR. See also, in the same folder, draft letter from George Frampton to the *Denver Post* disavowing tree spiking, with marginal comment from "Ben" asking, "Do we really want to be so harsh?"

102. Gary Steele, "My response to Williams terrorism accusation," n.d., DF.

103. Mary Beth Nearing and Brian Heath, "Oregon Update," *Earth First!*, March 20, 1986, 7.

104. Dave Foreman, "Editorial," and Pete Dustrud and Gary Snyder, letters to the editor, *Earth First!*, August 1, 1982, 2.

105. Judi Bari, *Timber Wars* (Maine: Common Courage, 1994), 269. See also Bari, "Spiking: It Just Doesn't Work," *Earth First!*, February 2, 1995; and Elliot Diringer, "Environmental Group Says It Won't Spike Trees," *San Francisco Chronicle*, April 11, 1990.

106. Gene Lawhorn, "Why Earth First! Should Denounce Tree Spiking," *Earth First!*, September 22, 1990, 9.

107. John Henry, letter to the editor, *Earth First!*, August 1, 1990, 3.

108. Paul Watson, "In Defense of Tree Spiking," *Earth First!*, September 22, 1990, 7–9.

109. "Northern California Earth First! Renounces Tree Spiking," n.d., DF.

110. Judi Bari, Darryl Cherney, and North Coast California Earth First!ers to All Earth First! Groups, Chapters, Individuals, etc., memorandum, n.d., DF.

111. Neither Erik Loomis nor Darren Speece finds any evidence that Bari's attempts at coalition-building yielded enduring alliances. See Erik Loomis, *Empire of Timber: Labor Unions and the Pacific Northwest Forests* (New York: Cambridge University Press, 2016), 227–228, and Speece, *Defending Giants*, 188.

112. Erik Ryberg, "Civil Disobedience: An Urgent Critique," *Earth First!*, May 1, 1991, 8.

113. Foreman, *Confessions of An Eco-Warrior*, 158.

114. Judi Bari, "Monkeywrenching," *Earth First!*, February 2, 1994, 8.

115. On the Earth Liberation Front, see Craig Rosebraugh, *Burning Rage of a Dying Planet: Speaking for the Earth Liberation Front* (New York: Lantern, 2004); and Leslie James Pickering, *The Earth Liberation Front: 1997–2002* (Portland, OR: Arissa, 2007).

116. Bari was in this sense close to the anarcho-syndicalists of the nineteenth century, who favored direct action but shed the anarchists' resistance to working within the industrial system. On anarcho-syndicalism and the "timber wars," see Graham Purchase, *Anarchism and Environmental Survival* (Tucson: See Sharp, 1994).

117. Harris, *The Last Stand*, 273–276.

118. Bari, *Timber Wars*, 188–192.

119. Harris, *The Last Stand*, 276–277.

120. On Bari, Cherney, and the bombing, see Zakin, *Coyotes and Town Dogs*, 386–396; Bari, *Timber Wars*, 25–54, 193–195, 286–328; Kate Coleman, *The Secret Wars of Judi Bari: A Car Bomb, the Fight for the Redwoods, and the End of Earth First!* (San Francisco: Encounter, 2005), 8–13, 151–185; "The Bombing: What Happened?" and "Someone Tried to Kill Us, the Cops Tried to Frame Us," both in *Earth First! Extra*, Summer 1990; and Judi Bari, "For F.B.I., Back to Political Sabotage?" *New York Times*, August 23, 1990. On the makeup of the bomb itself, see Harris, *The Last Stand*, 328–329.

121. The Oakland district attorney eventually dropped the case for lack of evidence, and the FBI investigation never found a convincing suspect. For Earth First!, it remained an article of faith that the FBI targeted Bari and Cherney, going to great effort to prove the activists were responsible for their own bombing. Unsubstantiated theories about who set the bomb have included logging companies; antiabortion protesters targeting Bari's pro-choice activism; Bari's ex-husband, Mike Sweeney; and the FBI itself. On Greenpeace and the reaction to the Oakland bombing, see Mike Roselle, *Tree Spiker*, 130–131. On the larger environmental movement's response, see Paul Rauber, "No Second Warning," *Sierra*, January/February 1991.

122. Howie Wolke, "FOCUS on Wilderness," *Earth First!*, September 22, 1990, 7.

123. Dave Foreman and Nancy Morton, "Good Luck, Darlin'. It's Been Great," *Earth First!*, September 22, 1990, 5.

124. Judi Bari, "Expand Earth First!" *Earth First!*, September 22, 1990, 5.

125. Mikal Jakubal, " 'Live Wild or Die'—The Other EF!" *Fifth Estate*, Winter 1988/ 1989, 10.

126. Fennell, "The Split in Earth First!" 5.

127. "A Challenge to the Fifth Estate: Environmentalism and Revolution," *Fifth Estate*, Winter 1990–1991, 18.

128. Stephen Jay Gould, "Our Natural Place," in Gould, *Hen's Teeth and Horse's Toes: Further Reflections on Natural History* (New York: W. W. Norton, 1983), 25.

129. James Berry, "Is the Sky Falling?" *Earth First!*, December 21, 1982, 17.

130. Abbey, *Hayduke Lives!*, 186–212.

131. Abbey, *Desert Solitaire*, 214–215.

6. THE LIMITS AND LEGACY OF RADICALISM

1. On human understandings of redwoods and redwood forests, see Elliott Norse, *Ancient Forests of the Pacific Northwest* (Washington, D.C.: Island, 1990); Reed Noss, ed., *The Redwood Forest: History, Ecology, and Conservation of the Coast Redwoods* (Washington, D.C.: Island, 2000); John Evarts and Marjorie Popper, eds., *Coast Redwood: A Natural and Cultural History* (Los Olivos, CA: Cachuma, 2001); and Richard Preston, *The Wild Trees: A Story of Passion and Daring* (New York: Random House, 2007).

2. Jared Farmer, *Trees in Paradise: A California History* (New York: Norton, 2013), 5.

3. On conservationists and redwoods, see Evarts and Popper, eds., *Coast Redwood*, 123–163; Farmer, *Trees in Paradise*, 60–108; and Susan Schrepfer, *The Fight to Save the Redwoods: A History of Environmental Reform, 1917–1978* (Madison: University of Wisconsin Press, 1983).

4. On orthodoxy and change within the Forest Service, see Samuel Hays, *Wars in the Woods: The Rise of Ecological Forestry in America* (Pittsburgh: University of Pittsburgh Press, 2007). For a rich discussion of assumptions about sustainability and yield, see Nancy Langston, *Forest Dreams, Forest Nightmares: The Paradox of Old Growth in the Inland West* (Seattle: University of Washington Press, 1995).

5. On Franklin and DeBonis, see William Dietrich, *The Final Forest: Big Trees, Forks, and the Pacific Northwest* (Seattle: University of Washington Press, 1992), 106–125, 174–190.

6. Hays, *Wars in the Woods*.

7. Paul Hirt, "Dissension Within the Ranks," *Earth First!*, May 1, 1990, 7. On Mumma, see Paul Rauber, "The August Coup," *Sierra*, January/February 1992.

8. See Michael Soulé and Bruce Wilcox, *Conservation Biology: An Evolutionary-Ecological Perspective* (Sunderland, MA: Sinauer Associates, 1980); and David Quammen, *The Song of the Dodo: Island Biogeography in an Age of Extinction* (New York: Touchstone, 1996).

9. Dave Foreman and Howie Wolke to "The Hardcore," 1980, DF.

10. Reed Noss, "National Forum on Biodiversity: Is Anyone Listening?" *Earth First!*, November 1, 1986, 13.

11. Mitch Friedman, "Conservation Biology and the Greater North Cascades Ecosystem," *Earth First!*, May 1, 1988, 26.

12. Reed Noss, "Do We Really Want Diversity?" *Earth First!*, June 21, 1986, 20.

13. George Wuerthner, "Monarchs of Millenia: Old Growth Forests," *Earth First!*, December 21, 1986, 22. On changing views of forests and old growth, see Hays, *Wars in the Woods*, 45–54; Kathie Durbin, *Tree Huggers: Victory, Defeat and Renewal in the Northwest Ancient Forest Campaign* (Seattle: The Mountaineers, 1996), 49–53; and Steve Erickson, "Forest Service Holds Old Growth Symposium," *Earth First!*, August 1, 1989, 7.

14. Pacific Northwest Research Station Old-Growth Definition Task Group, "Interim Definitions for Old-Growth Douglas-Fir and Mixed-Conifer Forests in the Pacific Northwest and California," July 1986, box 22, folder 5, WSR, 3.

15. Northwest Forest Resource Council, "Old Growth: Here Forever," March 1991, box 22, folder 7, WSR, 3. On the Wilderness Society, see "Old-Growth Douglas-Fir Definitions," May 13, 1987, box 22, folder 5, WSR.

16. For competing origin stories of the phrase "ancient forests," see Dietrich, *The Final Forest*, 223–229; and Brock Evans, "Wild Words, Wild Lands," *Wild Earth*, Spring 1999, 9–11.

17. Turner, *The Promise of Wilderness*, 280–189; Durbin, *Tree Huggers*, 146–155; and " 'The Big One' Educates America," *Earth First!*, August 1, 1989, 8.

18. Mitch Freedman [*sic*], "Old Growth Strategy Revised," *Earth First!*, December 21, 1988, 7.

19. For a brief summary of the controversy over the northern spotted owl and old growth, see Douglas Bevington, *The Rebirth of Environmentalism: Grassroots Activism from the Spotted Owl to the Polar Bear* (Washington, D.C.: Island, 2009), 114–123; on environmental pressure, see Wallace Turner, "Endangered Owl is Focus of Meeting," *New York Times*, August 29, 1987.

20. John Muir, *My First Summer in the Sierra* (New York: Mariner, 1998 (1911)), 157.

21. George Frampton, memorandum, July 15, 1991, box 22, folder 7, WSR. On industry estimates, see Northwest Forest Research Council, "Northern Spotted Owl," n.d., box 22, folder 7, WSR. On environmentalists' claims, see Sallie Tisdale, "Marks in the Game," *Sierra*, July/August 1992.

22. On environmental strategy, see Turner, *The Promise of Wilderness*, 280–289; and Durbin, *Tree Huggers*, 87–94.

23. Erik Loomis, *Empire of Timber: Labor Unions and the Pacific Northwest Forests* (New York: Cambridge University Press, 2016).

24. Mitch Freedman, "Spotted Owl EIS Out," *Earth First!*, September 23, 1986; and Mitch Friedman and Lizzie Zemke, "Earth First! Digs in in Washington," *Earth First!*, November 1, 1986.

25. On the "rider from hell," see Durbin, *Tree Huggers*, 106–110; and Karen Wood, "Hatfield Tries to End Controversy, Owls, Old Growth," *Earth First!*, September 22, 1989. On mainstream environmentalists' response, see Mitch Friedman, "The 1989 Timber Compromise: Will Environmentalists Ever Learn?" *Earth First!*, February 2, 1990.

26. On the various Thomas committees, see Durbin, *Tree Huggers*, 111–118, 197–208.

27. Justin Time, "Option 9: Mainstream Groups Sell Out," *Earth First!*, November 1, 1983, 1.

28. Paul Rauber, "Improving on Nature," *Sierra*, March/April 1995, 72.

29. On the timber wars, see Darren Frederick Speece, *Defending Giants: The Redwood Wars and the Transformation of American Environmental Politics* (Seattle: University of Washington Press, 2017); David Harris, *The Last Stand: The War Between Wall Street and Main Street Over California's Ancient Redwoods* (San Francisco: Sierra Club, 1996); and Bevington, *The Rebirth of Environmentalism*.

30. Mike Roselle, "Tree Huggers Save Redwoods," *Earth First!*, November 1, 1983, 4.

31. See David Cross, "Sally Bell Redwoods Protected!" *Earth First!*, February 2, 1987.

32. For useful discussions of Pacific Lumber's practices, see Speece, *Defending Giants*, 124–132; and Harris, *The Last Stand*, 8–20.

33. On the Maxxam raid, see Harris, *The Last Stand*; Speece, *Defending Giants*; and Phil Garlington, "Predator's Maul," *Outside*, December 1988.

34. See Speece, *Defending Giants*, 124–142; and Garlington, "Predator's Maul," 42. On criticism of Pacific Lumber, see Robert Lindsey, "Ancient Redwoods Fall to a Wall Street Takeover," *New York Times*, March 2, 1988.

35. Harris, *The Last Stand*, 177–179.

36. "Greg King's Statement," *Earth First!*, September 23, 1987, 6.

37. Howie Wolke, "Save Our National Forests!" *Earth First!* supplement, March 20, 1988, n.

38. Speece, *Defending Giants*, 41–42, 154–158. See also Harris, *The Last Stand*, 284–285.

39. On Forests Forever, see Speece, *Defending Giants*, 179–184; and Paul Rauber, "Losing the Initiative?" *Sierra*, May/June 1991.

40. Speece, *Defending Giants*, 191–196

41. Reed McManus, "Logging Without Looking," *Sierra*, July/August, 1996, 30.

42. Jeanne Trombly email to David Brower, July 2, 1996, carton 23, folder 20, DRB.

43. Reed Noss, "Florida's National Forests: Our Last Chance," *Earth First!*, March 21, 1989, 21.

44. George Wuerthner, "A New Sagebrush Rebellion," *Earth First!*, May 1, 1989, 24.

45. Darryl Cherney, "Debt for Nature, Jail for Hurwitz," *Earth First!*, December 21, 1993.

46. Ed Wayburn to Dianne Feinstein, September 5, 1995; Barbara Boxer to Ed Wayburn, March 28, 1996; and Alice Goodman to Dianne Feinstein, August 29, 1995, carton 11, folder 3, EW.

47. See Speece, *Defending Giants*, 229–237; and Bevington, *The Rebirth of Environmentalism*, 62–66.

48. Michael Passoff email to Mikael Davis, September 30, 1998, carton 100, folder 28, DRB.

49. Carl Pope email to Michael Dorsey et al., July 14, 1998, carton 11, folder 3, EW.

50. See Richard Brewer, *Conservancy: The Land Trust Movement in America* (Lebanon, NH: University Press of New England, 2003).

51. Sally Fairfax, Lauren Gwin, Mary Ann King, Leigh Raymond, and Laura Watt, *Buying Nature: The Limits of Land Acquisition as a Conservation Strategy, 1780–2004* (Cambridge, MA: MIT Press, 2005), 5.

52. On the two meetings, see Greg Hanscom, "Visionaries or Dreamers?" *High Country News*, April 26, 1999; and David Johns, "North American Wilderness Recovery Strategy," *Wild Earth*, Winter 1991/1992.

53. On TWP, see Dave Foreman, *Rewilding North America: A Vision for Conservation in the 21st Century* (Washington, D.C.: Island, 2004); David Clarke Burks, ed., *Place of the Wild: A Wildlands Anthology* (Washington, D.C.: Island, 1994); and Turner, *The Promise of Wilderness*, 303–311.

54. Mitch Friedman to TWP board and staff, October 27, 1997, carton 24, folder 8, SCSW.

55. "The Wildlands Project Mission Statement," *Wild Earth* (special issue, n.d.), 4.

56. Dave Foreman, "Dreaming Big Wilderness," *Wild Earth*, Spring 1991, 12–13.

57. Reed Noss, "Biodiversity, Wildness, and The Wildlands Project," in Burks, ed., *Place of the Wild*, 38.

58. "Proposal: Sky Islands/Greater Gila Nature Reserve Network," November 18, 1997, carton 24, folder 10, SCSW.

59. David Johns, "Protecting the Wild Heart of North America: The Politics of Y2Y," carton 24, folder 9, SCSW, 1.

60. "Wildlands Implementation Workshop: Designing Strategies for On-The-Ground Protection," carton 24, folder 8, SCSW.

61. Howard Schneider, "Conservationists Take Stock of the Land," *Washington Post*, October 27, 1997.

62. "Wilderness Preserve System," *Earth First!*, June 21, 1983, 9.

63. Dave Foreman, "Wilderness Areas Are Vital," *Wild Earth*, Winter 1995/1995, 68 (italics in original). See also Dave Foreman and Howie Wolke, *The Big Outside: A Descriptive Inventory of the Big Wilderness Areas of the U.S.* (Tucson: Ned Ludd, 1989).

64. Dave Foreman, "Around the Campfire," *Wild Earth*, Summer 1993, inside cover.

65. On cores, corridors, and carnivores, see Foreman, *Rewilding North America*, 128–143; and Caroline Frasier, *Rewilding the World: Dispatches from the Conservation Revolution* (New York: Metropolitan, 2009).

66. Dave Foreman, *Rewilding North America*, 229.

67. On these various efforts, see Jonathan Adams, *The Future of the Wild: Radical Conservation for a Crowded World* (Boston: Beacon, 2006); Mitch Friedman and Paul Lindholdt, eds., *Cascadia Wild: Protecting an International Ecosystem* (Bellingham, WA: Greater Ecosystem Alliance, 1993); Foreman, *Rewilding North America*; and Frasier, *Rewilding the World*.

68. Amy Irvine, "Strange Bedfellows for Wilderness: Science and Faith," *Southern Utah Wilderness Alliance*, Summer 1999, 4.

69. "Proposal: Sky Islands/Greater Gila Nature Reserve Network."

70. Daniel Simberloff to Dave Foreman, November 23, 1997, carton 24, folder 8, SCSW.

71. Brock Evans, letter to the editor, *Wild Earth*, Winter 1996/1997, 10.

72. Keith Lampe to David Brower, April 18, 1994, box II: 103, folder 25, GS.

73. Keith Lampe to David Brower, November 14, 1986, box II: 103, folder 17, GS. See also unnamed Lampe newsletter, July 6, 1985, box II: 103, folder 7, GS.

74. John Davis, "Ramblings"; and David Brower, "The Politics of Environmental Compromise," both in *Earth First!* (February 2, 1990), 2, 26.

75. On zero cut, see Bevington, *The Rebirth of Environmentalism*, 111–159; and Turner, *The Promise of Wilderness*, 315–326.

76. On the Shawnee, see Orin Langelle, "Shawnee Timber Sale Stopped," *Fifth Estate*, Winter 1990–1991, 7.

77. Margaret Young, "What the Big 10 Don't Tell You," *Wild Earth*, Spring 1991, 50. See also Margaret Young, "Nightmare on Polk Street: ASCMEE Acts Up," *Wild Earth*, Winter 1991/92; and Keith Schneider, "Logging Policy Splits Membership of Sierra Club," *New York Times*, December 26, 1993.

78. Chad Hanson email to David Brower, February 16, 1996, carton 23, folder 20, DRB.

79. This story is told in Bevington, *The Rebirth of Environmentalism*, 134–138.

80. David Brower, "Public Trees," September 3, 1994, carton 103, folder 17, DRB.

81. Dave Foreman, "Around the Campfire," *Wild Earth*, Spring 1996.

82. Karl Drexel, "Will the Real Sierra Club Please Stand Up?" *Christian Science Monitor*, May 24, 1996.

83. Chad Hanson and Carl Pope, letter to the editor, *Christian Science Monitor*, June 13, 1996. On ongoing zero cut issues, see "Emily," memorandum, August 13, 1997, carton 23, folder 34, DRB.

84. On zero cud, see Kirsten Bovee, "Zero-Cow Initiative Splits Sierra Club," *High Country News*, February 26, 2001; and Lynn Jacobs, "An Open Letter to the Sierra Club and Range Activists," *Earth First!*, August 1, 1988, 16.

85. David Brower to Jim McNeill, November 29, 1994, carton 5, folder 110, DRB. On NREPA, see Turner, *The Promise of Wilderness*, 311–315; and "NREPA Reintroduced, Pronounced 'Dead on Arrival,'" *Big Sky Sierran*, July 1993, 4.

86. Dave Foreman, "The Northern Rockies Ecosystem Protection Act and the Evolving Wilderness Area Model," *Wild Earth*, Winter 1993/1994, 57.

87. Dave Foreman, "Evolving Wilderness Area Model," 57.

88. James Conner, memorandum, August 17, 1993, carton 23, folder 7, DRB.

89. Bruce Hamilton, "An Enduring Wilderness," *Sierra*, September/October 1994, 48. On the Club's change of heart see also Jenny Martin to "Sierrans," May 25, 1994, carton 23, folder 7, DRB.

90. Brooks Martin to David Brower, November 23, 1992, carton 23, folder 7, DRB.

91. Mark Davis to David Brower, 1993, carton 103, folder 17, DRB.

92. David Brower, "Free Trade: Environment in the Balance?" n.d., carton 5, folder 117, DRB.

93. Carl Pope, "Paying the Price for Free Trade," *Sierra*, June/August 1997, 15.

94. See Julie Beezley et al., email chain, July 24–31, 1996, carton 23, folder 21, DRB.

95. Chad Hanson email to David Brower et al., August 27, 1996, carton 23, folder 21, DRB. On Werbach's intervention, see Tom Elliott email to David Brower et al., October 1, 1996, carton 23, folder 21, DRB.

96. Tim Hermach to "friends and colleagues," October 18, 1996, carton 23, folder 21, DRB.

97. David Brower, "Let the River Run Through It," *Sierra*, March/April 1997; Christopher Franklin, "Un-Dam It!" *Wild Earth*, Fall 1997.

98. On dam removal in the 1990s, see Timothy Egan, "Heralding a New Era, Babbitt Chips Away at Harmful River Dams," *New York Times*, July 15, 1998; Reed McManus, "Down Come the Dams," *Sierra*, May/June 1997; Brad Knickerbocker, "Turning Man-Made Creations Back to Nature," *Christian Science Monitor*, September 26, 1997; and William Lowry, *Dam Politics: Restoring America's Rivers* (Washington, D.C.: Georgetown University Press, 2003). On reactions to the Sierra Club's proposal, see Scott Miller, "Undamming Glen Canyon: Lunacy, Rationality, or Prophecy?" *Stanford Environmental Law Journal* 19, no. 1 (January 2000), 123. For a favorable view, see Daniel Beard, "Dams Aren't Forever," *New York Times*, October 6, 1997. Beard was commissioner of the Bureau of Reclamation—the largest dam-building agency in the world—from 1993 to 1995, and a senior vice-president at the National Audubon Society.

99. David Brower, "Let the River Run Through It," 42.

100. Jennifer Hattam, "Thinking Big: Five Bold Ideas for the New Century," *Sierra*, January/February 2000, 58.

101. On environmental justice, see Luke Cole and Sheila Foster, *From the Ground Up: Environmental Racism and the Rise of the Environmental Justice Movement* (New York: New York University Press, 2001); Robert Gottlieb, *Forcing the Spring: The Transformation of the American Environmental Movement* (Washington, D.C.: Island, 1993); Robert Bullard, *Dumping in Dixie: Race, Class, and Environmental Quality* (Boulder, CO: Westview Press, 1990); Mark Dowie, *Losing Ground: American Environmentalism at the Close of the Twentieth Century* (Cambridge: MIT Press, 1995), 125–174; and Eileen Maura McGurty, "From NIMBY to Civil Rights: The Origins of the Environmental Justice Movement," *Environmental History* 2 (July 1997).

102. Dowie, *Losing Ground*, 133–135.

103. On Chavis, see "A *Sierra* Roundtable on Race, Justice, and the Environment," *Sierra*, May/June 1993, 52.

104. Garrett Hardin, "Living on a Lifeboat," in Garrett Hardin and John Baden, eds., *Managing the Commons* (New York: W. H. Freeman, 1977).

105. Regular meeting of the board of directors, minutes, February 5–6, 1972, carton 4, folder 12, SCR.

106. Organizational meeting of the board of directors, minutes, May 7–8, 1977, carton 4, folder 17, SCR.

107. Organizational meeting of the board of directors, minutes, May 6–7, 1978, carton 4, folder 17, SCR.

108. . B. Meredith Burke, "Sierra Club Schism: The Limits of Sharing," *Christian Science Monitor*, April 21, 1998. On shifts in Club population policy more generally, see "Population," n.d., carton 23, folder 32, DRB.

109. For Li quote, see Hannah Creighton, "Not Thinking Globally," *Race, Poverty and the Environment*, Summer 1993, 28, carton 40, folder 4, SCOED; Julie Beezley to "Sierra Club friends," March 10, 1995, carton 23, folder 15, DRB.

110. "Proposed Resolution for Neutral Position on Immigration Control," n.d., carton 40, folder 4, SCOED.

111. John Tanton, letters to the editor, *The Atlantic*, May 1992, 11.

112. "Population," n.d., carton 23, folder 32, DRB.

113. On SUSPS, see Alan Kuper to SUSPS members, February 13, 1998, carton 24,

114. On the 1998 vote, see John Cushman, "An Uncomfortable Debate Fuels a Sierra Club Election," *New York Times*, April 5, 1998; and Glen Martin, Ramon McLeod, and Chronicle staff, "Sierra Club Divided by Vote on Immigration," *San Francisco Chronicle*, February 23, 1998. For the text of the competing proposals, see "Sierra Club Bulletin," *Sierra*, January/February 1998, 105–106.

115. Bill McKibben, "Immigrants Aren't the Problem. We Are," *New York Times*, March 9, 1998.

116. Hilda Solis to Carl Pope, October 28, 1997, carton 23, folder 32, DRB.

117. Roy Hengerson email to Anne Ehrlich, November 20, 1997, carton 23, folder 32, DRB.

118 David Brower, "What Causes Migration?" n.d., carton 6, folder 4, DRB. Julie Beezley email to David Brower, October 24, 1997, carton 23, folder 32, DRB. Alan Kuper email to Chris Franklin and David Brower, October 31, 1997, carton 23, folder 32, DRB.

119. Dave Foreman to Alan Kuper, August 29, 1996, carton 40, folder 8, SCOED;

120. David Johns, "Protecting the Wild Heart of North America: The Politics of Y2Y," n.d., 7, carton 24, folder 9, SCSW.

121. "Cultural Diversity Issues at TWP," June 10, 1998, carton 24, folder 9, SCSW.

122. Bonnie Sharpe to Michele Perrault and Sue Lowry, April 26, 1994, carton 40, folder 4, SCOED.

123. Ric Oberlink email to unknown, November 3, 1997, carton 23, folder 32, DRB.

124. See Michael Soulé and Gary Lease, eds., *Reinventing Nature?: Responses to Postmodern Deconstruction* (Washington, D.C.: Island Press, 1995), 10.

125. William Cronon, "The Trouble with Wilderness; or, Getting Back to the Wrong Nature," in William Cronon, ed., *Uncommon Ground: Rethinking the Human Place in Nature* (New York: Norton, 1995), 79.

126. John Davis to Gary Snyder, August 15, 1996, box II: 204, folder 44, GS.

127. Cronon, "The Trouble with Wilderness," 88.

128. Donald Waller, "Wilderness Redux," *Wild Earth*, Winter 1996/1997, 38.

129. On the roadless rule, see Turner, *The Promise of Wilderness*, 351–362.

130. Foreman, *Rewilding North America*, 158.

131. Foreman, *Rewilding North America*, 208.

132. On La Manta Mojada, see *Nature More: The Newsletter of Earth First*, July 1980, DF.

133. Bart Koehler, "Democracy at Work: Thoughts on Wilderness, Democracy, Freedom, and Patriotism," in Wilderness Support Center, *Stand by Your Land: An Activists Guide to Helping People Protect America's Wild Places*, n.d., personal collection of Bart Koehler. On SEACC, see Durbin, *Tree Huggers*, 145–146; on the Wilderness Support Center, see Turner, *The Promise of Wilderness*, 380–391.

CONCLUSION

1. Abe Streep, "The Trials of Bidder 70," *Outside*, December 2011.

2. Kirk Johnson, "No 'Choice of Evils' Defense in Oil Lease Case, Judge Rules," *New York Times*, November 17, 2009. On DeChristopher's popularity, see Streep, "The Trials of Bidder 70."

3. On the Middle Santiam, see Mike Roselle, "Oregon Trials: The Middle Santiam Tries Oregon," *Earth First!*, December 21, 1984.

4. Mike Roselle, "Deep Ecology and the New Civil Rights Movement," *Earth First!*, May 1, 1988, 23.

5. Maxine McCloskey, ed., *Wilderness: The Edge of Knowledge* (San Francisco: Sierra Club, 1970), 254.

6. Philip Berry, address before Education for Environmental Awareness Conference, February 28, 1971, carton 4, folder 51, EA.

7. George Marshall to Philip Berry, November 19, 1969, carton 6, folder 7, SCR.

8. David Brower, Tom Turner, and Connie Parrish, "What's in a Name?: Yes," *Not Man Apart*, October 1983, 2.

9. Bill Devall and George Sessions, "Direct Action," *Earth First!*, November 1, 1984, 19.

10. David Brower, "Foreword," in Maxine McCloskey and James Gilligan, eds., *Wilderness and the Quality of Life* (San Francisco: Sierra Club, 1969), vii-vii.

11. Dipesh Chakrabarty, "The Climate of History: Four Theses," *Critical Inquiry* 35 (Winter 2009), 206. See also Dipesh Chakrabarty, "Postcolonial Studies and the Challenge of Climate Change," *New Literary History* 43 (Winter 2012). For a rich discussion of Chakrabarty's views, see Jeremy Davies, *The Birth of the Anthropocene* (Oakland: University of California Press, 2016).

12. Chakrabarty, "The Climate of History," 208, 210.

13. Amitav Ghosh, *The Great Derangement: Climate Change and the Unthinkable* (Chicago: University of Chicago Press, 2016), 92, 111.

14. Davies, *The Birth of the Anthropocene*, 57.

15. Davies, *The Birth of the Anthropocene*, 198–202.

16. Ghosh, *The Great Derangement*, 158–159.

17. Ghosh, *The Great Derangement*, 31.

18. Mike Roselle, draft statement, n.d., carton 93, folder 25, DRB. See also Karen Pickett, "Roselle Gets 4 Month Sentence," *Earth First!*, March 20, 1988.

19. On CGZ, see Tricia Shapiro, *Mountain Justice: Homegrown Resistance to Mountaintop Removal for the Future of Us All* (Oakland: AK, 2010).

Index

Abbey, Edward, 185–88; anarchism of, 160–61, 188, 189fig; anti-immigration stance, 196, 204; and Black Mesa, 211, 212; vs. Bookchin, 192, 197, 234; on the breakdown of representative democracy, 222; on cowboy life, 172; *Desert Solitaire*, 187, 234; and Earth First!, 121–22, 124, 185, 189fig, 204; and the Glen Canyon Dam, 123; *Hayduke Lives!*, 185, 234; *The Journey Home*, 123; *The Monkey Wrench Gang*, 121–22, 129, 141, 185, 269; on patriotism, 281; on terrorism vs. sabotage, 142

Adams, Ansel, 15, 17–18, 26, 38

Adams, Brock, 246

AIDS epidemic, 196

air quality, xi, 24, 84. *See also* Clean Air Act; pollution

Alaska: Alaska Natives, 109, 127, 212–13; atomic bombs tested in, 130–31; battle over public lands, 108–10, 114, 116, 117, 127, 149, 324–25n23; highlighted in 1969 wilderness conference, 39–40; trans-Alaska pipeline, 58

Alaska Coalition, 109–10, 116

Alaska National Interest Lands Conservation Act (ANILCA), 109–10, 316n45. *See also* Alaska: battle over public lands

Alaska Native Claims Settlement Act (1971), 109

Alexander, George, 223

Alien-Nation (anarchist group), 204–5, 233, 335n51

Alliance for the Wild Rockies, 266

Allison, James Robert, III, 336n67

All-Species Projects, 100

Alternatives (journal), 103

Amchitka atomic testing ground (Alaska), 130–31

America and the New Era (SDS), 32

American Indian Movement (AIM), 211–12

anarchism, 188–92; as critique of democratic principles, 310n65; deep ecology criticized by anarchists, 204–8; Earth First! and, 144–45, 159, 160–61, 164, 188, 189fig, 204–6 (*see also* Earth First!); *Fifth Estate* editors' views, 197–98 (see also *Fifth Estate*); radical environmentalism and, 7, 144–45,